T0155584

Maker Innovations Series

Jump start your path to discovery with the Apress Maker Innovations series! From the basics of electricity and components through to the most advanced options in robotics and Machine Learning, you'll forge a path to building ingenious hardware and controlling it with cutting-edge software. All while gaining new skills and experience with common toolsets you can take to new projects or even into a whole new career.

The Apress Maker Innovations series offers projects-based learning, while keeping theory and best processes front and center. So you get hands-on experience while also learning the terms of the trade and how entrepreneurs, inventors, and engineers think through creating and executing hardware projects. You can learn to design circuits, program AI, create IoT systems for your home or even city, and so much more!

Whether you're a beginning hobbyist or a seasoned entrepreneur working out of your basement or garage, you'll scale up your skillset to become a hardware design and engineering pro. And often using low-cost and open-source software such as the Raspberry Pi, Arduino, PIC microcontroller, and Robot Operating System (ROS). Programmers and software engineers have great opportunities to learn, too, as many projects and control environments are based in popular languages and operating systems, such as Python and Linux.

If you want to build a robot, set up a smart home, tackle assembling a weather-ready meteorology system, or create a brand-new circuit using breadboards and circuit design software, this series has all that and more! Written by creative and seasoned Makers, every book in the series tackles both tested and leading-edge approaches and technologies for bringing your visions and projects to life.

More information about this series at https://link.springer.com/ bookseries/17311.

Norman Dunbar

Arduino Interrupts

Harness the Power of Interrupts in Your Arduino
and ATmega328 Code

apress®

Norman Dunbar
Rawdon
West Yorkshire, UK

ISBN-13 (pbk): 978-1-4842-9713-1   ISBN-13 (electronic): 978-1-4842-9714-8
https://doi.org/10.1007/978-1-4842-9714-8

Managing Director, Apress Media LLC: Welmoed Spahr
Acquisitions Editor: Miriam Haidara
Development Editor: James Markham
Editorial Assistant: Jessica Vakili

Cover designed by eStudioCalamar

Cover image by Freepik (www.freepik.com)

Distributed to the book trade worldwide by Springer Science+Business Media New York, 1 New York Plaza, Suite 4600, New York, NY 10004-1562, USA. Phone 1-800-SPRINGER, fax (201) 348-4505, e-mail orders-ny@springer-sbm.com, or visit www.springeronline.com. Apress Media, LLC is a California LLC and the sole member (owner) is Springer Science + Business Media Finance Inc (SSBM Finance Inc). SSBM Finance Inc is a Delaware corporation.
For information on translations, please e-mail booktranslations@springernature.com; for reprint, paperback, or audio rights, please e-mail bookpermissions@springernature.com.
Apress titles may be purchased in bulk for academic, corporate, or promotional use. eBook versions and licenses are also available for most titles. For more information, reference our Print and eBook Bulk Sales web page at http://www.apress.com/bulk-sales.
Any source code or other supplementary material referenced by the author in this book is available to readers on GitHub (github.com/apress). For more detailed information, please visit https://www.apress.com/gp/services/source-code.

Paper in this product is recyclable

Writing books is not an easy task, especially if you have other commitments, like family, work, a dog, and suchlike. I would like to thank my wife Alison for allowing me some spare time to get my thoughts down on paper (or PDF) and also to everyone involved in the Arduino universe, be that hardware, software, or even just a LaTeX file to get Arduino IDE code formatting styles available in a LyX document.[1]

---

[1] https://github.com/trihedral/ArduinoLatexListing

Contents

About the Author

Norman Dunbar is a retired Oracle database administrator who lives with his wife, Alison, and a cockapoo dog, Wesley, to keep him out of trouble.

Norman has had a long-running relationship with electronics since childhood and with computers since the late 1970s, and the Arduino was a perfect marriage of the two interests. With a love of learning new things, examining and explaining the Arduino Language and the hardware became a bit of a hobby. As his piles of notes expanded, Apress published the results of his findings in *Arduino Software Internals*, in April 2020.

Since then, Norman has been diving into the slightly trickier aspects of the Arduino, interrupts, with a view to documenting them for his own ease of use. Once more, his notes have become a book.

Because he never remembers how hard it is to write a technical book, Norman is currently writing a third book about the Arduino.

Norman's motto continues to be *don't think, find out.*

About the Technical Reviewer

Farzin Asadi received his BSc in Electronics Engineering, MSc in Control Engineering, and PhD in Mechatronics Engineering. Currently, he is with the Department of Electrical and Electronics Engineering at Maltepe University, Istanbul, Turkey. Dr. Asadi has published more than 40 papers in ISI/Scopus indexed journals. He wrote 25 books as well. His research interests include switching converters, control theory, robust control of power electronics converters, and robotics.

Acknowledgments

I would like to thank everyone at Apress and Springer who were involved in the production of this book. Some names that spring to mind are Miriam Haidara, my Commissioning Editor, who thought this would be a good book; Sowmya Thodur who has had to suffer keeping me organized and on the straight and narrow; Jessica Vakili who has had the misfortune to have to work with me on two books now; James Markham, my Development Editor; and especially to all the unsung heroes behind the scenes who converted my files into something you can hold in your hand and read in the bath!

Open source has played a big part in this book too. The book was written using the LyX editor (www.lyx.org/).

Graphics for various circuit schematics and breadboard layouts are courtesy of the Fritzing tool for circuit design (https://fritzing.org/).

Arduino code highlighting is facilitated by the Arduino Latex Listing project run by "Trihedral" on GitHub (https://github.com/trihedral/ArduinoLatexListing/).

Code for the book was developed using both the Arduino IDE versions 1.8.6 and 2.1.0 (www.arduino.cc/) and PlatformIO, my preferred development system (https://platformio.org/).

Finally, I must thank my Technical Reviewer, Farzin Asadi, who kindly read and commented on my code and pointed out a, thankfully, small number of errors and improvements.

Preface

Interrupts seem to be a bone of contention with some makers, but they are actually quite simple (famous last words?) and have the bonus effect of allowing almost instantaneous response to certain events happening, which a polling application might miss, depending on what else it was doing at the time.

Much of the Arduino code you see in books or on pages on the Internet seem to avoid interrupts, which tends to give the impression that they are somehow difficult. This could not be further from the truth!

Interrupts actually help make your code simpler as you only have to code the normal chain of events in your main loop and then write small, very small for best results, functions to handle one interrupt event each. For example, consider a small Arduino robot which wanders around its environment and has a pair of switches attached to it to detect obstacles – similar to the antennae on some insects.

The main code in the `loop()` function should concentrate on driving the robot, most likely in a forward direction but based on a variable which tells it which way to drive. Interrupts would be used to detect when the collision switches had been "pressed" (by hitting something) and update the variables used in the `loop()` to change direction and turn away from the detected obstacle.

This book will hopefully make Arduino (ATmega328P) interrupts a lot less "difficult" and easier to use in your own code.

1   Code and Listings

Inline code, within the text, will be formatted as typewriter text, `like this`.

Code segments and listings in the rest of the book will be shown as follows:

Listing 1 Example code listing

```
const byte ledFlash = 13;
const byte ledOnOff = 8;
const byte onPin  = 2;
const byte offPin = 3;


void setup() {
    // LED pins are obviously outputs.
    pinMode(ledFlash, OUTPUT);
    pinMode(ledOnOff, OUTPUT);
```

```
    // D2 and D3 are inputs with pullup (to save me using
    // external resistors.)
    pinMode(onPin, INPUT_PULLUP);
    pinMode(offPin, INPUT_PULLUP);
}
```

Hopefully, you will note that the code formatting is in the same style as the code in the Arduino IDE environment.

This is thanks to `arduinoLanguage.tex`, a small LATEX file, which is available from my GitHub repository.[2] Of course, this was not all my own work; I forked the original repository owned by "Trihedral."[3] I am extremely grateful to "Trihedral" for making the code available as it saved me no end of work, not least trying to figure out the color codes! I have slightly amended my version to highlight the ATmega328P's register and bit names in addition to the Arduino Language highlighting.

If the code in Listing 1 is *not* highlighted as it would normally appear in the Arduino IDE, then I humbly apologize; the production processes in converting my PDF files into a proper book appear to have overwritten the Arduino style with their own in-house style. C'est la vie.

You are permitted to reuse the code listed in this book as you see fit – it's here to help you, so use it! And if you want to credit me, then feel free to do so as well – but it's not mandatory.

The code repository for this book is located at https://github.com/Apress/arduino-interrupts.

2   Arduino and AVR Code

Some of the examples in this book are obviously written for the Arduino IDE – those examples will need to be compiled within the IDE or using the new Arduino-cli utility[4] of course!

The non-Arduino examples will be found in folders named "PlatformIO."[5] This is another development system for Arduino and AVR projects, and I thoroughly recommend it. The project files, included in this book's code repository, will mainly be configured for either my Arduino Duemilanove or my Arduino Uno boards and may need to be slightly edited to suit your particular Arduino board. It will *not* be necessary for you to create a new project and then copy my files from the `src`, `lib`, and/or `include` directories into your project's similarly named directories as all you need to do is edit the supplied `platformio.ini` file in each project to suit your board.

If you only have the Arduino IDE and you wish to try out the PlatformIO (plain AVR C++ in other words) versions of the sketches in the examples, then you can easily do this if you start a new sketch in the Arduino IDE and copy the code from the PlatformIO source file(s) into it, replacing all the standard code that the IDE creates for you.

When you compile the code, it will still compile all the Arduino files that it would normally do, but it *will not* link them into the finished binary (hex) file. You will get the same sized executable ready for uploading as you would get with the PlatformIO system installed.

What you will not get is any of the Arduino Language features such as `millis()`, `delay()`, `setup()`, `loop()`, and so on, and there's none of the nice hand-holding that you get from the Arduino Language – *you* are firmly in control now! (Have fun!)

---

[2]https://github.com/NormanDunbar/ArduinoLatexListing

[3]https://github.com/trihedral/ArduinoLatexListing

[4]https://github.com/arduino/arduino-cli

[5]https://platformio.org/

Oh yes, for the sake of keeping things simple, most, if not all, of the example sketches and code just flash an LED. Everyone knows how to do this, don't they? LEDs are a fairly simple method of showing how something works without needed masses and masses of sometimes impenetrable code. Out there in the real world, things are a bit more involved than just blinky lights – but hopefully, I'll have explained things in a good enough way for you to go off and make your own, interrupt-driven, projects. Good luck and have fun!

3   Admonitions

If I want to draw your attention to something or emphasize some fact from the main body of the text, I will use a note, as follows:

> **Note**
> This is a note that I want to bring to your attention.

If there is something that you really need to be aware of, you will see this:

> **Warning**
> This is some text that I want to bring to your attention. It may help prevent your Arduino from releasing the magic blue smoke that makes it work, or it may explain the reason why your code fails to do what was expected.

And finally, if I have a useful tip or helpful hint, I will do this:

> **Tip**
> Never run with scissors!

Terminology

Terms like "master" and "slave" are deemed to be no longer acceptable, and many organizations have been amending their documentation to replace those terms with other, more acceptable ones.

In the data sheet for the ATmega328P,[6] the existing "master" and "slave" terms are still in place. In this book, I will avoid those terms, unless I am directly quoting from the data sheet or using the name of a register or bit within a register.

I will be replacing "slave" with "sensor" or "peripheral" and "master" with "controller" as appropriate and as is currently the new standard.

---

[6]At the time of writing, 2020.

Introduction

This book is intended to be a guide, for beginners and moderately experienced Arduino makers, into the *slightly scary* world of Arduino Interrupts. Actually, it's not *actually* the Arduino, it's the Arduino's *microcontroller*, the ATmega328P. However, I'll be using one or two of my Arduino boards as test beds throughout.

Interrupts do not feature much[7] in the Arduino Language, but are an integral part of the AVR hardware itself. They are what allows your sketch, or application code, to apparently do two things at once. Consider, for example, that your laser cutter has a powerful and exceedingly destructive laser beam. You would like the beam to cut off immediately when you hit the *Big Red PANIC! Switch* – it's no good to you, or anyone else, if the beam carries on until the end of the programmed cut and *then* checks to see if the switch has been pressed.

That switch is almost 100% certain to be attached to an interrupt, and that interrupt will "fire" as soon as the switch is hit, cutting off the beam immediately.

There are times when polling a sensor is acceptable, but in doing so, you waste the microcontroller's time and resources when it should be left to get on with whatever the main task is, and only process the sensor input when the sensor has some to offer.

Do you sit in your lounge at home regularly checking the front door to see if someone is there? Or do you wait for the doorbell to chime, *interrupting* whatever you are doing at the time? That's the difference between polling and interrupts in a nutshell.

The main body of code continues as programmed, doing what it does best, and without checking the "front door" all the time. When the "doorbell" chimes, the program is interrupted, saves its place in the code, goes off to see who is at the door, and then comes back to continue from where it left off. There's no specific place that it can be interrupted; it can happen at any place in the code, and it will be handled correctly – if programmed to do so.

In the forthcoming chapters, I will explain the vast majority of the interrupts[8] available on the microcontroller used in the Arduino Uno, Nano, and my favorite, the Duemilanove, the Atmel (now Microchip) ATmega328P. In each case, where relevant, I will explain what the interrupt is for; how it works; how, or if, it can be used in an Arduino sketch; and how it can be used in plain AVR C++ code. In addition, if I feel like showing off, I will show it in AVR Assembly Language. All the demonstration code will be available for download from the book's GitHub account.

---

[7]Only the functions `attachInterrupt()` and `detachInterrupt()` allow you access to the INT0 and INT1 interrupts, and nothing else. The `millis()` and `micros()` functions are facilitated by the overflow interrupt for Timer/counter 0, but all that happens in the background, hidden from your view. Arduino serial communications, of course, *do* use interrupts.

[8]With only one exception, SPM!

Where appropriate, each demonstration will be accompanied by a Fritzing[9] project in which only the breadboard layout is of any relevance. For those readers without a Fritzing installation (and why not?), there will be a PNG image, exported from the project, to show the breadboard layout.

---

[9]http://fritzing.org

Arduino Interrupts

1

This chapter will introduce you to the concept of interrupts on the Arduino. More specifically, the interrupts are actually part of the ATmega328P used on many Arduino boards such as the Uno. Here you will learn all about how the ATmega328P processes interrupts and returns to your code afterwards.

1.1   Interrupt Concepts

There are many interrupts available on the ATmega328P; Table 1-1 shows them all. Each interrupt vector is two *instruction words* in size. On the ATmega328P, an instruction word is two bytes in size, so there are four bytes for each interrupt vector in Table 1-1.

The Interrupt Vector Table, if present, is usually located at address 0 in the Flash RAM – unless you have set fuses to relocate it of course. More on that later. On an Arduino board, the vectors do indeed reside at address 0, and this is considered "standard" – at least, if you are using the *avr-gcc* C++ compiler, which sets up the Interrupt Vector Table for you.

The reason for this necessity is that the ATmega328P, in your Arduino, always starts executing at the Reset vector when power is applied. The device has to know instinctively where to begin executing when power is applied, and so it starts at address 0.[1] If the user presses the reset button or grounds physical pin 1 on the ATmega328P, then execution jumps to the Reset vector address, to follow the instructions there. Usually, address 0 will contain a "jump" instruction to the real start of the code. The jump instruction, JMP, is a 32-bit instruction, which is four bytes or two instruction words – just the right size to fit into the Interrupt Vector Table.

> **Note**
> If you are interested, the JMP instruction uses the highest 10 bits of the lowest word in memory for the opcode; the next 6 bits of the same word are used for the high-order 6 bits of the destination address with the second word of the instruction being the low-order 16 bits of the address. The address is therefore 22 bits in size and allows for up to 2^{22} *words* of address space to be addressed. As the ATmega328P only has 32 KB (16 K words) of Flash RAM, 22 bits is suitably large enough to cover the entire address space.

---

[1] Of course, this depends on the fuse settings; it may be at the start of the bootloader address space.

© The Author(s), under exclusive license to APress Media, LLC, part of Springer Nature 2024
N. Dunbar, *Arduino Interrupts*, Maker Innovations Series,
https://doi.org/10.1007/978-1-4842-9714-8_1

Table 1-1 ATmega328P interrupts

Vector	Name	Description
0	RESET	Reset from power-on, Watchdog reset, Brown Out reset, or RST pin grounded.
1	INT0	External Interrupt request 0.
2	INT1	External Interrupt request 1.
3	PCINT0	Pin Change Interrupt request 0.
4	PCINT1	Pin Change Interrupt request 1.
5	PCINT2	Pin Change Interrupt request 2.
6	WDT	Watchdog Timer Interrupt.
7	TIMER2 COMPA	Timer/Counter 2 Compare Match A.
8	TIMER2 COMPB	Timer/Counter 2 Compare Match B.
9	TIMER2 OVF	Timer/Counter 2 Overflow.
10	TIMER1 CAPT	Timer/Counter 1 Input Capture Event.
11	TIMER1 COMPA	Timer/Counter 1 Compare Match A.
12	TIMER1 COMPB	Timer/Counter 1 Compare Match B.
13	TIMER1 OVF	Timer/Counter 1 Overflow.
14	TIMER0 COMPA	Timer/Counter 0 Compare Match A.
15	TIMER0 COMPB	Timer/Counter 0 Compare Match B.
16	TIMER0 OVF	Timer/Counter 0 Overflow.
17	SPI STC	SPI Serial Transfer Complete.
18	USART RX	USART Receive Complete.
19	USART UDRE	USART Data Register Empty.
20	USART TX	USART Transmit Complete.
21	ADC	ADC Conversion Complete.
22	EE READY	EEPROM Ready.
23	ANALOG COMP	Analog Comparator Interrupt.
24	TWI	Two-Wire (I^2C) Serial Interface.
25	SPM READY	Store Program Memory. *This interrupt is not covered in this book due to a lack of available information regarding its use.*

The table is in order of the interrupt priority – the Reset interrupt is the one with the highest priority, `INT0` is next, then `INT1`, and so on.

Interrupts will only be available if the device has been initialized in such a way that the *Global Interrupt flag* is configured on. For projects developed in the Arduino Language, this is done automatically; for other development systems, you may have to do this explicitly in your code. The global interrupt flag is the "I" (for interrupt) bit in the ATmega328P's *Status Register* (`SREG`).

In addition to the global interrupt flag, each interrupt has itself to be enabled, normally by setting a bit in a register deep inside the ATmega328P.

On Arduinos, some interrupts are set up for you, behind the scenes,[2] and without you having to do anything. These are

- Interrupts are enabled globally.
- Timer/counter 0 is configured with its overflow interrupt enabled. This is used for the `millis()`, `micros()`, and `delay()` functions.

---

[2]By the `init()` function, called at startup.

- If your sketch uses the Serial port (the USART), then two of the three available USART interrupts will be in use while there is data to transmit or receive; these are
  - USART RX: This interrupt, the *USART Receive Complete* interrupt, executes when a new byte of data is received into the USART. On Arduinos, the byte is copied into the Arduino's receive buffer, if there is space for it, or quietly dropped otherwise. The data byte remains in the Arduino's receive buffer until the sketch reads it out using a `Serial.read()` function call.
  - USART UDRE: This interrupt, the *USART Data Register Empty* interrupt, executes when transmitting data, and the previous byte has been passed from the UDR0 register into the USART's internal shift register ready to be transmitted. There is now room for another byte to be loaded into the UDR0 register.

1.2   Interrupt Processing

What exactly happens when an interrupt is received by a working program? It depends on the type of interrupt that has been fired. There are two separate interrupt types:

- Edge-triggered interrupts
- Level-triggered interrupts

Edge-triggered interrupts are detected when an "edge" is found on a pin or are any interrupts which are not level interrupts! Think of a square wave, for example, the edges are where it changes from low to high or from high to low. Levels are where the wave is high or low and stays there for a time.

In *most* cases, when an interrupt occurs, the "I" bit in the Status Register is cleared, and thus all further interrupt processing is disabled. The bit is cleared by the ATmega328P hardware, not any running software. An interrupt flag bit is set to indicate that the particular interrupt has occurred. Most interrupts have a flag bit.

If, and only if, you know what you are doing, you *can* change the global interrupt flag back to a 1 in your interrupt handling code so that *nested interrupts* are enabled. This means that your current interrupt handler could itself be interrupted. It is probably advisable to avoid this situation. The Arduino interrupt handling routines do not re-enable the global interrupt flag during interrupt handling.

The *Program Counter* register (PC) is the address of the next instruction to be executed; it has its value copied onto the stack for safe keeping and is loaded with the address of the appropriate interrupt vector in Table 1-1. Execution continues from that address. The hardware also clears the interrupt flag that was previously set to show that the interrupt had occurred.

It takes a minimum of four system clock cycles to initiate an interrupt. If the ATmega328P was sleeping when the interrupt occurred, the wake-up time from that sleep mode will be increased by a further four clock cycles to accommodate the interrupt.

As each interrupt vector has room for two, and only two, instruction words or space for one 32-bit instruction, the entries in the table are usually a JMP to some other address in the code where the real interrupt handling code begins.

Note

If you are writing in Assembly Language, it is your responsibility to set up the Interrupt Vector Table correctly. You only need to define the RESET interrupt – so that the device knows where to start executing at power-on or after a reset – and any further interrupts that your application code uses. Unused space in the interrupt vector table can be used for application code. This means that if you are not using *any* interrupts, the application code can begin at address 0 and will start executing there on a reset or after a power-on.

If you are using *avr-gcc* to compile your C++ code, then that will set up the entire Interrupt Vector Table automatically. Unused vectors will be filled with a dummy interrupt handler which handles any spurious interrupts detected by the device. The dummy handler simply assumes a really bad error was detected – after all, the detected interrupt was not coded for – and forces the device to reset.

The code that handles the interrupt, the *Interrupt Service Routine* (ISR), should then

- Save the Status Register and any other registers that it intends to use on the stack
- Carry out the required processing to actually handle the interrupt
- Restore the working registers and the Status Register from the stack
- Exit by executing a RETI instruction, *RETurn from Interrupt*

The global interrupt flag is set again by the hardware when the RETI is executed. The PC is restored from the stack, and execution continues from that address – the instruction immediately after the one that was interrupted.

When an ISR returns to the main program, at least one (machine code) instruction will be fully executed before any pending, or further, interrupts are processed *in priority order*. A pending interrupt is one which occurred while the ISR was in progress.

It takes a further four clock cycles to return from an ISR after processing.

Normally, while the ISR is executing, further interrupts are *not* processed. The current interrupt is usually permitted to run to completion. However, *all* interrupts available to the ATmega328P have a flag bit to indicate that it has occurred – whether the global interrupt flag is set or not. While this bit records the fact that a particular interrupt has occurred, it does not record how many times it occurred. This is a fact worth remembering, and I will explain why later.

Note

According to the data sheet for the ATmega328P, the interrupting stimulus can be detected on a pin, for example, and, if so, will set the interrupt's flag as appropriate. *Only* if the flag is set, *and* the interrupt itself has been enabled, *and* the global interrupts are also enabled, then the ISR for that interrupt will be executed, interrupting the main code. In this case, the flag bit will be automatically cleared.

In order for the interrupt stimulus to be noticed by the ATmega328P, it must remain in place for at least one clock cycle. On an Arduino Uno, for example, the clock runs at 16 MHz or 16 million cycles per second. Each cycle takes 1/16,000,000ths of a second, or 0.0625 microseconds, to execute. That's pretty quick!

While an ISR is executing, further interrupts of the same kind will simply set the appropriate flag. Other, different interrupts will likewise set their own flags. As long as the ISR is executing, these will have no effect on the device. They will be processed, if enabled, after the current ISR completes and returns to the main code, but only after one machine instruction has been fully executed.

Interrupt flags can be manually cleared by writing a 1 to the flag bit position(s) to be cleared. If an ISR is processing the interrupt, this is done automatically for you. If, on the other hand, there isn't an ISR, then the sketch software should explicitly clear the flag.

> **Note**
>
> You may be puzzled by the statement that a 1 is to be written to the bit? Surely that should be a 0? No, I'm afraid not, and I'm as equally puzzled as you are! The ATmega328P hardware requires these, and many other, flag bits to be cleared by the writing of a 1 to the appropriate bit.

Level interrupts do not necessarily set the interrupt flag but simply continue to trigger as long as the interrupt condition *is present*. If the interrupt triggering event ceases before the interrupt is actually triggered, then the interrupt will not be triggered. The stimulus which triggers these level interrupts must ensure that the triggering event remains in place for at least five clock cycles. On the Arduino Uno again, five clock cycles is a massive 0.3125 microseconds, so that's how long the interrupting stimulus has to remain in force so that the ATmega328P recognizes it.

The data sheet for the ATmega328P warns that

> The Status Register is not automatically stored when entering an interrupt routine, nor restored when returning from an interrupt routine. This must be handled by software.

This is not something you need to worry about unless you are coding in Assembly Language. The code generated by the C++ compiler (*avr-g++* and/or *avr-gcc*) generates the correct code.

1.3   Interrupts While Processing Interrupts

I mentioned previously that the interrupt flags don't record how many times an interrupt occurred, only that it occurred. This is an important point to remember. Consider a system set up to toggle an LED by pressing a switch. Switches, by their very nature, have a tendency to *bounce* when making or breaking contact. This is caused by the contacts being forced together, or apart, inside the switch and bouncing off of each other a few (dozen!) times before they settle down, stop bouncing, and finally make, or break, contact.

- Let us consider a "push to make, release to break" switch. When the button is pressed, the very first "make" triggers the interrupt, and the ISR starts executing with the result that the LED is about to be toggled on.
- While the ISR is running the code to toggle the LED on, the button switch's internals are *still* bouncing – making and breaking lots of times – before settling down to a "pressed" state. If one or more of the bounces last long enough to trigger the interrupt, then the interrupt flag bit is set again.
- The current ISR execution completes and the LED is lit, for example. The main code continues by executing its next instruction, and then the ISR executes again because the interrupt flag bit was set by the multiple "makes" of the bouncy switch.
- The LED is now toggled off again by the ISR's second execution.

This leaves the user wondering why the LED *sometimes* doesn't come on when the switch is pressed. The same can happen when the LED is expected to be extinguished; sometimes, it works, while at other times it doesn't.

I admit that this is a slightly contrived example, but it is valid in that regardless of the number of times the interrupt stimulus happens while an ISR is executing, the flag bit only records that it effectively happened once more, so the ISR will be executed one more time after the current execution completes.

I did actually suffer from this problem while writing my book *Arduino Software Internals*.[3] The Arduino website has an example of using a switch to light an LED, which I was using as an example. It doesn't work properly if the switch bounces. It works perfectly if you debounce the switch.

> **Tip**
> Switch debouncing is an important topic and is discussed in some detail in Appendix C, "Debouncing Switches."

1.4   Interrupts While Not Configured

As you now know, many interrupts have a flag bit in a register somewhere. This flag bit will always be set when the interrupt stimulus is registered in the appropriate place – on a pin, after a USART transmission, and so on – and will remain set *until cleared*.

This is something you might want to take note of. On power-up, or reset, almost all registers are cleared to have zeros in all their bits. Global interrupts are also disabled. This obviously leads to the system being configured in a default state. The *Analog Comparator*, for example (see Chapter 11, "Analog Comparator Interrupt"), is configured by default to compare the voltage on pin D6 with that on D7 and to set the ACO bit in the ACSR register whenever the output from the comparator changes.

Setting or clearing the ACO bit is a stimulus that *would* trigger an interrupt had the device been differently configured and global interrupts enabled. However, even though no such configuration took place, the AC interrupt flag, bit ACI in the ACSR register, will still show that the stimulus for the *Analog Comparator* interrupt has been received and noted.

If interrupts for the Analog Comparator and global interrupts were subsequently enabled, the ISR for the *Analog Comparator* interrupt would immediately fire because the ACI bit is set.

Depending on the interrupt being captured, and what its ISR is coded to do, this might not be what you want. It is therefore always advisable to clear the appropriate interrupt flag bit before enabling the interrupt that you are interested in.

In addition, without interrupts being enabled and appropriate ISRs written, the flag bit will remain set until cleared by your code. Normally, this entails writing a one value to the bit, which is confusing to many people who are accustomed to clearing bits in registers by writing a zero. Atmel decided otherwise, so that's what we have to do. If the interrupts are enabled, then the flag bit will be cleared automatically by the hardware when the ISRs execute.

---

[3] Available from Apress and all good bookshops around the world!

1.5 Interrupt Coding – Points to Note

This section discusses a number of relatively important points that should be kept in mind when writing code which uses or handles interrupts.

1.5.1 Do You Really Need Interrupts?

An interesting question, especially in a book about interrupts! However, it does require bearing in mind given how the ISR interrupts your sketch code every time the interrupt is triggered. If the ISR code takes too long to execute, then your sketch's main purpose will suffer as the interrupt handler takes up almost all the processing time.

Equally, if your sketch spends most of the `loop()` function just waiting for an interrupt to occur, then perhaps it would be better if it polled the interrupt flag to see if it has occurred and then handle it as appropriate on detection.

It should be obvious that if the sketch sends the ATmega328P to sleep, rather than sitting in the `loop()` constantly doing "not very much," then an interrupt will be useful in waking the board when required. I use this method on an ATtiny85 night light. The Analog Comparator interrupt wakes the sleeping board when the light level falls below a user set limit. It will then turn on the night light LED and immediately go back to sleep. When it gets light again, the board wakes up once more and turns the LED off. Apart from the LED usage, very little power is required, and the battery lasts that little bit longer.

An interrupt is necessary to wake the board, in this case, as it spends most of the time fast asleep.

For best results, interrupts should be used when they are expected to occur rarely, so as not to impinge on the performance of the sketch's actual purpose – the aforementioned *Big Red PANIC! Switch*, for example, is not expected to be triggering frequently, but must be actioned as soon as it is triggered.

If the interrupt is expected to occur frequently, then the interrupt should really be tested for and handled in the normal code as opposed to using an ISR. The setup and pull-down[4] of the ISR function will again degrade performance; however, when the `loop()` function polls for, and handles, the interrupt stimulus, there is no setup and pull-down to execute, saving time on each and every execution.

1.5.2 Delays and Serial Input/Output

Beware when executing code within an interrupt handler, on an Arduino board, programmed using the Arduino Language. Within an interrupt handling ISR, interrupts are turned off. This means that attempting to call a `delay()` or `Serial.println()` or similar will not work as these rely on interrupts to function. This is the usual advice given with respect to Arduino projects. However, that's not *strictly* true. You *can* call `Serial.println()` and so on, from an ISR, *provided* you print fewer characters than the amount of free space in the transmit buffer. If you fill the buffer, which is

---

[4]When an ISR is executed, the code executing will save certain registers on the stack before executing any of the ISR's useful code. On completion, it has to restore all those registers. Code generated by the *gcc* compiler, used by the Arduino IDE, etc., preserves the SREG plus every one of the 32 general-purpose registers on entry to an ISR and restores them all on exit. That's a lot of work before the useful code in the ISR can get started. This happens regardless of whether or not the registers are used by the ISR code.

63 bytes in size by default, `Serial.print()` will hang waiting for an interrupt to send the data to the USART and to clear space in the buffer. As the interrupt will never occur, the buffer overflow will never clear, and the system will be stuck!

1.5.3 Keep ISRs Short

ISR code must be kept as short as possible to avoid unnecessary delays to the main code. This is discussed in upcoming chapters where the individual interrupts themselves are explained.

1.5.4 Variables May Be Volatile

Variables used in the ISR code should be declared as `volatile` if they are also accessed in the main code so that the compiler doesn't optimize them away, leading to interesting bugs in your application.

1.5.5 Interrupt Vectors Can Be Relocated by Fuse Settings

There is one fuse bit which affects the location of the *Reset* interrupt vector. Bit 0 in the ATmega328P's *High Fuse Byte* is the BOOTRST fuse bit. When BOOTRST is programmed, or zero, then the Reset interrupt vector will be located in the first four bytes of the Bootloader location in Flash RAM. When BOOTRST is not programmed, or 1, the Reset interrupt vector will be located at address 0 in the Flash RAM.

> **Tip**
> A fuse bit is considered to be programmed when it is *zero*, not one. Bear this in mind.

The location of the remainder of the Interrupt Vector Table is determined by the IVSEL bit in the *MCU Control Register,* MCUCR. If IVSEL is zero, the table is located in Flash RAM at address 2, while if it is set to 1, the table immediately follows after the location of the Reset interrupt vector, wherever that is located. Table 1-2 shows the four options available.

Table 1-2 Interrupt Vector Table options

BOOTRST	IVSEL	Reset Vector Address	Vector Table Address
0	0	Boot Loader Address	Flash RAM Address 2
0	1	Boot Loader Address	Reset vector address + 2
1	**0**	**Flash RAM Address 0**	**Flash RAM Address 2**
1	1	Flash RAM Address 0	Reset vector address + 2

The default, and the option described in the remainder of this book, is the third option – the Reset address is at address 0 with the rest of the interrupt vectors following on immediately after it. The option is highlighted in bold text in Table 1-2.

> **Note**
>
> Don't forget, Flash RAM is *word* addressed. Address 0 is bytes 0 and 1. Address 1 is bytes 2 and 3 and so on. The 2 added in the Vector Table Address calculation is two *words*. A word is 16 bits in this case. Two words, or four bytes, are required because an interrupt vector is always 32 bits, two words or four bytes.

1.5.6 The Arduino Doesn't Make Interrupts Easy

Many of the interrupts available on the ATmega328P are not *easily* available to the Arduino Language; however, it's not really a huge problem, you just have to get used to some *interesting* coding.

1.6 Key Takeaways

In this chapter, we learned that

- An interrupt will cause the current sketch or application code to be paused while the interrupt routine is serviced by the *Interrupt Service Routine*, the ISR.
- The Interrupt Vector Table is normally located at address 0 in the Flash RAM – unless you have set the fuses to relocate it.
- An ISR will only be executed if
  - Global interrupts are enabled.
  - The specific interrupt is itself enabled.
  - The interrupt's triggering criteria are met.
- When an interrupt is triggered, it takes a minimum of four clock cycles to initiate the ISR. If the system is in one of its sleep modes when the interrupt occurs, the usual wake-up time for that sleep mode is increased by these four cycles. The completion of an ISR and its return to the main code adds a further four clock cycles.
- When an ISR is executing, global interrupts are disabled. This prevents nested interrupts. The sketch or application code is, however, free to enable interrupts within an ISR which will permit further interrupts of a higher priority to interrupt the current ISR.
- When ISR processing is complete and control returns to the sketch or application code, at least one machine instruction will be fully executed before any pending or further interrupts are processed. A pending interrupt is one which occurred while the previous ISR was in progress.
- Interrupts can be edge triggered or level triggered. Level-triggered interrupts will trigger the ISR for as long as the triggering level remains present.
- Whenever an ISR for a particular interrupt executes, the flag bit for that interrupt will be automatically cleared. If the interrupt is not enabled, the ISR obviously will not be triggered, but the flag bit *will* still be set – as a *pending* interrupt – if the appropriate criteria for that interrupt are met. In this case, the sketch or application code *should* clear the flag bit by writing a 1 to it. This will prevent the pending interrupt from immediately triggering the ISR in the event of the interrupt subsequently being enabled.
- The Arduino Language doesn't *easily* permit the use of most interrupts.

1.7   Coming Up

In the next chapter, we will begin our investigation of the actual interrupts present on the ATmega328P, by looking at what happens when the device is reset.

Reset Interrupt

2

In this chapter, we begin our dive into the specific interrupts available on the ATmega328P by taking a look at the Reset interrupt. This is the interrupt which triggers when the board is powered on or reset in some manner, so it's a good place to start our investigations. You will learn here how to determine why the board was reset but also how the bootloader installed on your board might just hide those details from you.

2.1 Resetting the Board

The vector for this interrupt is located at address 0 in the Interrupt Vector Table, and as such, the *Reset* interrupt is the interrupt with the highest priority. There are a number of reasons why the system might execute this interrupt:

- At power-on: The ATmega328P needs to have somewhere to start executing! It will normally start from address 0 in the Flash RAM; however, with suitable fuse and register bit settings, the interrupt vector table can be moved elsewhere in memory, into the bootloader address space.
- When the reset pin, physical pin 1 on the ATmega328P, is grounded: Normally, this pin is held at VCC by judicious use of a $10 \, K\Omega$ resistor; however, when the reset switch is pressed, the pin is grounded and the interrupt occurs.
- When the *Watchdog Timer* (WDT) times out and forces a reset: There is an explanation of the WDT in Chapter 5, "Watchdog Interrupt."
- If the power supply dips below a certain voltage for too long a time, the *Brown Out Detector* (BOD) will hold the microcontroller, internally, in a reset mode until the voltage rises to a workable level again. On the return of a working voltage, BOD will release the internal reset hold, and the system will reset. If you had a logic analyzer or oscilloscope on the reset pin, you would not see it being held at GND potential while BOD was controlling the resetting of the board.

© The Author(s), under exclusive license to APress Media, LLC, part of Springer Nature 2024
N. Dunbar, *Arduino Interrupts*, Maker Innovations Series,
https://doi.org/10.1007/978-1-4842-9714-8_2

- In an Arduino sketch, the Interrupt Vector Table is filled with any vectors that are explicitly used in the sketch; plus the *Timer/counter 0 Overflow* interrupt used for the `millis()`, `micros()`, and `delay()` functions; and, if Serial is used, the *USART Receive Complete* and *USART Data Register Empty* interrupts. All remaining unused vectors are pointed at a "bad interrupt" routine. This causes the Arduino to be reset on the occurrence of an interrupt which it was not expecting.
- Arduinos connected to the IDE's Serial Monitor will be reset when the monitor screen is opened.
- Arduinos being programmed via the bootloader will be reset in order to activate the bootloader which looks for incoming communications of a certain protocol. If none are forthcoming, the main sketch is executed; otherwise, the bootloader begins writing the new sketch into program memory.
- ATmega328Ps, whether on an Arduino board or not, being programmed by an In-Circuit System Programmer (ICSP) device will be reset.

After the system has been reset, the *MCU Status Register* (MCUSR) can be used to find out why the reset happened. There are four bit flags in this register (which is not the Status Register or SR mentioned previously) which are of interest:

- The WDRF bit shows that the system was reset by the Watchdog Timer timing out.
- The BORF bit shows that the system was reset by the Brown Out Detector.
- The EXTRF bit shows that the system was reset by the reset pin being grounded.
- The PORF bit shows that the system was powered on. A power-on reset will clear the other bits of the MCUSR register.

Warning
In a break with tradition, these four flag bits are cleared, if required, by the sketch code writing a zero – yes, zero this time – to the bits in question. This is the complete opposite to just about every other flag in the ATmega328P!

The data sheet for the ATmega328P advises that

To make use of the Reset Flags to identify a reset condition, the user should read and then reset the MCUSR as early as possible in the program. If the register is cleared before another reset occurs, the source of the reset can be found by examining the Reset Flags.

This advice means that an Arduino sketch *should*[1] be able to determine how it was reset or started. Let's see how that works. Figure 2-1 shows the very simple breadboard layout I used for this sketch. It is a simple setup where I have four LEDs and four 330 Ω resistors to indicate which of the bits in the MCUSR register were set when the Arduino reset.

---

[1] Do you feel a "but" coming soon? I do!

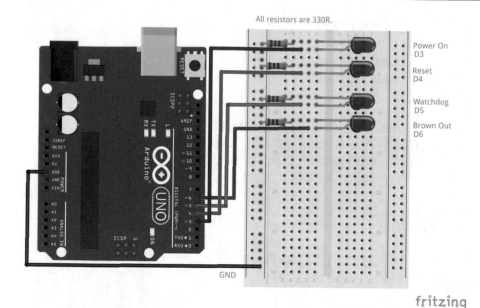

Figure 2-1 Reset interrupt bit checker

Listings 2-1 to 2-4 are taken from a sketch which examines the MCUSR register to determine why the Arduino board was reset. My Duemilanove and my Uno give rather surprising results!

Listing 2-1 ResetInterrupt – defines

```
// Easy defines.
#define POWER_ON_RESET(x)  ((x) & (1 << PORF))
#define POWER_ON_RESET_PIN 3
#define EXTERNAL_RESET(x)  ((x) & (1 << EXTRF))
#define EXTERNAL_RESET_PIN 4
#define WATCHDOG_RESET(x)  ((x) & (1 << WDRF))
#define WATCHDOG_RESET_PIN 5
#define BOD_RESET(x)       ((x) & (1 << BORF))
#define BOD_RESET_PIN    6
```

Listing 2-1 is just a few defines to make it more understandable when I come back to the code in six months' time! Just in case I forget what PORF and so on actually mean.

Listing 2-2 ResetInterrupt – lightLED() function

```
void lightLED(uint8_t led) {
    digitalWrite(led, HIGH);
}
```

The lightLED() function (see Listing 2-2) is there to simply light up the LED(s) corresponding to the bits which were found to be set in MCUSR after the device restarted.

Listing 2-3   ResetInterrupt – setup() function

```
void setup() {
    // Get current MCUSR & reset it.
    uint8_t mcusr = MCUSR;
    MCUSR = 0;

    pinMode(POWER_ON_RESET_PIN, OUTPUT);
    pinMode(EXTERNAL_RESET_PIN, OUTPUT);
    pinMode(WATCHDOG_RESET_PIN, OUTPUT);
    pinMode(BOD_RESET_PIN, OUTPUT);

    Serial.begin(9600);
    delay(1000);

    Serial.print("MCUSR = 0b");
    Serial.println(mcusr, BIN);

    if (POWER_ON_RESET(mcusr)) {
        Serial.println("Power on reset detected.");
        lightLED(POWER_ON_RESET_PIN);
    }

    if (EXTERNAL_RESET(mcusr)) {
        Serial.println("External reset detected.");
        lightLED(EXTERNAL_RESET_PIN);
    }

    if (WATCHDOG_RESET(mcusr)) {
        Serial.println("Watchdog reset detected.");
        lightLED(WATCHDOG_RESET_PIN);
    }

    if (BOD_RESET(mcusr)) {
        Serial.println("Brown out reset detected.");
        lightLED(BOD_RESET_PIN);
    }
}
```

The `setup()` function is where the real work takes place. Reading through Listing 2-3, we can see that if the board was reset by one of the four main reasons, we should get a message on the Serial Monitor, and a certain number of LEDs will be lit up.

Listing 2-4 ResetInterrupt – loop() function

```
void loop() {
  // Not much going on here...
}
```

The `loop()` function, in this sketch, does very little – as you can see from Listing 2-4. In fact, it does nothing.

While testing the sketch on an Uno with a bootloader present, absolutely no LEDs lit up, and the Serial Monitor showed that `MCUSR` was always zero. I suspected that the bootloader was getting in the way. The Uno uses the Optiboot bootloader, and looking at the code there, I see the code extract shown in Listing 2-5.

Listing 2-5 Optiboot extract

```
    ....
  // Adaboot no-wait mod
  ch = MCUSR;
  MCUSR = 0;

 if (!(ch & _BV(EXTRF))) appStart();

  ...

void appStart() {
  watchdogConfig(WATCHDOG_OFF);
  __asm__ __volatile__ (
#ifdef VIRTUAL_BOOT_PARTITION
    // Jump to WDT vector
    "ldi r30,4\n"
    "clr r31\n"
#else
    // Jump to RST vector
    "clr r30\n"
    "clr r31\n"
#endif
    "ijmp\n"    );
}
```

We can see from the bootloader code that on the Uno, running with the Optiboot bootloader, the `MCUSR` register is already examined and reset to zero *before* our sketch gets hold of it. The `ResetInterrupt.ino` sketch is therefore no good on an Uno running with that bootloader. After zeroing out the `MCUSR` register, the bootloader checks if the reset was not caused by an external reset and jumps to the `appStart()` function if that was the case (not an external reset).

At `appStart()`, the `R30` and `R31` registers are cleared to zero, and an indirect jump made to the address held in the `R30:R31` registers combined, which is the Reset vector at address 0. The Uno's bootloader takes the "Jump to RST vector" path through the `appStart()` code.

Note
The IJMP instruction does assume that the Reset vector is located at address 0, which is the case with the Arduino's default fuse settings; however, it is not impossible for users to change the vector locations as described in Table 1-2.

I also program my boards with a USBtiny In-Circuit System Programmer (ICSP) device. So, let's cut the bootloader out of the equation and go direct. Immediately after programming the Uno via the ICSP, I no longer have a bootloader.

- When the sketch has finished uploading via the USBtiny, the LED for an external reset lights which is because the ICSP resets the board by pulling the RST pin low after programming is complete.
- Powering up via the USB socket lights up the LED for a power-on reset.
- Powering up, but not programming, using the USBtiny programmer socket lights up both the LED for a power-on reset and the Brown Out Detector LED. This is interesting as it implies that the power being supplied by the ICSP wasn't stable enough, and the BOD held the board in an internal reset state until it was, finally, stable enough to allow the board to run normally.
- Pressing the reset button lights the external reset LED.

It is not possible to test what happens when the Serial Monitor is opened as there is no communication without the bootloader.

The Duemilanove uses a different bootloader; let's see what happens with that device, first with a bootloader present:

- When the sketch has finished uploading via the bootloader, I see the LED for an external reset lit up.
- Powering up via the USB socket lights up the LEDs for a power-on reset, external reset, and brown out detected. It seems that the Duemilanove is a bit heavy on power, somehow,[2] and the BOD gets involved in keeping things stable.
- Powering up via the USBtiny programmer socket also lights up the LEDs for a power-on reset, external reset, and brown out detected. At least the Duemilanove is consistent in its startup power drain.
- Pressing the reset button lights the external reset LED.
- Opening the Serial Monitor lights the external reset LED. This makes sense because when the Serial Monitor opens, the connected board is reset.

With the bootloader overwritten, the results are as follows:

- When the sketch has finished uploading via the bootloader, I see the LED for an external reset lit up.
- Powering up via the USB socket lights up the LEDs for a power-on reset and brown out detected – this is different when the bootloader is present as the external reset LED is not lit in this configuration.

---

[2]"Somehow" is author speak for, "I don't know what or why this is happening. Yet!"

- Powering up via the USBtiny programmer socket lights up the LEDs for a power-on reset, external reset, and brown out detected.
- Pressing the reset button lights the external reset LED.

Table 2-1 summarizes the results for my Uno, while Table 2-2 summarizes the results for my Duemilanove.

Table 2-1 Uno – Reset results summary

	With Bootloader			Without Bootloader		
	Power	Reset	BOD	Power	Reset	BOD
After upload	–	–	–	–	✔	–
Reset button	–	–	–	–	✔	–
USB power-up	–	–	–	✔	–	–
ICSP power-up	–	–	–	✔	–	✔
Serial Monitor	–	–	–	N/A	N/A	N/A

Table 2-1 shows that the bootloader definitely interferes with the ability of an Uno board to determine its own startup status. It is interesting that there should be a difference between powering the board using the USB connection and using the six-pin ICSP header where the latter displays a BOD detected reset as well as the power-on reset – two for the price of one.

It's clear from Table 2-2 that the bootloader used in the Duemilanove is different from that used in the Uno (although you *can* edit the `boards.txt` file to use the Uno bootloader on the Duemilanove and save some Flash RAM in the process).

Table 2-2 Duemilanove – Reset results summary

	With Bootloader			Without Bootloader		
	Power	Reset	BOD	Power	Reset	BOD
After upload	–	✔	–	–	✔	–
Reset button	–	✔	–	–	✔	–
USB power-up	✔	✔	✔	✔	–	✔
ICSP power-up	✔	✔	✔	✔	✔	✔
Serial Monitor	–	✔	–	N/A	N/A	N/A

Sadly, the Duemilanove seems to suffer from multiple reasons for just about every different method of resetting it – apart from just pressing the reset button. I'm thinking that this particular board needs a bit more "oomph" to get started, and this drags down the power a bit, causing the BOD to kick in and hold the board in reset until the supply stabilizes again.

In summary then, the ability for a sketch to determine how it was started up is not much use on any Arduino[3] which is using a bootloader as some bootloaders get in the way and fiddle with the MCUSR register, so we can't really tell why the device was reset with any great level of accuracy. Shame.

Of course, if we were to write all the code in Assembly Language, *we* would be in total control and able to determine *exactly* how the device was restarted – but we'd still have to lose that bootloader on the Arduino!

---

[3] Well, on my Arduinos at least. Your mileage, as they say, may differ. Try it and see.

> **Note**
> You will note that the Watchdog option is sadly missing from Tables 2-1 and 2-2. This is because we have yet to discuss the Watchdog – but that's coming soon in Chapter 5, "Watchdog Interrupt."

2.2   Register Summary

The single register used by the Reset interrupt is described, in summary only, in this section. Only the bits relevant to the interrupt are considered here. While other bits may be used elsewhere, they are marked here as not applicable. Consult the data sheet for full details of the registers involved.

2.2.1   MCU Status Register

Only the *MCU Status Register*, MCUSR, is used by the Reset interrupt.

7	6	5	4	3	2	1	0
N/A	N/A	N/A	N/A	WDRF	BORF	EXTRF	PORF

Bits 4 through 7 are not used and will always be read as zero. The remaining bits are set to indicate what condition caused the reset.

WDRF   If set, the Watchdog Timer (WDT) caused the reset.

BORF   If set, the Brown Out Detector (BOD) caused the reset.

EXTRF   If set, the External Reset pin was grounded to cause the reset.

PORF   If set, the reset was caused by the device being powered on.

2.3   Key Takeaways

- The Reset interrupt has the highest priority of any interrupt.
- The Reset interrupt can be triggered by
  - Powering on the ATmega328P
  - Pulling pin 1 of the ATmega328P, the reset pin, to ground potential
  - The Watchdog Timer, WDT, causing a reset
  - The Brown Out Detector, BOD, causing a reset
  - A bootloader forcing a reset
  - A bad interrupt being detected – if the code running was created with the *avr-gcc* compiler
  - Opening the Arduino's Serial Monitor utility
  - Programming the AVR with an ICSP
- The MCU Status Register, MCUSR, can be read to determine what exactly caused the reset to occur.
- Some Arduino bootloaders overwrite the MCU Status Register which corrupts the reset information.
- The Duemilanove seems to be a bit power-hungry at startup.

2.4 Coming Up

That was somewhat easy – there's nothing to set up or configure; the interrupt "just" happens as and when required. The next two chapters take a look at the external interrupts – those triggered by something happening outside of the ATmega328P.

Read on for a description of a pair of interrupts which the Arduino boards can easily configure so that a function in your sketch is automatically called whenever *something*[4] happens on pins D2 and D3.

---

[4]That's a technical term!

External Interrupts INT0/INT1

3

In this chapter, we will investigate the first pair of external interrupts. External interrupts are triggered by some stimulus applied to the pins in question. External interrupts cover INT0 and INT1, to be discussed in this chapter, and the Pin Change interrupts covered in the following chapter. The Arduino software makes INT0 and INT1 available for use, but hides the names from you. After reading this chapter, you will have a better understanding of what the Arduino is doing behind the scenes and hiding from you.

3.1   Interrupts INT0 and INT1

The INT0 and INT1 interrupts are located in Vectors 1 and 2 in the Interrupt Vector Table.

The ATmega328P has two external interrupts available, these being INT0 and INT1. These are the highest priority interrupts after the Reset interrupt, with INT0 being a higher priority interrupt than INT1.

> **Note**
> These interrupts will fire even if the appropriate pin is configured as an output pin, and the pin changes state in such a way as to match the interrupt stimulus. This feature effectively allows your code to trigger an interrupt almost at will.

3.2   Setting Up Arduino Interrupts

Other than the Reset interrupt described in the previous chapter, these two interrupts are probably the easiest to set up when you are using an Arduino board or at least using the Arduino Language to program the sketch. The Arduino Language provides a function named `attachInterrupt()` which does all the setup necessary.

On the other hand, if you occasionally decide to write code for your Arduino board using plain AVR C++, then you will need to write all the code to do the required register setup and also write the Interrupt Service Routine (ISR) – one for each of the two interrupts in use by your sketch – as described in Section 3.3, "Setting Up AVR Interrupts."

© The Author(s), under exclusive license to APress Media, LLC, part of Springer Nature 2024
N. Dunbar, *Arduino Interrupts*, Maker Innovations Series,
https://doi.org/10.1007/978-1-4842-9714-8_3

On an Arduino, the INT0 interrupt is attached to pin D2, while the INT1 interrupt is attached to pin D3. Normally, these two pins are used for I/O, and no interrupts are used; however, the `attachInterrupt()` function links a function in your sketch to the pin(s) so that the function is called whenever the appropriate stimulus is seen by the pin.

The `attachInterrupt()` function requires three parameters:

- An interrupt number, 0 or 1 only. This corresponds to INT0 and INT1.
- A function address to be called when the interrupt is fired.
- A stimulus to fire the interrupt.

3.2.1   Interrupt Number

The Arduino website warns against calling `attachInterrupt()` and passing 0 or 1 directly for the interrupt number; instead, it advises passing the appropriate pin number to `digitalPinToInterrupt()` and using that function's result as the interrupt number parameter of `attachInterrupt()`. Calling `digitalPinToInterrupt()` will return the correct interrupt number for the pin passed or a *negative* error code if the wrong pin is passed as a parameter.

> **Note**
> This raises a slight problem as `attachInterrupt()` requires an `unsigned` value for the interrupt number. If called via `digitalPinToInterrupt()`, as advised, then it will work, but it's not correct C++ code.

For example:

```
attachInterrupt(digitalPinToInterrupt(onPin), ledOn, FALLING)
```

would connect the `onPin` pin to the `ledOn()` function which would be automatically called every time that there was a high to low change on the `onPin` pin.

In the event that the pin number passed is out of range, only pins numbered 2 and 3 are permitted with an ATmega328P, then the code will not raise any errors, and the interrupt code in the attached function would not be executed.

3.2.2   Interrupt Function

The interrupt function parameter is a *pointer* to any appropriate function within your sketch. The function must be defined as `void` and take no parameters, for example, `void ledOn()`. When passed as a parameter to `attachInterrupt()`, however, it is the *address* of the function we want, not a function call – so don't use the parentheses. If your function name is `ledOn()`, for example, then pass the *address*, `ledOn`, and not the *result* of the function being called, which would be `ledOn()` *with* the parentheses.

A couple of points to bear in mind when writing interrupt-driven code:

- Interrupt handling functions should be kept as short as possible. This is the case regardless of whether you are writing code in the Arduino Language, plain AVR C++, or even Assembly Language. Keep it short and keep it simple.
- Variables which are accessed in both the main body of the sketch and within the interrupt functions must be declared as `volatile` to prevent the compiler optimizing them out of the sketch altogether, for example, `volatile uint8_t ledStatus;`.
- While keeping the interrupt functions short and sweet, use them to set a flag variable that the main code in the `loop()` function checks and acts upon – if at all possible.

Of course, in the examples which follow, I will occasionally completely ignore some of that advice. This is because the ISRs are very short indeed (and are even shorter when I use AVR C++ rather than the Arduino Language).

3.2.3 Interrupt Stimulus

There are four different stimuli that can be used to trigger the interrupts:

- **LOW** will trigger the interrupt *whenever* the pin is low, and the interrupt will fire constantly for as long as the pin is held low. If a sketch sets the pin low, then the interrupt routine will keep firing until the pin is taken high again.
- **CHANGE** will trigger the interrupt whenever the pin changes value from high to low or from low to high. The interrupt will not know what the state of the pin is, only that it changed. If you need this information, you will have to execute a `digitalRead()` function call on the appropriate pin to find out.
- **RISING** will trigger the interrupt whenever the pin goes from low to high.
- **FALLING** will trigger the interrupt whenever the pin goes from high to low.

Of these stimuli, `LOW` is deemed to be a Level interrupt and as such *will not set a flag bit* to say that it occurred; it will simply keep on firing for as long as the pin remains low. The other three stimuli will set an appropriate flag bit.

3.2.4 Arduino Polling Example

The demonstration sketch for these two interrupts is one in which a switch attached to pin D2 turns an LED on, and another switch attached to pin D3 turns it off again. At the same time, the main loop of the program is flashing the built-in LED for five seconds at a time. The main loop is using the usual `delay()` function call.

The sketch in Listings 3-1 to 3-3 and the breadboard layout in Figure 3-1 are an example of how it can be done with code which polls for input each time around the loop. However, you will find it extremely difficult to get the sketch to turn the green LED on and off as there is only a brief interval in the main loop where the two switches are polled. If you miss your opportunity, you have to wait, at the very least, another five seconds, maybe even ten, before the switch will be polled again.

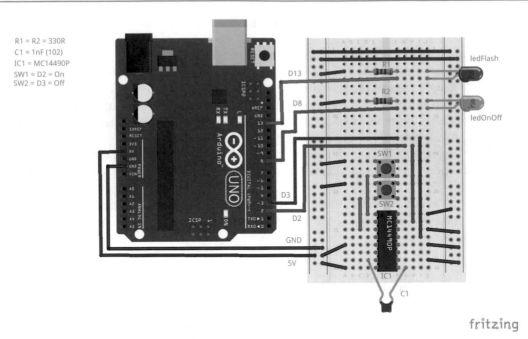

R1 = R2 = 330R
C1 = 1nF (102)
IC1 = MC14490P
SW1 = D2 = On
SW2 = D3 = Off

Figure 3-1 PollingSwitches sketch – breadboard layout

Note
Don't dismantle this setup too soon; we will be using it again in the next chapter.

I am using an MC14490P to debounce up to six switches. You don't have to use one, but it helps avoid spurious effects if your switches, like mine, tend to bounce a lot. If you don't have, or wish to use, the MC14490P, either connect the two switches directly to D2 and D3 – you will probably find difficulties in getting things to work as expected – or refer to Appendix C, "Debouncing Switches," which has details on a couple of simple methods to debounce switches.

I cannot get either switch to register a press unless I physically press and hold the switch down until it turns the LED on or off, depending on which switch I'm holding. This is not acceptable. Had one of the buttons been the "panic" button on a powerful laser cutter, for example, then it would be a very unsafe laser cutter indeed.

Listing 3-1 PollingSwitches sketch – constants

```
// D13 is flashed for 5 seconds by loop().
const byte ledFlash = 13;

// D8 is controlled by interrupts. D2 = on, D3 = off.
const byte ledOnOff = 8;

// D2 and D3 are switch pins.
const byte onPin  = 2;
const byte offPin = 3;
```

Listing 3-1 simply defines a few constants which makes reading and amending the code at a later date a bit easier than just having "magic" numbers embedded in the code. In the sketch, pins D2 and D3 are mandatory – we have no choice as those two pins are the only ones on which the Arduino Language can use interrupts. D13, the built-in LED, will be flashed at five-second intervals by the loop() function, while another LED attached to pin D8 is controlled by the two switches attached to D2 and D3; D2 turns the LED on, while D3 turns it off.

Note

There's actually no need to use two switches; a single switch could have been used for both purposes; however, this chapter demonstrates two separate interrupts, hence the two switches.

Listing 3-2 PollingSwitches sketch – setup() function

```
void setup() {
    // LED pins are obviously outputs.
    pinMode(ledFlash, OUTPUT);
    pinMode(ledOnOff, OUTPUT);

    // D2 and D3 are inputs with pullup (to save me using
    // external resistors.)
    pinMode(onPin, INPUT_PULLUP);
    pinMode(offPin, INPUT_PULLUP);
}
```

Listing 3-2 sets up the sketch. There's nothing much to see here other than taking note that the switches are configured with the input pull-up resistors enabled. This has two effects:

- Calling digitalRead() on either of the two pins will return high when the switches are not pressed.
- The call will return low when the switches are pressed.

This always feels back to front to me, but using the built-in pull-up resistors saves a couple of pennies in component costs, per switch.

Listing 3-3 PollingSwitches sketch – loop() function

```
void loop() {
    digitalWrite(ledFlash, HIGH);
    delay(5000);

    // Poll switches. The code is in the middle but it
    // makes no difference as there will always be a
    // 10 second loop time, no matter where I place the
    // code to poll.
    if (digitalRead(onPin) == HIGH)
        digitalWrite(ledOnOff, HIGH);
```

```
    if (digitalRead(offPin) == HIGH)
        digitalWrite(ledOnOff, LOW);


    digitalWrite(ledFlash, LOW);
    delay(5000);

}
```

The `loop()` function is there to show an example of "work" being done. The fact that all it does is flash the built-in LED is only because it's simple enough to follow – everyone knows the blink sketch after all. If this was a laser cutter or a 3D printer, for example, the work being done would be different. It's easier for me to show work by flashing LEDs for longer periods of time.

The LED is turned on for five seconds, then the two switches are polled, then the LED is turned off for five seconds. You don't get much time to press the switch before it is ignored for another ten seconds. You need to press and hold the switch before it will be registered as pressed – unless you get really lucky of course. (In which case, buy a lottery ticket!)

We can see that the sketch works, but works very badly indeed. It is not responsive, and if one of the switches was a safety switch, it would be next to useless. We need a better solution – enter the interrupts.

3.2.5   Arduino Interrupt Example

The polling example sketch should be changed as follows:

- The `setup()` function should be changed to that shown in Listing 3-4.
- The `loop()` function should be changed to that shown in Listing 3-5.
- Two new functions have been added to execute the interrupt code for the switches. Those are shown in Listing 3-6.

Listing 3-4 InterruptSwitches sketch – setup() function

```
void setup() {
    // LED pins are obviously outputs.
    pinMode(ledFlash, OUTPUT);
    pinMode(ledOnOff, OUTPUT);

    // D2 and D3 are inputs with pullup (to save me using
    // external resistors.)
    pinMode(onPin, INPUT_PULLUP);
    pinMode(offPin, INPUT_PULLUP);

    // D2 and D3 have an ISR each to turn the LED on and off.
    attachInterrupt(digitalPinToInterrupt(onPin),
                ledOn, FALLING);
```

```
        attachInterrupt(digitalPinToInterrupt(offPin),
                        ledOff, FALLING);
}
```

As you may notice, the only differences between the `setup()` function in Listings 3-4 and 3-2 are the two calls to the function `attachInterrupt()`, which has been described previously.

Listing 3-5 InterruptSwitches sketch – loop() function

```
void loop() {
    digitalWrite(ledFlash, HIGH);
    delay(5000);
    digitalWrite(ledFlash, LOW);
    delay(5000);
}
```

In Listing 3-5, calling `digitalRead()` on two switches is now gone; `loop()` is only concerned with flashing the built-in LED now. It doesn't need to know or care about the switches anymore.

Listing 3-6 InterruptSwitches sketch – interrupt handling functions

```
void ledOn() {
    digitalWrite(ledOnOff, HIGH);
}


void ledOff() {
    digitalWrite(ledOnOff, LOW);
}
```

Listing 3-6 is new. These two small functions are responsible for actioning whatever we want to do when one or the other of the two switches is pressed.

On the Arduino, pin D2 is the on switch and pin D3 is off. D2 is attached to the `ledOn()` function, and D3 is attached to `ledOff()`. All that these two functions do is to set the green LED to on or off accordingly. Sounds too good to be true? Try it – run the polling example first and see how frustrated you get attempting to get the LED on and off, then upload the interrupt version. The difference is literally chalk and cheese as the interrupt sketch instantly reacts to the switches.

3.3   Setting Up AVR Interrupts

Using the Arduino Language is the easy way to set up these two interrupts, but sometimes it's nice to get down and dirty with the hardware; it also saves precious Flash RAM! This section effectively describes what the Arduino's `attachInterrupt()` function does for you.

3.3.1   Register Usage

The registers used in setting up the INT0 and INT1 interrupts are

- The *External Interrupt Mask Register* (EIMSK) which has two bits reserved to enable one or both of the interrupts. All other bits are unused and will be read as 0 if the register is read by your code. The bits in question here are named INT0 in bit position 0 and INT1 in bit position 1.
- The *External Interrupt Control Register A* (EICRA) which has four bits reserved for use, two for each interrupt. Each interrupt has its stimulus defined by a combination of the two bits assigned to the interrupt. The bits are ISC00 in bit position 0 and ISC01 in bit position 1 for INT0 and ISC10 in bit position 2 and ISC11 in bit position 3 for INT1. The other bits in the register, bits 4 to 7, are unused and will be read as 0 if your code reads the register. Table 3-1 shows the settings of the two bits and which stimulus will fire the interrupts.
- The *External Interrupt Flag Register* (EIFR) which has two bits set aside to indicate that an INT0 or an INT1 occurred. The bits used as INTF0 and INTF1 and all other bits are unused and will be 0 if the register is read.

Table 3-1   INT0 and INT1 stimulus settings

ISCn1:ISCn0	Description
00	**LOW** – the interrupt will fire and keep firing as long as the pin is held low.
01	**CHANGE** – the interrupt will fire when the pin changes from high to low or from low to high.
10	**FALLING** – the interrupt will fire when the pin changes from high to low.
11	**RISING** – the interrupt will fire when the pin changes from low to high.

3.3.2   Configuring the Interrupt

Configuring the INT0 and INT1 interrupts is relatively simple. You have to decide what stimulus will fire them and which of the two interrupts you want to use. Once that is decided, simply set a couple of bits in a couple of registers, and after writing the ISR code, you are done.

The first stage is to disable global interrupts, then configure the stimulus you require to fire the interrupt. Table 3-1 shows the bits that are required to be set. If you are using INT0, then you have to set bits ISC00 and ISC01, while for INT1 you need bits ISC10 and ISC11 to be set. For example, for a FALLING interrupt stimulus, ISCn1 would be set to 1, while ISCn0 would be 0.

For INT1, this is as simple as

```
EICRA |= (1 << ISC11);
EICRA &= ~(1 << ISC10);
```

and for INT0

```
EICRA |= (1 << ISC01);
EICRA &= ~(1 << ISC00);
```

Both examples preserve the other bits in the EICRA register, leaving other configuration bits unchanged.

3.3.3 Enabling the Interrupt

Prior to enabling the interrupt, it is advised to clear the flag bit for the appropriate interrupt. This will prevent spurious execution of the ISR if, while the configuration was in progress, the stimulus to trigger the interrupt was detected.

To enable the INT0 and INT1 interrupts, all that is required is to set the appropriate bit, or bits, in the External Interrupt Mask Register (EIMSK). You would set bit INT0 to enable the INT0 interrupt and bit INT1 to enable the INT1 interrupt. It's not at all confusing that the interrupts and the enabling bits have the same name, is it?

Finally, *make sure that global interrupts are enabled*. On Arduinos, this is done in the background; however, if you are writing AVR code, then it is your responsibility to do this. Listing 3-9 shows this being done with the sei() function call.

3.3.4 Interrupt Service Routines

Interrupt Service Routines are set with the ISR macro defined in avr/interrupt.h. That header file must be included in your source code if you are not using the Arduino Language. Listings 3-7 and 3-8 show a pair of very simple examples.

3.4 AVR Interrupt Example

The code in Listings 3-7 to 3-9 show an AVR version of the InterruptSwitches.ino sketch from Listings 3-4 to 3-6.

> **Tip**
> Read on for a description of how you can use plain AVR code in an Arduino sketch and get it to compile to *exactly* the same size as it does under PlatformIO *without* needing to install PlatformIO.

The AVR application, InterruptSwitches, starts with Listing 3-7 which contains the included header files and the ISR for the INT0 interrupt. This interrupt handler is being used to turn on the LED on Arduino pin D8, AVR pin PB0.

Listing 3-7 InterruptSwitches AVR application – INT0 ISR

```
#include <avr/io.h>
#include <avr/interrupt.h>
#include <util/delay.h>


ISR(INT0_vect) {
```

```
    // LED on Arduino D8 = Port B, pin 0.
    PORTB |= (1 << PORTB0);
}
```

Listing 3-8 shows the ISR for the INT1 interrupt. This interrupt handler is being used to turn off the LED on Arduino pin D8, AVR pin PB0.

Listing 3-8 InterruptSwitches AVR application – INT1 ISR

```
ISR(INT1_vect) {
    // LED on Arduino D8 = Port B, pin 0.
    PORTB &= ~(1 << PORTB0);
}
```

The main() function is shown in Listing 3-9

Listing 3-9 InterruptSwitches AVR application – main() function

```
int main() {
    // Setup D13 (PB5) and D8 (PB0) as output.
    DDRB |= ((1 << DDB5) | (1 << DDB0));

    // Setup Switches on D2 and D3 (PD2 and PD3).
    DDRD &= ~((1 << DDD2) | (1 << DDD3));

    // Configure INT0 and INT1 on a falling edge.
    EICRA = ((1 << ISC11) | (0 << ISC10) |
             (1 << ISC01) | (0 << ISC00));

    // Enable the INT0 and INT1 interrupts.
    EIMSK = ((1 << INT1) | (1 << INT0));

    // Clear flags.
    EIFR |= ((1 << INTF1)|(1 << INTF0));

    // VERY IMPORTANT - Enable global interrupts.
    sei();

    // Loop - flashes D13 (PB5) every 5 seconds.
    while (1) {
        // Use the PIN register to toggle D13.
        PINB |= (1 << PINB5);
        _delay_ms(5000);
    }
}
```

The code compiles to only 228 bytes of program space in the Flash RAM, compared with the Arduino's 1264 bytes of program size plus 13 bytes of Static RAM for variables.

As I mentioned previously, I'm ignoring my own advice and not bothering to set flags and so on in the ISRs because each ISR is a single statement to turn on or off the LED attached to pin PB0 – that's port PORTB and pin PORTB0 on that port – which is equivalent to the Arduino pin D8. Why am I using these pins? Because Figure 3-1 is exactly the layout that corresponds to the code!

3.4.1 Compiling AVR Code in the Arduino IDE

I previously mentioned that the InterruptSwitches AVR code is *expected* to be compiled and uploaded using PlatformIO. The PlatformIO system does away with all the Arduino hand-holding and gives the maker total control over the generated code being uploaded. There is no hand-holding when using plain AVR C++ and PlatformIO.

> **Tip**
>
> I say *expected*, but read on, you might be surprised at what you can actually do within the Arduino IDE.

The Arduino Language does a lot of work behind the scenes to make life easy for the beginner – it sets up interrupts, configures the three ATmega328P timer/counters to allow PWM on six pins, and so on. You can, if you wish, do away with all this hand-holding and still use the Arduino IDE to develop your code.

Briefly, here's all you need to do to compile and run the previous AVR code in the Arduino IDE *unchanged*:

- Open the Arduino IDE and select File->New.
- Click into the editor and press CTRL+A to select all text.
- Press the DEL key to delete the default text.
- Paste (or load) the code from the PlatformIO file main.cpp into the editor. This will contain both ISRs and the main() function.
- Click the compile/verify button – it compiles! If you don't want to save it before compiling, just click the "cancel" button when prompted to save the sketch. Did you notice that it now compiles to just 228 bytes?
- Click the upload button to upload it to your device. If you still don't want to save it, again click the "cancel" button when again you are prompted to save the sketch.
- Press the buttons on the breadboard – it just works.

What we have just done here is override the entire Arduino Language, and you have just possibly compiled your first ever AVR C++ source code. While all the Arduino code files in the background are still *compiled* – you can see this if you enable verbose compilations – they are not *linked* into the finished application. None of the Arduino hand-holding, or language, can be used; you are running with the wolves now!

If you decide to continue in this vein, you will need to speak[1] AVR C++ as the Arduino Language is no longer available – unless you go back to the old ways of course.

---

[1] Okay, *type*.

3.5   Interrupt Flags

As mentioned previously, there are flag bits which are set whenever an interrupt occurs, but *not* for those interrupts deemed to be level interrupts. For the INT0 and INT1 interrupts, fired by CHANGE, RISING, or FALLING stimulus, but *not* the LOW level stimulus, the flag register is named the *External Interrupt Flag Register* (EIFR).

The flag bits, of which there are only two, INTF0 and INTF1, take up bits 1 and 0 in the EIFR register. The other bits are not used (in the ATmega328P) and, if read, will always be read as 0.

If you have configured and enabled the INT0 and INT1 interrupts *and* enabled global interrupts, then these flag bits will be set when the appropriate interrupt occurs and then almost immediately cleared by the ISR and need not be bothered with further.

If, on the other hand, you have configured the INT0 and INT1 interrupts, but have not yet enabled them, and global interrupts are enabled, then if the stimulus is detected, the flag bits *will still be set*. It is then the responsibility of the code itself to clear the flag bits because if the interrupts are subsequently enabled, those ISRs *will* fire immediately, even if the stimulus has been removed at some point previously.

The flag bits are cleared by writing a 1 to the appropriate bit. Yes, a 1, and no, I don't know why either.

The one oddity here is that if the interrupts are configured as LOW, a level interrupt, then the flag bits will *never* be set regardless of whether the interrupts are enabled or not.

At power-up, or reset, the default setting for almost all registers is to be cleared to 0. This means that for the INT0 and INT1 interrupts, they will be configured as a LOW level interrupt. No matter how often the pins are held low, the interrupt flag bits will never be set.

Listing 3-10 is a sketch to show how the interrupt flags are affected for interrupts which are configured, but never enabled.

Listing 3-10   InterruptDisabled Sketch

```
void setup() {
    Serial.begin(9600);

    // Configure an interrupt on D2 and D3
    // but don't enable it.
    //
    // 00 = LOW
    // 01 = CHANGE
    // 10 = FALLING
    // 11 = RISING
    EICRA = ((0 << ISC11) | (1 << ISC10) |
             (0 << ISC01) | (1 << ISC00));
}

void loop() {
    // See if an "interrupt" occurred on D2 or D3.
    // Pressing a switch should change EIFR but not
    // clear it after release.
    Serial.print("EIFR=");
    Serial.println(EIFR, BIN);
```

```
  // Clear flags.
  EIFR = 3;
  delay(250);
}
```

I connected pins D2 and D3 to a pair of switches and tested all four configurations for the interrupt stimulus twice: once with the switches configured with pull-up resistors to VCC and then with the resistors pulling down to GND. Table 3-2 summarizes the results.

Table 3-2 InterruptDisabled sketch results

Stimulus	ISCn1:ISCn0	INTF0	INTF1
LOW	00	Never set	
CHANGE	01	Set on press and release	
FALLING – Pull up	10	Set on press	
FALLING – Pull down	10	Set on release	
RISING – Pull up	01	Set on release	
RISING – Pull down	11	Set on press	

We can see clearly from the results that even though we have never enabled the interrupts, only configured them, pressing one or both of the switches attached to pin D2 or D3 does set the appropriate flag bit in the EIFR register if the configuration settings are met.

It is also plain to see that when configured for a LOW level interrupt, the flag bits are never set.

For RISING and FALLING configurations, the point at which the interrupt flag is set depends upon the switch configuration – pull up or pull down.

3.6   Register Summary

The registers used for the two external interrupts are described, in summary only, in this section. Only the bits relevant to the two interrupts are considered. While other bits may be used elsewhere, they are marked here as not applicable. Consult the data sheet for full details of the registers involved.

3.6.1   External Interrupt Mask Register

The *External Interrupt Mask Register*, EIMSK, is used to enable or disable one or both of the two interrupts.

7	6	5	4	3	2	1	0
N/A	N/A	N/A	N/A	N/A	N/A	INT1	INT0

Bits 2 through 7 are not used and will always be read as zero. The remaining two bits are used to enable and disable the required interrupt.

INT1   If set, the INT1 interrupt is enabled. If clear, the interrupt is disabled.
INT0   If set, the INT0 interrupt is enabled. If clear, the interrupt is disabled.

3.6.2   External Interrupt Control Register A

The *External Interrupt Control Register* A, EICRA, is used to select the interrupt triggering criteria for the two interrupts.

7	6	5	4	3	2	1	0
N/A	N/A	N/A	N/A	ISC11	ISC10	ISC01	ISC00

Bits 4 through 7 are not used, while the remaining bits are set to enable the required interrupt.

ISC11:ISC10   Determine the trigger for the INT1 interrupt.
ISC01:ISC00   Determine the trigger for the INT0 interrupt.

See Table 3-1 for details of the available settings for each interrupt.

3.6.3   External Interrupt Flag Register

The *External Interrupt Flag Register*, EIFR, is used to determine if the ATmega328P has detected the triggering stimulus for one or both of these two interrupts.

7	6	5	4	3	2	1	0
N/A	N/A	N/A	N/A	N/A	N/A	INTF1	INTF0

Bits 2 through 7 are not used and are always read as zero. The two remaining bits are set to show if the appropriate interrupt stimulus was detected.

INTF1   Stimulus for the INT1 interrupt was detected.
INTF0   Stimulus for the INT0 interrupt was detected.

See Table 3-1 for details of the available settings for each interrupt.

3.7   Key Takeaways

In this chapter, we learned that

- There are two External Interrupts available on the ATmega328P, INT0 and INT1.
- INT0 is attached to physical pin 4, AVR pin PD2, Arduino pin D2.
- INT1 is attached to physical pin 5, AVR pin PD3, Arduino pin D3.
- The attachInterrupt() function is used in the Arduino Language to make these two interrupts usable in a sketch.

- The interrupts can be triggered by
  - The pin's voltage level rising from low to high
  - The pin's voltage level falling from high to low
  - The pin's voltage level rising or falling (changing)
  - The pin's voltage level being detected as low
- Configuring either of the two interrupts to be triggered by a low level *will not* set the appropriate flag bit in the flag register. Any of the three other triggers *will* set the flag bit.

3.8   Coming Up

You will have noticed in this chapter that the ATmega328P only has two pins which can be used in this manner to fire an interrupt. What do you do if you need more than two pins to trigger interrupts? The next chapter continues with external interrupts and looks at the *Pin Change* interrupts which can be configured to trigger interrupts on *almost* every pin on an ATmega328P.

Pin Change Interrupts

4

Pin Change interrupts are another example of the external interrupts discussed in the previous chapter. This time, instead of having only two special pins to use, we have 20 pins to play with. Unfortunately, instead of having two dedicated interrupts like INT0 and INT1, we have to share the interrupts between three different handlers. This requires a bit of thought in determining which of the covered pins triggered the interrupt – this chapter explains all.

4.1   Changing Pins

The three Pin Change interrupts are found in Vectors 3, 4, and 5 in the Interrupt Vector Table.

The ATmega328P has the ability to connect a *Pin Change* interrupt to almost all of the pins on the device. However, as only three interrupt vectors are available, and there are up to 20 pins, a bit of vector sharing has to take place. The three interrupt vectors are

- *Pin Change interrupt 0*, PCINT0, which looks after interrupts on pins PCINT0 to PCINT7. These are Arduino pins D8 to D13 and also AVR pins PB0 to PB5. The two "missing" AVR pins, PB6 and PB7, are used by the crystal oscillator and don't have an Arduino name.
- *Pin Change interrupt 1*, PCINT1, which looks after interrupts on pins PCINT8 to PCINT14. These are Arduino pins A0/D14 to A5/D19 and also AVR pins PC0 to PC5. The "missing" pin is the ATmega328P's reset pin, PC6, physical pin 1.
- *Pin Change interrupt 2*, PCINT2, which looks after interrupts on pins PCINT16 to PCINT23. These are Arduino pins D0 to D7 and also AVR pins PD0 to PD7.

It's not *really* confusing that they named the interrupt vectors the same as the first three pin names, is it? This isn't really a problem; in your code, you can refer to the pins by their PCINTx names or their Pxn names. For example, PCINT16 is PD0 for Arduino pin D0. Figure 4-1 will help make things a little more obvious.

© The Author(s), under exclusive license to APress Media, LLC, part of Springer Nature 2024
N. Dunbar, *Arduino Interrupts*, Maker Innovations Series,
https://doi.org/10.1007/978-1-4842-9714-8_4

Note

There is no interrupt covering pin `PCINT15` as that pin doesn't exist. `PCINT14` is on the RST pin, pin 1, and `PCINT7` and `PCINT6` are on the pins that the crystal is attached to on an Arduino board, so might not be usable.

These interrupts will fire even if the pin in question is configured as an output pin. This means that you can fire the interrupt from your own sketches if you configure the interrupts and then change the state of the pin.

Unlike the INT0 and INT1 interrupts in the previous chapter, pin change interrupts only respond to *changes* on the appropriate pin – if a pin goes from low to high, or high to low, and remains changed for the required minimum period of one clock cycle, then the interrupt will fire.

In order to determine which change took place, your code has to read the current state of the appropriate PINx register.

4.2   Arduino and ATmega328P Pinout

If you have an Arduino and are used to the Arduino Language, then terms like `PCINT0`, `PB0`, and so on probably don't mean much to you. Figure 4-1 shows a diagram of an ATmega328P and its pins.

ALT	Arduino	PCInt	AVR	Pin		Pin	AVR	PCInt	Arduino	ALT
RESET		PCINT14	PC6	1	U	28	PC5	PCINT13	D19/A5	SCL
RX	D0	PCINT16	PD0	2		27	PC4	PCINT12	D18/A4	SDA
TX	D1	PCINT17	PD1	3		26	PC3	PCINT11	D17/A3	
INT0	D2	PCINT18	PD2	4		25	PC2	PCINT10	D16/A2	
OC2B/INT1	D3/PWM	PCINT19	PD3	5		24	PC1	PCINT9	D15/A1	
XCK/T0	D4	PCINT20	PD4	6		23	PC0	PCINT8	D14/A0	
			VCC	7		22	GND			
			GND	8		21	AREF			
XTAL1/OSC1		PCINT6	PB6	9		20	AVCC			
XTAL2/OSC2		PCINT7	PB7	10		19	PB5	PCINT5	D13	SCK
OC0B/T1	D5/PWM	PCINT21	PD5	11		18	PB4	PCINT4	D12	MISO
OC0A/AIN0	D6/PWM	PCINT22	PD6	12		17	PB3	PCINT3	D11/PWM	OC2A/MOSI
AIN1	D7	PCINT23	PD7	13		16	PB2	PCINT2	D10/PWM	OC1B/SS
ICP1/CLKO	D8	PCINT0	PB0	14		15	PB1	PCINT1	D9/PWM	OC1A
ALT	Arduino	PCInt	AVR	Pin		Pin	AVR	PCInt	Arduino	ALT

Figure 4-1   ATmega328P pinout

The names of the Arduino pins are in the columns headed "Arduino" (No! Really?), and the Atmel/Microchip names are in the columns headed "AVR." You can ignore the other columns for now, apart maybe from the names in the column headed "PCInt" as those names are the ones we will need in this chapter.

When configured, the interrupts will fire if the appropriate stimulus is received on any of the pins.

4.3 Setting Up Arduino Interrupts

Unless you can find and use a library, then the Arduino Language doesn't make these interrupts easy, unlike the two external interrupts, INT0 and INT1, discussed in the previous chapter where the `attachInterrupt()` function can be used to link the two interrupt pins to a function in your sketch.

> **Tip**
> Open your library manager, select Sketch->Include Library->Manage Libraries..., and when you get the prompt, enter "pinchangeinterrupt" into the search box. Scroll down the results list and find the PinChangeLibrary by Nico Hood.

The rest of this section assumes that you have indeed installed Nico Hood's Pin Change interrupt library.

The sketch in Listings 4-1 through 4-4 demonstrates the use of the library and how a pin change interrupt, on Arduino pin D2, can be used to toggle an LED even while the main `loop()` of the sketch is busy elsewhere flashing the built-in LED on a five-second cycle. The breadboard layout is exactly the same as we used in the previous chapter, reproduced in Figure 4-2 for your convenience.

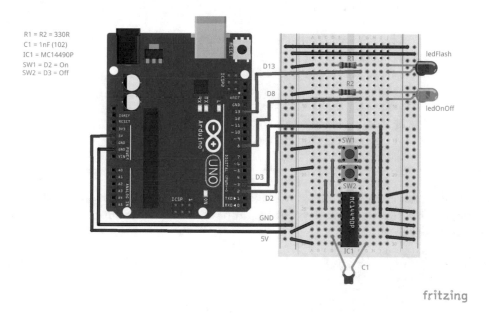

Figure 4-2 Pin Change interrupt sketches – breadboard layout

Listing 4-1 PinChangeSwitch sketch – constants

```
// We need this to use the PinChangeInterrupt library.
#include "PinChangeInterrupt.h"

// D13 is flashed for 5 seconds by loop().
```

```
const byte ledFlash = 13;

// D8 is controlled by interrupts. D2 = on/off.
const byte ledOnOff = 8;

// D2 is the switch pin.
const byte onOffPin  = 2;
```

We need to make sure we include the header for the new library, which we can easily do by typing in the `#include` statement shown just before the start of the definitions for the sketch's constants.

As with the similar sketch in the previous chapter, the built-in LED is flashed in five-second periods, and a second LED is controlled by the switch on D2. This new LED is attached to pin D8. There is only one switch in use in this implementation of the sketch; switch SW1 is unused in the circuit. Switch SW2 lights the LED when pressed and extinguishes it when released.

Listing 4-2 PinChangeSwitch sketch – setup() function

```
void setup() {
    // LED pins are obviously outputs.
    pinMode(ledFlash, OUTPUT);
    pinMode(ledOnOff, OUTPUT);

    // D2 is input with pullup (to save me using
    // external resistors.)
    pinMode(onOffPin, INPUT_PULLUP);

    // D2 has an ISR to turn the LED on and off.
    attachPCINT(digitalPinToPCINT(onOffPin),
                toggleLED, CHANGE);
}
```

In `setup()`, not much has changed. We still define our output and input pins for the LEDs and the switch, but this time we call a new function, `attachPCINT()`, to attach our `toggleLED()` function to the switch on D2.

Note
What's in a name? The function `attachPCINT()` is exactly the same as the function called `attachPinChangeInterrupt()` but is far easier to type!

The `attachPCINT()` function and the Arduino's `attachInterrupt()` are very similar and have the same effect – a function in the sketch is attached to an interrupt on a particular pin and will be executed when something happens to that pin. We can call `attachPCINT()` with the same stimuli as listed in the previous chapter, however:

- LOW has absolutely no effect and will do nothing; it is not a *pin change*. It will not raise an error.
- CHANGE will fire when the switch is pressed and again when it is released.

- RISING will fire as soon as the switch is being released from a press; nothing happens when it is pressed. This assumes that the switch is configured either as INPUT_PULLUP or with external pull-up resistors fitted.
- FALLING fires as soon as the switch is pressed; nothing happens when it is released. Once again, this assumes that the switch is configured either as INPUT_PULLUP or with external pull-up resistors fitted.

In our example, whenever the switch is pressed or released, the function toggleLED() will be executed – the LED will light when the switch is pressed and extinguish when it is released.

Listing 4-3 PinChangeSwitch sketch – loop() function

```
void loop() {
    digitalWrite(ledFlash, HIGH);
    delay(5000);
    digitalWrite(ledFlash, LOW);
    delay(5000);
}
```

The loop() function just sits there, repetitively lighting the built-in LED for five seconds, before turning it off for another five seconds. This is just a simulation of some work being done.

Listing 4-4 PinChangeSwitch sketch – toggleLED() function

```
void toggleLED() {
    digitalWrite(ledOnOff, !digitalRead(ledOnOff));
}
```

The toggleLED() function is called each and every time the switch on D2 is pressed or released. It simply lights or extinguishes the LED on pin D8.

If you wish to use pin change interrupts on an Arduino and don't have a suitable library installed, read on as the following sections describe how it is done in plain vanilla AVR C/C++ code.

4.4 Setting Up AVR Interrupts

I'm sure there are libraries available for the AVR coders among us. Sadly, my Google skills haven't turned any up yet – I might have to write one![1]

The steps involved in setting up pin change interrupts for an AVR application, or even for an Arduino sketch, are

- Choose the pin, or pins, you want to enable interrupts on.
- Set a mask to select those pins. If the pins are on different Pin Change interrupt vectors, you will need more than one mask.
- Enable one or more of the three main Pin Change interrupts.

---

[1] I eventually did!

- Write the ISR for each of the Pin Change interrupt vectors in use, and in that code determine the state of the pin(s) and whether or not the interrupt was caused by a CHANGE, RISING, or FALLING state, if necessary.

These steps are described in the following sections.

4.4.1   Choosing Pins, Setting Masks

If we continue with the previous example code, as seen in Listings 4-1 through 4-4, with a view to converting it to plain AVR code, we will choose the AVR equivalent to Arduino Pin D2 for our switch. We will still be using the same breadboard layout; see Figure 4-2 for a quick reminder.

- Pin D2 is AVR pin PD2 and has a Pin Change interrupt name of PCINT18.
- Pin PD2 is bit position PORTD2 on the PORTD register.
- PCINT18 is managed by Pin Change interrupt vector PCINT2.

As far as the interrupt is concerned, that is all we need. For the LEDs we will be lighting up, Arduino pin D13 is PB5 and pin D8 is PB0.

4.4.2   Enabling Pin Change Interrupts

To enable the Pin Change interrupts, we need to configure one, or more, of these registers:

- *Pin Change Interrupt Control Register*, PCICR
- *Pin Change Mask Register 0*, PCMSK0
- *Pin Change Mask Register 1*, PCMSK1
- *Pin Change Mask Register 2*, PCMSK2

There is also a flag register to show which, if any, of the Pin Change interrupts occurred.

- *Pin Change Interrupt Flag Register*, PCIFR

4.4.2.1 Pin Change Interrupt Control Register

This register has three bits available on the ATmega328P, these being PCIE2 in bit position 2, PCIE1 in bit position 1, and PCIE0 in bit position 0. All other bits are reserved and will be read as 0 if the register is read.

Setting one or more of these three bits will enable the corresponding Pin Change interrupt for the appropriate bank of pins:

- PCIE0 controls the bank of pins from PCINT0 through PCINT7.
- PCIE1 controls the bank of pins from PCINT8 through PCINT14.
- PCIE2 controls the bank of pins from PCINT16 through PCINT23.

Once you have set the PCICR register, you must then set a bit mask in the various pin change mask registers to enable the interrupt on the specific pins.

In our example program, PCINT18 is managed by bit PCIE2, so we will need to execute PCICR |= (1 << PCIE2) to enable the required interrupt.

4.4.2.2 Pin Change Mask Registers

There are three registers which are used to control which pins in each bank are to be enabled with a Pin Change interrupt:

- Register PCMSK0 controls pins PCINT0 through PCINT7.
- Register PCMSK1 controls pins PCINT8 through PCINT14.
- Register PCMSK2 controls pins PCINT16 through PCINT23.

You will write a 1 to the appropriate bit position in the register(s) to indicate which pins in each bank are enabled.

For our example sketch, pin PCINT18 is managed by bit PCINT18 in register PCMSK2, so we would have to enable that pin by executing PCMSK2 |= (1 << PCINT18).

4.4.3 Pin Change Interrupt Setup Summary

As we can see, there's a lot going on to configure the pin change interrupts and handlers in our code. We have to remember the Arduino pin name and how it maps onto the PCINTn pin name used in the data sheet; we need to pick the correct pin change interrupt control register, and the pin change mask register, for the pins we wish to use.

Wouldn't it be nice if we had a simple lookup table with all the information rather than having to trawl through the data sheet? Perhaps Table 4-1 will help make the various pin and register names a little more clear.

As our example uses Arduino pin D2 for the switch, we find D2 in Table 4-1 and note that

- It is AVR pin PD2 and/or pin PCINT18.
- It requires bit PCIE2 to be set in the PCICR register.
- It also requires bit PCINT18 in the PCMSK2 register to be set.
- The ISR will be written for PCINT2_vect.

As mentioned previously, the bits in the PCMSKn register can be referred to by either their PCINTx name or their AVR pin names. For D2, we can set bit PCINT18 or bit PD2 in PCMSK2 and get the same, working result.

4.4.4 Writing the ISR

When using pin change interrupts, there will be an ISR required for every bank of pins in which your code has enabled at least one pin as an interrupt pin.

As ever, code in the ISR should be kept short, and any variables shared with the main code must be declared as volatile to prevent weird problems when the compiler optimizes them away.

Always remember, the interrupt is triggered by a CHANGE; it is up to our code to determine if the change was RISING or FALLING, if this is relevant to the application.

Table 4-1 Pin Change interrupt setup

Arduino	AVR	PCINTn	PCICR	PCMSKn	Vector
D0	PD0	PCINT16	PCIE2	PCMSK2	PCINT2
D1	PD1	PCINT17	PCIE2	PCMSK2	PCINT2
D2	PD2	PCINT18	PCIE2	PCMSK2	PCINT2
D3	PD3	PCINT19	PCIE2	PCMSK2	PCINT2
D4	PD4	PCINT20	PCIE2	PCMSK2	PCINT2
D5	PD5	PCINT21	PCIE2	PCMSK2	PCINT2
D6	PD6	PCINT22	PCIE2	PCMSK2	PCINT2
D7	PD7	PCINT23	PCIE2	PCMSK2	PCINT2
D8	PB0	PCINT0	PCIE0	PCMSK0	PCINT0
D9	PB1	PCINT1	PCIE0	PCMSK0	PCINT0
D10	PB2	PCINT2	PCIE0	PCMSK0	PCINT0
D11	PB3	PCINT3	PCIE0	PCMSK0	PCINT0
D12	PB4	PCINT4	PCIE0	PCMSK0	PCINT0
D13	PB5	PCINT5	PCIE0	PCMSK0	PCINT0
N/A	PB6	PCINT6	PCIE0	PCMSK0	PCINT0
N/A	PB7	PCINT7	PCIE0	PCMSK0	PCINT0
A0/D14	PC0	PCINT8	PCIE1	PCMSK1	PCINT1
A1/D15	PC1	PCINT9	PCIE1	PCMSK1	PCINT1
A2/D16	PC2	PCINT10	PCIE1	PCMSK1	PCINT1
A3/D17	PC3	PCINT11	PCIE1	PCMSK1	PCINT1
A4/D18	PC4	PCINT12	PCIE1	PCMSK1	PCINT1
A5/D19	PC5	PCINT13	PCIE1	PCMSK1	PCINT1
N/A	PC6	PCINT14	PCIE1	PCMSK1	PCINT1

We can determine the state of the pin by checking its bit position in the appropriate PINx register. The value we find there will be the value that the pin *changed to*, so finding a 1 in a bit position shows that the pin changed to high, and finding a 0 shows that it changed to low.

4.4.4.1 Multiple Pin ISRs

While this situation is not relevant to the example I am discussing, there may be occasions when you have multiple pins in the same bank enabled to fire an interrupt. Your code must determine which pins changed state so that you can execute the appropriate code. This is quite simple to do.

Listings 4-5 and 4-6 show how the changing pins on Bank 2 can be determined. Listing 4-5 is a helper function to accept the previous and current state of the pins in a bank and will return a bit mask where a 1 indicates that the pin has changed state.

Listing 4-5 Pin Change ISR – which pins changed

```
// Function to return only those changed pins.
uint8_t whatChanged(uint8_t prevState, uint8_t currState) {
    return (prevState ^ currState);
}
```

The Exclusive OR bitwise function used here will only return a 1 where the bits differ. If a pin has the same state as before, it will return a 0.

It isn't necessary to have the code in whatChanged() as a separate function, unless you have to do the same thing in multiple ISRs as this will help reduce the size of your code – both source and compiled – at the slight cost of a function call in the affected ISRs.

Listing 4-6 uses the whatChanged() function to determine which pins changed between ISR calls. You will note that the previousState variable is declared as volatile – this allows it to be shared between the ISR and the main body of code, if necessary.

Listing 4-6 Pin Change ISR – multiple pin stimulus

```
// previousState will be initialised from PIND
// immediately before we enable global interrupts.
// For now, assume that this has been done!
volatile uint8_t previousState = 0;

ISR(PCINT2_vect) {
    uint8_t currentState = PIND;

    // What changed since last time?
    uint8_t changedPins =
        whatChanged(previousState, currentState);

    // Update previous state.
    previousState = currentState;

    // Did PD2/PCINT18 change?
    if ((changedPins & (1 << PCINT18))) {
        // Yes, PD2 changed.
        ...
    }
}
```

Note

The following three sections are only interested in a single pin on Bank 2, PCINT18, and the ISRs are written with the assumption that, elsewhere in the code, that pin was correctly set up in the PCMSK2 register.

4.4.4.2 Writing CHANGE ISRs

As already mentioned, all ISRs for the Pin Change interrupts react to a pin changing state. Because of this, CHANGE interrupts need not hold a previous state and can simply react to the interrupt by doing what is required. For example, Listing 4-7 shows an ISR where AVR pin PB5, Arduino pin D13, is toggled each and every time an interrupt occurs on PCINT18.[2]

---

[2]Although I should point out that if any other pin on Bank 2 is subsequently configured to trigger an interrupt, this code will toggle the LED regardless of which pin, of those configured, changed. These examples are for single pin configurations only.

Listing 4-7 Pin Change ISR – handling CHANGE stimulus

```
ISR(PCINT2_vect) {
    // PD2/PCINT18 changed, toggle PB5/D13.
    PORTB |= (1 << PORTB5);
}
```

Because the example code is assumed to have enabled *only* the PCINT18 pin on Bank 2, then the ISR doesn't need to check which exact pin triggered the interrupt as there can be only one.[3]

4.4.4.3 Writing FALLING ISRs
Listing 4-8 shows an ISR where AVR pin PB5, Arduino D13, is toggled each time a change occurs on *any pin* in Bank 2. The code is, however, only interested in a FALLING change on pin PCINT18 and so filters out that single pin.

Listing 4-8 Pin Change ISR – handling FALLING stimulus

```
ISR(PCINT2_vect) {
    // PD2/PCINT18 changed, toggle PB5/D13 if FALLING.
    if (!(PIND & (1 << PCINT18))) {
        PINB |= (1 << PINB5);
    }
}
```

Once again, the assumption that we have enabled a single pin applies. The code doesn't need to retain state as a low on pin PCINT18 would indicate that it changed from high to low – a FALLING change.

4.4.4.4 Writing RISING ISRs
Listing 4-9 shows an ISR where AVR pin PB5, Arduino D13, is toggled each time an interrupt occurs on *any pin* in Bank 2 but will only toggle the LED if pin PCINT18 is changing from low to high.

Listing 4-9 Pin Change ISR – handling RISING stimulus

```
ISR(PCINT2_vect) {
    // PD2/PCINT18 changed, if RISING toggle PB5/D13.
    if (PIND & (1 << PCINT18)) {
        PINB |= (1 << PINB5);
    }
}
```

In this ISR, the assumption remains that we have enabled a single pin to react to changes. The code doesn't need to retain state as a high on pin PCINT18 would indicate that it changed from low to high – a RISING change.

[3]Like the Highlanders! (Too dated?)

4.5   The AVR Sketch – Single Pin

Now that we can write ISRs which can determine which of multiple pins in a bank changed and whether the change was RISING or FALLING as necessary, we can write an AVR C++ application to emulate the Arduino sketch in Listings 4-1 through 4-4. Once again, we are using the breadboard layout as shown in Figure 4-2.

We want a switch on PD2 to light an LED when pressed and extinguish it when released. The LED will be on pin PB0 which corresponds to Arduino pin D8. Pin PD2 is in Bank 2, so we need to set bit PCIE2 in register PCICR to enable interrupts on this bank of pins. In addition, we need to set bit PCINT18 in register PCMSK2 to enable that one particular pin, and we will need an ISR for vector PCINT2_vect.

The interrupt we wish to capture is a CHANGE interrupt – we want to do something whenever it changes.

That's our research completed; let's write code!

Listing 4-10 demonstrates the same actions as the Arduino sketch. The LED will light on a switch press and extinguish when the switch is released – a CHANGE interrupt.

Listing 4-10 AVR_PinChange_CHANGE application

```
#include <avr/io.h>
#include <avr/interrupt.h>
#include <util/delay.h>


// PB0 is Arduino pin D8.
ISR(PCINT2_vect) {
    // PD2/PCINT18 changed, toggle PB0.
    PINB |= (1 << PINB0);
}


int main() {
    // Setup: Set pin modes.
    // PB0 and PB5 are outputs.
    DDRB |= (1 << DDB0) | (1 << DDB5);

    // PD5 is input with pullup.
    DDRD &= ~(1 << DDD5);
    PORTD |= (1 << PORTD5);

    // Setup. Pin PD2/PCINT18 to interrupt on change.
    cli();
    PCICR = (1 << PCIE2);
    PCMSK2 = (1 << PCINT18);
    PCIFR |= (1 << PCIF2)
    sei();

    // Loop. Flashes PB5/D13 every 5 seconds.
```

```
    while (true) {
        PINB |= (1 << PINB5);
        _delay_ms(5000);
    }
}
```

If you have PlatformIO, then the code in Listing 4-10 can be typed into a new project in the normal manner. If you don't (yet) have PlatformIO, and you want to try it out for yourself, then using the Arduino IDE, create a new sketch and then replace all the text in the editor with that in Listing 4-10, then just compile and upload in the usual manner.

Listings 4-11 and 4-12 illustrate FALLING and RISING pin change interrupt handlers. Listing 4-11 shows the handling of a FALLING interrupt while Listing 4-12 is the ISR code for a RISING interrupt. One or other of these two listings will replace the ISR in Listing 4-10 as appropriate in your sketch.

If you uploaded the code with the CHANGE interrupt configured, then the LED will immediately light up when the switch is pressed and immediately extinguish when it is released.

With a FALLING interrupt, the LED lights as soon as you press the switch. It remains lit until you next press the switch.

A RISING interrupt is similar, but the LED lights and extinguishes only when you release the switch.

Note
The latter two interrupts do this because the pin is configured as what the Arduino refers to as INPUT_PULLUP, so it held at 5 V when the switch is released and goes to GND when pressed.

Listing 4-11 will light/extinguish the LED immediately after the switch is *pressed*. This is probably what is desired from a push-on/push-off switch – you want the action to happen as soon as the switch is pressed.

Listing 4-11 *AVR_PinChange_FALLING application*

```
ISR(PCINT2_vect) {
    // PCINT18 changed, toggle PB0 if FALLING.
    if (!(PIND & (1 << PCINT18))) {
        PINB |= (1 << PINB0);
    }
}
```

Listing 4-12 will light/extinguish the LED immediately after the switch is *released*. If you hold the switch down for any length of time, it will not light (or extinguish) the LED until such time as you release it again.

Listing 4-12 AVR_PinChange_RISING application

```
ISR(PCINT2_vect) {
    // PCINT18 changed, toggle PB0 if RISING.
    if (PIND & (1 << PCINT18)) {
        PINB |= (1 << PINB0);
    }
}
```

4.6   The AVR Application – Multiple Pins

So far, so good as we only have a single pin configured to trigger the interrupt. What do we need to consider if the code has configured other pins on the same bank as PCINT18 to trigger interrupts?

Listings 4-13 and 4-14 show an application which configures multiple pins to trigger interrupts, but only wants to light our LED when the state of PCINT18 is FALLING.

Listing 4-13 contains the function whatChanged() and the ISR. The whatChanged() function returns an 8-bit value where a 1 bit indicates a changed pin in that position. A zero bit indicates that the pin corresponding to that bit position did not change.

The function uses the Exclusive OR bitwise function. If the two bits compared are the same, a zero will result. If the bits have different values, a 1 will result. By comparing the state of the pins before and after in this manner, the result of the function easily shows which pin or pins caused the interrupt to be triggered.

Listing 4-13 AVR_PinChange_FALLING_MULTI application – ISR

```
#include <avr/io.h>
#include <avr/interrupt.h>
#include <util/delay.h>

volatile uint8_t prevState = 0;

// Helper function to return only changed pins.
uint8_t whatChanged(uint8_t prevState, uint8_t currState) {
    return (prevState ^ currState);
}


ISR(PCINT2_vect) {
    // What changed?
    uint8_t currState = PIND;
    uint8_t chgdPins = whatChanged(prevState, currState);

    // Did PD2/PCINT18 change?
    if (chgdPins & (1 << PCINT18)) {

        // If so, was it FALLING?
        if (!(currState & (1 << PCINT18))) {
```

```
                // Must be FALLING, toggle PB0.
                PINB |= (1 << PINB0);
        }
    }

    // Do other pin checks here.
    // For example, check if PD3/PCINT19 changed.
    if (chgdPins & (1 << PCINT19)) {
        // do something
    }

    // Must remember to set previousState.
    prevState = currState;
}
```

The ISR compares the previous state of the PIND register, via prevState, with the current state, in currState, to see which pins have changed. If PCINT18 has changed and is FALLING, the LED on PB0 is toggled.

It then checks if PCINT19 changed in any way and, if so, "does something" – feel free to add some code to make it actually do something. Listing 4-14 contains the main() function for the application.

Listing 4-14 AVR_PinChange_FALLING_MULTI application – main() function

```
int main() {
    // Setup: Set pin modes.
    // PB0 and PB5 are outputs.
    DDRB |= (1 << DDB0) | (1 << DDB5);

    // PD5 is input with pullup.
    DDRD |= (0 << DDD2);
    PORTD |= (1 << PORTD5);

    // Setup. All Bank 2 pins will interrupt on change.
    cli();
    PCICR = (1 << PCIE2);
    PCMSK2 = 0xFF;
    PCIFR |= (1 << PCIF2)

    // Grab the initial state of PIND.
    prevState = PIND;
    sei();

    // Loop. Flashes PB5 every 5 seconds.
    while (true) {
        PINB |= (1 << PINB5);
        _delay_ms(5000);
    }
}
```

The `main()` function just sets the pins PB0 and PB5 as outputs, sets *all* pins on Bank 2 to trigger interrupts, and just before enabling interrupts, fetches the initial state of the pins on Bank 2. The ISR needs this to compare with the first time it is triggered by a pin on Bank 2 changing state. It's advisable to initialize `prevState` immediately before the interrupts are enabled.

The `main()` function then loops around flashing PB5 every five seconds. The ISR in Listing 4-13 will handle the lighting and extinguishing of the LED on PB0.

4.7   Interrupt Flags

The three Pin Change interrupts have a flag bit in the *Pin Change Interrupt Flag Register*, PCIFR. These bits are named

- PCIF0 for pins PCINT0 through PCINT7
- PCIF1 for pins PCINT8 through PCINT14
- PCIF2 for pins PCINT16 through PCINT23

As with other interrupt flags, the bit is set when the interrupt stimulus arrives – in this case, a pin has changed state – but if the global interrupt flag and/or the appropriate bit in the PCICR register is not set, then the interrupt will not trigger.

If the interrupt does not trigger, the flag bit will remain set until your application clears it in the normal "back to front" manner of writing a 1 to the bit in question.

If the interrupts are enabled correctly, then the bit will be cleared by the hardware when the ISR executes.

4.8   Register Summary

The registers used for the pin change interrupts are described, in summary only, in this section. Only the bits relevant to the interrupts are considered. While other bits may be used elsewhere, they are marked here as not applicable. Consult the data sheet for full details of the registers involved.

4.8.1   Pin Change Interrupt Control Register

The *Pin Change Interrupt Control Register*, PCICR, is used to enable or disable one or more of the three pin change interrupts.

7	6	5	4	3	2	1	0
N/A	N/A	N/A	N/A	N/A	PCIE2	PCIE1	PCIE0

Bits 3 through 7 are not used and will always be read as zero. The remaining three bits are used to enable and disable the appropriate interrupt.

PCIE0   If set, the interrupt monitoring changes on pins PCINT0 through PCINT7 is enabled. If clear, the interrupt is disabled.

PCIE1   If set, the interrupt monitoring changes on pins PCINT8 through PCINT14 is enabled. If clear, the interrupt is disabled.

PCIE2   If set, the interrupt monitoring changes on pins PCINT16 through PCINT23 is enabled. If clear, the interrupt is disabled.

Figure 4-1 shows the appropriate pins for each of the three pin change interrupt vectors and how they relate to both the AVR and Arduino naming conventions.

4.8.2   Pin Change Mask Registers

Each of the pin change mask registers defines which pin, out of the many each interrupt covers, will actually trigger the interrupt. When a particular bit is one, that pin will be able to trigger the interrupt. If a bit is zero, that pin cannot trigger the interrupt.

Table 4-1 shows the details of which pin is controlled by each bit in the three separate registers.

4.8.2.1 Pin Change Mask Register 0

Pin Change Mask Register 0, PCMSK0, controls pins PCINT16 through PCINT23. If a bit is enabled, that pin will be able to trigger the interrupt. If a bit is clear, it will not be able to trigger the interrupt. These pins trigger the PCINT0 interrupt and have the highest priority of the three pin change interrupts.

7	6	5	4	3	2	1	0
PCINT23	PCINT22	PCINT21	PCINT20	PCINT19	PCINT18	PCINT17	PCINT16

4.8.2.2 Pin Change Mask Register 1

Pin Change Mask Register 1, PCMSK1, controls pins PCINT8 through PCINT14. If a bit is enabled, that pin will be able to trigger the interrupt. If a bit is clear, it will not be able to trigger the interrupt. These pins trigger the PCINT1 interrupt. There is no pin to enable the pin PCINT15 as this pin is not part of the ATmega328P.

7	6	5	4	3	2	1	0
N/A	PCINT14	PCINT13	PCINT12	PCINT11	PCINT10	PCINT9	PCINT8

Bit 7, which would have been for pin PCINT15, is unused and will always be read as zero. Bit 6 is unlikely to be of use on an Arduino board nor indeed on an AVR setup as it controls the reset pin for the ATmega328P. It is possible to program a fuse which enabled the reset pin as an I/O pin, but this is not advised unless you have access to a high voltage programmer for subsequent reprogramming.

4.8.2.3 Pin Change Mask Register 2

Pin Change Mask Register 2, PCMSK2, controls pins PCINT0 through PCINT7. If a bit is enabled, that pin will be able to trigger the interrupt. If a bit is clear, it will not be able to trigger the interrupt. These pins trigger the PCINT2 interrupt and have the lowest priority of the three pin change interrupts.

7	6	5	4	3	2	1	0
PCINT7	PCINT6	PCINT5	PCINT4	PCINT3	PCINT2	PCINT1	PCINT0

Bits 7 and 6 of this register are unlikely to be of use on an Arduino as the physical pins that those bits control are used by the 16 MHz crystal and are not available for general I/O.

4.8.3 Pin Change Interrupt Flag Register

The *Pin Change Interrupt Flag Register*, PCIFR, records whether a pin change interrupt was detected and on which bank of pins.

7	6	5	4	3	2	1	0
N/A	N/A	N/A	N/A	N/A	PCIF2	PCIF1	PCIF0

Bits 3 through 7 are not used and will always be read as zero. The remaining three bits are used to indicate which interrupt or interrupts were detected.

PCIF0   If set, the PCINT0 interrupt is triggered.
PCIF1   If set, the PCINT1 interrupt is triggered.
PCIF2   If set, the PCINT2 interrupt is triggered.

This register *does not* indicate which physical pin triggered the interrupt, only that one or more pins in a particular bank of pins changed state and thus triggered the interrupt for that bank. It is the responsibility of the ISR code to determine which pins triggered the interrupt and what the state change for those pins happened to be: rising, falling, or change.

4.9   Key Takeaways

In this chapter, we learned that

- There are 23 pins on an ATmega328P which can trigger a Pin Change interrupt.
- Those 23 pins are arranged in three banks. Each bank has its own ISR and can be configured separately from the other banks.
- Of the 23, only 20 are generally available as two are used by the external crystal and one is for the reset pin, which can be "fused" to convert it to a general I/O pin.
- The ISRs will be triggered if any of the enabled pins detect a state change.
- The ISRs have to determine which pins in the bank triggered the interrupt and also what state change occurred.
- The interrupt can also be triggered by software changing the pin's state.

4.10   Coming Up

This chapter concludes the external interrupts. The remaining chapters describe the interrupts which are triggered by something happening within the body of the ATmega328P itself.

The first of these that we will be looking at in the next chapter is the Watchdog Interrupt.

Watchdog Interrupt

5

This chapter takes a look at the Watchdog Interrupt. The watchdog is a feature of the ATmega328P which sits quietly in the background and then, anytime the system appears to hang up, jumps into action and resets the board. The Arduino doesn't make use of this interrupt, so this chapter has the details you need to make your code more robust.

Most documentation covering the watchdog makes no mention of the interrupt, only the fact that the board will be reset if it goes wrong. This chapter resolves this issue and explains how the Watchdog Interrupt can be used in your code to do something useful, *without* resetting the board.

5.1   Watching the Board

The Watchdog Interrupt vector is found in Vector 6 in the Interrupt Vector Table.

The ATmega328P has a *Watchdog Timer*, WDT, to monitor the device, and when it determines that something has gone wrong, it can automatically reset the microcontroller and, hopefully, revert things to a stable and working state. This can be extremely useful if the device is located somewhere where it might be difficult to send an engineer to reset it manually, on a space probe somewhere, at the bottom of a well, or any similarly inaccessible location.

The Watchdog Timer usually works as follows:

- The ATmega328P is configured to start the Watchdog Timer with a specific timeout.
- It then begins executing the sketch or application.
- The Watchdog Timer counts down toward zero.
- At some point in the code, usually in the main loop, the Watchdog Timer's counter must be reset *before* the timer has fully counted down.
- If the Watchdog Timer reaches zero when counting, then either
  - An interrupt will be fired, then one more timeout period will be permitted before the device *possibly* resets.
  - The device will be immediately reset if the *Watchdog Timer* interrupt is not enabled.

N. Dunbar, *Arduino Interrupts*, Maker Innovations Series,
https://doi.org/10.1007/978-1-4842-9714-8_5

The Watchdog Timer can be configured with a number of settings ranging between 16 milliseconds and 8 seconds. When using the Watchdog Timer, your code must reset the Watchdog Timer counter, or your device may restart itself. The reset isn't required if your code is only using the *Watchdog Timer* interrupt and not the reset feature.

The Watchdog Timer interrupt comes into play just before a device reset. What happens, if the interrupt is enabled, is

- The *first* timeout period will expire and trigger the interrupt, causing the interrupt's ISR to be executed. The device *will not* reset at this point.
- If a second timeout occurs, *unless* reconfigured by the ISR that just executed, the ATmega328P will reset itself.
- On restarting, the Watchdog Timer will be configured to reset the device, as before, but now it will have the *minimum timeout period of 16 milliseconds* and not what was configured before the reset.

Warning
Hidden away in the data sheet is the information that if a device is reset by the Watchdog Timer, then when it restarts the Watchdog will still be enabled. This is good, except the timeout will be the shortest timeout available, 16 milliseconds, which might not be a good thing.

Because of this, setting up the Watchdog Timer should be considered the most important part of your code.

This could be a problem if the device has a bootloader, I'm looking at you Arduino Duemilanove, as that will take time to execute and will probably lead to a *Watchdog Timer Reset Loop* where the board simply resets constantly.

In theory, the interrupt is fired once to allow the device to preserve any information that must be saved between restarts, then after another timeout period, the device resets itself. The idea is that, on restarting, it will read the saved information and continue processing data from where it left off.

We can run the ATmega328P in four different ways:

- With the Watchdog Timer disabled, which obviously means that the watchdog will play no part in proceedings.
- With the Watchdog Timer running in *Watchdog Reset* mode, WDR, where the device will reset on the first timeout, no interrupt will be fired.
- With the Watchdog Timer running in *Watchdog Interrupt* mode, WDI, where the device will *not* reset, but the interrupt will fire every time the Watchdog Timer times out.
- With the Watchdog Timer running in *Watchdog Interrupt and Reset* mode, which hasn't got an official abbreviation so I have unofficially named it WDIR. In this mode, the interrupt fires on the first timeout, and the device resets on the second – unless a Watchdog reset or reconfiguration takes place first.

5.2   Setting Up the Watchdog Timer

The ATmega328P has a fuse bit named WDTON which if programmed – the fuse bit is a zero – then the Watchdog Timer is always enabled and cannot be disabled. The Arduino does not usually program this fuse bit, so the Watchdog Timer can be configured. On the Arduino, fuse bits are programmed quietly in the background when you select the Tools->Burn Bootloader option.

Assuming that the fuse is not programmed, then there are rules – there always are – about how to correctly set up the Watchdog Timer, with interrupts or otherwise. The data sheet makes this very clear:

- Disable global interrupts.
- Reset the Watchdog Timer.
- Clear bit WDRF in the MCUSR register.
- Write a 1 bit to the Watchdog Timer Control Register bits WDCE *and* WDE in the same instruction.
- *Within four system clock cycles*, write the desired configuration bits for the prescaler and interrupt bits, *and* write a 0 to the WDCE bit. *All* bits must be set or cleared in the same instruction.

This sequence of instructions is described fully in Section 5.2.3, "The Hard Method".

Because the Arduino Language doesn't "surface" any manner of setting this interrupt, Arduino sketches and AVR C/C++ code have to set it up in the same manner.

The Watchdog Timer can be set up and configured to operate in three different manners as previously described:

- *Watchdog Reset*, WDR, mode: The device will reset on the first timeout.
- *Watchdog Interrupt*, WDI, mode: The device will execute the ISR every time it times out, but will not reset the device.
- *Watchdog Interrupt and Reset*, WDIR, mode: The board will execute the ISR on the first timeout and reset the board on the second.

Of these three, the middle one, WDI, is interesting as it allows the Arduino to be put to sleep, to save power, and to use the interrupt to wake up, do some work, and go back to sleep. This can save a lot of battery power. I use this method on my plant watering system which looks after my citrus (lime) plant when I'm away from home for any length of time.

There are two ways to set up the Watchdog Timer: an easy way and a hard way. Assembly language programmers get the hard way only!

5.2.1   The Easy Method

The easy method uses the AVR library which is included with the Arduino software and also with most, if not all, other development environments. Unfortunately, this method is suitable only when setting up Watchdog Reset, WDR, mode. If this is what you need, then the steps are

- Include the avr/wdt.h header file in your code.
- In the setup() function (Arduino) or wherever your AVR code does its initialization, call wdt_reset() followed by wdt_enable() passing an appropriate timeout. (See Table 5-1 for the timeouts which are available.)

- In the `loop()` function (Arduino), or in your AVR code's main loop, ensure that a call to `wdt_reset()` is made. This applies to any long-running code elsewhere in the sketch/application too. You must never allow the timeout period to expire.

That's it. The Watchdog Timer is set and will reset the board if your code doesn't reset the timer before it times out.

"Hang on!" I hear you think, "What about interrupts? This *is* a book about interrupts after all!"

Ah, yes. We have a *slight* problem there. The AVR library doesn't actually give us any functions which we can use to configure the Watchdog Timer to fire an interrupt when it times out. To do that, we will need to get down and dirty in the hard way of doing things, but first we need to know about the *Watchdog Timer Control and Status Register*, `WDTCSR`. Read on.

5.2.2   The Watchdog Timer Control and Status Register

The `WDTCSR` is an eight-bit register buried deep in the bowels of the ATmega328P, which controls everything about the Watchdog Timer.

7	6	5	4	3	2	1	0
WDIF	WDIE	WDP3	WDCE	WDE	WDP2	WDP1	WDP0

WDIF   This is the interrupt flag bit and is described in Section 5.3, "Watchdog Timer Interrupt Flag".

WDIE   This bit enables or disables the Watchdog Timer interrupt.

WDP3   Prescaler, bit 3.

WDCE   This bit allows the Watchdog Timer to be configured. It must be set in conjunction with `WDE` to instigate a change to the configuration. It should be cleared at the same time as *all* the other configuration bits are being written.

WDE   This bit enables the Watchdog Timer and makes it reset the board when the timeout period expires.

WDP2   Prescaler, bit 2.

WDP1   Prescaler, bit 1.

WDP0   Prescaler, bit 0.

`WDP3:WDP0` are four bits which are used to define up to 16 different timeouts for the Watchdog Timer. See Table 5-1 for details. Sadly, only 10 of the 16 values have been made available by Atmel. The data sheet advises that the other six values are reserved.

The Watchdog Timer can be configured to time out after a period as short as 16 milliseconds or as long as 8 seconds. We cannot pick and choose our own timeout periods though; we have to use one of the ten preset values.

Table 5-1 Watchdog Timer prescaler settings

Setting	WDP3:WDP0	Timeout period
0	0000	16 milliseconds
1	0001	32 milliseconds
2	0010	64 milliseconds
3	0011	0.125 seconds
4	0100	0.25 seconds
5	0101	0.5 seconds
6	0110	1 second
7	0111	2 seconds
8	1000	4 seconds
9	1001	8 seconds

Tip

Given that eight seconds is the longest timeout, we can increase this by keeping a running count of how many timeouts have occurred, then when enough have been counted, do the task we require.

For example, if we configure a 2-second timeout and count 15 of those before executing the code we need to execute, we effectively get a 30-second timeout.

5.2.3 The Hard Method

If all your code needs is to reset the board after a timeout period has, well, timed out, then the easy method will suffice. If, on the other hand, you need the Watchdog Timer interrupt, then it unfortunately has to be done the hard way.

So, the hard way.

Listings 5-1 and 5-2 show a pair of small functions which can be used in an Arduino sketch, or in a plain AVR C/C++ application, to configure the Watchdog Timer to enable and disable its interrupt.

If you use these functions in a sketch, then you will also need to define some code as described in Listing 5-3 to actually handle the Watchdog Timer interrupt when it occurs.

Listing 5-1 WDT_Interrupt() function

```
#include "avr/wdt.h"

void WDT_Interrupt(uint8_t timeout) {
    // Save global interrupt flag
    uint8_t oldSREG = SREG;

    // Set the prescaler bits.
    uint8_t wdt_setting;
    timeout = (timeout > 9) ? 9 : timeout;
    wdt_setting = (timeout > 7) ? (1 << WDP3) : 0;
    wdt_setting |= (timeout & 7);
```

```
    // Disable Interrupts.
    cli();

    // Reset WDT.
    wdt_reset();

    // Clear RESET by WDT flag.
    MCUSR &= ~(1 << WDRF);

    // Do the timed sequence.
    WDTCSR |= ((1 << WDCE) | (1 << WDE));

    // Enable interrupts but not the reset.
    WDTCSR = (wdt_setting) | (1 << WDIE);

    // Restore global interrupt flag.
    SREG = oldSREG;
}
```

Note

This code does not enable the Watchdog Timer to reset the device. It only enables the Watchdog Timer interrupt or WDI mode. This allows the Watchdog Timer to execute something in your sketch, regularly – like flashing an LED – even while the main loop is in a delay, for example.

Listing 5-2 WDT_noInterrupt() function

```
void WDT_noInterrupt() {
    // Disable WDT interrupt leaving
    // everything else unchanged.
    WDTCSR &= ~(1 << WDCE);
}
```

Listing 5-2 doesn't need to perform the timed sequence mentioned previously as it is not changing the WDE bit, it simply clears the WDIE bit to disable the Watchdog Timer interrupt.

Of course, if you choose to use the WDT_Interrupt() and/or WDT_noInterrupt() functions, you will need to set up an ISR to handle the Watchdog Timer interrupt. This would resemble the code in Listing 5-3.

Listing 5-3 WDT ISR handler template

```
ISR(WDT_vect) {
    // Do something (short) here when the WDT
    // times out.
    ...
}
```

5.2.4   Watchdog Timer Reset Loop

In a moment of slight madness, I decided to add a second parameter to the function `WDT_Interrupt()`, in Listing 5-1, to indicate if the Watchdog Timer should reset the device or not. When I uploaded that sketch to a Duemilanove, with a one-second reset timeout, it all worked fine for as long as I was resetting the Watchdog Timer. When the code subsequently executed a `delay(1500)`, the board reset as I expected.

On restarting, I encountered a *Watchdog Timer Reset Loop* because the bootloader took longer than 16 milliseconds to execute, which caused the Watchdog to reset the board after 16 milliseconds. That caused the bootloader to restart; it again took too long to execute, which caused the Watchdog Timer to issue a reset ... rinse and repeat!

The reset loop happened even though my `setup()` function attempted to configure the Watchdog Timer as its very first action. It sadly never got that far in the code because the bootloader hadn't handed control over to my `setup()` code by the time the Watchdog Timer counted down and reset the board again.

It also turned out to be incredibly difficult to reprogram the board as it still kept resetting in the bootloader. In the end, I resorted to programming it with an ICSP, which resolved the issue as the programmer didn't have to wait for the bootloader to notice it and start programming.

A Watchdog Timer Reset Loop is a definite possibility if you are using the Watchdog Timer to reset your board, and your board has a bootloader present. It *is* possible to use the Watchdog Timer in WDR mode with the Uno as it uses a different bootloader from the Duemilanove and reconfigures the Watchdog Timer from within the bootloader itself.

5.3   Watchdog Timer Interrupt Flag

The `WDIF` bit is set in the `WDTCSR` register when the Watchdog Timer times out and the Watchdog Timer has had its interrupt enabled. If global interrupts are also enabled, then the ISR for the interrupt will be fired, and the hardware will clear this bit automatically.

If global interrupts are not enabled, then your sketch has to clear the bit manually – in the time-honored fashion of writing a 1 to the bit. If the bit is not cleared, the Watchdog Timer interrupt will fire if global interrupts are subsequently re-enabled.

Clearing the `WDIF` bit doesn't need to use the timed sequence of instructions that was required to initially configure the Watchdog Timer.

5.4   Arduino Watchdog Timer Interrupt Sketch

The WatchdogBlink sketch, in Listing 5-4, uses the function `WDT_Interrupt()` from Listing 5-1 to fire an interrupt from the Watchdog Timer, every second. The ISR for the interrupt will toggle the built-in LED (Arduino pin `D13`).

Listing 5-4 WatchdogBlink sketch

```
#include "avr/wdt.h"

void WDT_Interrupt(uint8_t timeout) {
    // Not shown here in full, unchanged from the text.
```

```
}

void setup() {
    pinMode(LED_BUILTIN, OUTPUT);
    WDT_Interrupt(WDTO_1S);
}


void loop() {
    while (true) ;
}


ISR(WDT_vect) {
    digitalWrite(13, !digitalRead(13));
}
```

The function WDT_Interrupt(), from Listing 5-1, has already been discussed and should be fresh in your memory! Just to test you, I've removed the contents!

The setup() function has little to do; it simply calls WDT_Interrupt() with a one-second timeout and makes sure that the built-in LED on D13 is an output pin.

The loop() function is once again completely unremarkable and does nothing – the Watchdog Timer interrupt is where all the hard work is being done; that is the code in the ISR(WDT_vect) which simply toggles pin D13.

5.5   AVR Watchdog Timer Interrupt Application

The WatchdogBlink sketch, in Listing 5-4, is good for an Arduino sketch. If you needed to do the same sketch in AVR C++ instead, then it could be written as shown in Listing 5-5. Note that the function WDT_Interrupt() remains completely unchanged and, as such, is not reproduced in full.

Listing 5-5 WatchdogBlink AVR application

```
#include "avr/io.h"
#include "avr/interrupt.h"
#include "avr/wdt.h"

void WDT_Interrupt(uint8_t timeout) {
    // Not shown here in full, unchanged from the text.
}


int main() {
    // setup.
    DDRB |= (1 << DDB5);
    WDT_Interrupt(WDTO_1S);
```

```
    // This is needed here because the
    // AVR code doesn't do it for you
    // unlike the Arduino.
    sei();

    // Loop. (Does nothing.)
    while (true) ;
}


ISR(WDT_vect) {
    PINB |= (1 << PINB5);
}
```

We need to include the files `avr/io.h`, `avr/interrupt.h`, and `avr/wdt.h` to allow the register names and the `cli()` and `sei()` functions to be used and to allow the use of the Watchdog Timer functions.

The `main()` function contains the setup and loop code, all in one place. The setup part calls out to `WDT_Interrupt()` as before, with a one-second timeout. It also sets Arduino pin D13, AVR pin PB5, to be an output pin.

The loop part of the `main()` function has nothing to do as the Watchdog Timer is doing the hard work of flashing the LED using the ISR. The ISR is just toggling the LED, perhaps in an unusual manner? Why is it writing a 1 to the `PINB` register when this is an output pin – it should be writing to the `PORTB` register surely?

There is a useful feature of the ATmega328P whereby if a pin is defined as an output pin, its PINx register, normally used for input pins, is redundant. The designers of the AVR microcontrollers decided that if an output pin has its PINx bit set to 1 at any time, then that output pin would toggle its state.

As the Arduino's built-in LED is on pin D13, and we know that is the ATmega328P's PINB5 bit in the `PINB` register, then writing a 1 to `PINB5` in port `PINB` will toggle the pin.

> **Note**
> It's not just the PINx register that has a use for the times that it is not being used – if that makes any sense?
>
> The PORTx register, used only for output pins, is also used in a similar manner. If a pin is defined as input, but subsequently has a 1 bit written to its PORTx register bit, then the pin will be defined as being input with the pull-up resistors enabled – the Arduino calls this `INPUT_PULLUP`.

5.6   Watchdog Reset Sketch

In Chapter 2, "Reset Interrupt", we created a small sketch to light up some LEDs based on the manner in which the Arduino board was reset/started up. In that chapter, we didn't know about the Watchdog Timer, so now that we do, it's time to add a couple of extra lines to the sketch to enable us to see a Watchdog Timer reset in action.

To make the code from Chapter 2 work with Watchdog Timer timeouts, we first need to add a header file, `avr/wdt.h`, just prior to the `lightLED()` function, as shown in Listing 5-6.

Listing 5-6 WatchdogReset sketch – lightLED() function

```
// ADD THIS LINE:
#include "avr/wdt.h"

void lightLED(uint8_t led) {
    digitalWrite(led, HIGH);
}
```

Then we need to change the `setup()` function to add additional three lines: three code lines and a pair of comments to mark where they are to be inserted. This is shown in Listing 5-7.

Listing 5-7 WatchdogReset sketch – setup() function

```
void setup() {
    // Get current MCUSR & reset it.
    uint8_t mcusr = MCUSR;
    MCUSR = 0;

    // *** ADD THESE TWO LINES ***
    wdt_reset();
    wdt_enable(WDTO_8S);

    ...

    if (WATCHDOG_RESET(mcusr)) {
        // *** ADD THIS LINE ***
        wdt_disable();

        Serial.println("Watchdog reset detected.");
        lightLED(WATCHDOG_RESET_PIN);
    }

    ...
}
```

The first line added makes sure that the Watchdog Timer is reset – in case it has been enabled elsewhere – so that it will not fire as we are adjusting its manner of operation.

The second new line sets the timeout to eight seconds. This means that if the device doesn't call `wdt_reset()` before each eight-second timeout has expired, the board will reset itself.

The `wdt_disable()` function call turns all subsequent Watchdog Timer operations off as we are no longer interested – we have, or should have, an LED lit up to show that a restart was caused by the Watchdog Timer.

> **Warning**
>
> Do not upload this sketch to a board which has a bootloader. It *will* cause a Watchdog Timer Reset Loop when restarting as the Watchdog Timer timeout will be reset to 16 milliseconds.
>
> It will be *almost impossible* to reprogram your Arduino using the bootloader if this happens due to the bootloader taking too long to recognize that a new program is being uploaded before the Watchdog Timer times out and resets the board. Again! (Ask me how I know?)
>
> In the event of a Watchdog Timer Reset Loop, you will probably only be able to get the device reprogrammed using an ICSP or another Arduino as an ICSP.
>
> If you upload this sketch using an ICSP device instead, you will delete the bootloader and the sketch *will* work.

The breadboard layout remains the same as before. To save you looking back to Chapter 2, "Reset Interrupt", I've reproduced it in Figure 5-1.

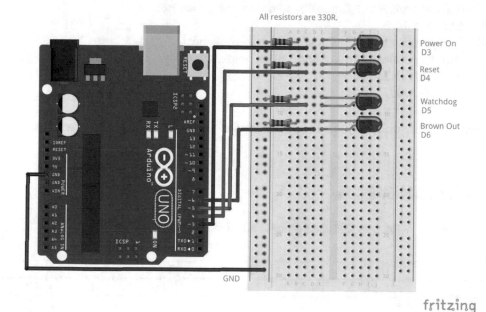

Figure 5-1 Reset interrupt bit checker

Testing *without* a bootloader on both my Duemilanove and Uno shows that the Watchdog Timer does indeed reset the device after an eight-second delay as no matter which LEDs are lit by the appropriate power-on/reset methods listed in Chapter 2, those LEDs all go out and the Watchdog Reset LED lights.

5.7   Register Summary

There are two registers used or affected by the Watchdog Timer.

5.7.1   Watchdog Timer Control and Status Register

The *Watchdog Timer Control and Status Register*, WDTCSR, controls the configuration of the Watchdog Timer and also contains the interrupt flag bit.

7	6	5	4	3	2	1	0
WDIF	WDIE	WDP3	WDCE	WDE	WDP2	WDP1	WDP0

WDIF   This bit indicates that the Watchdog Timer interrupt has occurred.
WDIE   This bit enables or disables the Watchdog Timer interrupt.
WDP3   Prescaler, bit 3.
WDCE   This bit allows the Watchdog Timer to be configured.
WDE   This bit enables the Watchdog Timer Reset functionality.
WDP2   Prescaler, bit 2.
WDP1   Prescaler, bit 1.
WDP0   Prescaler, bit 0.

Bits WDP3:WDP0 are used to define the timeout period for the Watchdog Timer. See Table 5-1 for details.

5.7.2   MCU Control Register

The *MCU Control Register,* MCUCR, has a single bit related to the Watchdog Timer.

7	6	5	4	3	2	1	0
N/A	N/A	N/A	N/A	WDRF	N/A	N/A	N/A

Bits 4 through 7 are not used and will always be read as zero. Bits 0 through 2 are used elsewhere, but are not related to the Watchdog Timer.

WDRF   If set, the Watchdog Timer caused the reset.

Note
Some Arduino bootloaders clear the register on startup. This bit may not be available in an Arduino sketch in those occasions. It will be available if the device was programmed with an ICSP, which doesn't require the presence of a bootloader.

5.8   Key Takeaways

In this chapter, we learned that

- The Watchdog Timer can be used to reset the ATmega328P after a certain timeout has passed, unless the device resets the counter.
- The Watchdog Timer can be used to trigger an interrupt, one time, before resetting the device. This can be used to save important data, possibly to the EEPROM, before the reset occurs.
- The Watchdog Timer can be used to trigger an interrupt, repeatedly, without resetting the device.
- The Watchdog Timer has a limited number of timeout periods available.
- If the Watchdog Timer has reset the device, then after everything restarts, the timeout will be reconfigured to the *smallest possible* time setting, 16 milliseconds. This can cause an Arduino, with a bootloader, to enter a Watchdog Timer Reset Loop.
- The ATmega328P has a fuse bit named WDTON which if programmed, the bit is zero, then the Watchdog Timer is always enabled and cannot be disabled. This does not affect Arduino boards.
- Enabling the Watchdog Timer requires a special timed sequence of instructions. Disabling it does not.

5.9   Coming Up

That's enough of the Watchdog for now. In the next chapter, we will look into the three timer/counters and their associated interrupts. See you there.

Timer/Counter Interrupts

6

Timers/counters are very useful features of the ATmega328P and can be used for many different purposes in your code – if you know how. The Arduino uses them to facilitate `analogWrite()` and the `millis()`, `micros()`, `delay()`, and `delayMicroseconds()` functions; however, it doesn't give you much access to the individual timer/counters for your own, alternative, uses. This chapter will expand your knowledge of these useful devices and show how they can be used in various different modes.

6.1   Timers and Counters

The are ten different timer/counter interrupts on an ATmega328P; they are located in Vectors 7 through 16 in the Interrupt Vector Table.

The ATmega328P has three separate and independent timer/counters named Timer/counter 0, Timer/counter 1, and Timer/counter 2. Timer/counter 1 is a 16-bit timer/counter, while the other two are only 8 bits. Both of the eight-bit timer/counters have three interrupts and, thus, three vectors in the table, while Timer/counter 1 has the same three interrupts as the other two timer/counters plus an additional interrupt for its *Input Capture Unit* (ICU).

Timer/counter 0 has interrupt vectors 14, 15, and 16 in Table 1-1; Timer/counter 1 has vectors 10, 11, 12, and 13, while Timer/counter 2 has vectors 7, 8, and 9. Why they are in this order I don't know, but it puts Timer/counter 2 higher in priority than the other two timer/counters.

The interrupts that all three timer/counters have in common are

- Timer/counter *Overflow* interrupt
- Timer/counter *Compare Match A* interrupt
- Timer/counter *Compare Match B* interrupt

Timer/counter 1 also has

- *Input Capture Event* interrupt

© The Author(s), under exclusive license to APress Media, LLC, part of Springer Nature 2024
N. Dunbar, *Arduino Interrupts*, Maker Innovations Series,
https://doi.org/10.1007/978-1-4842-9714-8_6

6.2   Timer/Counter Bits and Pieces

Before we dive into the various interrupts available with the three timer/counters, well, three as we are discussing the ATmega328P, we need to think about some of the registers internally used by the timer/counters.

The first register to consider is the TCNTn register. This register is 8 or 16 bits wide, depending on the timer/counter and holds the current count value for the timer/counter. Timer/counter 1 is 16 bits wide, and the other two are 8 bits. The "n" part of the register name refers to the timer/counter number – so TCNT0 is the register for Timer/counter 0.

The other two registers we will be looking at in this chapter are the OCRnA and OCRnB registers. Again, the "n" part of the name refers to the timer/counter number. These two registers are the *Output Compare Registers* for the timer/counter. These two registers are 8 or 16 bits wide, depending on the timer/counter in question, with Timer/counter 1 being 16 bits wide.

In the remainder of this chapter, if you see me refer to TCNTn or OCRnx, then I'm speaking in general, whereas if I refer to TCNT2 or OCR2A, then I'm being specific about a certain timer/counter. The text formatting will also help; actual register names are formatted in monospaced font, while generic names are not.

6.3   Overflow Interrupt

All three timer/counters have the *Overflow* interrupt available to them. This interrupt will trigger each and every time that the particular TCNTn "rolls over" from its maximum value to zero – it has overflowed in other words. The interrupt fires on the same clock cycle in which TCNTn becomes zero and sets the timer/counter's interrupt flag bit to show that the interrupt has been noted.

As with other interrupt flags, if there's an ISR and the appropriate interrupt is enabled, the flag bit will be automatically cleared by the hardware. If interrupts are disabled – either at the global or timer/counter level, then the flag bit must be cleared by your code, by writing a 1 to it.

How often does the overflow occur? That depends on

- The clock speed of the device you are using
- The individual timer/counter's prescaler
- The timer/counter's maximum value, known as TOP or MAX depending on the mode that the timer/counter is running

You will notice, when looking at the data sheet for the ATmega328P, especially in the section regarding timer/counters, a lot of references to BOTTOM, MAX, and TOP. These are

- BOTTOM is the lowest value that the timer/counter can take in whichever mode the timer/counter is configured. It is *always* zero.[1]
- MAX is the highest possible value that the timer/counter can take in the current mode which the timer/counter is configured. For the 8-bit timer/counters 0 and 2, this is always 255, while for the 16-bit Timer/counter 1, it is one of
    - 255 or 0xFF when running in any of the 8-bit modes
    - 511 or 0x01FF when running in any of the 9-bit modes

---

[1] Which makes me wonder why they didn't just say "zero" rather than giving it a name!

- – 1023 or 0x03FF when running in any of the 10-bit modes
- – 65,535 or 0xFFFF when running in any of the 16-bit modes
- • TOP is the highest possible value that the timer/counter can take in its current mode. It is set depending on the mode and varies. In some timer/counter modes, the TOP value is set by the value in another register.

If we consider an Arduino, the system clock speed is 16 MHz as that's the rating of the crystal oscillator attached to the ATmega328P. Timer/counters 0 and 2 are eight bits and have an absolute maximum value of 255 – they will overflow on the 256th count. Timer/counter 1 has an absolute maximum value of 65,535 and will overflow on the 65,536th count.

All three timer/counters have various prescalers – these divide the system clock speed down from 16 MHz to some other more useful value. Of course, not all timer/counters have the same set of prescalers. Table 6-1 shows the prescalers for each of the three timer/counters on the ATmega328P.

Table 6-1 Timer/counter prescalers

Prescaler	Timer 0 CS02:CS00	Timer 1 CS12:CS10	Timer 2 CS22:CS20	Timer frequency	Timer period
Off	000	000	000	–	–
Divide by 1	001	001	001	16 MHz	0.0625 uS
Divide by 8	010	010	010	2 MHz	0.5 uS
Divide by 32	–	–	011	500 KHz	2 uS
Divide by 64	011	011	100	250 KHz	4 uS
Divide by 128	–	–	101	125 KHz	8 uS
Divide by 256	100	100	110	62.5 KHz	16 uS
Divide by 1024	101	101	111	15.625 KHz	64 uS
External Falling	110	110	–	–	–
External Rising	111	111	–	–	–

The three "Timer n CSn2:CSn0" columns are the three bits that need to be set in the timer/counters' registers to set that prescaler speed. The timer/counters are disabled when the bits are all zero. The three bits in question are located in the appropriate *Timer/Counter Control Register B*, TCCRnB, where "n" is the timer/counter number.

Timer/counters 0 and 1 can be clocked externally either on a falling or a rising edge. This must be applied to a particular pin of which two are available. We will not be discussing this further here as it is not really relevant to the interrupt handling.

The "*Frequency*" column shows how fast the timer/counter's clock will be operating, based on a system clock of 16 MHz, and the "*Period*" column shows how often the timer/counter will increment its internal count register – TCNTn.

The calculation to work out how often the timer/counter's overflow interrupt will be triggered is

$$(MAX + 1) * Period$$

Table 6-2 shows how long each timer/counter will take to overflow at each available prescaler.

Table 6-2 Timer/counter overflow timings

Prescaler	8 bits	9 bits[1]	10 bits[1]	16 bits[1]
Divide by 1	16 uS	32 uS	64 uS	4.096 mS
Divide by 8	128 uS	256 uS	512 uS	32.768 mS
Divide by 32[2]	512 uS	–	–	–
Divide by 64	1.024 mS	2.048 mS	4.096 mS	262.144 mS
Divide by 128[2]	2.048 mS	–	–	–
Divide by 256	4.096 mS	8.192 mS	16.384 mS	1.048576 S
Divide by 1024	16.384 mS	32.768 mS	65.536 mS	4.194304 S

Notes
1. Timer/counter 1 only
2. Timer/counter 2 only

6.3.1   Configuring Timer/Counter 1

Because the Arduino Language has no facilities for linking timer/counter overflow interrupts to your sketch, you will have to configure the timer/counters the hard way – the same as AVR C++ programmers have to do – if you need or wish to use the overflow interrupts in your sketches.

There are a few steps that we must go through in order to set up a timer/counter with an overflow interrupt; these are

- Choose a timer/counter mode.
- Clear the interrupt flag.
- Enable the interrupt.
- Set the prescaler to start the timer/counter.
- Write the ISR.

For the example code in this section, I will be looking at using Timer/counter 1 only. This is simply because the other two timer/counters overflow far too quickly – as you can see from Table 6-2 – and any flashing of LEDs will be far too quick for the eye to see; they will just appear to be constantly on.

6.3.1.1 Choose a Timer/Counter Mode

Timer/counters have a number of modes available. If all we want the timer/counter to do is to generate the overflow interrupt, then normal mode will suffice. The Arduino uses Timer/counter 0 with an overflow interrupt but also uses its waveform generator to generate fast hardware PWM, for the `analogWrite()` function, on pins D5 and D6, so it is using the timer/counter for three different things.

Using the different modes is beyond the scope of this book[2] but is discussed fully in the ATmega328P's data sheet and in my book *Arduino Software Internals*. We will concentrate on running the chosen timer/counter in normal mode for the example code.

Setting normal mode involves nothing more than setting three, or four, bits in a couple of the timer/counter's registers to all zero. Normal mode is mode zero and is the default when the device is reset or powered on, but on an Arduino board, the timer/counters have been reconfigured from the default – our code will need to explicitly set the values we want.

The registers in question are the *Timer Counter Control Register A*, TCCRnA, and *Timer Counter Control Register B*, TCCRnB, and the bits are WGMn2 in TCCRnB and WGMn1 and WGMn0 in

---

[2]Sounds like a cop-out to me!

register TCCRnA. Timer/counter 1 has an extra bit to use, WGM13 also in TCCRnB. This is because Timer/counter 1 has up to 16 modes; the others have up to 8 – although some mode values are not used as they are reserved by Atmel/Microchip.

6.3.1.2 Clear the Interrupt Flag

I previously mentioned that if the conditions that would fire an interrupt are detected, even with interrupts disabled, the interrupt flag bit would be set anyway. As this flag being set would cause a spurious interrupt if interrupts were subsequently enabled, we must (or should) clear the interrupt flag bit *before* enabling the interrupt.

For the timer/counters, the flag bit is bit TOVn in the *Timer/Counter Interrupt Flag Register*, TIFRn.

In the unusual manner that Atmel deemed normal when they designed the AVR microcontrollers, we clear this flag by writing a 1 to it.

6.3.1.3 Enable the Overflow Interrupt

Another register to remember, the *Timer/Counter Interrupt Mask Register*, TIMSKn, is where we find the Timer/counter's Overflow interrupt enable bit, TOIEn. Setting this bit will enable the interrupt for the appropriate timer/counter.

6.3.1.4 Set the Prescaler

On startup or reset, the timer/counters' prescaler defaults to value zero, which disables the timer/counters. To set the prescaler as we desire, we need to select a value from Table 6-1. For our example Arduino sketch/AVR application, we wish to divide the system clock by 256 to get approximately one second between overflows. That means we need to set Timer/counter 1s prescaler bits to 100 in binary of course!

6.3.1.5 Configuring Timer/Counter 1

We are now ready to pull all of the required steps together and write a function to configure Timer/counter 1 to run in normal mode with a prescaler of 256 giving us an interrupt approximately every one second. Listing 6-1 shows the enableTimer1() function which will be used by the Arduino sketch and the AVR C++ code which follows in the remainder of this chapter.

Listing 6-1 EnableTimer1() function

```
//=================================================================
// A function for Arduino and AVR to enable Timer/counter 1
// in normal mode and with a 256 prescaler and the overflow
// interrupt enabled. The interrupt will trigger every 1.048576
// seconds.
//
// NOTE: This will mess up PWM on pins D9 and D10 if used in an
// Arduino sketch, Timer/counter 1 allows analogWrite() on
// those two pins.
//=================================================================

void enableTimer1() {
    // Choose a timer/counter mode.
    // This overrides the Arduino setup.
```

```
    TCCR1A = ((0 << WGM11) | (0 << WGM10));
    TCCR1B = ((0 << WGM13) | (0 << WGM12));

    // Clear the interrupt flag.
    TIFR1 = (1 << TOV1);

    // Enable the Overflow Interrupt.
    TIMSK1 = (1 << TOIE1);

    // Choose a prescaler to start the timer/counter.
    // Divide by 256 is chosen.
    TCCR1B |= ((1 << CS12) | (0 << CS11) | (0 << CS10));
}
```

You will notice, I hope, that I have completely initialized the TCCR1A, TCCR1B, TIFR1, and TIMSK1 registers when giving them their initial values. This has to be done because, on an Arduino, these registers are already used to initialize the timer/counter in eight-bit Phase Correct PWM mode, allowing analogWrite() for pins D9 and D10. By explicitly writing a new value, the code makes sure that the registers have a known value – I don't want to merge my new settings into a potentially unknown value in the registers. Not only that, I want Timer/counter 1 to be running in 16-bit normal mode – it will have been configured in eight-bit mode by the Arduino Language's init() function.

In addition, when I subsequently OR a couple of zeros into CS11 and CS10 to set the prescaler to divide by 256, I obviously don't *need* the two zero bits to be there as they have no effect. However, I need the prescaler setting to be 100_{bin}, so having them there is documentary. Those two zero bits are already zero thanks to the previous initialization of the TCCR1B register.

6.3.2   Arduino Overflow Interrupts

As with almost all interrupts, the Arduino Language doesn't allow easy access to these interrupts. If you need to use them in a sketch, then you will have to work with code at the AVR level as shown in Listing 6-1, or something similar, according to your needs.

The Arduino does, however, *use* the Timer/counter 0 Overflow interrupt. It is used to maintain the counters for the micros() and millis() functions which are used by the delay() function.

> **Note**
> If your Arduino sketch needs to use the Timer/counter 0 Overflow interrupt, then, unfortunately, you cannot. Because the Arduino initialization configures the interrupt and sets up an ISR for it, your code will register as a duplicate and will fail to compile.
>
> You can either use Timer/counter 2 which is another eight-bit timer/counter or Timer/counter 1 which is 16 bits or write the code using AVR C++ instead, which gives you total control over the microcontroller.

In normal use, at least on the Arduino boards based on the ATmega328P microcontrollers, Timer/counter 0 is configured with the prescaler set to divide the system clock by 64, giving an overflow period of 1.024 mS and the overflow interrupt enabled.

The ISR for the overflow interrupt accumulates the count of milliseconds so far, since the device was reset or restarted. As the overflow interrupt occurs every 1.024 mS, this means that account needs to be taken of the extra fractions of a millisecond, and indeed the code does exactly that – adding in an extra millisecond every time the fractions add up.

With that aside out of the way, let's get back to the example code. Looking at Table 6-2, we can see that if we wanted to use an overflow interrupt to do something roughly every second while the main CPU was busy elsewhere, Timer/counter 1 is the only one that has a period close to one second while running with a prescaler of 256.

We will use this setting, just because we have already created Listing 6-1 to cause an interrupt roughly every second, and create a sketch that lets the main `loop()` flash the built-in LED every five seconds while the timer/counter flashes another LED every second – well, every "just over" a second. Figure 6-1 shows the breadboard layout we will be using for this sketch.

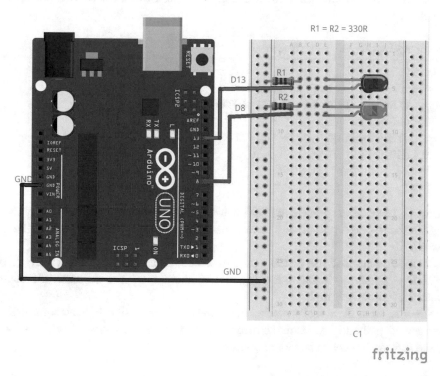

Figure 6-1 Timer1 overflow blink

Listings 6-2 through 6-4, plus Listing 6-1, will be the entire sketch. Listing 6-2 is the first and shows the ISR we will be using to blink the LED on Arduino pin D8.

Listing 6-2 Timer1Blink sketch – ISR

```
ISR(TIMER1_OVF_vect) {
    // Flash D8 every 1.048576 seconds.
    digitalWrite(8, !(digitalRead(8)));
}
```

As you can see from the comment, this function will be executed every 1.048576 seconds and will toggle the LED attached to pin D8.

Listing 6-3   Timer1Blink sketch – setup() function

```
void setup() {
    pinMode(LED_BUILTIN, OUTPUT);
    pinMode(8, OUTPUT);
    enableTimer1();
}
```

The setup() function makes sure that pins D13 (where the built-in LED is attached) and D8 are both OUTPUT pins. It then initializes Timer/counter 1 as per Listing 6-1 to overflow approximately every second.

Listing 6-4   Timer1Blink sketch – loop() function

```
void loop() {
    // Flash D13 every 5 seconds.
    digitalWrite(LED_BUILTIN, HIGH);
    delay(5000);
    digitalWrite(LED_BUILTIN, LOW);
    delay(5000);
}
```

The loop() function does the usual hard work of flashing the built-in LED every five seconds. As ever, while the delay() function is executing, only interrupts can make use of the CPU to do "useful" work.

If you compile and upload the sketch, you will see the built-in LED flashing every five seconds, while the LED attached to pin D8 is flashing around about every second under the control of the timer/counter's overflow interrupt.

The problem is, what if we really needed the second LED to flash every second *exactly*? Luckily enough, we can adapt the ISR to make the timer/counter a bit more accurate. Listing 6-5 shows what I changed the ISR to, in order to be more accurate.

Listing 6-5   Timer1BlinkAdjusted sketch – ISR

```
ISR(TIMER1_OVF_vect) {
    // Adjust the flash rate to every second.
    TCNT1 = 3036;

    // Flash D8 every 1.048576 seconds.
    digitalWrite(8, !(digitalRead(8)));
}
```

Because the Arduino's digitalRead() and digitalWrite() functions take quite a long time to execute, I am resetting the TCNT1 counter first in this version of the ISR. This makes sure that the counter is updated as soon as possible within the ISR. If it was done after the function calls, the flash period wouldn't be accurate, and working out the actual count value would have been wasted time.

How did I work out the value 3036? Well, from Table 6-1 we know that with a prescaler of 256, Timer/counter 1 takes 16 microseconds to count once. We want it to count up enough times to trigger the interrupt every second. To do this, we need to start counting from a different value rather than zero. We calculate the value as

$$65,536 - (1,000,000/16)$$

Why this calculation? We know that each count in TCNT1 takes 16 microseconds, and we want to overflow every second, which is 1,000,000 microseconds. Dividing that figure by 16 gives 62,500 counts of Timer/counter 1 in every second. As the timer/counter has to count from 0 to 65,535 plus 1 in order to overflow, a total of 65,536 counts, that's far too many. As we get an overflow interrupt every time that TCNT1 rolls over to zero, we can use the ISR for that interrupt to flash the LED and reset the value in TCNT1 so that there are only 62,500 counts until the next overflow.

We therefore calculate that there are 62,500 counts of 16 microseconds in a second, so if we set the internal counter to 3036, then it will overflow after 65,536 minus 3036 counts and flash the LED every second.

Except, it still doesn't work *properly*!

Running the sketch with the value 3036 set in the Timer/counter after every interrupt, my cheap "EspoTek Labrador" oscilloscope[3] shows me that I'm getting a period of 1.98 seconds, and not 2 seconds. Why not?

The timing calculations we see in the data sheet are for non-Arduino systems where the code is written in plain C++. The Arduino has to execute digitalRead() and digitalWrite() in the ISR, and because those functions do validation checks, disable interrupts, preserve registers, and so on, they take longer to execute. The interrupt still triggers every second,[4] but the Arduino code takes longer to toggle the LED, so we get a slower response. We need to code in plain AVR C++, if not in the whole sketch, at the very least in the ISR.

We could simply adjust the timing value again, but the main CPU clock (CLK_{cpu}) is not necessarily exactly 16,000,000 MHz, and as the Timer/counter's own clock is running off of the CPU clock, then that won't necessarily be exact either. Sometimes, it might be more accurate than at other times depending on various environmental factors such as temperature, but none of this is guaranteed.

Listing 6-6 shows an additional amendment to the sketch, and with this code in the ISR, we do indeed get the proper one-second flash that we were after. I have commented out the Arduino code lines and replaced them with the one required line of AVR code.

Listing 6-6 Timer1BlinkAdjustedAgain sketch – ISR

```
ISR(TIMER1_OVF_vect) {
    // Flash D8 every 1.048576 seconds.
    // digitalWrite(8, !(digitalRead(8)));
    PINB |= (1 << PINB0);

    // Adjust the flash rate to every second.
    TCNT1 = 3036;
}
```

[3]https://espotek.com/labrador/product/espotek-labrador-board/
[4]And a bit!

Now the ISR is executing a single instruction (which corresponds to two Assembly Language instructions) rather than two entire Arduino Language functions with numerous statements and which compile to a large number of Assembly Language instructions. Remember I said that one of the rules of writing interrupt handlers is short, concise code?

6.3.3   AVR Overflow Interrupts

In the AVR code, initializing Timer/counter 1 as required has not changed. We still use the code in the `enableTimer1()` function shown in Listing 6-1. Listing 6-7 shows the ISR's code to flash the LED but without using any of the Arduino Language functions and, thus, avoiding any overhead. Figure 6-1 shows the breadboard layout.

Listing 6-7 Timer1BlinkAVR application – ISR

```
#include "avr/io.h"
#include "avr/interrupt.h"
#include <util/delay.h>


ISR(TIMER1_OVF_vect) {
    // Flash D8 every 1.048576 seconds.
    PINB |= (1 << PINB0);

    // Adjust the timer to flash every second.
    TCNT1 = 3036;
}


void enableTimer1() {
    // Nothing has changed here.
    ...
}
```

The changes here are to include a number of required header files and to replace the Arduino Language functions to toggle the LED with a single instruction. Listing 6-8 is the `main()` function which does the setup and main loop of the AVR version of the sketch.

Listing 6-8 Timer1BlinkAVR application – main() function

```
int main() {
    // setup.
    // PB0 and PB5 are output.
    DDRB = ((1 << DDB0) | (1 << DDB5));
    enableTimer1();
    sei();

    // Loop. Flash PB5 every 5 seconds.
    while (true) {
```

```
        PINB |= (1 << PINB5);
        _delay_ms(5000);
    }
}
```

In the `main()` function, the setup is the same except we have to remember to enable interrupts,[5] and in the loop, we just use AVR C++ to flash the built-in LED every five seconds.

With this code uploaded to my Duemilanove, the oscilloscope now shows a period of two seconds – one second with the LED on and one second with it off.

The discrepancy between the Arduino and the AVR C++ code does illustrate how much work the Arduino Language functions are carrying out in the background on your behalf.

Note

The Overflow interrupt can be used in conjunction with the other timer/counter interrupts and/or timer/counter modes. The Arduino does this in that it uses Timer/counter 0 to count the `millis()` and uses the timer/counter's waveform generator to generate PWM on two of the Arduino pins. This does, however, depend upon the timer/counter's mode as some modes don't allow the count to reach MAX, so the timer/counter will *never* overflow or trigger the overflow interrupt.

6.4   Compare Match A/B Interrupt

Each of the three timer/counters has two *Compare Match* interrupts – one on channel A and one on channel B. These act independently of each other, and when the value in the appropriate match register corresponds to the timer/counter's current count, an interrupt will be triggered – if configured to do so.

You should however note that in some timer/counter modes, the count register will be cleared to zero when the channel A value matches it. This will prevent any interrupts on the B channel from triggering if that happens to have a higher value than the A channel does.

To avoid any confusion (on my part), I shall continue as in the previous section, but considering only the normal timer/counter mode. If you need details of other modes, the data sheet[6] has all you need to know.

6.4.1   Compare Match Pins

Table 6-3 shows the details of the pins that might be affected by a Compare Match for the three timer/counters. This is not really relevant to the use of the interrupts, but might be useful if you can get the timer/counter to do the hard work rather than your interrupt's ISR code – you might find that you don't actually need the interrupt.

---

[5]Yes, I did forget, again!

[6]Or *Arduino Software Internals*!

Table 6-3 Timer/counter compare match pins

Name	Arduino pin	AVR pin	Physical pin
OC0A	D6	PD6	12
OC0B	D5	PD5	11
OC1A	D9	PB1	15
OC1B	D10	PB2	16
OC2A	D11	PB3	17
OC2B	D3	PD3	5

These pins can be configured to perform an action when the TCNTn counter matches the value in the OCRnx registers. The actions are *in addition* to triggering the appropriate interrupt and are

- No action is taken – the interrupt will fire, but the affected pins will be, ahem, unaffected.
- The pins will toggle each time there is a match.
- The pins will be set to GND potential, or low, each time there is a match.
- The pins will be set to VCC potential, or high, each time there is a match.

In order to select the required action, your code must configure the COMnx1 and COMnx0 bits in the timer/counters' TCCRnA register. The settings have different actions when the timer is running in one of the PWM modes or in a non-PWM mode. We are only considering the non-PWM modes as the others are out of scope for this book.[7] Table 6-4 shows the settings for non-PWM modes.

Table 6-4 Timer/counter compare match pin settings

COMn1A	COMn1B	Action
0	0	No action. The pin will not be affected
0	1	The pin will toggle
1	0	The pin will be set low
1	1	The pin will be set high

Warning
As already mentioned, these settings are only valid for non-PWM timer/counter modes. See the data sheet if you have a need to use the feature with any of the PWM modes.

If, for example, you simply need an LED to blink when there is a match, then the interrupt will not be required – get the timer/counter hardware to blink the LED for you. For the sake of our example code, which is still to come, the interrupts will "manually" blink the LEDs without getting the timer/counter hardware involved. (This book is, after all, about interrupts!)

You will find that the interrupt is useful if you need to toggle, for example, an LED on a different pin to those listed in Table 6-3 because the timer/counter hardware can only action those specific pins.

---

[7]Cop out!

6.4.2   Timer/Counter Configuration

Unfortunately, the Arduino Language has no facility to enable these two interrupts for use in your sketches, so you will need a small piece of code in your setup() function to configure the chosen timer/counter in the manner you need. Something like Listing 6-9 will suffice.

For the example sketch, we will look at configuring Timer/counter 1 with a divide by 256 prescaler giving a 1.048576 second period in which the counter will count up and then reset to zero. At some point in this period, we will get a match on the OCR1A and OCR1B registers and use the interrupts to toggle different LEDs.

> **Note**
> Yes, I could toggle the appropriate pins just using the timer/counter hardware and do away with the interrupt, but for the sake of demonstration, I'm using LEDs attached to different pins from those the hardware controls (in case you were wondering!).

Bear in mind that the LEDs will both flash at the same rate. The counter is taking just over one second to count up and then overflow, so there will be one match on each of the OCR1A and OCR1B register values, in each one (and a bit) second period. This is true whether we are using interrupts or getting the timer/counter hardware to toggle our LEDs.

Listing 6-9 EnableTimer1CompMatch() function

```
//================================================================
// A function for Arduino and AVR to enable Timer/counter 1
// in normal mode and with a 256 prescaler and the compare A/B
// interrupts enabled. The interrupts will trigger every
// 1.048576 seconds.
//
// NOTE: This will mess up PWM on pins D9 and D10 if used in
// an Arduino sketch, Timer/counter 1 allows analogWrite() on
// those two pins.
//================================================================

void enableTimer1CompMatch(uint16_t ocr1a, uint16_t ocr1b) {
    // Choose normal timer/counter mode.
    // This overrides the Arduino setup.
    TCCR1A = ((0 << WGM11) | (0 << WGM10));
    TCCR1B = ((0 << WGM13) | (0 << WGM12));

    // Clear the interrupt flags.
    TIFR1 = ((1 << OCF1A) | (1 << OCF1B));

    // Set the compare match registers.
    OCR1A = ocr1a;
    OCR1B = ocr1b;

    // Enable both the Compare Match Interrupts.
```

```
    TIMSK1 = ((1 << OCIE1A) | (1 << OCIE1B));

    // Choose a prescaler to start the timer/counter.
    // Divide by 256 is chosen here.
    TCCR1B |= ((1 << CS12) | (0 << CS11) | (0 << CS10));
}
```

Who spotted that the initialization of TCCR1A and TCCR1B could have simply been an assignment of zero to the two registers? Well done, you were paying attention. However, in doing it this way, I know that the bits I'm interested in are set how I want them. Self-documenting code – I occasionally write it!

The enableTimer1CompMatch() function can be used from Arduino sketches or from a plain AVR C++ application – with any required minor changes to enable different prescalers and so on. Obviously, the two interrupts have been enabled, so a separate ISR for each will be required. This will be shown in Listing 6-12 in the Arduino sketch.

We are now ready to create an Arduino sketch to make use of the two Compare Match Interrupts.

6.4.3   Arduino Compare Match Interrupts

The example sketch, shown in Listings 6-10 through 6-12, will toggle pins D7 and D8 each and every time that there is a match between the TCNT1 register and either of the OCR1A or OCR1B registers.

Listing 6-10 shows the enableTimer1CompMatch() function, which is unchanged from Listing 6-9, and the setup() function.

Listing 6-10 Timer1CompBlink sketch – setup() function

```
//===============================================================
// An Arduino Sketch to flash an LED on pin D8 and another on
// D9 using Timer/counter 1 in normal mode, with a 256
// prescaler and using the two compare match interrupts.
//
// NOTE: This will mess up PWM on pins D9 and D10.
//
// Norman Dunbar
// 26 February 2020.
//===============================================================

void enableTimer1CompMatch(uint16_t ocr1a, uint16_t ocr1b) {
    // Function unchanged from text.
    ...
}


void setup() {
    // Enable LED pins D8, D9 & D13.
    pinMode(8, OUTPUT);
    pinMode(9, OUTPUT);
```

```
    pinMode(LED_BUILTIN, OUTPUT);

    // Enable Timer/counter 1.
    // D8/PB0 = COMP1A toggles at 43,692 roughly 2/3 of MAX.
    // D9/PB1 = COMP1B toggles at 21,845 roughly 1/3 of MAX.
    enableTimer1CompMatch(43692, 21845);
}
```

In the `setup()` function, there's nothing much to be noted. We do the usual `pinMode()` calls to make sure our LEDs are on output pins, and then `enableTimer1CompMatch()` is called, passing values of 43,692 and 21,845 for the `OCR1A` and `OCR1B` registers. These values are approximately one and two thirds of the full count of 65,535 available for Timer/counter 1 in normal mode.

Listing 6-11 is, by now, the standard `loop()` function to do the "real work" of flashing the built-in LED every five seconds.

Listing 6-11 Timer1CompBlink sketch – loop() function

```
void loop() {
    // Flash the built in LED every 5 seconds.
    digitalWrite(LED_BUILTIN, HIGH);
    delay(5000);
    digitalWrite(LED_BUILTIN, LOW);
    delay(5000);
}
```

Listing 6-12 shows the two ISRs for the Compare Match Interrupts on Timer/counter 1. Please be aware that, as previously discussed, I am using plain AVR code to toggle the pins as interrupt code must be kept short and sweet. I could use Arduino Language to toggle the pins, but you will remember from Listing 6-2, which did so, that it took too long to execute and affected the timings. This is obviously not a major problem when toggling LEDs, but depending on the application, it could be significant.

Listing 6-12 Timer1CompBlink sketch – compare match ISRs

```
ISR(TIMER1_COMPA_vect) {
    // Toggle pin D8 (PB0) every interrupt.
    PINB |= (1 << PINB0);
}

ISR(TIMER1_COMPB_vect) {
    // Toggle pin D9 (PB1) every interrupt.
    PINB |= (1 << PINB1);
}
```

> **Tip**
> Although I'm not showing it here, you could, if you needed to, enable the Overflow interrupt as well and use that to adjust the value in the counter so that you have a better control over how long it takes to toggle the LEDs, similar to how we adjusted the timer/counter's overflow period in the previous section.

Figure 6-2 is the breadboard layout being used for the sketch.

When uploaded and running, you should see that the LEDs on D8 and D9 flash every second or so, while the built-in LED on D13 flashes every five seconds as it has done in all previous sketches. The LED on D9 will flash first after a reset or power-on, then the LED on D8 will light up.

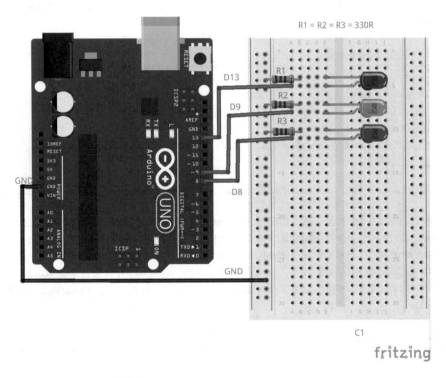

Figure 6-2   Timer1 compare match blink

6.4.4   AVR Match Interrupts

Converting the Arduino Timer1CompBlink sketch to plain AVR code is quite simple. Listings 6-13 and 6-14 show the result. The breadboard layout is exactly the same as that in Figure 6-2. We start with Listing 6-13 containing the two ISRs and other helper functions.

Listing 6-13 Timer1CompBlink – AVR application – helper functions

```
//================================================================
// An AVR application to flash an LED on pin D8 and another on
// D9 using Timer/counter 1 in normal mode, with a 256
// prescaler and using the two compare match interrupts.
//
// Norman Dunbar
// 26 February 2020.
//================================================================

#include "avr/io.h"
#include "avr/interrupt.h"
#include <util/delay.h>


ISR(TIMER1_COMPA_vect) {
    // Toggle pin PB0 every interrupt.
    PINB |= (1 << PINB0);
}


ISR(TIMER1_COMPB_vect) {
    // Toggle pin PB1 every interrupt.
    PINB |= (1 << PINB1);
}


void enableTimer1CompMatch(uint16_t ocr1a, uint16_t ocr1b) {
    // Function unchanged from text.
    ...
}
```

There's nothing very special or difficult here; the two ISRs will toggle their associated pins every time an interrupt occurs.

Listing 6-14 Timer1CompBlink – AVR application – main() function

```
int main() {
    // setup.
    // PB0, PB1 and PB5 are output pins.
    DDRB = ((1 << DDB0) | (1 << DDB1) | (1 << DDB5));

    // Enable Timer/counter 1.
    // PB0 = COMP1A toggles at 43,692 roughly 2/3 of MAX.
    // PB1 = COMP1B toggles at 21,845 roughly 1/3 of MAX.
    enableTimer1CompMatch(43692, 21845);
    sei();
```

```
// Loop. Flash PB5 every 5 seconds.
while (true) {
    PINB |= (1 << PINB5);
    _delay_ms(5000);
}
}
```

This simple application doesn't do anything differently from the Arduino sketch – except the very important step of enabling global interrupts – but it does do it in a much smaller size, 254 bytes Flash RAM and no Static RAM as opposed to 1044 bytes Flash RAM plus 9 bytes of scarce Static RAM.

When uploaded and running, you should see that the LEDs on PB0 and PB1 flash every second or so, while the built-in LED on PB5 flashes every five seconds as it has done in all previous sketches. The LED on PB1 will flash first after a reset or power-on, then the LED on PB0 will light up.

6.5   Input Capture Event Interrupt

Timer/counter 1 has one more feature, with an interrupt, which the other timer/counters do not have. This is the *Input Capture Unit* (ICU) and the *Input Capture Event* interrupt. The ICU is connected to a single pin on the ATmega328P – pin ICP1 – which corresponds to Arduino pin D8, a.k.a. PB0, which is physical pin 14 on the device.

This pin can be configured to listen for a RISING or FALLING edge and when detected can trigger the interrupt in addition to the usual action of recording the current value of the TCNT1 register, which is copied to the ICR1, the *Input Capture Register*. The *Input Capture Flag* bit, ICF1, is set to 1 in the same clock cycle in which the ICR1 is set to TCNT1's value. This flag will be automatically cleared by the ISR if enabled or in code by writing a 1 to it.

The Analog Comparator (see Chapter 11, "Analog Comparator Interrupt") can also cause an event to be recorded by the ICU.

As an aside, this is not as useful as it might sound. The event's timestamp is just the TCNT1 value and nothing more. Depending on the prescaler setting and the system clock speed, Timer/counter 1 will roll over very quickly – approximately every four seconds with a 16 MHz clock and a 1024 prescaler. You will have to write some code to be able to determine exactly in which four-second period the event arrived!

6.5.1   Timer/Counter 1 Configuration

Have you guessed? Yet again, the Arduino Language has no facility to allow the use of the Input Capture Unit interrupt easily in a sketch, so we are required to come up with an AVR style C++ function to configure Timer/counter 1 to enable the *Input Capture Unit* interrupt. Listing 6-15 shows such a function, enableTimer1ICU(), which can be used unchanged in either an Arduino sketch or in AVR code.

The enableTimer1ICU() function configures Timer/counter 1 with a 1024 prescaler, allowing for a period of 4.194304 seconds between overflows, and with the *Input Capture Unit* interrupt enabled. No other interrupts are in force, for the purposes of this example.

Listing 6-15 Timer1ICUBlink sketch – EnableTimer1ICU() function

```
//================================================================
// A function for Arduino and AVR to enable Timer/counter 1 in
// normal mode and with a 1024 prescaler and the input capture
// interrupt enabled. The interrupt will trigger every 4.194304
// seconds.
//
// NOTE: This will mess up PWM on pins D9 and D10 if used in an
// Arduino sketch, Timer/counter 1 allows analogWrite() on
// those two pins.
//================================================================
void enableTimer1ICU() {
    // Choose a timer/counter mode, with ICU enabled. The ICU
    // is a falling edge trigger. (ICES1 = 0).
    // This overrides the Arduino setup.
    TCCR1A = ((0 << WGM11) | (0 << WGM10));
    TCCR1B = ((0 << WGM13) | (0 << WGM12) | (0 << ICES1));

    // Clear the ICU interrupt flag.
    TIFR1 = (1 << ICF1);

    // Enable the Input Capture Interrupt.
    TIMSK1 = (1 << ICIE1);

    // Choose a prescaler to start the timer/counter.
    // Divide by 1024 is chosen
    TCCR1B |= ((1 << CS12) | (0 << CS11) | (1 << CS10));
}
```

> **Note**
> The Input Capture Unit has a noise canceling feature, which we are not using here. It is fully
> described in the data sheet, but means that an event has to be sampled four times with the same
> value to be registered. This takes four system clock cycles.

6.5.2 Arduino Input Capture Interrupts

For the demonstration sketch, we will not be bothering with the event's timestamp. All we will do is toggle an LED attached to pin D9 when an event is recorded on pin D8 – in other words, we will use the Input Capture Unit as a switch to turn an LED on and off. Figure 6-3 is the breadboard layout, and you can see that I'm once again using an MC14490P IC to avoid switch bounce.

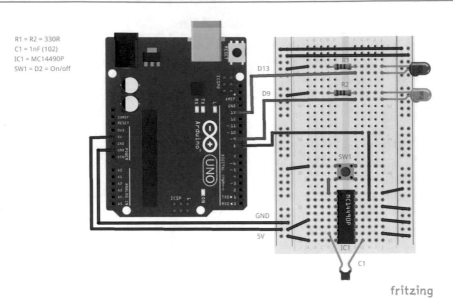

R1 = R2 = 330R
C1 = 1nF (102)
IC1 = MC14490P
SW1 = D2 = On/off

Figure 6-3 Timer1 ICU blink

Listings 6-16 through 6-18 show the various functions in the Arduino sketch. The function enableTimer1ICU() is unchanged from Listing 6-15 and so is not shown in full in the listing. It will, of course, be present in the sketch in the book's code download.

Listing 6-16 Timer1ICUBlink sketch – setup() function

```
//===============================================================
// A sketch to toggle an LED when an Input Capture Unit (ICU)
// interrupt is received on Arduino pin D8. The LED will be on
// D7 and the built in LED on D13 will be flashing on a 5
// second cycle.
//
// Norman Dunbar
// 27 February 2020.
//===============================================================


void enableTimer1ICU() {
    // Function unchanged from text.
    ...
}


void setup() {
    // Enable input and output pins.
    // D9 and D13 are OUTPUT.
    pinMode(9, OUTPUT);
    pinMode(LED_BUILTIN, OUTPUT);
```

```
    // D8 is INPUT_PULLUP.
    pinMode(8, INPUT_PULLUP);

    // Enable the ICU and interrupt.
    enableTimer1ICU();
}
```

In this version of the `setup()` function, pins D9 and D13 are output pins, while D8 is an input pin with the pull-up resistor enabled. This means that while the switch is not pressed, pin D8 will be held high. The Input Capture Unit is configured to trigger the interrupt on a `FALLING` edge, which will happen when the switch is first pressed. Timer/counter 1 is configured with a 1024 prescaler and with the Input Capture Unit enabled along with its interrupt.

Listing 6-17 is the ISR which will fire every time the Input Capture Unit registers a `FALLING` edge on its pin.

Listing 6-17 Timer1ICUBlink sketch – ISR

```
//================================================================
// Toggle D9 every time an event is recorded by the ICU.
//================================================================
ISR(TIMER1_CAPT_vect) {
    // Toggle pin D9 (PB1) every interrupt.
    PINB |= (1 << PINB1);
}
```

The ISR simply toggles pin D9 on every interrupt; this means that the Input Capture Unit is effectively a toggle switch which will turn the LED on the first interrupt and off on the next.

I am using AVR code in the ISR, rather than `digitalRead()` and `digitalWrite()` for the simple reason that those two functions will affect the timing of the interrupt handler due to the amount of low level code they compile down to. This is not a problem just to toggle an LED, but other applications may be detrimentally affected.

You may recognize the code in Listing 6-18. It's the same old loop which flashes the built-in LED every five seconds over and over again!

Listing 6-18 Timer1ICUBlink sketch – loop() function

```
void loop() {
    // The usual flash built in LED every 5 seconds.
    digitalWrite(LED_BUILTIN, HIGH);
    delay(5000);
    digitalWrite(LED_BUILTIN, LOW);
    delay(5000);
}
```

When this sketch has been uploaded to your Arduino, it will allow you to turn the LED on and off with the switch, all the while the built-in LED is taking up all of the main CPU's time, flashing and delaying. In the manner to which I hope you are becoming accustomed, you will see that the interrupts respond "instantly" no matter what the main CPU is doing.

Now, it's time to do it all again, only without the Arduino Language, just plain AVR C++.

6.5.3   AVR Input Capture Interrupts

Listing 6-19 is the AVR version of the Timer1ICUBlink sketch in the previous section.

Listing 6-19   Timer1ICUBlink – AVR application

```
//================================================================
// A sketch to toggle an LED when an Input Capture Unit (ICU)
// interrupt is received on pin ICP1/PB0. The LED will be on
// PB1 and the built in LED on D13 will be flashing on a 5
// second cycle.
//
// Norman Dunbar
// 27 February 2020.
//================================================================

#include "avr/io.h"
#include "avr/interrupt.h"
#include <util/delay.h>


ISR(TIMER1_CAPT_vect) {
    // Toggle pin PB1 every interrupt.
    PINB |= (1 << PINB1);
}


void enableTimer1ICU() {
    // Function unchanged from text.
    ...
}


int main() {
    // setup.
    // PB1 and PB5 are output pins.
    DDRB = ((1 << DDB1) | (1 << DDB5));

    // PB0 is input with pullup.
    DDRB |= (0 << DDB0);          // Not strictly necessary!
    PORTB |= (1 << PORTB0);

    // Enable Timer/counter 1 with ICU interrupt.
```

```
    enableTimer1ICU();
    sei();

    // Loop. Flash PB5 every 5 seconds.
    while (true) {
        PINB |= (1 << PINB5);
        _delay_ms(5000);
    }
}
```

6.6   Register Summary

There are a number of registers used or affected by the various Timer/counter interrupts. There are actually a number of registers involved in configuring and using the three Timer/counters. The register summary that follows only references those registers, or bits within registers, which affect or are affected by interrupts. See the data sheet for full details of the other registers and bits used by the Timer/counters.

6.6.1   Timer/Counter Interrupt Mask Registers

There are three *Timer/Counter Interrupt Mask* registers, one for each timer/counter. They are TIMSK0, TIMSK1, and TIMSK2 for Timer/counters 0, 1, and 2.

6.6.1.1 Timer/Counter Interrupt Mask Register 0

7	6	5	4	3	2	1	0
N/A	N/A	N/A	N/A	N/A	OCIE0B	OCIE0A	TOIE0

All bits marked as "N/A" are reserved and will be seen as zero if the register is read.

OCIE0B   Setting this bit to 1 will enable Timer/counter 0s Compare Match B interrupt.
OCIE0A   Setting this bit to 1 will enable Timer/counter 0s Compare Match A interrupt.
TOIE0   Setting this bit will enable Timer/counter 0s Overflow interrupt.

6.6.1.2 Timer/Counter Interrupt Mask Register 1

7	6	5	4	3	2	1	0
N/A	N/A	ICIE1	N/A	N/A	OCIE1B	OCIE1A	TOIE1

All bits marked as "N/A" are reserved and will be seen as zero if the register is read.

ICIE1   Setting this bit to 1 will enable Timer/counter 1s Input Capture interrupt.
OCIE1B   Setting this bit to 1 will enable Timer/counter 1s Compare Match B interrupt.
OCIE1A   Setting this bit to 1 will enable Timer/counter 1s Compare Match A interrupt.
TOIE1   Setting this bit will enable Timer/counter 1s Overflow interrupt.

6.6.1.3 Timer/Counter Interrupt Mask Register 2

7	6	5	4	3	2	1	0
N/A	N/A	N/A	N/A	N/A	OCIE2B	OCIE2A	TOIE2

All bits marked as "N/A" are reserved and will be seen as zero if the register is read.

OCIE2B   Setting this bit to 1 will enable Timer/counter 2s Compare Match B interrupt.

OCIE2A   Setting this bit to 1 will enable Timer/counter 2s Compare Match A interrupt.

TOIE2   Setting this bit will enable Timer/counter 2s Overflow interrupt.

6.6.2   Timer/Counter Interrupt Flag Registers

There are three *Timer/Counter Interrupt Flag* registers, one for each timer/counter. They are TIFR0, TIFR1, and TIFR2 for Timer/counters 0, 1, and 2.

6.6.2.1 Timer/Counter Interrupt Flag Register 0

7	6	5	4	3	2	1	0
N/A	N/A	N/A	N/A	N/A	OCF0B	OCF0A	TOV0

All bits marked as "N/A" are reserved and will be seen as zero if the register is read.

OCF0B   If this bit is read as a 1, then there has been a compare match between the count in the TCNT0 register and the OC0B register.

OCF0A   If this bit is read as a 1, then there has been a compare match between the count in the TCNT0 register and the OC0A register.

TOV0   If this bit is read as a 1, then the TCNT0 register has overflowed to zero.

6.6.2.2 Timer/Counter Interrupt Flag Register 1

7	6	5	4	3	2	1	0
N/A	N/A	ICF1	N/A	N/A	OCF1B	OCF1A	TOV1

All bits marked as "N/A" are reserved and will be seen as zero if the register is read.

ICF1   If this bit is read as a 1, then there has been an Input Capture Event on the ATmega328P's ICP1 pin (Arduino pin D8, AVR pin PB0).

OCF1B   If this bit is read as a 1, then there has been a compare match between the count in the TCNT1 register and the OC1B register.

OCF1A   If this bit is read as a 1, then there has been a compare match between the count in the TCNT1 register and the OC1A register.

TOV1   If this bit is read as a 1, then the TCNT1 register has overflowed to zero.

6.6.2.3 Timer/Counter Interrupt Flag Register 2

7	6	5	4	3	2	1	0
N/A	N/A	N/A	N/A	N/A	OCF2B	OCF2A	TOV2

All bits marked as "N/A" are reserved and will be seen as zero if the register is read.

OCF2B If this bit is read as a 1, then there has been a compare match between the count in the TCNT2 register and the OC2B register.

OCF2A If this bit is read as a 1, then there has been a compare match between the count in the TCNT2 register and the OC2A register.

TOV2 If this bit is read as a 1, then the TCNT2 register has overflowed to zero.

6.7 Key Takeaways

In this chapter, we learned that

- There are three separate Timer/counters in an ATmega328P, and they account for 10 of the microcontroller's 26 interrupts.
- Each of the three Timer/counters has
  - An Overflow interrupt
  - A Compare Match A interrupt
  - A Compare Match B interrupt
- In addition to these three interrupts, Timer/counter 1 also has an *Input Capture Event* interrupt.
- When using the features of a Timer/counter's interrupts, we can also use the other features of the Timer/counter at the same time. The Arduino does this to count the millis() in a sketch and also to generate PWM for analogWrite().
- Timer/counters do not count unless a suitable prescaler has been configured.
- The Analog Comparator can cause Timer/counter 1s *Input Capture Unit* interrupt to be triggered.

6.8 Coming Up

That was a big chapter; there's a lot going on in the Timer/counter interrupt realm. In the next chapter, we will take a look at the *SPI Serial Transfer Complete* interrupt.

SPI Interrupt

7

In this chapter, we will take a look at the SPI interrupt. This is another interrupt that you don't see in the Arduino Language, but after reading this chapter, hopefully, you will be better armed and able to use it to good effect in your own code. SPI is the Serial Peripheral Interface and is used to exchange data with a peripheral, one bit at a time, using shift registers. The information on the following pages will help you realize that when using other shift registers such as the SN74HC595, you can actually talk to them over SPI rather than using the Arduino's shiftIn() and shiftOut() functions.

7.1   I SPI with My Little Eye

Vector 17 in the Interrupt Vector Table is where we will find the SPI interrupt.

There is a single interrupt for the SPI system. Its purpose is to execute whenever an SPI transfer is complete and a data byte has been received or transmitted. Bear in mind, however, that whenever there is a communication taking place on the SPI bus, there is *always* a simultaneous transmission *and* receipt of data, which means that every time the interrupt fires, one byte has been transmitted and one received. Whether or not the received byte is of any use depends on the peripherals in use at the time—SPI requires data to be *exchanged*.

Data are exchanged between the controller and the peripheral one bit at a time, but at extremely high speeds.

7.2   SPI Background

The next few sections explain much about the internal workings of SPI. Much of what is described is taken care of automatically by the SPI hardware in the ATmega328P. You don't *need* to know most of this information, but it can help you to better understand what is going on. Read on!

SPI is normally implemented as a shift register in each device. Communications involving SPI is basically two shift registers connected together. One bit at a time is clocked into both shift registers as another bit is shifted out. The protocol is known as *synchronous* as it is clocked. Unlike the USART, when the Arduino is writing or reading the Serial Interface, there are no baud rates,[1] start bits, parity bits, or stop bits.

---

[1] Although there is a speed to be considered.

© The Author(s), under exclusive license to APress Media, LLC, part of Springer Nature 2024
N. Dunbar, *Arduino Interrupts*, Maker Innovations Series,
https://doi.org/10.1007/978-1-4842-9714-8_7

The controlling device controls the clock for the communications. Only three wires need to be connected, in addition to power and ground. These are

- MISO—*Master In, Slave Out*: Data from the peripheral is transmitted to the controlling device on this line. You may see this labeled as CIPO, *Controller In, Peripheral Out*, in more recent documentation. The latest data sheets from Microchip, at the time of writing, have yet to make this change.
- MOSI—*Master Out, Slave In*: Data from the controlling device is transmitted to the peripheral on this line. You may also see this labeled as COPI, *Controller Out, Peripheral In*.
- SCK—SPI clock: This is generated by the controlling device and synchronizes both devices to shift each data bit onto the MISO and MOSI lines at the same time.

Given that numerous peripheral devices can be connected to the SPI bus at the same time, how does each one know when it is being addressed? Well, there needs to be one additional line between the controller and each peripheral. This is the CS (chip select), or SS (slave select), line. When this is pulled *low*, the peripheral knows it is being addressed. This means that the controller needs to have one spare pin for each of the peripherals it may wish to communicate with.

> **Note**
> The ATmega328P has a pin labeled SS. This is Arduino pin D10, AVR pin PB2.
>
> This pin is used when the ATmega328P is configured as a peripheral in an SPI communication. The pin will be connected to (one of) the controlling device's GPIO pins and pulled low when the controller wishes to address this device as a peripheral.
>
> In this chapter, when I use the term SS I am referring to this specific pin on the *controller*. When I refer to CS, then I am referring to *any* GPIO pin that is being used to indicate to an SPI peripheral that it is now being addressed as a peripheral.
>
> Also, and very importantly, when configuring the Arduino/ATmega328P as a controlling device, you can avoid spending many hours debugging your sketch as to why it is not working correctly, if you remember to configure the controller's SS pin as an output!

Figure 7-1 shows how an example circuit could be set up to connect an Arduino Uno to three separate 25LC010 EEPROMs using a separate CS line for each EEPROM—Arduino pins D2, D3, and D4 are used as the three CS lines, each one controlling a separate EEPROM.

All three EEPROMS have their SCK, MISO (data out), and MOSI (data in) lines connected together and are connected to the Arduino pins D13/SCK, D12/MISO (data in), and D11/MOSI (data out), respectively.

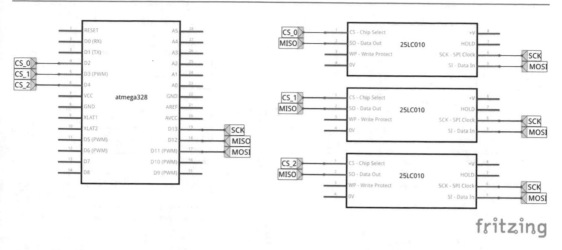

Figure 7-1 SPI EEPROM example

> **Note**
>
> If you are unfamiliar with the way the circuit diagram is laid out in Figure 7-1, all you need to know is that any connection with a label attached is electrically joined to *every* other connection with the same label. For example, in Figure 7-1, all the component pins labeled SCK are electrically connected together.
>
> This manner of drawing a circuit reduces the number of potentially confusing lines that need to be drawn to connect components together. I *know* it's confusing as I originally drew the circuit with lines rather than net labels!

If there are more peripherals in the circuit than there are spare ATmega328P pins to be used as CS lines, then there are a couple of options which can help get around the pin shortage. You could use a three-to-eight multiplexer or a shift register.

In Figure 7-2, I show the use of an SN74HC595 shift register which only requires three pins to switch up to eight separate peripherals. Figure 7-2 shows the circuit where an ATmega328P is connected to six 25LC010 EEPROMs. Up to eight EEPROMs (or other SPI peripherals) can be connected in this configuration. Not shown in the schematic are the 10 KΩ pull-up resistors on the OE and MR pins of the SN74HC595; those pins are active low and should be pulled up to avoid spurious resets and suchlike.

If even more peripherals are required to be connected, shift registers can be cascaded together to give further eight additional peripheral CS lines for each additional shift register added to the circuit. The ATmega328P will still only require three pins as shown in Figure 7-2. The number of SPI peripherals that an ATmega328P microcontroller can address, using only three of its pins, is effectively unlimited given enough shift registers.

> **Note**
>
> Don't forget, the SPI protocol requires the peripheral's CS line to be pulled low. The code running to select CS_5, for example, should write a value of (0b11011111) to the shift register to pull that one CS line low.

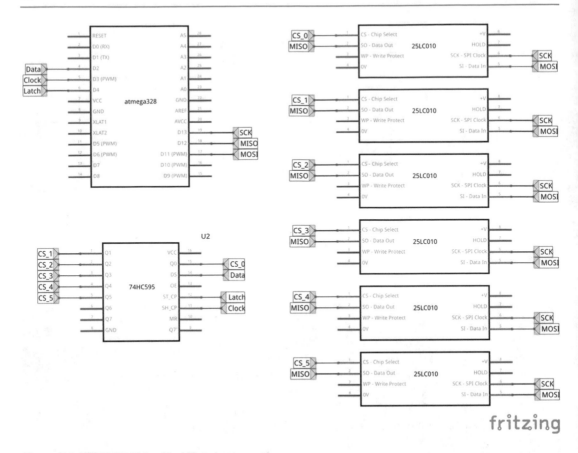

Figure 7-2 SPI EEPROMs with shift register example

Please bear in mind, your Arduino board or ATmega328P-based board can be configured as either a controller or a peripheral. Many SPI sensors and suchlike can only be configured as a peripheral. The data sheet for the appropriate device will have full details.

What do we need to know in order to talk SPI with a sensor?

There are four pieces of information we need to be able to set up SPI between two devices:

- What speed should we communicate at? Can we generate this speed based upon our ATmega328P/Arduino's system clock rate? We must communicate at the slowest rate of all the devices attached to the SPI bus.
- Is data shifted in/out with the most significant bit (MSB) or least significant bit (LSB) first?
- Which edges of SCK are the data bits written and read? (Phase.)
- Is SCK idle when high or low? (Polarity.)

7.2.1   SPI Clock

The SCK pin is used to connect the peripherals to the controller's SPI clock signal. This clock is generated only by the controller and is used to synchronize communications between the controller and the peripheral so that both shift a bit of data onto the bus at the same time, and both read a data bit

Table 7-1 SPI clock prescalers

SPI2X	SPR1	SPR0	SCK frequency	Arduino frequency
0	0	0	F_CPU/4	4 MHz
0	0	1	F_CPU/16	1 MHz
0	1	0	F_CPU/64	250 KHz
0	1	1	F_CPU/128	125 KHz
1	0	0	F_CPU/2	8 MHz
1	0	1	F_CPU/8	2 MHz
1	1	0	F_CPU/32	500 KHz
1	1	1	F_CPU/64	250 KHz

into their receiving shift register at the same time. The ATmega328P has *seven* different clock rates, all based upon a division of the main system clock. Looking at the data sheet for the ATmega328P, we can see in the SPI chapter that it *appears* that the ATmega328P is an upgraded microcontroller to a previous device. Why do I say this? Well, the prescaler for the SPI clock is a little on the weird side!

Table 7-1 shows the eight different prescaler settings. Yes, eight—even though the data sheet states that SPI has *seven* programmable bit rates. What's amiss? Looking closely at Table 7-1, you will notice that there are two different prescaler settings that generate "divide by 64."

Table 7-1 shows the SCK frequencies which can be obtained when using the standard Arduino 16 MHz crystal.

The weirdness I mentioned previously is related to the order of the prescaler divisors. It appears that there may only have been four different prescalers in the past, but the use of the SPI2X bit in the *SPI Status Register*, SPSR, as a "speed doubler" has given us the additional speeds. It just so happens that by doubling the clock speed, one of the existing options, $F\_CPU/128$, doubles up to provide an already existing speed, $F\_CPU/64$.

7.2.2 SPI Frequency

Table 7-1 shows the various prescalers that are able to be used on an ATmega328P, as fitted to many Arduino boards. These prescalers allow various SPI clock speeds between 125 KHz and 8 MHz. Obviously, if your ATmega328P is clocked at a different frequency, those SPI speeds will vary. My *NormDuinos*,[2] running at 8 MHz, can only manage SPI clock frequencies of between 62.5 KHz and 4 MHz as my clock frequency is half that of an Arduino Uno, for example.

Some SPI devices can be run at frequencies up to 100 MHz.[3]

Contributing to the higher speeds of some SPI devices is the fact that *every* bit transferred is a *useful* bit. When sending data over the USART, for example, there are the data bits, and wrapped around them are the framing bits—stop, start, and parity bits. These have to be transmitted but then stripped off at the receiving end. With a start bit, eight data bits, no parity, and one stop bit, there are ten bits transmitted of which eight are of interest—20% of the transmission is "wasted" bits. Add on a parity bit, and this goes up to 27.27% of your transmission being wasted.

Setting the SPI frequency is done by choosing a suitable prescaler for the SPI clock. This is done by writing to bit SPI2X in the *SPI Status Register*, SPSR, and bits SPR1:SPR0 in the *SPI Control Register*, SPCR. The values to write are those in Table 7-1.

---

[2]Homemade "Arduino" with the crystal removed, allowing for two extra pins, running on the internal 8 MHz oscillator.

[3]Reference: Elliot Williams, *Make: AVR Programming*, 2014. ISBN: 978-1-4493-5578-4.

The frequency configured should always be within the range of the *slowest* device in the conversation.

7.2.3   Bit Ordering

SPI exchanges data bit by bit between the controller and the peripheral. Each device transmits one bit of data per SCK pulse. Data can be sent in either the least significant bit first or most significant bit first. The LSB of a data byte is bit 0, while the MSB is bit 7.

Setting the bit order is a simple case of writing to the DORD bit in the *SPI Control Register*, SPCR. Writing a zero to DORD configures MSB first, while writing a one configures LSB first.

It should be obvious that the controller cannot configure the peripheral's bit ordering, so remember to consult the data sheet for the peripheral to determine the expected order that it needs to receive data and the order in which it will transmit data.

7.2.4   Phase, Polarity, and SPI Mode

Setting polarity and phase is done by writing to bits CPOL (polarity) and CPHA (phase) in the *SPI Control Register*, SPCR. What exactly do these bits control?

Polarity defines the idle state of the SPI clock. The clock must be in this idle state at the point when the peripheral's CS pin is pulled low to initiate a transfer of data. If the peripheral requires the clock to idle low, then CPOL must be zero; if idle is high, then CPOL will be one. If the clock idles low, then the leading edge of a clock pulse will be rising and the trailing edge falling. The opposite is true for a clock which idles high. The clock is used when data are being exchanged between the controller and the peripheral. When not actively exchanging data, the clock is usually pulled either high or low, according to CPOL, to indicate that the bus is idle.

The clock edges—where it changes from one state to the other—are important as they are used by the hardware in both devices to output the data line's new state on one edge and to read the data state on the other edge. This is the *phase* of the data exchange and controlled by the CPHA bit.

If the CPHA bit is zero, then the data bit is written onto the bus on the trailing edge of the *previous* clock pulse and is read on the leading edge of the *current* clock cycle. This means that the data line needs to be set up correctly for the first bit before the clock is started. The data line must then remain valid until it is read, and the next data bit will then be asserted on the trailing edge of the current clock cycle.

If CPHA is one, then the data bit is written onto the bus on the leading edge of this clock pulse and is read on the trailing edge of the same clock cycle. The data line will remain valid until the leading edge of the *following* clock cycle whereupon the next data bit will be output.

Depending on which documentation you read, you may find the terms latched, asserted, or set up for output and shifted, read, or sampled for input. Both devices will be simultaneously writing a single bit on the same clock edge, and both will be simultaneously reading a bit on another clock edge.

Some data sheets do not mention phase and polarity at all. They mention SPI modes instead. There are four different modes, and they relate to the various binary combinations of polarity and phase, where phase takes the role of the least significant bit and polarity the most significant bit.

7.2.4.1 Mode 0

In this mode, both polarity and phase are zero:

- As polarity is zero, the clock idles low and a cycle begins when it transitions to a high state. The leading edge is rising; the trailing edge is falling.
- As phase is also zero, a data bit is output onto the bus on the trailing edge of the *previous* clock cycle, and a data bit is input from the bus on the leading edge of the current clock cycle.

7.2.4.2 Mode 1

In this mode, polarity is zero and phase is one:

- As polarity is zero, the clock idles low and a cycle begins when it transitions to a high state. The leading edge is rising; the trailing edge is falling.
- As phase is one, a data bit is output onto the bus on the leading edge of a clock cycle, and a bit is input on the trailing edge of the same clock cycle.

7.2.4.3 Mode 2

In this mode, polarity is one and phase is zero.

- As polarity is one, the clock idles high and a cycle begins when it transitions to a low state. The leading edge is falling; the trailing edge is rising.
- As phase is zero, a data bit is output onto the bus on the trailing edge of the *previous* clock cycle, and a data bit is input from the bus on the leading edge of the current clock cycle.

7.2.4.4 Mode 3

In this mode, both polarity and phase are one.

- As polarity is one, the clock idles high and a cycle begins when it transitions to a low state. The leading edge is falling; the trailing edge is rising.
- As phase is also one, a data bit is output onto the bus on the leading edge of a clock cycle, and a bit is input on the trailing edge of the same clock cycle.

7.3   Data Transfers

When a device is transmitting data, there is no buffering involved. This means that the transmitter must wait for the current transmission to complete before attempting to write another byte to the *SPI Data Register*, SPDR. If a new data byte is written to SPDR before the current byte is finished being output, then a data collision will result. This will set the Data Collision flag bit, WCOL, in the *SPI Status Register*, SPSR. See Section 7.5,Write Collision Errors, later in this chapter for more detail.

When a device is receiving data, it *is* double buffered. This allows for one byte to be waiting in SPDR to be read by the code, while a second byte is being received. However, if the first byte is not read from SPDR, then it will be overwritten when the incoming byte has been fully received.

On each clock cycle, on the appropriate edge, one bit of data will be read from the appropriate input data line and shifted into the least significant bit of the internal shift registers on the two devices. As each new bit is clocked in, the other bits are shifted up one place to make room. The oldest bit is lost, unless the device has some means to shift it out to other devices.

7.4   Controller and Peripheral Modes

There are two modes that a device can be operated in when communicating over SPI. These are

- Controller mode
- Peripheral mode

Depending on the chosen mode, some of the SPI pins are automatically configured by the SPI hardware when the SPI is enabled. Only the pins required as inputs are configured in this manner. Output pins must be configured as such by the code. The data sheet advises that this configuration setup is required to avoid damage through driver contention.

7.4.1   Controller Mode

In order to take control of the SPI bus and control the communication, a device must become the controller. This is done by setting the *Master* bit, MSTR, in the *SPI Control Register*, SPCR. When configured as a controller, then as the data sheet advises, the SS pin can be configured as either an input or an output. This has certain connotations as the data sheet makes clear.

- If SS is configured to be an output pin, then the SPI hardware—and communications—are not affected. The pin can be used as a normal GPIO pin if required.
  The data sheet states that

  Typically, the pin will be driving the SS pin of the SPI peripheral.

  This is fine, provided there's only one peripheral!
- If the SS pin is configured as an input pin, it must be held high to ensure that the SPI hardware acts as a controller. If the SS pin is ever driven low by peripheral circuitry, then the SPI hardware will interpret this as *bus contention* on the SPI bus. It will assume that another controller has attempted to select this device as a peripheral and wishes to start exchanging data. To avoid this potential bus contention, the SPI hardware will
  - Clear the MSTR bit in the SPCR register. The device becomes an SPI peripheral and loses controller status. As a result, the MOSI and SCK pins are reconfigured as input pins.
  - Set the SPIF bit in SPSR to indicate that SPI communications have occurred. If the SPI interrupt has been enabled by setting the SPIE bit in the SPCR register, and global interrupts are enabled, the ISR will execute.
  As a result of all the reconfiguration, any interrupt-enabled SPI communications in controller mode must check in the ISR that the MSTR bit is still set. If the MSTR bit has been cleared by a slave select, it must be set by the user to re-enable SPI Master mode. This is only necessary if there is any possibility that SS can be driven low by any feature of the circuitry that the microcontroller is part of. For best results, and to avoid the need to keep checking the MSTR bit, configure the SS pin as an output.

In controller mode, only the MISO pin is automatically configured when SPI is enabled. The remaining SPI pins, MISO, SCK, and SS, are not configured—it is the responsibility of the code to configure these as outputs.

7.4.2   Peripheral Mode

If the device is not configured as a controller, then it must be configured as a peripheral. When configured thus, the SS pin is always an input pin, or the device would not be able to know when it was being addressed by the controller.

For as long as SS remains high, all SPI pins are considered inputs, and the SPI hardware will not be able to receive any incoming data.

Whenever SS is pulled low by the controller, the peripheral's SPI hardware is activated. Activating SPI on the peripheral means that the MISO pin must be configured as an output prior to activation. All other SPI pins will remain as inputs.

After communications end, the controller will pull the peripheral's SS pin high again, and this will reset the SPI hardware in the peripheral which will cause MISO to revert to an input pin.

The data sheet notes that

> The SS pin is useful for packet/byte synchronization to keep the slave bit counter synchronous with the master clock generator. When the SS pin is driven high, the SPI slave will immediately reset the send and receive logic, and drop any partially received data in the Shift Register.

In peripheral mode, the MISO pin is not configured when SPI is enabled. All of the remaining SPI pins, MISO, SCK, and SS, are automatically configured as inputs. The code needs only to configure MISO as an output.

7.5   Write Collision Errors

As I mentioned previously, if the SPDR register is written to while a data transfer is currently in progress, this could corrupt the data being transmitted. This is possible as the SPDR register is not double buffered when transmitting data, only when receiving. The corruption would occur because the data written to SPDR is immediately written into the shift register used to transfer the data out, overwriting what is already there.

If the SPI hardware detects an attempt to write to SPDR while a transmission is in progress, it will set the Write Collision flag bit in the SPI Status Register, SPSR, which has the effect of preventing the new data from being written to the SPDR, and, thus, no corruption should occur.

The WCOL flag is cleared in the following manner, and not by writing a one bit in the usual manner:

- Read the *SPI Status Register*, SPSR, while WCOL is still set.
- *Access* the *SPI Data Register*, SPDR. What does "access" mean exactly? Reading? Writing? The data sheet doesn't say, but my testing has shown that reading the register is sufficient.

Note
Clearing the WCOL flag in this manner has the side effect of also clearing the SPIF flag.

Application note *AVR151: Setup and Use of the SPI* advises that

> A write collision is normally a peripheral error as the peripheral has no control over when a controller will initiate a transfer. A controller knows when a transfer is in progress and should not cause write collisions. However, the SPI logic can detect write collisions in controllers and peripherals.

7.6   Interrupts

So, having discussed all of the preceding, you should be aware that the ATmega328P's SPI hardware takes care of *most* of the hard work.

All we developers have to do, from the controlling device's point of view, is set up the devices in the manner we need to. To do this, we simply

- Configure SPI controller mode.
- Configure the SCK, SS, and MOSI pins as outputs and make sure that SS is pulled high.
- Configure the SPI clock frequency to match the slowest device in the communication—this should be available in the peripheral's data sheet.
- Configure the phase and polarity to match the peripheral—this should be available in the peripheral's data sheet.
- Configure the data transfer endianness, MSB or LSB first—this should be available in the peripheral's data sheet.
- Enable SPI.
- Pull the CS line for the chosen peripheral low to start the communication.

Once this is done, the SPI hardware will take care of the timings for the setup and latch of the data bits and so on. It's always nice when the hardware does things for us, so we don't have to.

Of course, for this book's subject matter, we also need to set up an interrupt handler and configure SPI to make use of it. To do this, we simply need to set a single bit in the SPCR register. The bit in question is the SPIE bit which enables the SPI interrupt.

Given that an interrupt is to be generated every eight SPI clock ticks, it's possible that using an interrupt in the controller can lead to performance problems overall. If the code was written in C/C++, then every time the ISR is executed

- All 32 of the Atmega328P's general-purpose registers and the status register will be preserved on the stack by the compiler-generated code.
- The ISR code executes.
- All those preserved registers will be restored again.

If you wrote the code in Assembly Language, on the other hand, then you will know exactly which registers are used by the ISR, and, thus, only those are required to be preserved and restored, saving a little time in each execution of the ISR.

There is much discussion on the Internet about this matter, and the general consensus appears to be to use interrupts when running a peripheral device, but use polling in the controller. This is fine if the peripheral is another microcontroller, for example, as that can be configured accordingly. Unfortunately, not all SPI peripherals have this ability.

When a byte of data has been completely exchanged between the two devices, the SPIF flag will be set in the SPSR register. If global interrupts and the SPI interrupt have been enabled, then the ISR will be executed and the flag automatically cleared.

In non-interrupt sketches, this flag should be polled so that the code knows when a new data byte has been transmitted or received, ready for the next one. The flag must be cleared in a different manner from the usual method of writing a one to the bit. To clear the flag, the code must

- Read the *SPI Status Register*, SPSR, while SPIF is still set.
- Access the *SPI Data Register*, SPDR. Reading the register is sufficient to clear the flag.

Normally, you would wish to read the received data when your own data byte had been transmitted, so this is actually an efficient manner of clearing the flag. You would be reading SPSR in the polling loop to determine the end of this data byte's transmission, then reading the received byte from SPDR so the flag will be almost automatically cleared. You get your data sent and received and the interrupt flag cleared all in the normal execution of the code.

> **Note**
> Clearing the SPIF flag in this manner has the side effect of also clearing the WCOL flag, if a write collision has occurred.

When using the SPI interrupt, it is usual for the controller to execute in non-interrupt mode and the peripheral to use interrupts. This is for the simple reason that the peripheral has no idea when the controller will wish to communicate with it. The controller, obviously, knows when it wishes to communicate. This is not to say that the controller cannot use interrupts of course.

7.6.1 Controller Interrupts

Application note *AVR151: Setup and Use of the SPI* has a reasonably helpful flowchart of the steps involved in initializing and using SPI interrupts on the controller. Unfortunately, some steps are omitted. I have included them all here.

7.6.1.1 Initialization
The controller initialization steps are

- Disable global interrupts.
- Configure MOSI, SCK, SS, and all CS pins, one for each peripheral, as output pins. Ensure that the SS pin is pulled high whether it is being used to control the peripheral or not.
- Enable SPI in controller mode by setting bits SPE and MSTR in the SPCR register.
- Select the SPI clock speed by setting bits SPR1:SPR0 in the SPCR register, plus, if necessary, bit SPI2X in the SPSR register.
- Configure phase and polarity by setting the CPHA and CPOL bits in the SPCR register.
- Enable the SPI interrupt by setting bit SPIE in the SPCR register.
- Clear the SPI interrupt flag by reading the SPSR register, followed by a read of the SPDR register.
- Enable global interrupts.

7.6.1.2 Interrupt Handler
In controller mode, the interrupt handler will be executed every eight ticks of the SPI clock. This indicates that a byte of data has been transmitted, and a byte has also been received. The received byte, if required, should be copied somewhere safe and a new data byte for transmission written to SPDR. If all communications are ended, disable SPI by clearing the SPE and SPIE bits (and the MSTR bit, if desired) in SPCR.

7.6.2 Peripheral Interrupts

The steps outlined in the following are from those occasions where you have complete control over the peripheral device, perhaps when two Arduinos are communicating over SPI. It is highly unlikely that you will be able to configure most SPI sensors in the described manner.

7.6.2.1 Initialization
The peripheral initialization steps are

- Disable global interrupts.
- Configure MISO as an output pin.
- Configure peripheral mode by clearing the MSTR bit in the SPCR register.
- Configure phase and polarity by setting the CPHA and CPOL bits in the SPCR register.
- Enable SPI and the SPI interrupt by setting bits SPE and SPIE in SPCR.
- Clear the SPI interrupt flag by reading the SPSR register, followed by a read of the SPDR register.
- Enable global interrupts.

7.6.2.2 Interrupt Handler
In peripheral mode, the interrupt handler will be executed every eight ticks of the *controller's* SPI clock. This indicates that a byte of data has been received from the controller and that a byte has also been transmitted to the controller. The received byte should always be read, and if required, should be copied somewhere safe and a new data byte for transmission written to SPDR. If all communications are ended, the controller should terminate the communication.

7.7   Controller Mode—Interrupt LED Driver

In the age-old tradition of blinking LEDs, the first SPI example sketch will use SPI to communicate with a Texas Instruments SN74HC595 Shift Register. The code will be simple and will blink eight LEDs attached to the SN74HC595 using only four wires, plus VCC and GND, on the Arduino. Shift registers can be cascaded to give more outputs, so the number of LEDs that we can blink with only four wires is almost unlimited.[4]

You didn't know that the SN74HC595 was SPI?[5] Read on.

7.7.1   The SN74HC595 Shift Register

The SN74HC595 shift register can be considered to consist of two main parts:

- The (internal) shift register which holds eight bits of data: New data bits, based on the state of the SER pin, *are clocked into the shift register each time the SRCLK pin is pulled high.* In addition, the "oldest" bit in the shift register will also be shifted out through pin QH' allowing multiple SN74HC595s to be cascaded together.

---

[4]However, don't draw too much current from the Arduino's 5 V and GND pins if you do decide to blink many, many LEDS!

[5]Neither did I!

- The storage register: This is connected to the output pins and is refreshed when the RCLK pin is pulled high. This need not necessarily change the state of the output pins though. The state of the output pins will only reflect the data in the storage register when ~OE pin is pulled low.

Why have I emphasized some text in the first bullet point? Because the data sheet for the SN76HC595 doesn't mention which SPI modes that it operates with. It does mention that the data are clocked on a rising edge; this means that we should be using mode 0 (CPOL = CPHA = 0) or mode 3 (CPOL = CPHA = 1) only. I have used both settings and both work fine.

In operation as an SPI device, RCLK would be pulled low to prevent the shift register data from being copied to the storage register; this acts like the CS pin. ~OE would normally be pulled high to avoid having potentially incorrect data on the output pins.

Data will be shifted in automagically by the SPI hardware, setting the data, SER, and clock, SRCLK, lines as appropriate and according to phase and polarity.

After all eight bits have been shifted in, the RCLK would be pulled high to deselect the SN74HC595 from the SPI bus and copy the new data from the internal shift register to the storage register. Depending on the state of the ~OE pin, this may also change the state of the output pins. If ~OE is pulled low, then the output pins would take on the same state as the storage register.

Figure 7-3 shows the pins on the SN74HC595 shift register. Some Arduino tutorials use different names for the pins for some reason; the names I have used in Figure 7-3 are those from the Texas Instruments data sheet for the device. Table 7-3, later in this chapter, cross-references these pin names with those of another data sheet which I have found on the Web. In the text, I will refer to the pin names as per Figure 7-3.

Figure 7-3 SN74HC595
pins

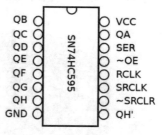

If you want to find out more about shift registers, then you may wish to watch these videos on YouTube:

- www.youtube.com/watch?v=HQ0ntNkBTYk: Shift registers and SPI
- www.youtube.com/watch?v=6fVbJbNPrEU: How shift registers actually work

7.7.2   The LED Driver Circuit

In the circuit for this example (see Figure 7-4), the output pins QA, the least significant bit of the SN74HC595, through QH, the most significant bit, are each connected to an LED via a 560 Ω resistor. The LED cathodes connect directly to ground.

The output pins on the SN74HC595 are wired slightly weirdly; the first bit of the output is on pin 15, while the second through eighth bits are on pins 1 through 7.

When data are shifted into the SN74HC595, output pin QA always receives the first bit of each data byte shifted in, and output pin QH receives the final bit.

Table 7-2 shows how the outputs will reflect the bits of the value 0b11010100, which is 212 decimal, for both LSB and MSB first shift directions.

Table 7-2 MSB or LSB first

	QA	QB	QC	QD	QE	QF	QG	QH
LSB first	0	0	1	0	1	0	1	1
MSB first	1	1	0	1	0	1	0	0

Figure 7-4 shows the breadboard layout for the LED Driver circuit. There are quite a few wires flying around, so it's a bit of a mess. I colored the wires for the various output pins to hopefully make things clearer about where each of the connections goes. It's not visible on the image, but the notch on the surface of the SN74HC595, indicating pin 1, is at the end closest to the eight 560 Ω resistors.

In Figure 7-4, I have the LEDs wired with QA at the top, down to QH at the bottom. In the code to follow, DORD is set to 1 to shift the MSB first, so QA reflects bit 7 through to QH which reflects bit 0 of the value shifted. The reason for this is simple; my viewpoint on the LEDs is from the right side of the image, so when I look at it, the LEDs light up, in binary values, with the lowest bit on the left as is normal. If your viewpoint is from the left side instead, then simply set DORD to 0 to shift the LSB first, and all will be well.

The breadboard circuit in Figure 7-4 uses the SN74HC595's RCLK pin as the CS pin. By pulling that low, the SN74HC595 will be usable as an SPI device.

Table 7-3 summarizes the connections for the sketch as the breadboard layout, in Figure 7-4, is a tad crowded with wires obscuring components and so on. As there are at least two different naming

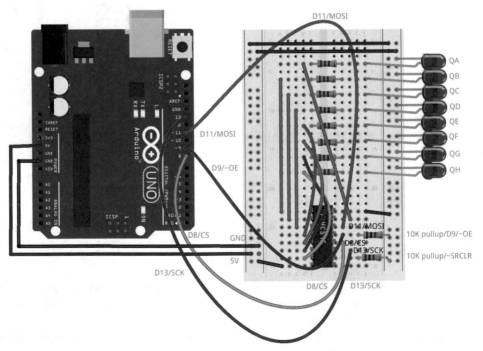

Figure 7-4 SPI_LEDs breadboard layout

"standards" for these shift registers, I have listed the physical pin numbers and two of the pin naming conventions that I am aware of.

Table 7-3 SN74HC595 pins and connections

Pin	Name	Alt name	Connect to
15,1–7	QA–QH	Q0–Q7	560 Ω resistor and LED anodes
8	GND	GND	Arduino GND
9	QH'	Q7'	Not connected
10	~SRCLR	~MR	10 KΩ pull-up to VCC
11	SRCLK	SH_CP	Arduino D13/PB5/SCK
12	RCLK	ST_CP	Arduino D8/PB0 (using this pin for CS)
13	~OE	~OE	10 KΩ pull-up to VCC and Arduino D9/PB1
14	SER	DS	Arduino D11/PB3/MOSI
16	VCC	VCC	Arduino 5 V

It is, unfortunately, quite uncommon to see the ~OE and ~SRCLR pins being pulled up to VCC in many Arduino tutorials. This can be a bit of a nuisance, to say the least, as leaving these pins floating causes all sorts of problems. I have a batch of these shift registers, and five of them do not function at all without having the pull-ups in place. The remainder fluctuates randomly. Adding the two pull-ups removed all problems, and the "dead" chips immediately burst into life again. The ~OE and ~SRCLR pins are active low, hence the need to pull them up to VCC to prevent them from floating.

Should ~OE and ~SRCLR be pulled up via a resistor or wired directly to VCC? That is the question. The answer is "it depends"!

- If you simply wish to make life easy and are not bothered by the odd flickering LED, then wire ~OE directly to VCC. Any data shifted into the SN74HC595 will automatically be seen on the output pins and LEDs, possibly causing a bit of flicker.
- If you have no intention, in your sketch code, of using the ~SRCLR pin to clear the SN74HC595's data at any point, then wire it directly to VCC.
- If you wish to avoid flickering LEDs, or have some other device(s) attached to the output pins, and need to have stable data before the output pins are changed, then wire ~OE to VCC via a 10 KΩ resistor, and your code can pull the pin to GND to enable the output pins all at once when the data are stable.
- If you need your code to control the clear data feature of the SN74HC595, then wire ~SRCLR to VCC using a 10 KΩ resistor, and your code can also pull this pin low to clear the data.
- You can, of course, tie one or other, or both, pins to VCC with a pull-up resistor, even if you have no need to control the pins from software. In Figure 7-4, you can see that the ~OE pin is pulled up via a resistor and is under control of the sketch, while ~SRCLR is not controlled by code, but is also pulled up via a resistor.

Warning
If you have these pins pulled high directly, without a resistor, never ever attempt to have the code connect the pins to ground. This will short out the power supply and may damage your Arduino. It is safest to always use a resistor.

7.7.3 The LED Driver Code

The code in Listings 7-1 through 7-5 are written in AVR C++ format rather than using the Arduino Language. If you are using the Arduino IDE, simply start a new sketch, Edit ▷ Select All, Edit ▷ Cut, then paste in or type the code in the following listings. If you really need to see the code in the Arduino Language—which will be much larger in size—there is a sketch named SPI_LEDs.ino in the code repository for this chapter.

We begin with the initialization of the sketch. Listing 7-1 shows the various header files we will need, especially if we are using the Arduino IDE, and sets up a few macro definitions.

Please note, the majority of comments have been removed from the listings here, but are available in the code files in the book's repository.

Listing 7-1 SPI_LEDs sketch—constants

```
#include <avr/io.h>
#include <util/delay.h>
#include <stdint.h>
#include <avr/interrupt.h>


// Pin definitions.
#define DDB_SCK     DDB5     // Clock pin.
#define DDB_MOSI    DDB3     // Data pin to 74HC595.
#define DDB_SS      DDB2     // Controller's SS pin.

// And extras for the 74HC595.
#define HC595_OE    DDB1     // D9/PB1 = 74HC595 output enable.
#define HC595_CS    DDB0     // D8/PB0 = 74HC595's CS pin.

// A small delay
#define SHORT_DELAY 100
```

As we are looking at interrupts in this book, we need an ISR to handle the SPI interrupt. Listing 7-2 shows the full code for this. You should note that the ISR's name is SPI_STC_vect. If you type this incorrectly, you will not get a compilation error, but the code will simply not work. Yes, that's *exactly* what happened to me when testing.

When using an SN74HC595 as a peripheral device, this ISR is called every time eight bits have been shifted out to it. All the ISR has to do is latch the data from the shift register to the storage register and enable the output pins. This will cause the LEDs to take on the state of the newly arrived byte of data.

Latching the data into the storage register has the added effect of ending the communication with the SN74HC595, which is facilitated by pulling its CS[6] pin high. The storage register data byte is then written to the output pins when we pull the ~OE pin low.

If we were communicating with a peripheral which had the ability to transmit data back to the controller, then we would read the received data from SPDR and add it to a buffer somewhere. As the SN74HC595 doesn't have this ability, we can ignore this; however, I am reading it in the ISR

---

[6]Actually, the pin we are using as a CS pin, the RCLK pin.

regardless—just to demonstrate where you would normally perform this action in a "real" SPI sketch or application.

Listing 7-2 SPI_LEDs sketch—ISR

```
// The SPI interrupt handler triggers when a byte has been
// transmitted and received.
ISR(SPI_STC_vect) {
    // Read, and ignore data received from SN74HC595.
    volatile uint8_t ignoreMe = SPDR;

    // Disable the 74HC595 from SPI.
    PORTB |= (1 << HC595_CS);

    // Then latch the new data onto the 74HC595's output pins.
    PORTB &= ~(1 << HC595_OE);
}
```

Listing 7-3 shows the code I am using to configure the SPI hardware.

The code begins by making sure that global interrupts are turned off, after which it initializes the SPI hardware using the details outlined in the data sheet and elsewhere in this section. The comments show the settings used.

After initializing the SPI hardware, the interrupt flag is cleared and global interrupts re-enabled.

Listing 7-3 SPI_LEDs sketch–setupSPI() function

```
void setupSPI() {
    // Disable global interrupts.
    cli();

    // Enable SPI as a controller;
    // Shift data MSB first;
    // F_CPU / 128 = 125 KHz;
    // SPI interrupts are enabled.
    // Phase and polarity are 0|0 or 1|1
    // as we need to clock data on a rising edge.
    SPCR = (1 << SPE)  | (1 << MSTR) |
           (1 << DORD) |
           (1 << SPR1) | (1 << SPR0) |
           (0 << CPOL) | (0 << CPHA) |
           (1 << SPIE);

    // Clear SPI interrupt flag.
    volatile uint8_t ignoreMe = SPSR;
    ignoreMe = SPDR;

    // Enable global interrupts.
    sei();
}
```

Listing 7-4 shows the `displayNumber()` function, which sends its parameter `value` to SPI to be displayed by the SN74HC595 on the output LEDs. It takes a `uint8_t` as we only have eight bits of data space available in the SN74HC595. If we were cascading these devices, we could send larger values, but we would still have to send them in eight-bit chunks.

The function enables the SN74HC595 by pulling the pin we are using as CS, the RCLK pin, low and pulls the ~OE pin high to prevent flicker on the LEDs as the new value is shifted in.

The value we wish to transfer to the LEDs is written to the SPDR register, and this initiates the SPI transfer. When all eight bits have been transferred, the interrupt flag will be set, and our ISR will execute to terminate the SPI communication and latch the new data onto the output pins.

Listing 7-4 SPI_LEDs sketch—displayNumber() function

```
void displayNumber(uint8_t value) {
    // Enable the 74HC595.
    PORTB &= ~(1 << HC595_CS);

    // while disabling its output latch.
    PORTB |= (1 << HC595_OE);

    // Load the value into the data register.
    SPDR = value;
}
```

Listing 7-5 is the equivalent of the Arduino's `setup()` and `loop()` functions, which, in AVR C++, is simply the `main()` function.

As per the data sheet, when configuring an SPI controller, the MOSI, SCK, and SS pins must be configured as outputs, and the SS pin should be pulled high. We are also configuring a couple of additional output pins to act as the CS pin for the SN74HC595 and to control when the new data appears on the device's output pins.

In order to prevent flicker, or other unwanted effects, the SN74HC595 is disconnected from SPI, and its output pins are disabled. The output pins will be re-enabled by the ISR when a new byte of data has been completely received.

Listing 7-5 SPI_LEDs sketch—main() function

```
int main() {
    // MOSI, SCK and SS need to be output.
    DDRB = (1 << DDB_MOSI) | (1 << DDB_SCK)  |
           (1 << DDB_SS)   | (1 << HC595_OE) |
           (1 << HC595_CS);

    // Make sure our SS is pulled high.
    PORTB |= (1 << DDB_SS);

    // Ensure 74HC595 is disconnected from SPI.
    PORTB |= (1 << HC595_CS);

    // Disable 74HC595's output pins before SPI is setup.
    PORTB &= ~(1 << HC595_OE);
```

```
    setupSPI();

    while (1) {
        // Display 0 - 255 with a delay between each digit.
        for (uint8_t i = 0; i <= 255; i++) {
            displayNumber(i);
            _delay_ms(SHORT_DELAY);
        }
    }
}
```

The main loop of the sketch simply sends all permissible eight-bit values to the SPI hardware to be displayed upon the SN74HC595's output pins.

7.8   Peripheral Mode—LED Driver

The next example sketch uses two Arduinos, which in my case are a Duemilanove and an Uno. The Duemilanove is configured as the controller, while the Uno is the peripheral. The controller sends the text of a message, one byte at a time over SPI, while the Uno receives the data bytes and outputs them onto a set of eight LEDs attached to the D0 through D7 pins as well as optionally displaying the received characters on the Serial Monitor. Figure 7-5 shows the breadboard layout for this experiment.

If you do not have enough LEDs,[7] then simply omit the breadboard and all the resistors and LEDs, just connect the two Arduinos together using Figure 7-6, and display the received message on the Serial Monitor instead.

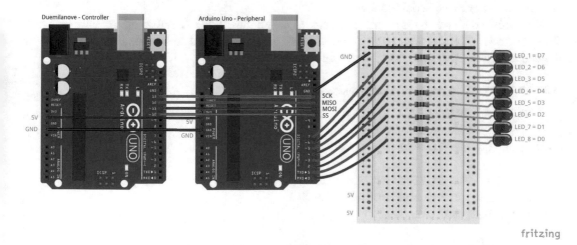

Figure 7-5 SPI_LEDs_peripheral breadboard layout

---

[7]Alternatively, if you do have enough LEDs but can't be bothered setting them all up!

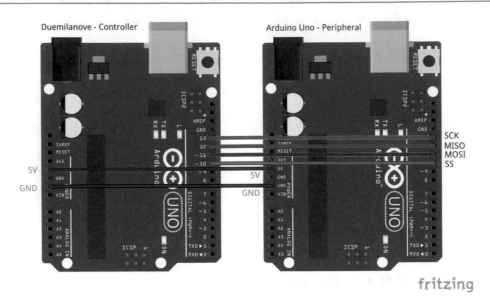

Figure 7-6 SPI_LEDs_peripheral alternative breadboard layout

The code for this sketch is shown in Listings 7-6 through 7-10.

Listing 7-6 defines the CONTROLLER macro. If this is one, then this device is the controller; if zero, then the device will be the peripheral. If the device is the controller, then a message is created to hold the data that will be transferred over SPI to the peripheral. If the device is the peripheral, the variable receivedByte is defined and will be used to store each byte received from the controller. A boolean flag is also defined, newByteReceived, to indicate to the loop() that it is safe to send another character to the Serial Monitor.

The code continues by defining a macro to determine if the Serial Monitor will be used, USE_SERIAL. If Serial is to be used, the PRINT macro is defined to be Serial.print() or defined as nothing if Serial output is not required.

Listing 7-6 SPI_LEDs_peripheral sketch—constants

```
// Define CONTROLLER as 1 or 0 to set things up correctly
// for each Arduino board.
#define CONTROLLER 1

// Define USE_SERIAL as 1 to use the SERIAL Monitor, or 0
// to just flash the LEDs.
#define USE_SERIAL 1

// Define a macro to print, or not, as requested.
#if USE_SERIAL
    #define PRINT(a) Serial.print(a)
#else
    #define PRINT(a)
#endif
```

```
#if CONTROLLER
    // A message to be flashed on the peripheral's LEDs.
    const char *message = "The quick brown fox jumps"
                          " over the lazy dog!\n";
#else
    // Store a single character from SPI.
    char receivedByte = 0;
    bool newByteReceived = false;
#endif

// Pin definitions. These are not setup in <avr/io.h> and
// its siblings. These are the pins that must be configured
// as only MISO is done automatically when this device is
// an SPI controller.
#define DDB_SCK    13      // Clock pin.
#define DDB_MISO   12      // Data in.
#define DDB_MOSI   11      // Data out.
#define DDB_SS     10      // Controller's SS pin.

// Short is the delay between characters.
#define THE_DELAY 100
```

After sorting out Serial output, the various SPI pins are defined, and the delay between sending each character is defined to be 100 milliseconds. Feel free to make this larger or even smaller, as you wish. It's only there to allow you to see the characters displayed on the LEDs as they arrive on the peripheral, rather than the LEDs simply flickering at a high frequency.

Following on from the initialization code, we have Listing 7-7, which is the interrupt handler for both the controller and peripheral. Yes, I'm going against accepted Internet advice and using an interrupt for both sending and receiving SPI data!

Listing 7-7 SPI_LEDs_peripheral sketch—ISR

```
#if CONTROLLER
// The SPI interrupt handler triggers when a byte has been
// transmitted and received. All we have to do here is
// disconnect the UNO from SPI.
ISR(SPI_STC_vect) {
    // Disable the Uno from SPI.
    digitalWrite(DDB_SS, HIGH);
}
#else
ISR(SPI_STC_vect) {
    // When the peripheral receives a byte, save it.
    receivedByte = SPDR;
    newByteReceived = true;

    // D0 to D7 are all output for the LEDs.
    for (byte p = 0; p < 8; p++) {
```

```
            digitalWrite(p, (!!(receivedByte & (1 << p))));
    }
}
#endif
```

For the controller device, all that is required is to cease transmission after each byte has been sent. To do this, we simply pull the controller's SS pin high. That's connected to the peripheral's own SS pin, used as the CS pin, which disconnects the peripheral.

For the peripheral, the interrupt triggers when a data byte has been received. The byte is copied from SPDR to receivedByte and the newByteReceived flag set to let loop() know it's safe to send the new byte to the Serial Monitor. The LEDs are then set according to each bit in the received byte. The use of the "!!" operator saves a shift operation and extracts a one or a zero depending on the value of each bit in the binary form of the received data byte.

Listing 7-8 shows the code to set up both devices in the appropriate SPI mode. The SPI hardware is set up as before, but this time we also pass a parameter to indicate if we are setting up as a controller or peripheral. This only affects the setting of the MSTR bit, used only by the controller.

Listing 7-8 SPI_LEDs_peripheral sketch—setupSPI() function

```
void setupSPI(bool controller) {
    // Disable global interrupts.
    noInterrupts();

    // Enable SPI as a controller;
    // Shift data MSB first;
    // F_CPU / 128 = 125 KHz;
    // SPI interrupts are enabled.
    // Phase and polarity are 0|0 or 1|1
    // as we need to clock data on a rising edge.
      SPCR = (1 << SPE)  |
             (1 << DORD) |
             (1 << SPR1) | (1 << SPR0) |
             (0 << CPOL) | (0 << CPHA) |
             (1 << SPIE);

      if (controller) {
          SPCR |= (1 << MSTR);
      }

    // Clear SPI interrupt flag, if set. Volatile to stop
    // compiler optimising it away.
    volatile uint8_t ignoreMe = SPSR;
    ignoreMe = SPDR;

    // Enable global interrupts.
    interrupts();
}
```

Listing 7-9 shows the setup function for both devices. Once again, CONTROLLER is used to differentiate between the two SPI modes. As discussed previously in this chapter, when a device is acting as an SPI controller, then its SCK, MOSI, and SS pins must be configured as output pins. MISO is automatically reconfigured by the hardware and needs no further configuration. Prior to configuring as a controller, the peripheral's CS pin is pulled high to disconnect it from SPI.

For the peripheral device, only MISO needs to be configured as an output because the SPI hardware only automatically configures input pins. After configuring the SPI hardware as a peripheral device, the Serial Monitor is initialized if it has been requested. Finally, all eight pins for the LEDs are initialized as output pins. You can leave this code present, even if you are not using the LEDs, no harm will come to your board.

Listing 7-9 SPI_LEDs_peripheral sketch–setup() function

```
void setup() {
#if CONTROLLER
    // MOSI, SCK and SS need to be output. MISO is
    // correctly configured already automatically.
    // WARNING: If the SS pin for the Arduino is
    // not an output pin, then SPI will not work!
    pinMode(DDB_SCK, OUTPUT);
    pinMode(DDB_MOSI, OUTPUT);
    pinMode(DDB_SS, OUTPUT);

    // Make sure our SS is pulled high. This
    // disconnects the peripheral, the Uno, from SPI.
    digitalWrite(DDB_SS, HIGH);

    // Now configure the Duemilanove as a controller.
    setupSPI(true);
#else
    // MOSI, SCK and SS are automatically configured
    // as inputs. Only MISO needs to be configured as
    // an output
    pinMode(DDB_MISO, OUTPUT);

    // Set up the Uno as a peripheral.
    setupSPI(false);

#if USE_SERIAL
    // Fire up the Serial Monitor.
    Serial.begin(9600);
#endif

    // D0 to D7 are all output for the LEDs.
    for (byte p = 0; p < 8; p++) {
        pinMode(p, OUTPUT);
    }
#endif
}
```

Finally, we come to the `loop()` function in Listing 7-10. The controller device simply enables the peripheral by pulling its own `SS` pin low, copies each byte to `SPDR`, and delays for a bit between characters. This is not to allow SPI to catch up; SPI is probably already finished by the time the delay starts! The delay is there to allow you to see the LEDs flashing at a reasonable rate as each character arrives at the peripheral. Feel free to remove it—but the LEDs won't be of much use if you do; they will just flicker very quickly. In case you are wondering, the controller's ISR disconnects the peripheral after each byte—which is not strictly necessary, but is harmless.

In the peripheral's `loop()`, the `newByteReceived` flag is checked, and if set, the data byte in `receivedByte` is sent to the Serial Monitor. Without this test, the output in the Serial Monitor would show an awful lot of repeated characters as the loop is running without a delay, whereas the controller has a delay of 100 milliseconds built in by default. If the LEDs are in use, or even if they are not present, on receipt of a space character, the LEDs are blanked. You are able to see the spaces between words on the LEDs with this "feature." After sending each received character to Serial and the LEDs, the `newByteReceived` flag is cleared to show that the `loop()` need not send any more characters until a new one has been received.

Listing 7-10 SPI_LEDs_peripheral sketch—loop() function

```
void loop() {
#if CONTROLLER
    // Copy some data to SPI. (Need to lose constness!)
    char *p = (char *)message;

    while (*p) {
        // Enable the Uno.
        digitalWrite(DDB_SS, LOW);

        // Copy each byte of the message to SPI.
        SPDR = *p;
        delay(THE_DELAY);

        // Don't forget to increment to the next character!
        p++;

        // The interrupt handler will disconnect between each byte

    }
#else
    // The peripheral will output the received byte. If a space
    // is received, turn off the LEDS.
    if (newByteReceived) {
      #if USE_SERIAL
        PRINT(receivedByte);
      #endif
        if (receivedByte == 0x20) {
            PORTD = 0;
        }
        newByteReceived = false;
```

```
    }
#endif
}
```

To compile the sketch, connect up the board you wish to use as the controller. Make sure that the CONTROLLER macro is defined as 1; compile and upload the code to the controller device.

Now connect up the peripheral device, redefine CONTROLLER to be 0 and USE_SERIAL as desired, then compile and upload the code to the peripheral board.

Open the Serial Monitor on the *peripheral* device, set it to 9600 baud if required, and watch as the messages sent from the controller appear on the Serial Monitor output. The LEDs will be flashing up the ASCII code of each character received, apart from spaces, which blank out all the LEDs.

If you set up the breadboard as per Figure 7-5 and you have chosen to use the Serial Monitor, you will notice that the LEDs attached to pins D0 and D1 tend to remain on constantly. This is due to those two pins being "stolen" by the USART for transmission and reception of data. It is unfortunate that of the three PORTx registers in the ATmega328P, only the PORTD register has eight usable bits, or pins, but only six when the Serial Monitor is being used. If you redefine USE_SERIAL to be 0, recompile, and upload to the peripheral device, you will see the LEDs on D0 and D1 flashing correctly again.

Going completely against accepted advice, it is possible to send the received byte directly to Serial *from within the ISR*! Yes, I know, this is normally frowned upon, and with good reason. However, you can send data to Serial from an ISR, even though interrupts are disabled for the duration of the ISR's execution, provided *you don't fill the USART transmit buffer*. Given that a 64-byte buffer, the Arduino Uno default buffer size, has room for 63 characters, sending 1 byte at a time from the ISR should usually be OK. Obviously, this depends on how long the delay between characters has been configured on the controller—the shorter the delay, the more chance there is to fill the buffer if the Serial Monitor isn't pulling them out and displaying them quickly enough.

You may be wondering why, in all the examples in this chapter, data are sent one byte at a time. It's simply because that's how I wrote it. There is no need to do it this way; you can simply pull the peripheral's CS low, in the setup(), and never pull it high again until you are completely finished transmitting data. As an exercise for the reader, why not amend the code in this chapter to select the peripheral or shift register, transmit all the data, and disconnect the peripheral or shift register—it will still work.[8]

7.9   What About Plain AVR C++?

If you are not a user of the Arduino IDE, then there is a suitable conversion of this sketch on the PlatformIO directory in the book's code repository. There is a foible here in that we have not yet looked at writing data to the USART for display on the Serial Monitor, but fear not, I have provided a few files in the lib directory for the project to make this happen. You don't need to look there, the main.cpp file is all you need at the moment.

Coincidentally, we will be looking at the USART in the next chapter.

The project file for this example is shown in Listing 7-11. This is very useful as it allows the same source code to be compiled either as a controller or a peripheral; and allows Serial output to be included or otherwise, without having to edit the code to change defines in the source beforehand.

---

[8]And be faster!

The `env` environment holds configuration that is common to every other environment in the file. We are using the Atmel AVR platform for both the controller and the peripheral boards, so this is common to both.

The `env:peripheral` environment holds configuration that is particular to the peripheral device. In this setup, we have specified the board to be an Uno. If your controller is also an Uno, you could move the board setting into the common environment. The Serial Monitor speed is defined to be 9600 baud, which must match up with the setting used in the main sketch code. The `build_flags` determine whether this is a controller or not and whether Serial Monitor output is required.

The `env:controller` environment holds configuration that is particular to the controller device. In this setup, we have specified the board to be a Duemilanove[9] with an ATmega328P microcontroller. If your controller device is different to mine, you will need to edit this setting. The `build_flags` determine whether this is a controller or not.

Listing 7-11   AVR C++ SPI_LEDs_peripheral application—project file

```
; Common to both build environments.
[env]
platform = atmelavr

[env:peripheral]
; This is the peripheral board, the Arduino Uno.
; Compile this one, using the -e command line option, or
; pick from the drop down in VSCode, to build the peripheral.
board = uno
monitor_speed = 9600
build_flags = -DCONTROLLER=0 -DUSE_SERIAL=1

[env:controller]
; This is the controller board, the Arduino Duemilanove.
; Compile this one, using the -e command line option, or
; pick from the drop down in VSCode, to build the controller.
board = diecimilaatmega328
build_flags = -DCONTROLLER=1
```

It is the use of the `build_flags` which saves us having to edit the source code before compiling the code for the two devices.

7.9.1   Compiling and Uploading

To compile the code for both the controller and the peripheral, you can run the following command in a terminal session after changing the current working directory to the directory where the `platformio.ini` file exists:

```
cd where_platformio.ini file is located
pio run
```

---
[9]Or an Arduino Dieci with an ATmega328P.

If you only wish to compile the peripheral variant of the code, the command to select the correct environment is

```
pio run -e peripheral
```

Likewise, to compile for the controller only, use this command:

```
pio run -e controller
```

To upload the code, you must obviously select the correct version—there is no option to "upload compiled code to both boards"!

```
pio run -t upload -e peripheral
```

or

```
pio run -t upload -e controller
```

To see the Serial output, if selected

```
pio device monitor --baud 9600 --port /dev/ttyUSB0
```

The baud and port can be left off, they will default to 9600 and will try to find the port used to upload the code, but if you have problems, specify them as required. To exit from the device monitor, type CTRL+C.

Of course, some of my readers may not like or wish to use the command line. *Visual Studio Code* has an extension that allows PlatformIO to be used as a development system, even for plain Arduino projects. To compile and upload using *VSCode* is simple:

- Open the project folder as normal with File ▷ Open Folder.
- To compile both variants of the code, simply click the tick (✔) or check mark tool on the bottom toolbar.

You can compile the two variants separately of course, but it's a tiny bit more complicated:

- Click the Alien/Ant's head icon on the left-side toolbar. This opens the PlatformIO task list.
- Click the environment you want from the list that appears. This will be "controller" or "peripheral."
- Click "Build" to build the code.
- Click "Upload" to upload the compiled code.

To see the Serial Monitor output, if configured, click the bottom toolbar tool which has a US-style power plug icon. You will need the peripheral board connected of course. After a delay, the peripheral will be reset, and the received characters will start to arrive. Use CTRL+C to exit from the monitor, then press any key, as advised on the window, to close it.

7.10   Register Summary

There are four registers involved in the setup and use of SPI. These are

- The *SPI Data Register*, SPDR, which holds the data to be transmitted or received
- The *SPI Control Register*, SPCR, which is used to set up communications between the two devices
- The *SPI Status Register*, SPSR, which is used to indicate the status of the SPI communication and to implement the "double speed" mode for the prescaler, used in setting the SPI frequency
- The *Data Direction B Register*, DDRB, which configures the input and output pins for SPI

7.10.1 SPI Data Register

The *SPI Data Register*, SPDR, is eight bits wide, and all eight bits are used to hold the data being shifted out onto the bus while also receiving the data from the other device involved in the communication.

7	6	5	4	3	2	1	0
MSB	Bit 6	Bit 5	Bit 4	Bit 3	Bit 2	Bit 1	LSB

7.10.2 SPI Control Register

The *SPI Control Register*, SPCR, is used to configure communications protocols for the SPI system. All eight bits are used in this register.

7	6	5	4	3	2	1	0
SPIE	SPE	DORD	MSTR	CPOL	CPHA	SPR1	SPR0

SPIE   This bit enables the SPI interrupt if set to one and disables the SPI interrupt if cleared to zero.

SPE   Writing a one to this bit will enable the SPI system. Writing a zero will disable it.

DORD   This bit determines if data is exchanged with the MSB or LSB bit sent first. Setting this bit to one exchanges data with the LSB transmitted first; clearing it to zero exchanges data with the MSB first.

MSTR   Writing a one to this bit will configure the device as the controller for the SPI communication. Clearing it to zero, the default, configures the device as the peripheral.

CPOL   This bit sets the polarity for the communication. Setting this bit to one configures the SPI clock to be idle when the SCK pin is high; zero configures it to idle when the pin is low.

CPHA   This bit sets the phase for the communication. Setting to one writes a data bit up on the leading edge of the SPI clock and reads it on the trailing edge. Clearing to zero writes a data bit on the trailing edge of the SPI clock and reads on the following leading edge of the clock.

SPR1   This bit is used to set the prescaler for SPI communications and is used in conjunction with SPR1 and SPI2X in the *SPI Status Register* (SPSR). Table 7-1 has the various SPI clock frequency settings available.

SPR0 This bit is used to set the prescaler for SPI communications and is used in conjunction with SPR0 and SPI2X in the *SPI Status Register* (SPSR). Table 7-1 has the various SPI clock frequency settings available.

7.10.3 SPI Status Register

The *SPI Status Register*, SPSR, has only three bits in use for SPI communications. Two are flag bits and the third enables double speed mode. All other bits are unused and are read only, always returning a zero in the unused bit positions.

7	6	5	4	3	2	1	0
SPIF	WCOL	N/A	N/A	N/A	N/A	N/A	SPI2X

SPIF This flag bit is set to 1 when a byte has been transmitted/received. It will be automatically cleared if the SPI interrupt has been enabled by setting bit SPIE in register SPCR. If the SPI interrupt is not enabled, then the flag can be cleared by first reading the SPSR register while SPIF is still set, then reading the SPDR register. This will also clear the WCOL bit if set. The normal AVR manner of writing a 1 to a flag bit to clear it does not apply in this instance.

WCOL This flag bit is set if the SPDR register is written to while a data transfer is still in progress. The WCOL bit should be cleared by first reading the SPSR register while WCOL is still set, then reading the SPDR register. This will also clear the SPIF bit if set. The normal manner of writing a 1 to a flag bit to clear it does not apply in this instance.

SPI2X This bit is used to set the prescaler for SPI communications and is used in conjunction with SPR0 and SPR1 in the *SPI Control Register*, SPCR. Table 7-1 has the various SPI clock frequency settings available. This bit enables double speed mode when written to one and single speed mode when cleared to zero.

7.10.4 Data Direction B Register

The *Data Direction B Register*, DDRB, has four bits used for SPI communications. All other bits are unused by SPI and can be used to configure other GPIO pins on PORTB, perhaps to use to select the SS pins on the SPI peripherals with which we are communicating.

Bit No.	7	6	5	4	3	2	1	0
Name	DDB7	DDB6	DDB5	DDB4	DDB3	DDB2	DDB1	DDB0
Controls	N/A	N/A	SCK	MISO	MOSI	SS	N/A	N/A

DDB5 This bit is set to 1 to ensure that the SPI clock pin, SCK, is correctly configured as an output. This is required only when the device is being configured as an SPI controller. When configuring an SPI peripheral, the pin will be automatically configured as an input and will overwrite any manual configuration by the sketch.

DDB4   This bit is set to 1 to ensure that the `MISO` pin is correctly configured as an output. This setting is not required when the device is being configured as an SPI controller as it will be automatically reconfigured as an input pin. For an SPI peripheral, the pin should be configured as an output.

DDB3   This bit is set to 1 to ensure that the `MOSI` pin is correctly configured as an output. This is required only when the device is being configured as an SPI controller. For an SPI peripheral, the pin will be automatically configured as an input.

DDB2   This bit is set to 1 to ensure that the `SS` pin is correctly configured as an output. This is required only when the device is being configured as an SPI controller—if you forget to configure this pin as an output, then SPI will not work on the controller. For an SPI peripheral, the pin will be automatically configured as an input.

7.11   Key Takeaways

In this chapter, we learned all we need to know about SPI, in particular:

- Phase and polarity and how it may require configuring for different devices. The four different modes were discussed and differences between them indicated. In most cases, it is enough to consult the data sheet where the phase and polarity details will be given or listed as the available modes.
- Data ordering, MSB or LSB first when shifting data, according to the peripheral's needs.
- Setting the SPI clock frequency to match that required by the slowest device involved in the communication.
- SPI flag bits are not cleared in the normal manner of writing a 1 to them. The interrupt flag is automatically cleared in the normal manner if SPI interrupts are configured. Other SPI flags are cleared by reading the status register containing the set flag, `SPSR`, and then *accessing* the data register, `SPDR`.
- When I referred to the `SS` in this chapter, I was referring to the controller's `SS` pin. When I referred to the `CS` pin, I was referring to the peripheral's chip select pin, which, in the case of a second Arduino board, just happens to be its `SS` pin as well!
- SPI data can be sent one byte at a time, disconnecting the peripheral from the SPI bus between each byte, or sent as a sequence of bytes with no disconnection until the end.
- The SN74HC595 shift register is able to be used as an SPI peripheral.

7.12   Coming Up

In the next chapter, we will take a look at the interrupts which we can use to carry out serial communications over the USART; there are three to get our heads around, but in practice, we only really need two of them.

USART Interrupts

8

The USART has three separate interrupts available for use in your code, and this chapter will examine those. However, most applications that I have come across which use USART interrupts only use two of the available interrupts. This chapter is no different as the third interrupt tends to be a little more inefficient than its alternative. All will be revealed!

The USART may appear to be quite a complicated beast even without interrupts, but polling for data is a bad idea when communications are involved.

Bear in mind also that using the USART requires more than just setting up an interrupt or two and setting the code running. There are baud rates, error percentages, parity, and lots more to consider before data can be transmitted or received. This chapter covers all of this in some detail.

Hopefully, by the end of this chapter, you will be a USART interrupt expert.

8.1 The USART

The three USART interrupts are found in Vectors 18, 19, and 20 in the Interrupt Vector Table. The individual vectors are

- Vector 18 is the *USART Receive Complete* interrupt vector.
- Vector 19 is the *USART Data Register Empty* interrupt vector.
- Vector 20 is the *USART Transmit Complete* interrupt vector.

You can see from this that the ATmega328P considers receiving data to be more important and have a higher priority than the transmission of data. The receipt of data has a single interrupt, while transmission has two.

8.2 USART Configuration

To configure the USART, there are four separate registers involved, not including the *USART Data Register*, UDR0, which is not used in configuring the USART. Some devices in the AVR range have more than one USART; the Mega 2560, for example, has four. The ATmega328P only has one, but it is named USART0 and all the registers controlling it are likewise named with a zero.

The USART configuration and status registers are discussed in the following sections.

© The Author(s), under exclusive license to APress Media, LLC, part of Springer Nature 2024
N. Dunbar, *Arduino Interrupts*, Maker Innovations Series,
https://doi.org/10.1007/978-1-4842-9714-8_8

8.2.1   Register UCSR0A

The *USART Control and Status Register A*, UCSR0A, is an eight-bit register with the following bit usage:

7	6	5	4	3	2	1	0
RXC0	TXC0	UDRE0	FE0	DOR0	UPE0	U2X0	MPCM0

The bits we are concerned with are bits 7 through 1; bit 0 is not being considered here. Bit 0 is a *Multiprocessor Communication Mode* bit, MPCM0.

UCSR0A is the main "go-to" register when checking for errors or the status of the USART. The only configuration bits in this register are bits 1, U2X0, and 0, MPCM0. All the other bits are status bits, and those are

- The *Receive Complete* bit, RXC0, which indicates that a new byte has arrived and is ready for retrieval from the UDR0 register. This bit may be used to trigger the *USART Receive Complete* interrupt.
- The *Transmit Complete* bit, TXC0, which indicates that the previous byte has been fully framed and transmitted and the UDR0 register can be loaded with a new data byte. This bit may be used to trigger the *USART Transmit Complete* interrupt.
- The *USART Data Register Empty* bit, UDRE0, which indicates that the USART's data register is ready to accept a new byte for transmission. This bit may be used to trigger the *USART Data Register Empty* interrupt. After a reset, this bit is set to 1 to indicate that the transmitter is ready to be loaded with data. This implies that as soon as you enable this interrupt, it will immediately trigger, assuming that global interrupts are also enabled.

All three of these bits can cause an interrupt to be triggered. If the corresponding interrupt is not being used in your code, the bit must be cleared in the normal manner of writing a 1 to its bit position in the register.

The remaining three bits of interest in this register are

- The *frame error* bit, FE0: This bit indicates that a framing error has been detected in a received byte of data. The test is effectively looking to see if the first stop bit of the data was a zero.
- The *data overrun* bit, DOR0, is set whenever a data overrun condition is detected. This means that the two-byte receive buffer is full, and a new start bit has been detected on the RX pin.
- The *parity error* bit, UPE0, is set if the next character in the receive buffer had a parity error when it was fully received but only if parity checking was enabled.
- The FE0, DOR0, and UPE0 bits remain valid until the UDR0 register is read, so application code must check this bit *before* reading UDR0. These bits must be written as zero when writing to UCSR0A.
- The double speed bit, U2X0, is set if the transmission of data is to use the USART's double speed mode. On the Arduino, this mode is enabled by default, but turned off if the configuration deems it necessary. The main reason for using this mode is due to the configuration of baud rates leading to smaller error rates between the baud rate requested and the actual baud rate able to be generated. This is explained in detail in Section 8.2.4, Register UBRR0.

8.2.2   Register UCSR0B

The *USART Control and Status Register B*, UCSR0B, is an eight-bit register with the following bit usage:

7	6	5	4	3	2	1	0
RXCIE0	TXCIE0	UDRIE0	RXEN0	TXEN0	UCSZ02	RXB80	TXB80

The bits we are concerned with are bits 7 through 2; bits 1 and 0 are not being considered in this book. Those two bits are the *Receive bit 8* bit, RXB80, and the *Transmit bit 8* bit, TXB80, which are used when communicating in nine data bit mode. The data sheet has all the detail you will need if you wish to investigate further.

Registers UCSR0B and UCSR0C control most of the USART configuration.

The bits we are concerned with are

- The *USART Receive Complete Interrupt Enable* bit, RXCIE0: As its name suggests, this bit enables the *USART Receive Complete* interrupt.
- The *USART Transmit Complete Interrupt Enable* bit, TXCIE0: This bit enables the *USART Transmit Complete* interrupt.
- The *USART Data Register Empty Interrupt Enable* bit, UDRIE0: This bit enables the *USART Data Register Empty* interrupt.
- The *Receive Enable* bit, RXEN0, which allows the USART to receive data.
- The *Transmit Enable* bit, TXEN0, which allows the USART to transmit data.

The remaining, interesting bit is the *Character Size 2* bit, UCSZ02, which is combined with bits UCSZ01 and UCSZ00 in the USCR0C register to determine the data bit size in the communications. These bits will be discussed in the following section.

8.2.3   Register UCSR0C

The *USART Control and Status Register C*, UCSR0C, is an eight bit register with the following bit usage:

7	6	5	4	3	2	1	0
UMSEL01	UMSEL00	UPM01	UPM00	USBS0	UCSZ01	UCSZ00	UCPOL0

The bits we are really only concerned with are bits 2 and 1 in this register. The other bits all default to zero after a reset which configures the USART in the desired asynchronous mode with one stop bit and no parity.

The data sheet has all the detail you will need if you wish to investigate the other bits further.

Registers UCSR0B and UCSR0C control most of the USART configuration.

The two bits we are concerned with are UCSZ01 and UCSZ00, which, when combined with bit UCSZ02 in register UCSR0B, make up a three-bit binary number which defines the data size in the USART communications. Table 8-1 shows the appropriate configuration for the differing data widths with the eight bit setting highlighted in bold. We are only interested in eight bit communications.

Table 8-1 USART data widths

UCSZ02:UCSZ00	Data width
000	5
001	6
010	7
011	**8**
100	Reserved
101	Reserved
110	Reserved
111	9

After a reset, the USART defaults to eight-bit data width, so our USART code won't always have to define the data width we require. In this chapter, our data will always be eight bits wide.

8.2.4   Register UBRR0

The *USART Baud Rate Register*, UBRR0, is used to generate the timing signals for the baud rate required for the USART communications.

UBRR0 is a pair of registers combined into a 12-bit register. The two parts of the UBRR0 register are named UBRR0H and UBRR0L. The high register contains the top four bits of the value, while all eight bits of the low register are used for the value. The top four bits of the high register are reserved and must be written as zeros when writing to the register.

The UBRR0 register is used to calculate the baud rate for the USART by setting the baud rate generator's "down counter" inside the ATmega328P. You must always write to the high register, UBRR0H, first, and then you may write to the UBRR0L register. As soon as UBRR0L is written, the baud rate generator *immediately* reconfigures itself and starts using the new down counter value to produce a new baud rate. This will cause corruption if any communications are currently in progress.

If you are programming in Assembly Language, it is your responsibility to ensure that you write to the two registers in the correct order. C++ programmers don't have to worry as the compiler handles the order of writing; we just have to set a value in the UBRR0 register and not worry at all about UBRR0H and UBRR0L.

I previously mentioned that the value set in the UBRR0 register is a down counter value for the baud rate generator. The generator begins counting as soon as UBRR0L is set, and when the counter reaches zero, a clock pulse will be generated, and the down counter will be reinitialized to the original UBRR0 value. These generated pulses are used by both the transmit and receive sides of the USART to communicate at the requested baud rate.

There are three steps involved in calculating a baud rate for the USART:

- Calculate UBRR0 for the *desired* baud rate.
- Calculate the *actual* baud rate with the UBRR0 setting just calculated.
- Calculate the error percentage.

The three steps are interlinked in that the value calculated for UBRR0 may not give the exact baud rate that is desired. The actual baud rate is then calculated based on the new UBRR0 value. Once the UBRR0 and the actual baud rate are known, we can check the error percentage and reject the desired baud rate if the error rate is out of range.

8.2.4.1 Calculating UBRR0

We need to first calculate UBRR0. There is a simple formula for this when the *USART Transmission Double Speed* bit, U2X0, in register UCSR0A is set:[1]

$$\left(\frac{F\_CPU}{8 * BAUD}\right) - 1$$

> **Note**
> Change the multiplier from 8 to 16 if the USART is configured to run in *USART Transmission Single Speed* mode. This is the number of times the RX pin will be sampled to determine if it is a 1 or a 0 bit being received.

On an Arduino, F_CPU is the system clock frequency and is normally 16 MHz, or 16,000,000 Hz. If we need a baud rate of 9600, the value is calculated to be

$$\left(\frac{16,000,000}{8 * 9,600}\right) - 1$$

This results in a value of 207.333 recurring. In a register, this will be the value 207 as there are no fractions in a register. This rounding of the calculated value for UBRR0 will affect the actual baud rate which will be generated. We need to check the actual baud rate next.

8.2.4.2 Calculating Baud Rate

Once UBRR0 has been calculated, we must feed the value back into a formula to calculate the actual baud rate that will be configured using the UBRR0 value. The formula to calculate the actual baud rate when the *USART Transmission Double Speed* bit, U2X0, in register UCSR0A is set is

$$\frac{F\_CPU}{8 * (UBRR0 + 1)}$$

> **Note**
> Change the multiplier from 8 to 16 if the USART is configured to run in *USART Transmission Single Speed* mode.

Continuing with our example, the value 207 feeds back in and results in

$$\frac{16,000,000}{8 * (207 + 1)}$$

This gives

$$\frac{16,000,000}{1664}$$

---

[1]The Arduino default for most baud rates. Only 57,600 baud on 16 MHz systems uses single speed mode.

which finally results in an actual baud rate of 9615.384615 truncated to 9615. Not quite the 9600 baud rate we requested. How bad is this value?

8.2.4.3 Calculating Error Percentages

As the preceding calculations have shown, we cannot exactly calculate a baud rate of 9600, but we can get close enough with 9615. It is now required that we find out how big an error we have created. The formula for the error percentage is

$$100 * \left(\frac{Actual\ Baud}{Required\ Baud} - 1 \right)$$

We required 9600, but the actual baud rate is 9615, so feeding those values into this formula shows that the error is 0.15625%. I can hear my old maths teachers saying "show your workings boy!", so here's how I got that figure:

$$100 * \left(\frac{9,615}{9,600} - 1 \right)$$

$$= 100 * (1.0015625 - 1)$$

$$= 100 * 0.0015625$$

$$= 0.15625$$

> **Note**
> The data sheet actually calculates 0.2% for this error. I *suspect* there is a bit of rounding going on. I tested quite a few of their calculated values for different baud rates, and there are errors in quite a few. I think that they have calculated all stages of the working with fractions and only truncated the final result.
>
> In my world, registers hold integer values, and fractions should be truncated as soon as they are generated, not at the end.

The data sheet states that error rates of $\pm 0.5\%$ should be used. In our example, the calculated error rate is much less than this, so we are safe to use 9600 as a baud rate.

> **Note**
> You may already have figured out that almost any 12-bit value can be loaded into the UBRR0 register to calculate pretty much *any* baud rate you wish, not just the standard ones. Make sure you always calculate error rates and reject any values which give a rate in excess of $\pm 0.5\%$.

8.2.5   Register UDR0

The *USART Data Register*, UDR0, is a dual register, used for both transmitting and receiving data. The register can only be written to if the USART has been enabled for transmitting; otherwise, writing to this register will simply be ignored. Good luck hunting down *those* bugs!

The UDR0 register is configured as a two-level FIFO, according to the data sheet, and this simply means that it has room for two bytes, and the first one into the register will be the first one out. This can be a problem when receiving data but not processing it quickly enough. If UDR0 has not been read and a third byte arrives, the USART will indicate a buffer overrun error, and data communications will be somewhat undefined afterward.

The data sheet warns that

> The receive buffer consists of a two level FIFO. The FIFO will change its state whenever the receive buffer is accessed. Due to this behaviour of the receive buffer, do not use Read-Modify-Write instructions (SBI and CBI) on this location. Be careful when using bit test instructions (SBIC and SBIS), since these also will change the state of the FIFO.

When transmitting, data is written to UDR0 when the register is signaled as being empty. There's an interrupt for this, the *USART Data Register Empty* interrupt, although code can poll the USART to determine when the register is empty.

The data in UDR0 will be sent from the register into the *Transmit Data Buffer* where it will be "framed" in start, stop, and, optionally, parity bits, before being sent to the USART's TX pin for actual transmission.

When receiving data, the *USART Receive Complete* interrupt can be used, but again this is optional, to retrieve the received data from the UDR0 register. When reading UDR0, the contents of the *Receive Data Buffer*, stripped of its frame bits, are returned to the code.

8.3   USART Transmitting

When the USART is configured to transmit data, two interrupts are made available to the application code.

8.3.1   USART Data Register Empty

This interrupt is triggered every time that the UDR0 register is empty and indicates that a new data byte can be written safely to UDR0 ready to be transmitted.

The transmitter copies the data byte into its own internal data buffer where it is wrapped, or framed, in a start bit, one or more stop bits, and an optional parity bit and then shifted out onto the TX pin for transmission. On an Arduino, the TX pin is pin D1 which, in AVR speak, is pin PD1.

This interrupt can, and will, be triggered even while the most recent data byte written to UDR0 is still being framed and actually transmitted "down the wire" to the receiving end of the communication.

> **Note**
> In the unlikely event that you are dealing with nine bits of data, you must write the ninth bit, bit 8 as it is named, into bit TXB80 in the UCSR0B register first, then write the remaining eight bits into UDR0.

The Arduino uses this interrupt to copy the next byte to be transmitted from a circular buffer into the UDR0 register, ready for transmission.

8.3.2   USART Transmit Complete

This interrupt is triggered each time that the transmission of the most recent data byte has completed and the UDR0 register is empty.

The interrupt can also be used to write another data byte to the UDR0 register, but in doing so, it will slow down the processing of the data. The *USART Data Register Empty* interrupt fires as soon as UDR0 is ready to accept another byte. The transmitter is most likely still framing and transmitting the previous byte.

The *USART Transmit Complete* interrupt, on the other hand, only fires after all the framing and transmitting has been done, so the UDR0 register could have been sitting empty for some time before this interrupt fires to indicate that another byte can be loaded.

The data sheet gives me the impression that the purpose of this interrupt is simply to terminate transmission when there's no more data to be sent and can be used to disable the USART's transmission interrupts.

The Arduino doesn't use this interrupt. However, as the flag bit for this interrupt, TXC0 in register UCSR0A, is set whenever the transmission of a data byte has completed, the flag bit is cleared in the normal manner by the Arduino code.

8.4   USART Receiving

When the USART is configured to receive data, a single interrupt is made available to the application code. I suspect that the reason there is only one interrupt is simple; the receiver has no way to know when the transmitter has finished sending as it is not in control. The *USART Receive Complete* interrupt's name is, therefore, a little misleading. I think it would be better named *USART Byte Receive Complete* instead.

8.4.1   USART Receive Complete

This interrupt will be triggered whenever a new data byte has been received by the USART, stripped of its framing bits and written into the UDR0 register ready to be retrieved by the application code.

> **Note**
> In the unlikely event that you are dealing with nine bits of data, you must extract the ninth bit, bit 8 as it is named, from bit RXB80 in the UCSR0B register first, then read the remaining eight bits from UDR0.

The three error detecting bits in the UCSR0A register, FE0, DOR0, and UPE0, should be read from register UCSR0A before reading data from UDR0 as they will be cleared when UDR0 is read. You must always read the UDR0 register regardless of whether an error was detected or not. The byte read will normally be thrown away on error.

Once UDR0 has been read, the USART will continue reading data from the RX pin. The receiver's data buffer is, as mentioned previously, only two bytes in size; if a third byte's start bit is seen on the RX pin while the buffer is full, there will be a data overrun error.

The Arduino uses this interrupt to copy the byte just received from the UDR0 register into a circular buffer, ready for the sketch to retrieve using any of the `Serial.read()` functions.

8.5   Using USART Interrupts on the Arduino

For once, the Arduino doesn't need anything in the way of configuration to use the USART interrupts. When you compile a sketch, the Arduino compilation environment will make sure that you get all that you need, and if you use the various Serial functions to communicate with the host PC, you are using already the USART interrupts.

Hidden within the Arduino's USART handling code, there are two 64-byte circular buffers which store any data received from, or ready to be sent to, the USART. The Arduino uses two of the three available USART interrupts:

- The *USART Data Register Empty* interrupt is used to send data from the transmit circular buffer to the UDR0 register, ready to be framed and transmitted.
- The *USART Receive Complete* interrupt is used to copy received data from the UDR0 register into the receive circular buffer, ready to be read by the sketch.

The remaining interrupt, *USART Transmit Complete*, is not used by the Arduino. So, let's look at some code instead.

8.5.1   Using the `printf()` Function

Normally, with the Arduino, if I wanted to print something like "The temperature of the room is nn degrees C." with a newline afterward, I'd have to do something along these lines:

```
int temperature = getCurrentTemperature();
...
Serial.print("The temperature of the room is ");
Serial.print(temperature);
Serial.println(" degrees C.");
...
```

Some output can take quite a few lines of `Serial.print()` calls. I'm quite competent in using C/C++ on Linux and occasionally, if I have to, on Windows. In those environments, I can do this instead:

```
int temperature = getCurrentTemperature();
...
printf("The temperature of the room is %d degrees C.\n",
    temperature);
...
```

This is by far much easier to use. So

- Open the Arduino IDE.
- Click Sketch ▷ Manage Libraries.
- In the dialog that appears, filter using "LibPrintf."
- One library by a developer named "Embedded Artistry" should appear. Install it in the normal manner.
- Your coding life is now much, much easier.

By default, the `printf()` function sends all its output to the Serial Monitor although this can be redirected to other devices or even to logging files, if necessary. The instructions are in the library documentation supplied. There is a GitHub repository[2] where you can keep up with updates, if desired. The library also works with other IDEs and development systems such as PlatformIO.

Using this library really does make coding for the Arduino a lot easier.

8.5.2   The Arduino Sketch

Listing 8-1 is a complete sketch that uses `printf()` and the USART interrupts to send and receive data over the serial network.

The sketch begins by defining a sign-on message to be printed to the Serial Monitor at startup time. The code proper continues with the `setup()` function, where the Serial Interface is initialized to use 115,200 baud and, by default, eight data bits, no parity, and a single stop bit. The sign-on message is then printed using `printf()`. The `printf()` function sends all its output to the Serial Monitor and that, in turn, sends the text to the USART via the *USART Data Register Empty* interrupt, deep in the Arduino firmware.

Following the sign-on message, there are a number of lines which have been commented out. Those lines were used when testing `printf()` with the Arduino. I have left them in, but commented out, so that you can see how `printf()` is used to print values in binary, hexadecimal, and so on. Feel free to uncomment these lines and recompile to see the output.

After the sign-on message, there's a prompt to the user to start typing text into the Serial Monitor, and this concludes the `setup()` function.

Listing 8-1   USART sketch—complete listing

```
//-------------------------------------------------------------
// This sketch demonstrates printing to the USART using the
// underlying interrupts. There's nothing unusual here - apart
// from the use of "printf()" which is not normally available
// on the Arduino. See the text (in the book) for details.
//
// Norman Dunbar.
// 1st June 2020.
//-------------------------------------------------------------

#include <LibPrintf.h>
```

---

[2]https://github.com/embeddedartistry/arduino-printf.

```
//------------------------------------------------------------
// A simple sign-on message.
//------------------------------------------------------------
const char Message[] = {"Welcome to Arduino interrupted"
                        " USART communications."};




//------------------------------------------------------------
// Initialise the Serial Monitor to 115200 baud and sign on.
// A few numerical examples of printf() are then exercised.
// Unless, of course, they are commented out!
//------------------------------------------------------------
void setup() {

    // Setup USART for 115200 baud.
    Serial.begin(115200);

    // Write sign-on message;
    printf("%s\n\n", Message);


// These lines were used in testing, feel free to uncomment
// them if you want to exercise some of the other functions
// available in "printf".
/*
    ...
*/

    // Let the user know we are ready.
    printf("\nPlease type some text...\n");
}




//------------------------------------------------------------
// Simply loop around copying user input back to the USART
//------------------------------------------------------------
void loop() {
    while(Serial.available()) {
        uint8_t c = Serial.read();
        printf("%c", c);
    }
}
```

In the `loop()` function, we wait for some text to be received by the USART and made available to the sketch. When data are present, we extract it from the receive buffer and display it on the Serial Monitor.

There are a couple of points to note with the Arduino's use of the USART.

You *should not* send or read data from the USART inside *any* interrupt handler because interrupts are turned off when executing an ISR. This applies to any interrupt handling code, including anything your sketch has attached using the `attachInterrupt()` function.

Tip

This is not *strictly* true. You can send data to the Serial Interface provided that you send fewer bytes than the remaining space available in the transmit buffer. By default, this buffer is 64 bytes in size, but only 63 are available at any time due to a peculiarity of circular buffers.

If you fill the transmit buffer from inside an ISR, then the system will hang up as the Arduino will attempt to wait for the *USART Data Register Empty interrupt* to empty the buffer by sending characters to the USART for transmission. However, that particular interrupt is not running as the current ISR has disabled global interrupts.

Do not attempt to transmit data to the USART in any ISR code unless it is absolutely necessary, and you can guarantee that the buffer will not fill up if you do so.

The circular buffers used by the Arduino for transmission and receipt of data are both 64 bytes long. Each buffer loses one character of capacity due to a foible of circular buffers when you only keep a head and tail pointer. Appendix A, Circular Buffers, explains why this is the case. When transmitting data, this is not a problem—except within an ISR as previously explained—but for receipt of data, it can cause loss of data if the sketch code is not extracting data from the receive buffer fast enough. The Arduino interrupt code checks for a full buffer and, if found, simply discards the character it has just received.

8.6   Using USART Interrupts in AVR Code

Those of us writing raw AVR C++ code have a little bit more work to do. The steps are

- Create some code to handle circular buffers.
- Write code to use the circular buffer code to add and remove data from a buffer.
- Write interrupt handling code for each of the three USART interrupts we are interested in using.

Circular buffers are, of course, not mandatory. They can be replaced by any similar buffering system that you may have written or have a library for. In this book, to match the Arduino, I shall be using circular buffers. Appendix A, Circular Buffers, explains circular buffers in some detail, should you need this.

8.6.1   Interrupt Handling

As I previously mentioned, there are interrupts for transmission and also for reception of data. I shall begin with the interrupt for transmitting data—which is the simplest. During the discussion, I shall make reference to the code that handles the interrupts in the main. Other code files, which you will find in the code repository for this chapter, deal with handling of circular buffers, which is explained fully in Appendix A, Circular Buffers, and will not be dealt with here in any great detail.

8.6.1.1 Transmitting Data

Our code to send data to the USART starts, as always, with a header file. The file is named USARTinterrupt.h, and we will be coming back to it and adding extra code to it as we progress. For data transmission, the code in Listing 8-2 is all that is required. Comments have been mostly removed from the listings.

The eagle-eyed among you will have noticed that I'm including printf.h. Yes, I have a version of the Arduino library that can be used in AVR code. I have made it available on the code repository for this book. In the example sketch, you will find it in the lib/printf directory.

Listing 8-2 USARTinterrupt.h—transmission constants

```
#ifndef USARTINTERRUPT_H
#define USARTINTERRUPT_H

#include <stdint.h>
#include <USARTbuffer.h>
#include <avr/interrupt.h>
#include "printf.h"


//================================================================
// USART TX Stuff follows.
//================================================================


//----------------------------------------------------------------
// This makes things look like function calls.
//----------------------------------------------------------------
#define START_UDRIE_INTERRUPT()  UCSR0B |= (1 << UDRIE0)
#define STOP_UDRIE_INTERRUPT()   UCSR0B &= ~(1 << UDRIE0)
#define STOP_TX()                UCSR0B &= ~(1 << TXEN0)

//----------------------------------------------------------------
// Initialise the USART. We always use 8N1 here -- this is
// just a demo after all.
//----------------------------------------------------------------
void USARTinit(uint32_t baudRate);

//----------------------------------------------------------------
// End usage of the USART.
//----------------------------------------------------------------
void USARTend();

//----------------------------------------------------------------
// Flush all data to TX from the buffer to the USART.
//----------------------------------------------------------------
```

```
void USARTflush();

//-------------------------------------------------------------
// Send a single byte to the USART.
// _putchar() is called internally by printf() and must be
// defined. USARTputChar() is just there for consistency!
//-------------------------------------------------------------
void _putchar(char ch);
void USARTputChar(uint8_t ch);
```

There's nothing much that's difficult here; I start by including the required header files and then defining three helper macros to make life easier:

- START_UDRIE_INTERRUPT() carries out a bitwise OR into the UCSR0B register to enable the *USART Data Register Empty* interrupt.
- STOP_UDRIE_INTERRUPT() carries out a bitwise AND into the UCSR0B register to disable the *USART Data Register Empty* interrupt.
- STOP_TX() disables all transmission.

There is no macro to start transmitting data. This is not done until there is at least one byte in the transmit buffer, so is not needed; if you need to see it, you will find it in the _putchar() function in the USARTinterrupt.cpp file.

Following the macro definitions, the function headers are declared for some functions involved in the USART initialization and data transmission. The header file in the code folder for this chapter has many more function definitions to enable transmitting of all kinds of data. They will not be mentioned here unless it is important. The functions are

- USARTinit() which completely initializes the USART and the two buffers required, one for transmission and one for reception of data.
- USARTend() which shuts down and powers off the USART after use.
- USARTflush() which flushes all data requested to be transmitted from the buffer into the USART.
- _putchar() which writes a single character into the transmission circular buffer for the interrupt to transmit. This is used internally by the printf() function.
- USARTputChar() is a duplicate of _putchar() but has a name that is consistent with other functions in the code.

We will be coming back to this header file later as we still have to consider the data receiving side of the USART, but for now, we need to look at the C++ code for the functions involved in transmitting data. These are in the code file named USARTinterrupt.cpp. The file begins as shown in Listing 8-3.

Listing 8-3 USARTinterrupt.cpp—headers and buffers

```
#include <avr/interrupt.h>
#include <stdlib.h>
#include "USARTinterrupt.h"
#include "USARTbuffer.h"
```

```
// The buffers live elsewhere.
extern   volatile circularBuffer rxBuffer;
extern   volatile circularBuffer txBuffer;
```

The header files included are required to implement the circular buffer handling and are similar to the code and files discussed in Appendix A, Circular Buffers, and to allow us to use the ISRs for the interrupt handling code.

Following on from the headers, we see the declaration of a pair of circular buffers, one for data reception and one for transmission.

You will notice that all of these are declared `extern volatile` as they are declared elsewhere, in the file `USARTbuffer.cpp`, and need to be accessed from both the main code and from the interrupt handling code.

The code continues with the `USARTinit()` function in Listing 8-4, and this function is responsible for setting up the USART and initializing the two circular buffers—which is a wee bit naughty—as the purists will say—but in my defense, the USART cannot work without the buffers!

Listing 8-4 USARTinterrupt.cpp—USARTinit() function

```
//--------------------------------------------------------
// Initialise the USART. For this example we only require the
// baud rate. We assume, always a bad idea, that we are using
// 8 bits of data, no parity and 1 stop bit.
// Calling here also initialises the two circular buffers.
//--------------------------------------------------------
void USARTinit(const uint32_t baudRate) {
    // Baud rate factor.
    uint16_t baudFactor;

    // Initialise the two buffers. Do it first to stop
    // occasional random garbage being transmitted by
    // the USART.
    cBufferInit(&rxBuffer);
    cBufferInit(&txBuffer);

    // Power up the USART.
    PRR &= ~(1 << PRUSART0);

    // Initialise the USART. This sets 1 stop bit and
    // no parity as a side effect. (They are the defaults.)
    UCSR0A = UCSR0B = UCSR0C = 0;

    // 8 bit data size.
    UCSR0C |= ((1 << UCSZ01) | (1 << UCSZ00));

    // Attempt high speed comms, required for 115200 baud
    // which doesn't work otherwise.
    UCSR0A = (1 << U2X0);
```

```
// Calculate baud rate factor from baud rate. Assumes
// high speed comms is in use.
baudFactor = (F_CPU / (8 * baudRate)) - 1;

// We need to keep the baudFactor below 4096 and
// on 16 MHz boards, we need low speed if baudRate is
// 57600.
if ((baudFactor > 4095) ||
    ((F_CPU == 16000000L) && (baudRate == 57600))) {
        UCSR0A = 0;
        baudFactor = (F_CPU / (16 * baudRate)) - 1;
}

// Set UBRR0 with correct factor.
UBRR0 = baudFactor;

// Enable and start RX, enable TX but don't start yet.
UCSR0B |= ((1 << TXEN0) | (1 << RXEN0) | (1 << RXCIE0));
}
```

Surprisingly, initializing the USART is quite simple and begins by initializing the two buffers used to transmit and receive data. This must be done before the interrupts are enabled, or we will get random garbage transmitted if the buffer hasn't been correctly configured when the USART is started up for transmission.

Following on from the buffer initialization, we need to ensure that the USART is actually powered up. We do this by disabling the power disable bit in the *Power Reduction Register*, PRR. We clear the bit by writing a zero to it.

While the USART is warming up, the three main configuration registers are cleared to zero. Doing this puts the USART into a known state with everything turned off and also, handily, sets the USART to one stop bit and no parity, which is what we are using here.

Unfortunately, this known state puts the USART into five-bit data mode, so we have to follow up and reset the data width to be eight bits, which we do in the USCR0C register.

We then request double speed USART communications by setting bit U2X0 in register UCSR0A and calculate the required double speed baud rate factor for the UBRR0 register which controls our baud rate.

If the factor value is above 4095, then it's not possible to use double speed mode for the USART because the UBRR0 register only has enough *usable* bits for values between 0 and 4095. It is also not possible to use double speed communications on boards running at 16 MHz and where a baud rate of 57,600 has been requested. In either case, we have to switch to single speed communications and recalculate the baud rate factor for the UBRR0 register.

Why do we attempt to use double speed mode first? Simple, the data sheet for the ATmega328P shows the various baud rates and error percentages for single and double speed. In almost all cases, the double speed error percentages are much, much less than the corresponding single speed error percentages.

What about the special case of 57,600 baud on 16 MHz systems? I have no idea! However, I have a hypothesis. Calculating the actual baud rate and error percentages for this combination results in exactly the same baud rate—58,823—in each case. The error percentage is also the same, as expected, at 2.12%. I suspect then that the single speed communications are slightly more reliable, given that the error percentage is well above the recommended maximum of 0.5%.

Once the UBRR0 register has been set to control the baud rate, we can configure the USART to transmit and receive data, but we only enable the *USART Receive Data Complete* interrupt. We do not enable the data transmission interrupt, *USART Data Register Empty*, as that will be done only after we have at least one byte in the transmission buffer. If we enable the interrupt now, the USART will keep transmitting whatever random data happens to be in the UDR0 register.

The next part of the file is shown in Listing 8-5 and is the USARTend() function which shuts down the USART after our application code has finished with it.

Listing 8-5 USARTinterrupt.cpp—USARTend() function

```
//----------------------------------------------------------------
// We are done with the USART. Stop the interrupts and power
// it down to save a couple of microamps. Waste not want not!
// This frees up pins PD0 and PD1 (D0 and D1) for GPIO.
//----------------------------------------------------------------
void USARTend() {
    // Make sure TX is completed.
    USARTflush();

    // Stop UDRIE interrupt, TX and RX.
    STOP_UDRIE_INTERRUPT();
    STOP_TX();
    STOP_RX();

    // Clear both buffers.
    cBufferInit(&txBuffer);
    cBufferInit(&rxBuffer);

    // Power off the USART.
    PRR |= (1 << PRUSART0);
}
```

Shutting down the USART involves flushing out any data still to be transmitted, and this happens when we call the USARTflush() function. That function simply blocks until the transmission buffer has been emptied by the USART interrupts. After the flush has taken place, the USART has its interrupts disabled and its ability to transmit or receive data disabled.

Both the transmit and receive buffers are then initialized, which has the effect of clearing them out leaving them empty. This step is not strictly necessary as initializing the USART again will do the clearing, but it's best to be explicit. Finally, the USART is powered off, saving a few microamps of current and making any battery power in use last just a little longer.

Writing data to the USART is facilitated by way of a circular buffer. Our application code writes to the buffer, and the interrupt handling code will copy the bytes from the buffer into the USART for transmission. As we are using the printf() library function, we must define the _putchar() function which will redirect all characters to be output by printf() to the USART by adding them to the transmit buffer. In addition, our application code might need to send binary data—integers and so on—to the USART; we therefore need a manner of writing any data type into the transmission buffer.

Listing 8-6 shows the code for a suitable _putchar() function and also a function named USARTputChar(), which our code will use to send individual bytes to the transmit buffer.[3]

Listing 8-6 USARTinterrupt.cpp—_putchar() function

```
//-----------------------------------------------------------
// This function is called from printf.c and is responsible
// for sending every character to be printed by printf, to the
// USART.
//-----------------------------------------------------------
void _putchar(char ch) {

    // Add data to the buffer. Will wait for space if full.
    cBufferAdd(&txBuffer, ch);

    // Fire up the UDRE0 interrupt.
    START_UDRIE_INTERRUPT();
}


//-----------------------------------------------------------
// This is not strictly necessary, we could just call
// _putchar() but as all the other USART functions are named
// USARTxxxx, this is consistent. That is all!
//-----------------------------------------------------------
void USARTputChar(uint8_t ch) {
    _putchar(ch);
}
```

There's really nothing complicated here; the character in the data buffer is copied into the transmission circular buffer ready to be sent to the USART. If the buffer becomes full, the code in cBufferAdd() will block waiting for space. Space is guaranteed to become available as the interrupt which empties the buffer into the USART is already running.[4]

The data byte is copied to the buffer using the buffer handling code as described in Appendix A, Circular Buffers. The buffer handling code is not discussed further here.

After writing the byte to the circular buffer, the *USART Data Register Empty* interrupt is enabled. This will cause the contents of the buffer to be sent to the USART for transmission. The USART will almost immediately begin sending the data.

Some of you may be wondering why my USARTwriteByte() takes a uint8_t parameter, while _putchar() takes a char instead. When I originally wrote my code, I used uint8_t throughout. I had separate functions to send different data types to the USART. After I discovered printf(), I realized that I could get rid of most of those functions and just use printf().

---

[3]This is not strictly required; we could simply call _putchar(), but all the other USART functions have a USARTxxxx() name format, so this is purely to be consistent.

[4]Unless someone attempted to write to the USART from inside another ISR. If that caused the buffer to fill up, then the code will block forever as the desired interrupt handler which frees space in the buffer will not be executing.

Unfortunately, `printf()` uses the old style parameters, and changing the header and implementation files caused the linker to fail and to produce a strange error that "_putchar() was not found." I have left well alone, and everything is working fine. A `char` is just an unsigned eight-bit variable, which is the same as `uint8_t` anyway.

There is often a need to cause an application to flush the transmission buffer and wait for it to completely empty. This is performed by the code shown in Listing 8-7, the `USARTflush()` function.

Listing 8-7 USARTinterrupt.cpp—USARTflush() function

```
//------------------------------------------------------------
// Flush the TX buffer to the USART and wait for completion.
//------------------------------------------------------------
void USARTflush() {
    volatile circularBuffer *tx = &txBuffer;
    if (tx->headIndex == tx->tailIndex)
        // Buffer empty.
        return;

    // Wait for interrupts to run down the buffer contents.
    while ((UCSR0B & UDRE0)) ;  // Wait ...
}
```

You should note that this function relies on a couple of assumptions:

- Global interrupts must be enabled.
- The *USART Data Register Empty* interrupt is enabled.
- The `TXEN0` bit has been set to enable the USART to transmit data.

`USARTflush()` checks if the transmission buffer is currently empty. If so, it makes a quick exit; otherwise, it "busy waits" until the *USART Data Register Empty* interrupt enable bit, `UDRIE0` in register `UCSR0B`, gets cleared at the end of the current transmission. All of this would eventually have happened, but this function allows the application code to wait for transmission to complete— shutting down the USART while data are being transmitted would result in an immediate halt to communications and an incomplete transmission. This is undesirable, so `USARTflush()` is called from `USARTend()` to ensure all data has been transmitted prior to closing down the USART.

The ISR which handles the *USART Data Register Empty* interrupt is next and can be seen in Listing 8-8.

Listing 8-8 USARTinterrupt.cpp—ISR(USART_UDRE_vect)

```
//------------------------------------------------------------
// Data Register Empty interrupt. Copy next byte to be sent
// from the txBuffer to UDR0. Will disable transmitter when we
// run out of bytes. No need for TX Complete interrupt.
//------------------------------------------------------------
ISR(USART_UDRE_vect) {
    // Grab next byte from txBuffer for transmission.
    volatile circularBuffer *tx = &txBuffer;
    int aByte= cBufferGet(tx);
```

```
    // Is txBuffer empty? Will be -1 if so.
    if (aByte != -1) {
        UDR0 = aByte;
    } else {
        // txBuffer is empty, disable UDRE interrupt.
        STOP_UDRIE_INTERRUPT();
    }

    // Clear the TX Complete interrupt flag.
    // The interrupt is unused but still sets the flag.
    UCSR0A |= (1 << TXC0);
}
```

When the ISR executes, it attempts to fetch the next byte to be transmitted from the transmission buffer. If the buffer is empty, −1 will be returned and the ISR will disable its own interrupt until the next time that there are data in the transmit buffer. The USART is still configured to transmit, TXEN0 is still set, but as there's currently nothing in the circular buffer to be transmitted, the interrupt might as well be disabled.

If there was a valid data byte in the buffer, it is copied into the UDR0 register ready to be framed and transmitted by the hardware.

If the *USART Transmit Complete* interrupt flag bit is set, as it could be even though we are not handling that particular interrupt,[5] we should clear it to avoid spurious execution of that interrupt in the event that it is subsequently enabled.

8.6.1.2 Receiving Data

Receiving data uses a single interrupt, the *USART Receive Complete* interrupt. This interrupt is triggered any time that data has been received by the USART and has been stripped of its framing bits (start, stop, and parity), and the remaining bits have been copied into the UDR0 register. There are three errors that can occur when receiving data:

- Parity error where there are not enough 1 bits in the received data to match the chosen parity. Most Arduino communications, and this includes AVR applications too, tend not to bother with parity.
- Data overrun where the two-byte receive buffer is full, and a new start bit is detected on the RX pin. This can occur when data are not being read from the UDR0 register quickly enough.
- Frame error where the USART detected that the first stop bit of the data was a zero.

When receiving data, the error bits in the UCSR0A register must be checked or copied before reading the UDR0 register. The error bits are valid only until the register is read.

Listing 8-9 is a continuation of the header file USARTinterrupt.h, which we started in Listing 8-2; it covers the addition of the details we require for receipt of data.

The changes begin with the addition of some macros for ease of use in the reception code. STOP_RX is used in the USARTend() function to shut down reception completely. The remaining macros are used, if required, for error checking.

---

[5]Remember, any time that the stimulus to trigger an interrupt is detected, the flag bit for that interrupt is set. This is true whether or not we are handling the interrupt for that case. Here, we are not handling the interrupt, but it will still set the flag—it is our responsibility to clear it. ISRs automatically clear their appropriate flag bit on execution.

Listing 8-9 USARTinterrupt.h—reception constants

```
. . .

//================================================================
// USART RX Stuff follows.
//================================================================


//----------------------------------------------------------------
// This makes things look like function calls.
//----------------------------------------------------------------
#define STOP_RX() UCSR0B &= ~((1 << RXEN0) | (1 << RXCIE0))

#define RX_ERROR_BITS ((1 << FE0) | (1 << DOR0) | (1 << UPE0))
#define USART_CHECK_ERRORS() UCSR0A & (RX_ERROR_BITS)

#define RX_FRAME_ERROR(x) (x) & (1 << FE0)
#define RX_OVERRUN(x) (x) & (1 << DOR0)
#define RX_PARITY_ERROR(x) (x) & (1 << UPE0)
#define RX_BUFFER_EMPTY -1


//----------------------------------------------------------------
// Read a single byte from the USART's rxBuffer. Returns -1
// on error - which means, buffer empty.
//----------------------------------------------------------------
int USARTreadByte();

//----------------------------------------------------------------
// Read a number of bytes into a buffer. Returns count of
// bytes actually read.
//----------------------------------------------------------------
int USARTreadBytes(uint8_t *buffer, int count);

//----------------------------------------------------------------
// Are there any data in the rxBuffer not yet read by the code
// if so, return how many bytes are available.
//----------------------------------------------------------------
uint8_t USARTavailable();


//----------------------------------------------------------------
// Any errors in the USART receiver?
//----------------------------------------------------------------
uint8_t USARTerror();

#endif // USARTINTERRUPT_H
```

The remaining changes to the header file are the function prototypes for the various
USARTread() functions.

The code for the USARTreadByte() function can be seen in Listing 8-10. There is not much to
see in this particular function as it simply passes back the result of the cBufferGet() function or
−1 in the event of an error which includes the receiver's circular buffer being empty.

Listing 8-10 USARTinterrupt.cpp—USARTreadByte() function

```cpp
//------------------------------------------------------------
// Read 1 byte of data from USART. Returns -1 on errors in
// receipt of the data, or buffer empty.
//------------------------------------------------------------
int USARTreadByte() {
    // This returns -1 on error.
    return cBufferGet(&rxBuffer);
}
```

Listing 8-11 shows the code for the USARTreadBytes() function which reads a number of
bytes from the received data buffer.

Listing 8-11 USARTinterrupt.cpp—USARTreadBytes() function

```cpp
//------------------------------------------------------------
// Read a number of bytes into a buffer. Returns count of
// bytes actually read. May include CR/LF characters in the
// output buffer.
//------------------------------------------------------------
int USARTreadBytes(uint8_t *buffer, int count) {
    int bytesRead = 0;
    int aByte;
    while (count) {
        aByte = USARTreadByte();
        if (aByte >= 0) {
            *buffer++ = aByte;
            count--;
            bytesRead++;
        } else {
            break;
        }
    }

    return bytesRead;
}
```

Unlike the Arduino code, which has a timeout, the code in Listing 8-11 does not have a timeout.
It will read characters into the supplied buffer until it has copied over the requested number of bytes,
or it has emptied the USART receiver's circular buffer. The number of bytes read is returned to the
caller.

The function `USARTavailable()` returns the count of data bytes remaining in the receive buffer. This count indicates data that have been received from the USART but which have yet to be read by the application code. Listing 8-12 shows the code for this function.

Listing 8-12 USARTinterrupt.cpp—USARTavailable() function

```
//------------------------------------------------------------
// Are there any data in the rxBuffer not yet read by the code
// if so, return how many bytes are available.
//------------------------------------------------------------
uint8_t USARTavailable() {
    return cBufferAvailable();
}
```

The `USARTerror()` function returns the most recent error detected by the *USART Receive Complete* interrupt handler. Listing 8-13 is the code for this function.

Listing 8-13 USARTinterrupt.cpp—USARTerror() function

```
//------------------------------------------------------------
// Any errors in the USART receiver?
//------------------------------------------------------------
uint8_t USARTerror() {
    return rxBuffer.lastError;
}
```

This function simply extracts and returns the error code for the USART's receiver. This value is set in the ISR (see Listing 8-14) in the event that a parity, data overrun, or frame error is detected when reading data from the USART into the circular buffer. Only bits 2, 3, and 4 are of interest; the remaining bits will all be zero.

Listing 8-14 shows the code responsible for handling the *USART Receive Complete* interrupt. This ISR is called each time a data byte is received by the USART, stripped of its framing and parity bits, and has been written into the UDR0 register. There is a two-byte buffer in the USART hardware which allows one byte to be stripped and copied to UDR0 while a second byte is still in the process of being received.

Listing 8-14 USARTinterrupt.cpp—ISR(USART_RX_vect)

```
//------------------------------------------------------------
// Receive complete interrupt. Copy data byte received to
// circular buffer. We must check for errors before reading
// the data from UDR0.
//------------------------------------------------------------
ISR(USART_RX_vect) {
    // Check for errors first.
    uint8_t errors = USART_CHECK_ERRORS();

    // Read data from USART.
    uint8_t aByte = UDR0;
```

```
    // If no errors, add the byte to the RX buffer, if
    // there is free space, otherwise just drop the byte.
    volatile circularBuffer *rx = &rxBuffer;
    if (!errors) {
        if (!cBufferFull(rx)) {
            cBufferAdd(rx, aByte);
        }
    } else {
        // Save the error bits in case the code is
        // interested.
        rx->lastError = errors;
    }
}
```

The ISR begins by extracting the error bits FE0, DOR0, and UPE0 from the UCSR0A register prior to reading the received data byte from UDR0. This must be done in the order given as the error bits are invalidated when UDR0 is read.

If any of the error bits were set, they are stored in the buffer's lastError field, then the byte just read is considered invalid and implicitly discarded. If the buffer is found to be full, then we cannot save the byte just read and it is discarded; otherwise, it is stored in the receive buffer—this is identical to how the Arduino handles a full receive buffer as it is not possible to wait for the buffer to empty—this buffer, unlike the transmit one, is not under interrupt control to empty it, only to fill it.

While the ISR takes care to update the buffer's lastError field, it is only the most recent error that is stored there. Any subsequent errors will overwrite the current one. A buffer full error is not saved, only wire errors.

An alternative course of action, left to the reader,[6] is to change the USART receiver's circular buffer to store 16-bit values instead of 8-bit values. The ISR would merge the error bits with the data byte received, with a shift and an OR, and save both together in the circular buffer. In this manner, each slot in the buffer would store the received data byte in the low byte and the error bits in the high byte.

The application code would then be aware of *all* errors in the receipt of the data, should it be necessary to do so.

8.6.1.3 Error Handling
Error handling in interrupt code is a somewhat tricky thing to get your head around; at least, I find this to be the case. This could be one of the reasons that some developers are not keen on interrupt code.

Transmission errors are easy. In our code in this chapter, we don't know if there were actual errors in transmitting the data. In fact, we cannot know as the USART doesn't report back at all, it simply feeds the data frame out onto the TX pin and that's all.

The only real error we could possibly see when attempting to transmit data is when we try to write some data to the circular buffer for transmission. The buffer might be full up and have no room.

---

[6]That sounds like a cop-out to me!

Even in this case it is a simple case to handle as the code that adds data to the buffer blocks (waits) for some space to become available, then carries on as if nothing had gone wrong. This processing is possible for these reasons:

- When the buffer is empty, the *USART Data Register Empty* interrupt is disabled as there is no data to transmit.
- As soon as a single byte is added to the buffer, the interrupt is turned on, and framing and transmission begin. This will continue until the buffer is completely empty again whereupon the *USART Data Register Empty* interrupt will be disabled until more data starts to fill the buffer.
- If the buffer is already full, we know that the interrupt must be running and will eventually create space for the new data, so we simply wait.
- There is no way that the buffer can have any space used in it, and the interrupt not be running, except for the time between the very first byte being added and the interrupt being started.

As you can see, transmission errors are covered by our code not having to do much at all as the *USART Data Register Empty* interrupt is emptying the buffer and that ISR handles errors perfectly well.

Errors in the receipt of data are a different matter. There are the three errors, known as wire errors, previously discussed; there is the possibility of the circular buffer being full and not being emptied fast enough; and there is the problem of getting errors out of the ISR itself.

When receiving data the interrupt is not emptying the buffer, it is filling it. We have to keep ISR code short and sweet, so what should we do if we see a wire error? Given that the transmission of the byte resulted in an error, the data received by the USART cannot be trusted, and the byte received should be dropped. The code in this chapter does this if a wire error was detected as can be seen in Listing 8-14.

Assuming no wire errors were seen, the USART will have successfully received the data byte, and the ISR should be able to add it into the buffer, ready to be read by the application code. If the buffer is full, then we cannot save the byte anywhere, and so the only reasonable course of action is to drop the recently received byte.

Reception errors in summary:

- Wire errors are handled by passing the most recent error back to the buffer's error variable. This will be overwritten if further errors are seen, which *may* be a problem.
- Wire errors *do not* add the received byte to the buffer; this *may* be a problem, but the byte cannot be relied upon to be valid if there were wire errors detected.
- Filling the buffer cannot cause the ISR to wait for the buffer to empty, unlike when transmitting. In this case, similar to the Arduino, *received data are simply lost*.
- If it is necessary to keep a record of the data byte received and any errors in the receipt of that particular data byte, the circular buffer handling code and the ISR would need to be amended to keep the error code with the data byte. The application would have to work out what to do in the event of an error, whether or not to drop the data byte.

8.7   AVR USART Example

We are now at a stage where we can convert the Arduino sketch in Listing 8-1 into AVR code for use with PlatformIO, for example.

Note
As discussed elsewhere, AVR C++ code, as used with PlatformIO and so on, can be compiled and executed from the Arduino IDE. Start a new sketch, select all the generated code, and delete it. Then type in the AVR code presented in the listings. Compile, upload, and be amazed!

Listing 8-15 is the example code to replace the Arduino code with our own. The example code attempts to replicate the Arduino sketch as closely as possible.

Listing 8-15   AVR example application—main() function

```
//------------------------------------------------------------
// This is a test application to demonstrate the use of an
// interrupt driven USART. This code demonstrates both TX and
// RX. This code has been tested with a buffer size ranging
// from 2 bytes (!) up to 64, all with no problems. The buffer
// size is a factor in how often it fills up, and this causes
// blocking waits when adding data to the buffer.
//
// Norman Dunbar.
// 1st June 2020.
//------------------------------------------------------------

#include <util/delay.h>
#include "USARTinterrupt.h"
#include "printf.h"

const char Message[] = {"Welcome to AVR interrupted"
                        " USART communications."};

int main() {

    // Setup USART for 115200 baud.
    USARTinit(115200);

    // Don't forget ...
    sei();

    // Write a message;
    printf("%s\n\n", Message);


// These lines were used in testing, feel free to uncomment
// them if you want to exercise some of the other functions
// available in "printf".
/*
    ...
*/
```

```
    // Let the user know we are ready.
    printf("\nPlease type some text...\n");

    // Infinite loop.
    while (1) {
        while(USARTavailable()) {
            uint8_t c = USARTreadByte();
            USARTputChar(c);
        }
    }
}
```

The setup part of Listing 8-15 sets the USART to run at 115,200 baud; the USART code itself, described previously in this chapter, configures eight-bit data, no parity, and a single stop bit. It then enables global interrupts; AVR code must do this if interrupts are required—I may have mentioned this already?[7]

The setup completes when the sign-on message and a prompt to the user to type some text are displayed.

The loop part of the code waits for data to be received from the USART and collects it into a small buffer of only 20 characters, plus one for a terminator. The loop ends by printing out, via the USART, the data bytes received.

This code suffers from exactly the same problem as the Arduino's serial reception; you can overload the buffer and lose data.

8.7.1   Did You See Something Slightly Weird?

You may have noticed that when using the Arduino IDE's Serial Monitor to communicate with the Arduino board, you get to type a full line of text and press the Return key, or click the "Send" button, to actually transmit the data from the Serial Monitor to the Arduino. Somehow, when you ran the AVR example code, everything you type appears instantly, so "Hello World" may appear spread over a number of lines, each containing one or more characters. Why is this?

The Arduino Serial Monitor is operating in "Line Mode" which means that typed text is buffered and only sent to the Arduino when the send button is clicked or Return is typed, whereas the AVR example code is not buffered and is talking directly to the Arduino. Each character typed is sent *immediately* to the USART. How do we recreate the Serial Monitor's behavior?

There are a number of options:

- Use PlatformIO's own monitor device.
- Use the Arduino IDE's Serial Monitor.
- Use *CoolTerm* in Line Mode.

---

[7]In just about every chapter!

I usually find that I don't have to bother setting anything in the `platformio.ini` project file to use the Arduino's Serial Monitor, or *CoolTerm*. In the descriptions that follow, if you find that the USART communications don't appear to be working, add one or more of the following settings to the `platformio.ini` file to force the usage of a particular port and baud rate for the communications:

- For the monitor port, use `monitor_port` although PlatformIO is pretty good at finding the monitor port by itself. However, it might be necessary in some cases to be explicit.
- For the baud rate, use `monitor_speed`. This must match the baud rate specified in the code.
- To display the characters you are typing, while you type them, use `monitor_echo`.
- For the different end-of-line character options, use `monitor_eol`.
- For special handling options, use `monitor_filters`.

The PlatformIO documentation[8] has details regarding the various monitor settings, if you need to consult the documentation.

Listing 8-16 shows the Serial Monitor parameters, in the `platformio.ini` file, to allow the monitor to communicate at 115,200 baud in line mode. Line mode is specified using the `send_on_enter` monitor filter setting. This lets you type a line of text and press the return key to send it to the USART, rather than sending each character as it is typed. Add these parameters to your own `platformio.ini` in order to run the example, if you wish.

Listing 8-16 Platformio.ini monitor settings

```
; Serial Monitor options
monitor_port = /dev/ttyUSB0
monitor_speed = 115200
monitor_filters = send_on_enter
monitor_echo = yes
monitor_eol = CRLF
```

8.7.1.1 Using the Arduino IDE's Serial Monitor

This is perhaps the easiest option especially if you already have the Arduino IDE installed. Open it up and configure it as if you were using it to create a sketch for your Arduino board. The most important configuration is to ensure that the port is correctly set. For my Uno, that would be `/dev/ttyUSB0`. *Do not* open the Serial Monitor yet. If you do, PlatformIO will not be able to upload the code.

Using the PlatformIO command line, or *VSCode*, upload the code to your board in the normal manner. Switch to the Arduino IDE, and open the Serial Monitor. Any text sent from the Arduino will appear on the display as normal, plus you are able to type text in Line Mode, to be sent to the Arduino when required.

Figure 8-1 shows the Arduino IDE's Serial Monitor communicating with my Uno running the AVR USART code.

---

[8]https://docs.platformio.org/en/latest/projectconf/section_env_monitor.html.

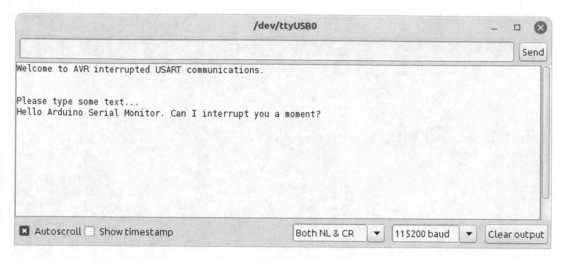

Figure 8-1 Arduino Serial Monitor

If you have to make changes to your code, you must close the Serial Monitor (but leave the Arduino IDE open) so that PlatformIO can upload using the same port.

8.7.1.2 Using CoolTerm

I have not been able to find any way of setting the Linux *Screen* utility into Line Mode, so I recommend the use of *CoolTerm* which is designed as a serial communications tool for embedded systems. *CoolTerm* is available from https://freeware.the-meiers.org/ and is free. There are versions for Windows, Linux, MacOS, and Raspberry Pi.

After downloading, unzip the file and check the Readme and OS-specific text files for any important details that you might need to be aware of, then execute the `CoolTerm` or `CoolTerm.exe` application, depending on your operating system.

Initially, you will not be connected, so first navigate to Connection ▷ Options on the main menu bar.

On the *Serial Port Options*, set the port as appropriate for your board. In my case, the port needs to be `/dev/ttyUSB0` and the baud rate 115,200, with eight data bits, no parity, and one stop bit as configured in the code. Leave everything else to default.

Under *Terminal*, set the Terminal Mode to Line Mode. You may choose to enable Local Echo if you wish to see your own typing echoed back to you. I left it disabled.

Click the OK button to save the settings.

Back on the main screen, click the Connect button. After a second or so, you should see the welcome text from the application.

Type some text into the line edit area at the bottom of the screen and press the Return key to send it to the USART. The text you typed will be displayed on the upper part of the *CoolTerm* display as displayed in Figure 8-2. This includes any spelling mistakes you might make while attempting to type "Hello"!

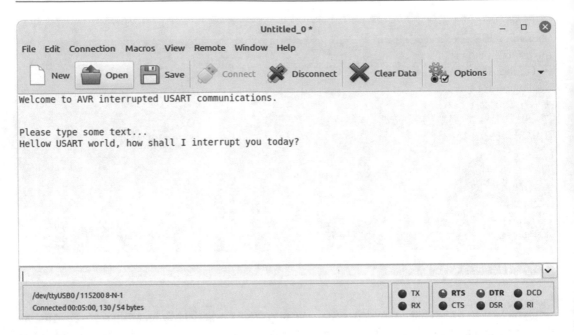

Figure 8-2 CoolTerm

Don't forget, if you type more characters than the USART buffer size, which is 64 characters less 1 for circular buffer reasons, and your baud rate is on the slow side, you *may* lose any characters after the 63rd.[9]

As with the Arduino IDE's Serial Monitor, if you need to change the code for any reason, you will have to disconnect the connection, or PlatformIO will not be able to upload the new code.

8.8   Interrupt Flags

All three USART interrupts have their own individual flag bits in the UCSR0A register. These have been described previously in this chapter, but are reproduced here for reference:

- The *Receive Complete* bit, RXC0, is set whenever a new byte has been received and is ready for retrieval from the UDR0 register. If enabled, this bit will trigger the *USART Receive Complete* interrupt.
- The *Transmit Complete* bit, TXC0, is set when the data byte in the UDR0 register has been fully framed and completely transmitted. If enabled, this bit will trigger the *USART Transmit Complete* interrupt.
- The *USART Data Register Empty* bit, UDRE0, is set when the UDR0 register is ready to accept a new byte for transmission. If enabled, this bit will trigger the *USART Data Register Empty* interrupt.

> **Note**
> After a reset, this bit is set to 1 to indicate that the transmitter is ready to be loaded with data.

---
[9]This is *exactly* the same as the Arduino does.

If the appropriate interrupt is enabled, these flag bits will be cleared by the hardware when the interrupt's ISR is executed. If any of these interrupts are not enabled, the flag bits must be cleared in the normal manner of writing a 1 to its bit position in the register.

On the Arduino, for example, the ISR for the *USART Data Register Empty* interrupt always clears the flag bit for the *USART Transmit Complete* interrupt which is not used by the Arduino code.

8.9   Register Summary

There are a number of registers used, or affected, by the various USART interrupts. The register summary that follows only references those registers, or bits within registers, which affect or are affected by interrupts. See the data sheet for full details of the other registers and bits used by the USART.

8.9.1   USART Baud Rate Register

The *USART Baud Rate Register 0*, UBRR0, is a pair of eight-bit registers, UBRR0H and UBRR0L, where only the lower four bits of UBRR0H are used in conjunction with all eight bits of UBRR0L. This register pair determines the baud rate for the USART.

8.9.2   USART I/O Data Register

The *USART I/O Data Register 0*, UDR0, holds each data byte to be transmitted or received. It is an eight-bit register, but when transmitting with fewer data bits, only the lower "n" bits are used. When transmitting, writing to UDR0 sends that data byte to the USART for transmission. When receiving data, the most recently received byte is available to read from UDR0. This is, it seems, a dual purpose register and is facilitated by there being two separate registers within the ATmega328P but both having the same I/O address. Internal logic determines the correct register to use depending on the direction data are being moved.

8.9.3   USART Control and Status Register A

The *USART Control and Status Register A*, UCSR0A, contains the three interrupt flag bits, the error bits, and the high speed mode bit:

7	6	5	4	3	2	1	0
RXC0	TXC0	UDRE0	FE0	DOR0	UPE0	U2X0	N/A

The bits related to interrupts are bits 7, 6, and 5.

RXC0   If this bit is read as a 1, then the USART has received a new byte of data, and it is ready to be retrieved from the UDR0 register. This bit, if interrupts are configured, will trigger the *USART Receive Complete* interrupt.

TXC0   If this bit is read as a 1, then the USART has finished framing the most recent byte to be transmitted, and the full frame has been completely transmitted. This bit will trigger the *USART Transmit Complete* interrupt if interrupts are enabled.

UDRE0   If this bit is read as a 1, then the UDR0 register is empty and the next byte to be transmitted can be written into it. This bit will trigger the *USART Data Register Empty* interrupt if configured to do so.

Of the remaining bits, we are not interested in bit 0, the Multiprocessor Communication Mode bit.

FE0   is the frame error bit. This will be set by the hardware if the USART detected a framing error in any received data bytes.

DOR0   is the data overrun error bit. The hardware sets this when there are two currently unread data bytes in the USART's *internal* buffer—not the application's receive buffer—and a start bit is detected for a third byte to be received.

UPE0   is the parity error bit. The hardware sets this if parity is being used and a data byte doesn't have enough 1s to ensure even or odd parity.

U2X0   is the bit which controls whether double speed communications will be used. If this bit is set, then double speed is in force.

8.9.4   USART Control and Status Register B

The *USART Control and Status Register B*, UCSR0B, has three bits related to interrupts, those being bits 7, 6, and 5. All other bits are not interrupt specific. See the data sheet for full details of those, if necessary.

7	6	5	4	3	2	1	0
RXCIE0	TXCIE0	UDRIE0	RXEN0	TXEN0	UCSZ02	N/A	N/A

The interrupt-specific bits in this register are

RXCIE0   Setting this bit to 1 will enable the *USART Receive Complete* interrupt.

TXCIE0   Setting this bit to 1 will enable the *USART Transmit Complete* interrupt.

UDRIE0   Setting this bit will enable the *USART Data Register Empty* interrupt.

Of the others, we are not interested in bits 1 and 0 as they are used for 9-bit data communications, which is beyond the scope of this book. The other bits in use are

RXEN0   which enables data receipt when set.

TXEN0   which enables data transmission when set.

UCSZ02   which, when combined with UCSZ01 and UCSZ00 in register UCSR0C, controls the data size we intend using for all communications.

8.9.5   USART Control and Status Register C

The *USART Control and Status Register C*, UCSR0C, has no bits related to interrupts, but the other bits control the features of the USART that we might be interested in using. These bits are:

7	6	5	4	3	2	1	0
N/A	N/A	UPM01	UPM00	USBS0	UCSZ01	UCSZ00	N/A

The interrupt-specific bits in this register are

UPM01:UPM00   These two bits determine the parity mode for communications. Permitted values are 0:0 for disabled, 1:0 for even parity, and 1:1 for odd parity. Any other values are reserved and must not be used.

USBS0   Setting this bit to 1 will enable the use of two stop bits when transmitting data. Leaving this bit clear enables one stop bit.

UCSZ01:UCSZ00   Setting these two bits, in conjunction with UCSZ02 in register UCSR0B, determines data size for the USART's communications. Setting both these bits to 1 and clearing UCSZ02 result in eight-bit data widths, the most common setting. For the other settings, the data sheet has full details.

8.10   Key Takeaways

In this chapter, we learned that

- The USART interrupts are used by the Arduino boards to facilitate the Serial interface.
- Transmitting data has little in the way of error checking and is basically "fire and forget."
- Receiving data does detect errors, and these must be checked before we read the received data byte from the UDR0 register.
- Using the *USART Transmit Complete* interrupt is not really required, as the *USART Data Register Empty* interrupt is faster in that it doesn't have to wait for the whole data *frame* to be transmitted, only for the UDR0 register to empty into the USART's transmit buffer.
- Circular buffers are used to handle transmission and reception as the USART cannot guarantee when data will arrive or be able to be transmitted. These buffers allow the application code to continue running while the USART deals with data communications in the background.

8.11   Coming Up

This was a busy chapter; it's time to settle back and take things easier for a bit. In the next chapter, we forget all about the USART and take a look into the Analog[10] to Digital Converter (ADC) interrupts.

---

[10]In the UK, we spell "analog" as "analogue." I am using the data sheet spelling here as it is polite to refer to things with the names their creator gave them. It does cause my spell checker some grief though!

Analog-to-Digital Converter Interrupt

9

The Analog-to-Digital Converter is the hardware feature of the ATmega328P which gives you the ability to execute Arduino code which calls the `analogRead()` function. It has a single interrupt which informs you when it has completed a conversion of the voltage on its input pin into a value your code can use. As far as the Arduino is concerned, that's it; however, there's more to the Analog-to-Digital Converter than the Arduino lets you know about.

This chapter takes a dive into the Analog-to-Digital Converter and shows you how to configure and use the Analog-to-Digital Converter interrupt easily and efficiently.

9.1   The ADC

Vector 21 in the Interrupt Vector Table is the location of the ADC interrupt.

The *Analog-to-Digital Converter* hardware, or ADC, in the ATmega328P, has a single interrupt available for use. This is known as the *ADC Conversion Complete* interrupt and has the vector name of "ADC." The name of the interrupt gives the game away; this interrupt will be fired whenever the Analog-to-Digital Converter has completed a conversion and the result is available.

In a C/C++ application, the result of the conversion can be obtained from the `ADCW` variable, which is an amalgamation of the `ADCH` and `ADCL` registers. These hold the high byte – actually only 2 bits – and the low byte of the result. The `ADCW` variable retrieves the conversion result by reading the `ADCH` and `ADCL` registers.

If you wish to read the two registers, rather than accessing `ADCW`, then beware of reading those in the wrong order. You *must* read the `ADCL` register first, then read `ADCH`, or you will get strange and incorrect results. The data sheet has the relevant details, but in brief

- The ADC returns a ten-bit result which can be left or right aligned.
- The result is read first from `ADCL` and then from `ADCH` in order to obtain the full ten bits, assuming the default right alignment. In this case, `ADCL` holds the lower eight bits of the result, while `ADCH` holds the two highest bits in bits 1 and 0 of the register.
- In left alignment, the `ADCH` register holds the lower eight bits, and the `ADCL` holds the remaining two bits in bits 1 and 0 of the register.

© The Author(s), under exclusive license to APress Media, LLC, part of Springer Nature 2024
N. Dunbar, *Arduino Interrupts*, Maker Innovations Series,
https://doi.org/10.1007/978-1-4842-9714-8_9

- After the `ADCL` register has been read by application code, the Analog-to-Digital hardware is prevented from accessing either of the ADC data registers until such time as the `ADCH` register is read.
- If a new conversion completes while register access is still prohibited, the new result is lost; however, the interrupt, if enabled, will still trigger.
- If you need less precision, eight bits, then the result should be left aligned and only `ADCH` need be read.

9.2   Setting Up Arduino Interrupts

The Arduino does not use the interrupt system to obtain results from the Analog-to-Digital Converter; instead, the `analogRead()` function uses a busy loop to poll the hardware for a result being made available, then returns it. When called, the function requests that the Analog-to-Digital Converter start a conversion, then the code waits in a tight loop, reading the state of the *ADC Start Conversion* bit, `ADSC`, in the *ADC Status Register A* register, `ADCSRA`. When the bit is cleared to zero, the result is ready and can be read from `ADCL` and `ADCH` or `ADCW`.

If an Arduino sketch requires to use the *ADC Conversion Complete* interrupt, it can do so with the `setupADC()` and `startADC()` functions in Listings 9-4 and 9-5, in Section 9.3, "Setting Up AVR Interrupts," in addition to a suitable ISR to process the interrupt.

The sketch in Listings 9-1 to 9-3 will use the `setupADC()` function to constantly update the PWM value of an LED attached to pin `D9` using the value that the Analog-to-Digital Converter reads from a potentiometer attached to pin `A0`.

The potentiometer in the breadboard layout is $100\,K\Omega$ linear, although any linear potentiometer that you have handy is also suitable; the value is not important.

The breadboard layout used is shown in Figure 9-1, and the sketch begins with the code in Listings 9-4 and 9-5, and following those, we have the global variable used by the ISR and the ISR itself in Listing 9-1.

Listing 9-1   ADCLED sketch – ISR

```
// Global storage for ADC result.
volatile uint16_t ADCReading = 0;


// The interrupt handler.
ISR(ADC_vect) {
    ADCReading = ADCW;
}
```

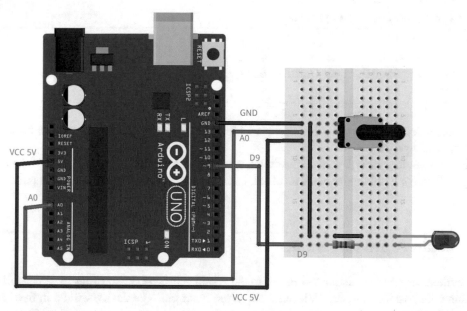

Figure 9-1 ADCLED breadboard layout

The setup() function in Listing 9-2 simply makes sure that pin D9 is an output pin, then initializes and starts the Analog-to-Digital Converter. The function setupADC() will be seen shortly in Listing 9-4 in Section 9.3, "Setting Up AVR Interrupts," while startADC() is to be found in Listing 9-5.

Listing 9-2 ADCLED sketch – setup() function

```
void setup() {
    // D9 has PWM, use it for the LED.
    pinMode(9, OUTPUT);

    // A0 is the input pin for the ADC.
    setupADC();

    // Start the first ADC conversion.
    startADC();
}
```

The loop() function in Listing 9-3 copies the most recently obtained value from the Analog-to-Digital Converter to pin D9. It must, as you can see, map the value read to a suitable value for the analogWrite() function, which only allows values between 0 and 255, whereas the Analog-to-Digital Converter is returning values between 0 and 1023.

Listing 9-3 ADCLED sketch – loop() function

```
void loop() {
    // Dim or brighten the LED.
    analogWrite(9, map(ADCReading, 0, 1023, 0, 255));
}
```

Once compiled and uploaded, this sketch will brighten and dim an LED on pin D9 based on the voltage applied to ADC pin A0.

In the next section, we will convert the sketch to use plain AVR C/C++ code instead of the Arduino Language. There's a little more work involved, but the code will be smaller when compiled, as well as quicker.

9.3   Setting Up AVR Interrupts

I have written the code in Listing 9-4 to set up the Analog-to-Digital Converter to run at full ten-bit resolution with Arduino pin A0, AVR pin PC0, as the input pin. The device will be in free "running mode" where the end of the current conversion will initiate a subsequent conversion. The code was originally written for my own devices; I have Arduino boards running at 16 MHz and some home-built *NormDuinos* running at 8 and 16 MHz. The code assumes that anything not running at 16 MHz is running at 8 MHz.

The remaining code in Listings 9-5 to 9-8 are the AVR version of the sketch in the previous section and simply fades an LED attached to Arduino pin D9, AVR pin PB1, up or down according to the value read by the Analog-to-Digital Converter. Once again, the breadboard layout is shown in Figure 9-1.

Listing 9-4 shows the code responsible for setting up the Analog-to-Digital Converter as described previously.

Listing 9-4 ADCLED application – setupADC() function

```
// Next 2 lines are NOT required for Arduino.
#include <avr/io.h>
#include <avr/interrupt.h>

void setupADC() {
    // Ensure ADC is powered.
    PRR &= ~(1 << PRADC);

    // Slow the ADC clock down to 125 KHz
    // by dividing by 128 or 64. 128 is for a 16 MHz Arduino
    // 64 for an 8 MHz NormDuino. Does not cater for other
    // clock speeds here. BEWARE.
    #if F_CPU == 16000000
        ADCSRA = (1 << ADPS2) | (1 << ADPS1) | (1 << ADPS0);
    #else
        // Non-standard 8 MHz clock in use.
        ADCSRA = (1 << ADPS2) | (1 << ADPS1) | (0 << ADPS0);
    #endif
```

```
    // Initialise the ADC to use the
    // internal AVCC 5 V reference voltage.
    ADMUX = (0 << REFS1) | (1 << REFS0);

    // Ensure result is right aligned.
    ADMUX &= ~(1 << ADLAR);

    // Use the ADC multiplexer input
    // ADC0 = Arduino pin A0.
    ADMUX |= ((0 << MUX3) | (0 << MUX2) |
              (0 << MUX1) | (0 << MUX0));

    // Disable ADC0 Digital input buffer.
    DIDR0 |= (1 << ADC0D);

    // Use the interrupt to advise when a result is available.
    ADCSRA |= (1 << ADIE);

    // Set auto-trigger on, and choose Free Running mode. As
    // we are not using the Analogue Comparator, we don't
    // care about the ACME bit in ADCSRB.
    ADCSRA |= (1 << ADATE);
    ADCSRB = 0;

    // Enable the ADC.
    ADCSRA |= (1 << ADEN);
}
```

Regardless of whether the interrupt is in use or not, or whether the Analog-to-Digital Converter is in free running mode, it *always* requires a manual start. Listing 9-5 shows the small function required to start the first conversion.

Listing 9-5 ADCLED application – startADC() function

```
void startADC() {
    ADCSRA |= (1 << ADSC);
}
```

The Arduino Language helpfully provides a number of useful functions, one of which is the analogWrite() function. In Plain AVR C/C++ code, we do not have anything similar, so we are required to set this up for ourselves. Listing 9-6 shows the code required to enable timer/counter 1 in *Phase Correct PWM* mode 3, so that we can create the equivalent of the Arduino's analogWrite() function.

Note

The Arduino uses timer/counter 1 to provide Phase Correct PWM in mode 1, which means that the highest value permitted is 255. We are not using mode 1, we are using mode 3 where the highest value is 1023. Timer/counter 1 provides PWM on Arduino pins D9 and D10; we are using D9 in the example code.

The details behind this setup are not really of too much interest here – we are really only interested in the interrupts after all, but in brief

- Timer/counter 1, the only 16-bit timer/counter, is initialized with a prescaler of 64.
- The timer/counter's mode is set to ten-bit Phase Correct PWM. This allows a range of values between 0 and 1023.
- Pin OC1A, Arduino pin D9, will be toggled on and off at the appropriate points.

The data sheet has full details.[1]

Listing 9-6 ADCLED application – setupPWM() function

```
void setupPWM() {
    // Clears everything to a known state.
    TCCR1A = TCCR1B = TCCR1C = 0;

    // Prescaler of 64.
    TCCR1B = ((1 << CS11) | (1 << CS10));

    // Phase correct PWM with TOP = 1023, sets pin
    // OC1A to toggle.
    TCCR1A = ((1 << WGM11) | (1 << WGM10) | (1 << COM1A1));
}
```

Unlike the Arduino sketch, the ISR doesn't use a global variable to hold the result of the Analog-to-Digital conversion as the value is sent directly to the OCR1A register which controls the duty cycle of timer/counter 1's PWM generation for pin OC1A. This can be seen in Listing 9-7.

Listing 9-7 ADCLED application – ISR

```
// The interrupt handler.
ISR(ADC_vect) {
    // OCR1A handles pin D9/PB1/OC1A.
    OCR1A = ADCW;
}
```

With all the peripheral code out of the way, Listing 9-8 is the setup and main loop for the application.

---

[1] As indeed does the book *Arduino Software Internals*.

Listing 9-8 ADCLED application – main() function

```
int main() {
    // PB1 is an Output pin.
    DDRB = (1 << DDB1);

    // We need PWM on PB1.
    setupPWM();

    // Initialise the ADC, using Pin PC0.
    setupADC();

    // Now, fire up the ADC.
    startADC();

    // Enable global interrupts.
    sei();

    // The main loop:
    while (1) {
        // Do nothing.
    }
}
```

Hopefully, you will notice in Listing 9-8 that the main loop does not have to do anything. The Analog-to-Digital Converter's ISR feeds the value read from the potentiometer directly into the `OCR1A` register, which controls the PWM duty cycle for pin `OC1A/D9/PB1` and allows timer/counter 1 to turn the LED on and off automatically as the value in the timer/counter's count register, `TCNT1`, matches the value in `OCR1A`.

The LED will be *off* when `TCNT1` matches the value in the `OCR1A` register while the timer/counter is counting *upward*; it will remain off until the count reaches the value in `OCR1A` while counting *downward*, at which point the LED will be turned *on*. As we adjust the value in the `OCR1A` register, we are affecting the duty cycle of the PWM waveform and brightening or dimming the LED as a result. The longer the LED is on, the brighter it appears to be.

Note
In Phase Correct PWM mode 3, the timer/counter counts upward from zero to TOP – 1023 in our example code – and then back down to zero again.

As the main loop is not busy at all, it could be put to better use doing *real work*, such as flashing the built-in LED every five seconds. The timer/counter hardware controls turning the LED on and off at the appropriate points in the cycle, while the Analog-to-Digital Converter controls the duty cycle of the PWM generated by changing the on and off points in the timer/counter's cycle.

9.4   Interrupt Flags

The ADC Conversion Complete interrupt sets the `ADIF` bit in *ADC Status Register A*, `ADCSRA`, each time a conversion is complete and the value is ready for retrieval. In the event that a sketch or application is not using interrupts, the Analog-to-Digital Converter will not start another conversion until the flag bit is cleared by code. This is done in the usual manner, by writing a 1 to the `ADIF` bit.

If the application code is using the ADC Conversion Complete interrupt, then the `ADIF` bit will be cleared automatically, and the Analog-to-Digital Converter will be free to begin another conversion.

9.5   Register Summary

There is one bit in one register, which is used to configure the Analog-to-Digital Converter interrupt. In addition, there is another single bit, in the same register, used as the interrupt's flag bit.

All other bits in the other Analog-to-Digital Converter registers are purely for configuring how the Analog-to-Digital Converter should work and are not related to the use of interrupts.

The register summary that follows only references the registers, and only the relevant bits, which affect or are affected by interrupts. See the data sheet for full details of all the other registers and bits used by the Analog-to-Digital Converter.

9.5.1   ADC Control and Status Register A

The *ADC Control and Status Register A*, `ADCSRA`, has two bits related to interrupts, those being bits 4 and 3. All other bits are not interrupt specific. See the data sheet for full details of those, if necessary.

7	6	5	4	3	2	1	0
N/A	N/A	N/A	ADIF	ADIE	N/A	N/A	N/A

ADIF   This bit is the flag bit which determines if the Analog-to-Digital Converter has completed a conversion and that the result is available. If this bit is read as a 1, then a result is waiting.

ADIE   Writing a 1 to this bit will enable the Analog-to-Digital Converter. Writing a 0 will disable it and throw away any pending conversion results.

9.6   Key Takeaways

- In this chapter, we learned how the Arduino uses the Analog-to-Digital Converter, without interrupts, to facilitate the `analogRead()` function.
- We learned how easy it was to enable the *Analog-to-Digital Converter* interrupt so that our code didn't have to hang around in a busy loop, waiting for the conversion to complete.
- We learned also how much other configuration is required before we can use the Analog-to-Digital Converter with or without interrupts!
- As a "by-product" of our playing with the Analog-to-Digital Converter, we saw how to set up the ATmega328P's 16-bit timer/counter to give us an `analogWrite()` equivalent function, but one with a wider range of values.

9.7 Coming Up

That's all for the Analog-to-Digital Converter. Coming up next, we have the *EEPROM Ready* interrupt which tells our code that a byte of data has been read from, or written to, the EEPROM and that it is ready to perform another read or write operation.

EEPROM Ready Interrupt

10

I have not come across many Arduino sketches which utilize the EEPROM built into the ATmega328P. There are a few but they all avoid using the EEPROM interrupt. This chapter attempts to resolve this issue.

By the end of this chapter, you will know how to use the EEPROM interrupt in your code and also whether you *should* be using it. You will also know just how difficult the Arduino makes life for you when you attempt to use EEPROM data. Currently, the Arduino IDE has no ability to allow you to upload EEPROM data without a little bit of messing about in code.

This chapter explains how you can use EEPROM data with your Arduino. It's not as simple as it is with other development systems, like PlatformIO.

10.1   The ATmega328P EEPROM

The EEPROM Ready interrupt resides in Vector 22 in the Interrupt Vector Table.

The interrupt is used to indicate that the EEPROM is ready for another read or write action to take place. The ATmega328P has 1 KB[1] of EEPROM memory available for storage of data – for example, a 3D printer needs to save settings somewhere and the EEPROM is as good a place as any, and it will keep the data secure between power cycles. EEPROMs are guaranteed to have a lifetime of at least 100,000 write cycles. There is no lifetime on read cycles to worry about.

To access the EEPROM from our own code, we need to get to know three new registers:

- The *EEPROM Address Register*, EEAR, which, because it is a 16-bit register, is made up of two 8-bit registers: EEARH which is the address high byte and EEARL which is the address low byte. Only two bits are actually used in EEARH as EEPROM addresses (on the ATmega328P) are 10 bits wide.
- The *EEPROM Data Register*, EEDR, which is either the byte to be written to the EEPROM or the byte just read from the EEPROM.

---

[1] My first computer, the Sinclair ZX81, had 1 KB of RAM in total.

© The Author(s), under exclusive license to APress Media, LLC, part of Springer Nature 2024   169
N. Dunbar, *Arduino Interrupts*, Maker Innovations Series,
https://doi.org/10.1007/978-1-4842-9714-8_10

- The *EEPROM Control Register*, EECR, which specifies, among other things, whether this EEPROM action is reading or writing, whether an erase will be done first, and, most importantly for this book, whether interrupts will be used.

10.1.1 Reading from the EEPROM

Unlike writing to the EEPROM, which will be explained in the next section, there are no special instruction sequences required when reading from the EEPROM. You may need to be aware that whenever the EEPROM is read from, the main CPU is halted for four clock cycles before the next instruction is executed.

To read data from the EEPROM, you simply have to

1. Wait until the *EEPROM Write Enable* bit, EEPE, in the EECR register becomes zero. This indicates that any previous write has completed and a new read or write operation can begin.
2. Write the EEPROM address to be read from to the EEAR register.
3. Write a 1 to EERE, the *EEPROM Read Enable* bit, in the EECR register.

The EEPROM is *byte addressable*, unlike the Flash RAM, so address 0 holds one eight-bit byte as does address 1 and so on.

Listing 10-1 is the data sheet example for reading an EEPROM without using interrupts, *very slightly* amended by me.

Listing 10-1 Data sheet EEPROMread() function

```
uint8_t EEPROMread(uint16_t EEaddress) {

    // Wait for existing write to complete.
    while(EECR & (1<<EEPE))
        ; // Wait here ...

    // EEPROM address.
    EEAR = EEaddress;

    // Trigger the read.
    EECR |= (1<<EERE);

    // Read the EEPROM byte.
    return EEDR;
}
```

As you can see, reading from the EEPROM is pretty simple. The next section explains how to write to the EEPROM – this is not so simple.

10.1.2 Writing to the EEPROM

In order to write to the EEPROM, we must follow a special procedure which helps avoid unintentional EEPROM writes, perhaps by a runaway or corrupted program or just bad code! The sequence of events that must be followed to write to the EEPROM is

1. Set the required write mode in the *EEPROM Programming Mode* bits EEPM1 and EEPM0 in the EECR register. Table 10-1 shows the required settings. After a reset or power-on, the register will be cleared to zero, and so the default mode is erase/write.
2. Wait until the *EEPROM Write Enable* bit EEPE in the EECR register becomes zero. This indicates that any previous write operations have now completed and a new one can begin.
3. Wait until bit SELFPRGEN in the SPMCSR register becomes zero to show that all writes to Flash RAM are complete.
4. Write the new EEPROM address to the EEAR register.
5. Write the EEPROM data byte to the EEDR register.
6. Write a 1 to EEPME, *EEPROM Master Write Enable* bit, while also writing a 0 to the EEPROM Write Enable bit, EEPE, both in the EECR register.
7. Within four clock cycles, write a 1 to the *EEPROM Write Enable* bit, EEPE, in the EECR register.

The order of steps 4 and 5 is not carved in stone; they can be switched around. However, take note of step 7; you have four clock cycles after step 6 in which to carry out step 7; if four clock cycles have passed and step 7 is not complete, then the EEPME will be reset by the hardware to zero, and the write to the EEPROM will fail.

What happens if there is an interrupt triggered between steps 6 and 7? The EEPROM write will inevitably fail because interrupt handling takes longer than four clock cycles. For this reason, it is best to disable interrupts prior to step 6 and re-enable them after step 7, if they were previously enabled of course!

Table 10-1 EEPROM programming mode bits

EEPM1	EEPM0	Operation	Timing
0	0	Erase current data, then write new.	3.4 milliseconds
0	1	Erase current data only.	1.8 milliseconds
1	0	Write new data only.	1.8 milliseconds
1	1	Reserved – do not use.	-

The data sheet warns, referring to the steps involved in writing to the EEPROM, that

> The EEPROM can not be programmed during a CPU write to the Flash memory. The software must check that the Flash programming is completed before initiating a new EEPROM write.
> Step 3 is only relevant if the software contains a Boot Loader allowing the CPU to program the Flash. If the Flash is never being updated by the CPU, step 3 can be omitted.

This seems to indicate that somehow it is possible to have a bootloader writing a new program to the Flash RAM *at the same time* as the application code is writing (or attempting to write) to the EEPROM. This also implies that the new program being written to the Flash RAM could be read from the EEPROM – this is indeed possible.

I think we can guarantee that our sketches will never attempt to do this, and we can forget about checking the SELFPRGEN bit in the SPMCSR register, as the data sheet example itself also does.

After a write to the EEPROM has taken place, the main CPU is halted for two clock cycles before the next instruction can be executed.

The data sheet has the example in Listing 10-2, ever so slightly modified by me, showing how to write to the EEPROM without using interrupts.

My amendments to the function show how to avoid writing to the EEPROM, and reducing its lifetime, by only writing the data when it is *different* from the current data present there. This is facilitated by the EEPROMread() function shown in Listing 10-1.

Listing 10-2   Data sheet EEPROMwrite() function

```
// Required for cli(), sei() etc.
#include <avr/interrupt.h>



void EEPROMwrite(uint16_t EEaddress, uint8_t EEdata) {

    // Check current data and return if the same
    // as we intend to write.
    uint8_t currentByte = EEPROMread(EEaddress);
    if (currentByte == EEdata)
        return;

    // Wait for existing write to complete. This should
    // be fine as we had to do it in EEPROMread().
    while(EECR & (1<<EEPE))
        ; // Wait here ...

    // EEPROM address.
    EEAR = EEaddress;

    // EEPROM Data byte.
    EEDR = EEdata;

    // Disable interrupts and set master write enable.
    // BUT: What about 0 in EEPE? It's already 0!
    uint8_t oldSREG = SREG;
    cli();
    EECR |= (1<<EEMPE);

    // You have 4 clocks to do this...
    // Will cause EEPROM to be written.
    EECR |= (1<<EEPE);

    // Restore interrupts - if they were on.
    SREG = oldSREG;
}
```

The code has one point to be aware of. Saving the current setting of the SREG prior to disabling interrupts and then restoring it after the timed instruction means that we always return the interrupt setting to how it was before we called the cli() function to disable them.

10.2   A Quick Arduino EEPROM Sketch

To demonstrate the use of the code in Listings 10-1 and 10-2 and show how relatively easy it is to write data to the EEPROM and read it back, Listings 10-3 to 10-5 show a quick Arduino sketch to do just that. The two EEPROM functions, EEPROMread() and EEPROMwrite(), are used unchanged from Listings 10-1 and 10-2 and have not been shown in Listing 10-3 in their entirety – to save space.

Listing 10-3 EEPROMpolling sketch – EEPROM functions

```
// Required for cli(), sei() etc.
#include <avr/interrupt.h>


// A function to read one byte of data from the EEPROM.
uint8_t EEPROMread(uint16_t EEaddress) {
    // Unchanged from text.
}


void EEPROMwrite(uint16_t EEaddress, uint8_t EEdata) {
    // Unchanged from text.
}
```

While we are not using interrupts for handling EEPROM communications, we do need to turn interrupts off, and this requires the avr/interrupt.h header file to be included. As previously mentioned, the two EEPROM handling functions are used unchanged and are not fully listed.

Listing 10-4 EEPROMpolling sketch – setup() function

```
void setup() {
    // Initialise the EEPROM control register
    // this should be already set, but better
    // to be explicit.
    EECR = 0;

    Serial.begin(9600);
    Serial.println("Writing data to the EEPROM");
    Serial.println("-------------------------");
    Serial.println();


    // Write some data to the EEPROM at address 0.
    uint8_t dataBuffer[] = "Hello EEPROM World!";
    uint8_t *p = dataBuffer;
```

```
    uint16_t EEAddress = 0;

    // Write the data count.
    EEPROMwrite(EEAddress++, (uint8_t)strlen(dataBuffer));

    while (*p) {
        Serial.print("Address ");
        Serial.print(EEAddress);
        Serial.print(" = '");
        Serial.print((char)*p);
        Serial.println("'");
        EEPROMwrite(EEAddress++, *p++);
    }

    Serial.println();
    Serial.println("Reading data from the EEPROM");
    Serial.println("---------------------------");
    Serial.println();
    delay(5000);
}
```

The `setup()` function, in Listing 10-4, initializes the EECR register to zero explicitly. This makes sure that the register is in a known state before we begin; then, after initializing the Serial Interface, it writes some data to the EEPROM using `EEPROMwrite()`. You should note that the number of bytes written – the length of the data – is written to the EEPROM first, then the bytes of the message are written.

The function concludes by writing some headings that the `loop()` will use and pausing to allow you to read the details it has written to the EEPROM.

As ever with an Arduino sketch, we need a `loop()`, and ours is shown in Listing 10-5.

Listing 10-5   EEPROMpolling sketch – loop() function

```
void loop() {
    // Read the EEPROM data back in the loop.
    uint16_t EEAddress = 0;

    // How many characters?
    uint8_t dataBytes = EEPROMread(EEAddress++);

    // Read back the characters.
    for (uint8_t x = 0; x < dataBytes; x++) {
        Serial.print("Address: ");
        Serial.print(EEAddress);
        Serial.print(" = '");
        Serial.print((char)EEPROMread(EEAddress++));
        Serial.println("'");
    }
```

```
    Serial.println("------------------------------");
    Serial.println();

    // And breathe!
    delay(5000);
}
```

The `loop()` is quite simple and doesn't even flash an LED. All it has to do is read back the number of bytes of data there are in the EEPROM, then read and display each byte. The data has to be cast to a `char` for printing to the Serial Monitor as `uint8_ts` are assumed to be numeric data. After reading and displaying the EEPROM data, there is a five-second pause before the process begins again.

Now, if you compile and upload this to your Arduino, the first time, and only the first time it is run, it will indeed write the data to the EEPROM. However, EEPROM data is safe through a power-off, so when the board is next started up with the same sketch loaded, the data will not be rewritten – unless it has changed. This preserves the lifetime of the EEPROM as it is guaranteed to have a minimum of 100,000 write cycles. That's to any one address, not in total, before that address might start showing signs of "wear" – data corruption in other words.

Warning
By default, when the Arduino IDE uploads a sketch using a bootloader, it *does not* erase the EEPROM as part of the process. To this end, if you upload a new sketch, the chances are pretty high that any EEPROM data you previously wrote will still remain – beware if this is not what you expect.

There is a fuse `EESAVE` which can be used to force the EEPROM to be erased – but this will count toward your total EEPROM writes *every* time you upload a new sketch and will reduce the life of the EEPROM.

Uploading with an ICSP device, on the other hand, *will* erase the EEPROM contents when the sketch is uploaded – unless you use the appropriate command-line option for your programmer to prevent this.

Now, the sketch we've just written is one way of reading and writing from the EEPROM. There are other ways. The AVRlib, supplied with the Arduino IDE, has a number of functions to read, write, and update EEPROM data without you having to worry about setting everything up correctly.

If you want to make life easy, I advise you to look at the documentation online at www.nongnu.org/avr-libc/user-manual/group__avr__eeprom.html for the full description. There is also the built-in EEPROM library, supplied with the Arduino IDE, but for some unknown reason, that doesn't come with many good recommendations online.

Different AVR devices have different EEPROM capacities. How can you tell what size you have? In the Arduino IDE, you can do this:

```
#include <EEPROM.h> // Must be upper case.
...
if (nextWriteAddress < EEPROM.length()) {
    do_something;
}
```

`EEPROM.length()` returns the total number of bytes in the EEPROM. In the case of the ATmega328P, this returns 1024, which allows addresses from 0 to 1023 to be written and read back. There is another way that doesn't require the EEPROM library, as follows:

```
...
if (nextWriteAddress <= E2END) {
    do_something;
}
```

In this case, `E2END` is defined according to the device in use and, on an ATmega328P, returns 1023, which is the highest available address that can be written or read.

10.3   Setting Up the EEPROM Interrupt

We already know the steps involved in writing to, or reading from, the EEPROM, and we have seen it in action. However, this is a book about interrupts, so we also need to be aware of the *EEPROM Ready Interrupt Enable* bit, `EERIE`, in the `EECR` register. This bit determines if we are using an interrupt routine to read or write the EEPROM data.

> **Note**
> To be perfectly frank, using an interrupt to write or read the EEPROM data is a bit of a faff and is most useful when reading or writing fairly large blocks of data – perhaps a string – to the EEPROM. If you only need to write a couple of bytes, then polling and/or using the AVRlib functions is *probably* a much better idea, especially as you usually want the data you have requested *right now*. However, this is a book about interrupts, so...

Using the interrupt stops your code having to constantly poll the `EEPE` bit to see if it is safe to read or write a byte of data. The EEPROM Ready interrupt is triggered anytime when it and global interrupts are enabled and when the `EEPE` bit is clear. This means that anytime your ISR code is executing, the EEPROM can safely be read and/or written. The interrupt usage also stops any likelihood of a further interrupt getting in the way of the write timings and aborting the write action. Interrupts are normally disabled during an ISR.

How does the ISR know when to read and when to write? Actually, it doesn't. Your code will need to inform the ISR whether it is supposed to be reading or writing the EEPROM data.

We will now begin to create a set of EEPROM handling functions, which can be used in Arduino sketches as well as in plain AVR code, to use interrupts to control access to the EEPROM.

10.3.1 EEPROM Structures

Listings 10-6 to 10-8 are extracted from a header file we will be using. The header file is named `EEPROMinterrupt.h` and can be found in the code repository for this chapter. The listings show some enumerations and a structure which will be used to communicate with the interrupt handling code, the ISR, telling it what action it is supposed to be carrying out under interrupt control. We only have a single EEPROM interrupt – it would be nice to have a separate interrupt for *ready to read* and *ready to write*, as other features of the ATmega328P have been given.

> **Note**
>
> I could have used another circular buffer for this chapter's example code; however, as we used circular buffers with the USART interrupt code, I thought a bit of variety would do us all a power of good!

Listing 10-6 is the enumeration of various status codes for the EEPROM interrupt functions.

Listing 10-6 EEPROM functions – status codes

```
// Various status codes that apply to EEPROM actions.
enum EEPROMstatus : uint8_t {
    EEPROM_ready = 1,          // Read for action. Not busy.
    EEPROM_writing,            // Busy - writing data.
    EEPROM_reading,            // Busy - reading data.
    EEPROM_error               // Oh dear, it went belly up.
};
```

A simple enough start, we only have a few status codes. I have deliberately avoided any code having the value zero as that is the default value for an uninitialized variable. I do not want to have that sort of problem occurring – if `EEPROM_ready` was zero, then at startup a sketch could imagine that the EEPROM was ready for action when, in fact, it was completely uninitialized.

The status codes I have been working with show that the EEPROM is ready and waiting for the next action, already writing data or reading it, or an error has been detected.

Listing 10-7 defines the error codes that may arise when using the EEPROM interrupt functions.

Listing 10-7 EEPROM functions – error codes

```
// Various error codes that apply to EEPROM actions.
enum EEPROMerror : uint8_t {
    EEPROM_noError = 1,        // No errors detected.
    EEPROM_busy,               // EEPROM in use, please wait.
    EEPROM_dataSize,           // Datasize is not >= 0.
    EEPROM_addressError,       // EEPROM address > E2END.
};
```

The error codes are also brief, and none of them have the value zero for the reasons given previously. I think the error codes are pretty much self-explanatory.

Listing 10-8 describes the `EEPROMinfo_t` structure type. A variable of this type will be used in our code to hold the metadata applicable to the EEPROM and the operation currently operating upon it.

Listing 10-8 EEPROM functions – EEPROMinfo structure

```
// This structure holds information about current
// EEPROM operations. It is volatile as it will be
// updated in the ISR.
typedef struct EEPROMinfo_t {
    uint8_t *bufferAddress;      // Read/write data here.
    uint16_t dataSize;           // Bytes to read/write.
    uint16_t currentByte;        // Bytes done so far?
    uint16_t rwAddress;          // Current EEPROM address.
    EEPROMstatus status;         // Current EEPROM status.
    EEPROMerror errorCode;       // Current EEPROM error code.
    uint16_t bytesProcessed;     // Bytes written or read.
} EEPROMinfo_t;
```

In this structure, we hold all the relevant information about the current operation on the EEPROM. We have

- The start address of the buffer to be written from or read into
- How much data is to be read or written
- Which byte in the buffer is the next one to be read or written
- The EEPROM address which we will start reading or writing from
- The current status of this EEPROM operation
- Any error codes we detect in this operation
- How many bytes we have currently processed in this operation

You may think that the number of bytes processed will always, in the absence of any errors, be the same as the data size. And you would be correct, except the code to be discussed doesn't always need to write *every* byte passed over. I have written a function to update the EEPROM only when the current data byte is different from the one I'm attempting to write. If they are the same, nothing is written and the number of bytes processed is not the same as the data size in those cases.

Sometimes, it's nice to define a macro to be used instead of some potentially misunderstood code. Listing 10-9 is an example.

Listing 10-9 EEPROM functions – interrupt start/stop macros

```
// This makes things look like function calls.
#define STOP_INTERRUPT() EECR &= ~(1 << EERIE)
#define START_INTERRUPT() EECR |= (1 << EERIE)
```

These two macro definitions convert the bit twiddling in the EECR register into what look like function calls in order to avoid typing mistakes while twiddling bits[2] and so that we don't have to look up the data sheet when you next come back to amend the code.

These two macros are used in a few places in the code that is to come. I think the names I've used make their purpose pretty clear.

I mentioned earlier that the structures and enumerations were extracted from a header file. The full header is to be found in the code directory for this chapter, if you feel the urge to read further. Now we are ready to look at the functions to manipulate EEPROM data.

10.3.2 Reading EEPROM Data

The first function we will look at is the EEPROMread() function, which is shown in Listings 10-10 to 10-12. The code in Listing 10-10 carries out a few sanity checks before we get down to the hard work of setting up to read data from the EEPROM.

Listing 10-10 EEPROMread() function – sanity checks

```
EEPROMerror EEPROMread(const uint8_t *buffer,
                       const uint16_t dataSize,
                       const uint16_t readAddress,
                       const bool waitComplete) {

    // Is EEPROM busy? Return if so.
    if (EEPROMinfo.status != EEPROM_ready) {
        return EEPROM_busy;
    }

    // Anything to read?
    if (!dataSize) {
        return EEPROM_dataSize;
    }

    // EEPROM address out of range?
    if ((readAddress > E2END) ||
        (readAddress + dataSize > E2END)) {
        return EEPROM_addressError;
    }
```

The first check performed is to be sure that no other EEPROM actions are in progress. To facilitate this check, the code checks that the EEPROMinfo structure is holding a status of EEPROM_ready. If not, the EEPROM read action is aborted, and an appropriate error code, EEPROM_busy, is returned.

An additional check is made to ensure that we actually have a valid request to read some data. If we are being asked to read zero bytes, we return the EEPROM_dataSize error code and, once again, abort the EEPROM read request.

---

[2]Yes! It was for exactly that reason I created these two macros!

The final check is to ensure that we are attempting to read within the boundaries of the EEPROM on the particular AVR microcontroller we are using. The EEPROM address must be in the range of zero to whatever value is defined for E2END. This check ensures that the whole request cannot run off the end of the EEPROM address range. If the check passes, the code continues into Listing 10-11; otherwise, it returns the EEPROM_addressError error code and aborts the read.

Listing 10-11   EEPROMread() function – continued

```
    // Set busy status, copy details and start interrupts.
    EEPROMinfo.status = EEPROM_reading;
    EEPROMinfo.bufferAddress = (uint8_t *)buffer;
    EEPROMinfo.dataSize = dataSize;
    EEPROMinfo.errorCode = EEPROM_noError;
    EEPROMinfo.rwAddress = readAddress;
    EEPROMinfo.currentByte = 0;
    EEPROMinfo.bytesProcessed = 0;
    START_INTERRUPT();
```

EEPROMinfo is a global and volatile structure holding full details of the current EEPROM action which is under control of interrupts. As previously discussed, there is a single interrupt assigned to the EEPROM, so we must inform the ISR, when it is triggered, which operation it is supposed to be carrying out. The EEPROMinfo structure holds all the relevant information.

The following metadata about the EEPROM read operation is set up in the structure:

- The status is set to show that an EEPROM read action is underway.
- The starting address of the buffer where the data should be read into is assigned.
- The number of bytes to be read from the EEPROM is assigned.
- The fact that no errors have yet occurred is set up.
- The address in the EEPROM where the read should begin is copied into the structure.
- The index into the buffer is initialized to the very first byte, counting from zero of course.
- The number of bytes processed so far is initialized to zero – we haven't started yet.

And finally, the EEPROM's interrupt is started. From here on, the ISR will process the data in the EEPROMinfo structure. The EEPROMread() function however has two choices now; it can wait for the read to complete, or it can carry on and leave the ISR to complete the action in the background. Listing 10-12 shows what happens next.

Listing 10-12   EEPROMread() function – continued

```
    // Should I wait or return I wonder? Check
    // the status if waiting.
    if (waitComplete) {
        while (EEPROMinfo.status == EEPROM_reading) {
            ; // Do nothing.
        }
    }
    return EEPROM_noError;
}
```

If the calling code requested that the function wait for completion, a busy loop is entered and will exit whenever the read completes or an error occurs. The ISR, discussed later, sets the status to EEPROM_ready when it completes the read or an error occurs, in which case the error code will be stored in the EEPROMinfo structure.

The EEPROMread() function will return with no errors. It is up to the calling code to check the EEPROMinfo structure to determine the success or failure of the read action.

10.3.3 Writing EEPROM Data

The EEPROMwrite() function is used to write data to the EEPROM. Listings 10-13 and 10-14 show the function. Listing 10-13 is not the complete listing as the function executes exactly the same sanity checks as shown in Listing 10-10, and as such, they are not shown here.

Listing 10-13 EEPROMwrite() function

```
EEPROMerror EEPROMwrite(const uint8_t *buffer,
                        const uint16_t dataSize,
                        const uint16_t writeAddress,
                        bool waitComplete) {

    // Sanity checks go here
    ...

    // Set busy status, copy details and start interrupts.
    EEPROMinfo.status = EEPROM_writing;
    EEPROMinfo.bufferAddress = (uint8_t *)buffer;
    EEPROMinfo.dataSize = dataSize;
    EEPROMinfo.errorCode = EEPROM_noError;
    EEPROMinfo.rwAddress = writeAddress;
    EEPROMinfo.currentByte = 0;
    EEPROMinfo.bytesProcessed = 0;
    START_INTERRUPT();
```

The following metadata about the EEPROM write operation is set up in the EEPROMinfo structure:

- The status is set to show that an EEPROM write action is underway.
- The starting address of the buffer where the data should be written from is assigned.
- The number of bytes to be written to the EEPROM is assigned.
- The fact that no errors have yet occurred is set up.
- The address in the EEPROM where the write should begin is initialized.
- The index into the buffer is initialized to the very first byte to be written.
- The number of bytes processed so far is initialized to zero.

And finally, the EEPROM's interrupt is started. From here on, the ISR will process the data in the EEPROMinfo structure and carry out the write in the background.

The `EEPROMwrite()` function now has two choices; it can wait for the read to complete, or it can carry on leaving the ISR to complete the action in the background. Listing 10-14 shows what happens next.

Listing 10-14 EEPROMwrite() function – continued

```
    // Should I wait or return I wonder? Check
    // the status if waiting.
    if (waitComplete) {
        while (EEPROMinfo.status == EEPROM_writing) {
            ; // Do nothing.
        }
    }
    return EEPROM_noError;
}
```

If the calling code requested that the function wait for completion, a busy loop is entered which will exit whenever the write completes or an error occurs. The ISR will set the status to `EEPROM_ready` when it has finished writing all the data to the EEPROM or if an error occurs.

The `EEPROMwrite()` function will return with no errors. It is up to the calling code to check the `EEPROMinfo` structure to determine the success or failure of the write action.

10.3.4 Updating EEPROM Data

EEPROMs have a limited lifetime when being written to.[3] This also applies to the EEPROM built in to the ATmega328P, and on average, a lifetime is 100,000 write operations. The data sheet advises that this is a minimum figure, so it is entirely possible that you will occasionally get more. 100,000 write actions work out at just over 11 writes per day, to run out after a year, which may or may not be appropriate, but this depends on your application or sketch. If you need more writes, then perhaps the use of some external Flash RAM might be more appropriate than the internal EEPROM.

The good news is the lifetime applies to each EEPROM address, and if one dies, you just need to start writing elsewhere. This could be difficult, trying to remember how many times a certain address has been written – you could save the number in the EEPROM, oh hang on! That's not going to work, is it?

One method of avoiding write operations to the EEPROM is simply not to do them. Why write a value to the EEPROM address if the value you are writing is already there? Listings 10-15 to 10-17 show the code in the `EEPROMupdate()` function which attempts to only write to EEPROM addresses where the new data differs from the old.

We begin with Listing 10-15 which carries out the same sanity checks as previously discussed, and as such, they are not shown in the listing nor discussed further. You may notice in Listing 10-15 that this function doesn't have the option to wait for completion; all will be explained.

Listing 10-15 EEPROMupdate() function

```
EEPROMerror EEPROMupdate(const uint8_t *buffer,
                         const uint16_t dataSize,
```

---

[3]Have I mentioned this already?

```
                              const uint16_t writeAddress) {
    // Sanity checks go here
    ...

    // Buffer for each character read from EEPROM.
    uint8_t oneCharacter;

    // Result of the read/write.
    EEPROMerror result;

    // How many bytes did we write?
    uint16_t bytesProcessed = 0;
```

The rest of Listing 10-15 declares a number of local variables to be used to hold data read from the EEPROM, one byte at a time, any error codes detected, and the running total of the number of bytes that have actually been written because the new data value differed from the old one.

The code continues in Listing 10-16 which shows the code in the main loop.

Listing 10-16 EEPROMupdate() function – continued

```
    // Scan the write buffer and the EEPROM to match
    // characters. Only write those which differ.
    // Always waits for completion - for obvious reasons!
    for (uint16_t x = 0; x < dataSize; x++) {
        result = EEPROMread(&oneCharacter,
                            1,
                            (x + writeAddress),
                            true);

        if (result != EEPROM_noError)
            return result;

        if (oneCharacter != buffer[x]) {
            result = EEPROMwrite(&buffer[x],
                                 1,
                                 (x + writeAddress),
                                 true);

            if (result != EEPROM_noError)
                return result;

            bytesProcessed++;
        }
    }
}
```

The code in Listing 10-16 reads the EEPROM, one byte at a time, and checks the byte read against the new byte for that address. If they are the same, nothing is done. Any errors detected will abort the function with an appropriate error code.

If the byte read from the EEPROM is different from that that is requested to be written there, then the new byte is written, and, if all went well, the running total of bytes processed will be updated. As with the previous read operation, any errors will abort the function.

After all characters have been checked and written, if necessary, the code continues into Listing 10-17.

Listing 10-17 EEPROMupdate() function – continued

```
    // Fiddle in the EEPROMinfo structure to show the
    // original requested bytes and buffers etc.
    EEPROMinfo.bufferAddress = (uint8_t *)buffer;
    EEPROMinfo.dataSize = dataSize;
    EEPROMinfo.rwAddress = writeAddress;
    EEPROMinfo.currentByte = dataSize + 1;
    EEPROMinfo.bytesProcessed = bytesProcessed;
    return EEPROM_noError;
}
```

The `EEPROMinfo` structure was updated when we called `EEPROMread()` and also `EEPROMwrite()`, so the totals are no longer valid for `EEPROMupdate()`'s usage. To this end, the data in the structure are now adjusted to show the correct details for the `EEPROMupdate()` call. The function then exits with no errors.

The reason that the `EEPROMupdate()` function has no option to wait for completion is simple. It must be allowed to complete due to the need to process each byte individually first reading it and then, if necessary, writing it.

10.3.5 Initializing the EEPROM Interrupt Functions

We are nearly done. We have two more sections of code to look at, and we can write a sketch to use the interrupt powered EEPROM functions.

The first small section of code is the `EEPROMinit ()` function as displayed in Listing 10-18. This is a tiny function which needs to be called once in the setup section of your sketch or application code. It sets the `EEPROMinfo` structure to a known state, ready for use, and initializes the `EECR` register to a known state.

Listing 10-18 EEPROMinit() function

```
void EEPROMinit() {
    EEPROMinfo.status = EEPROM_ready;
    EECR = 0;
}
```

The sanity checks carried out by the previously discussed functions will not allow the code to continue if the EEPROM is not ready. On initialization or startup of your code, this is not guaranteed.

Calling `EEPROMinit()` will ensure everything is in a known state. The EEPROM environment will be set up so that

- The programming mode is set to mode 0 as described in Table 10-1, which means that when data are written to an address, existing data will be erased first, then the new data written, all in one *atomic*, or indivisible, action. This is quicker than erasing and then writing as two separate actions.
- The EEPROM interrupt is disabled. We want the appropriate function to enable the interrupt when the environment is suitably ready.
- The various bits which permit reading or writing the EEPROM data are cleared, thus disabling those functions.

10.3.6 The EE_READY Interrupt ISR

The various functions discussed in the preceding sections have actually done nothing other than set up a global structure which allows the interrupt handler, the ISR, to process the various requests. Listings 10-19 to 10-21 show the code in the ISR to handle the EEPROM interrupt.

Listing 10-19 The EE_READY ISR

```
ISR(EE_READY_vect) {
    // Out of EEPROM memory? Flag error and terminate.
    // Sets the EEPROM_ready status in case further actions
    // are required.
    if (EEPROMinfo.rwAddress > E2END) {
        STOP_INTERRUPT();
        EEPROMinfo.errorCode = EEPROM_addressError;
        EEPROMinfo.status = EEPROM_ready;
        return;
    }
```

The ISR begins, in Listing 10-19, by checking that the current address being written to, or read from, has not exceeded the end of the EEPROM built in to the AVR microcontroller. In the unlikely event that it has, the interrupt is disabled to stop any further processing, the status is set to show that the EEPROM is ready for a new operation, and the appropriate error code is saved in the `EEPROMinfo` structure for the caller to use as required.

The ISR continues with the code in Listing 10-20, if the address was within range.

Listing 10-20 The EE_READY ISR – continued

```
    // Out of data? We must be finished.
    // Set the ready status and disable the interrupt.
    if (EEPROMinfo.currentByte >= EEPROMinfo.dataSize) {
        STOP_INTERRUPT();
        EEPROMinfo.status = EEPROM_ready;
        return;
    }
```

In Listing 10-20, we can see where the ISR checks for the end of the data to be written or read. The current byte to be processed in this pass through the ISR and the number of bytes to be processed in total are both held in the global EEPROMinfo structure. These are checked, and if the operation is complete, interrupts are disabled to prevent another pass, and the status is set to show that another operation may now be initiated.

If no early exit from the ISR is required, the code continues into Listing 10-21 to do the actual reading or writing of the next byte to be processed.

Listing 10-21   The EE_READY ISR – continued

```
    // Reads and writes need the next EEPROM address
    // and byte counter.
    EEAR = EEPROMinfo.rwAddress++;
    EEPROMinfo.currentByte++;
    EEPROMinfo.bytesProcessed++;

    // Reading or Writing?
    if (EEPROMinfo.status == EEPROM_reading) {
        // Reading: copy the data from EEPROM to buffer.
        EECR |= (1 << EERE);
        *EEPROMinfo.bufferAddress++ = EEDR;
    } else {
        // Writing. copy the data to the EEPROM.
        EEDR = *EEPROMinfo.bufferAddress++;
        EECR |= (1 << EEMPE);
        EECR |= (1 << EEPE);
    }
}
```

Listing 10-21 begins by setting the EEAR register to the next EEPROM address to be read or written, followed by an update to the current byte number – the offset into the read or write buffer in the calling code – and to the number of bytes processed by the ISR so far.

At this point, the ISR has to determine if it is going to read a byte from the EEPROM or write one to it. It does this by checking the EEPROMinfo structure's status field.

If the code is requesting a read from the EEPROM, the EERE bit, the EEPROM Read Enable bit, in the EECR register is set to trigger the read, and the data byte is read from the EEDR register into the data buffer assigned for read operations; the address is then incremented to be ready for the next pass through the ISR.

If the request was for a write to the EEPROM, then the byte of data is retrieved from the buffer and the buffer address incremented. Then the timed sequence of instructions is executed to enable the write. First, the EEPROM Master Write Enable bit, EEMPE, is set, then within four clock cycles, the EEPROM Write Enable bit, EEPE, is written to trigger the write.

Previously in this chapter, when discussing the steps that must be followed when reading from, or writing to, the EEPROM, I indicated that global interrupts should be disabled while the EEMPE and EEPE bits were being written. And yet, I'm not doing that here, why not? We are within an ISR, so interrupts are *already off*. There is no need to worry about interrupts when code is executing inside an ISR.

10.3.7 The Arduino Sketch

With the interrupt EEPROM code fully discussed, we can now build an Arduino sketch that uses it to read and write from the EEPROM. The plan is to use the `setup()` function to write some data to the EEPROM and the `loop()` function to repeatedly read it back and display it on the Serial Monitor. Listings 10-22 and 10-23 show the code.

In the IDE, create a new sketch in the normal manner. Save it with a suitable name; mine is called `EEPROMinterrupt.ino`. We now need to add two extra files, the header and code files we created in the previous sections. In the code repository for this chapter, you will find them free standing in the `EEPROM` directory. You will need a separate tab for `EEPROMinterrupt.h` and another for `EEPROMinterrupt.cpp`.

The easiest way to do this is to close the IDE once you have saved the main file of the sketch. Now, with the IDE closed, copy those two files into your directory where the file `EEPROMinterrupt.ino` currently is situated. You should have three files now. The IDE can be reopened and the sketch loaded in the normal manner. You should notice that there are three separate tabs in the IDE.

We start with Listing 10-22 where the code begins just above the `setup()` function where it includes the header file `EEPROMinterrupt.h`. Including this header will allow the sketch to use the interrupt code functions described earlier in this chapter.

A macro, `EEPROM_ADDRESS`, is then defined. This is the address in the EEPROM where we wish to write data to, and read data from, later in the code.

A message is defined next. This is the data we will write into the EEPROM and read back again in the `loop()` function. There's nothing stopping us reading it back in `setup()`, but the `loop()` function would have nothing to do then!

The macro, `READ_THIS_MUCH_DATA`, is defined next. This just allows the code in the `loop()` function to determine how much data we will retrieve from the EEPROM and write to the Serial Monitor. We don't have to read all 35 bytes of the original message if we don't want to; you can change it to less if required; try nine. If you make it more, the results will be undefined, and what you see on screen might contain "garbage" characters depending on whatever data was previously in the EEPROM. Try it and see.

Finally, an array named `loopBuffer` is created with enough space to hold the amount of data we wish to read from the EEPROM plus one extra byte. The extra byte is required in case the data in the EEPROM is not zero terminated as C/C++ strings should be; this is not required when writing numeric data, for example, `unit32_t` which is four bytes of data and doesn't require a terminator.

Listing 10-22 EEPROMinterrupt sketch – setup() function

```
#include "EEPROMinterrupt.h"

#define EEPROM_ADDRESS 0
char Message[] = {"Greetings Interrupted EEPROM world!"};

#define READ_THIS_MUCH_DATA 35
char loopBuffer[READ_THIS_MUCH_DATA + 1];

void setup() {
    Serial.begin(9600);
    EEPROMinit();
```

```
    EEPROMerror result = EEPROMupdate(Message,
                                      strlen(Message),
                                      EEPROM_ADDRESS);
    if (result != EEPROM_noError) {
        Serial.print("In setup(), EEPROMupdate() error: ");
        Serial.println(result);
        // Will carry on, but results undefined.
    }

    // INSERT DEBUG CODE HERE.

    Serial.println("In the loop....");
}
```

The setup() function continues by initializing the Serial Interface and then calls the EEPROMinit() function to initialize the EEPROM environment to a known state. We can now start using our recently developed EEPROM handling functions.

EEPROMupdate() is called to write some data, our message text, into the EEPROM at the desired address. The first time this sketch is uploaded, it will probably write all 35 bytes of data to the EEPROM; subsequent runs will not need to write anything unless you have overwritten the message text somehow. I will show you how to test this later in the code, but for now, the comment about inserting debug code is the place where we will be adding some code later.

If all went well in writing to the EEPROM, we will exit the function; otherwise, a message will be written to the Serial Monitor to alert you to the fact that a problem was detected.

The loop() function is next, and the code can be seen in Listing 10-23.

Listing 10-23   EEPROMinterrupt sketch – loop() function

```
void loop() {
    loopBuffer[0] = '\0';
    EEPROMerror result = EEPROMread(loopBuffer,
                                    READ_THIS_MUCH_DATA,
                                    EEPROM_ADDRESS,
                                    false);

    // Strings must be terminated.
    loopBuffer[READ_THIS_MUCH_DATA] = '\0';
    Serial.println(loopBuffer);
    delay(1000);
}
```

The loopBuffer variable is used to hold the bytes of data read back from the EEPROM. To ensure fairness, and avoid any doubt, the string is terminated with a zero byte at the start of the buffer. This effectively clears the string.

Next, the code initializes an EEPROM read by calling the EEPROMread() function, passing the buffer start address, how many bytes to read, the EEPROM address, and a flag to say "don't wait up." With the small number of bytes we are reading, by the time that the code reaches the line after the call to EEPROMread() then the data will have been read. In this case, I have not checked on errors returned from EEPROMread(), but I should have.

Tip
If your data is longer, or your clock speed slower, you might wish to delay progress until the data have been read from the EEPROM. To do this, simply pass true to the final parameter in the call to EEPROMread(). In that case, EEPROMread() will not return until an error has occurred or all the requested data was read from the EEPROM.

After the call to EEPROMread(), the data in the buffer is terminated and displayed on the Serial Monitor. There is a one-second delay before we go around again.

10.3.7.1 Debugging the EEPROM Code

I mentioned that we could insert some code to do a little debugging, and I left some space in the setup() function to add some debugging code. I had to use this when debugging the sketch as I had made a silly mistake in EEPROMupdate() which resulted in no data being written to the EEPROM.

The first step in adding the debugging code is to enable the sketch to access the EEPROMinfo structure. Add the single line of code in Listing 10-24 underneath the existing comment in the setup() function.

Listing 10-24 EEPROMinterrupt sketch – debugging code

```
// INSERT DEBUG CODE HERE.
extern EEPROMinfo_t EEPROMinfo;
```

With this line added, our sketch can access the EEPROM environment we have been using for the interrupt handling functions and code. Now add a few more lines to the function as shown in Listing 10-25.

Listing 10-25 EEPROMinterrupt sketch – debugging code continued

```
Serial.print("CHECKING: Bytes Requested: ");
Serial.println(EEPROMinfo.dataSize);
Serial.print(" Bytes Processed: ");
Serial.println(EEPROMinfo.bytesProcessed);
```

That's it. Compile and upload the new sketch and watch the Serial Monitor. In the code in Listing 10-25, we are printing the bytes required to be written and the bytes actually written. They may be different.

If you had this code present the first time the sketch was uploaded, you would have seen 35 for both values. Press the reset button, and you will see 35 and 0 – the data did not need to be written to the EEPROM as it had not changed. This will help prolong the life of your EEPROM.

10.3.8 The AVR Application

The AVR version of the Arduino sketch obviously doesn't have the ability to use the Serial Monitor. This is not such a huge problem as we have written the code already in Chapter 8, "USART Interrupts." Listings 10-26 through 10-28 show the code from the Arduino sketch converted to plain AVR C/C++.

As an added bonus, this application uses two different sets of interrupts in the same code; we have interrupts driving the USART for the AVR equivalent of writing to the Serial Monitor and another interrupt reading and writing from the EEPROM.

Listing 10-26 shows the various headers that the AVR code must include.

Listing 10-26   EEPROMinterrupt AVR application – headers and defines

```
#include "EEPROMinterrupt.h"
#include "USARTinterrupt.h"
#include <util/delay.h>
#include <string.h>


#define EEPROM_ADDRESS (const uint16_t)0
const char Message[] = {"Greetings Interrupted AVR"
                        " EEPROM world!"};


#define READ_THIS_MUCH_DATA 40
char loopBuffer[READ_THIS_MUCH_DATA + 1];
```

Following the various headers, the EEPROM address is defined along with a message to be written to, and read from, the EEPROM. This is a slightly longer message than the Arduino sketch used, so the READ_THIS_MUCH_DATA macro and the buffer used to read the data back from the EEPROM both need to be a little bit bigger than the Arduino required.

Listing 10-27 is the setup part of the main() function and begins by initializing the interrupts for the USART and the EEPROM. Global interrupts are also enabled as AVR code doesn't do this automatically, unlike Arduino code.[4]

Listing 10-27   EEPROMinterrupt AVR application – main() function

```
int main() {

    // Setup USART for 9600 baud.
    USARTinit(9600);

    // Setup EEPROM
    EEPROMinit();

    // Don't forget interrupts!
    sei();

    EEPROMerror result;
```

---

[4]I might have mentioned this before, but I keep forgetting myself!

```
result = EEPROMupdate((const uint8_t *)Message,
                      strlen(Message),
                      EEPROM_ADDRESS);

if (result != EEPROM_noError) {
    USARTwriteText("In main(), EEPROMupdate() error: ");
    USARTwriteInt(result);
    USARTwriteText("\r\n");
    // Will carry on, but results are undefined.
}
```

Once all the interrupts are enabled, the code writes a new message into the EEPROM and checks for any errors. If there were any detected, the code writes details to the AVR's equivalent of the Serial Monitor, but carries on. The main() function continues in Listing 10-28, where we find the loop.

Listing 10-28 EEPROMinterrupt AVR application – main() function continued

```
while (1) {
    loopBuffer[0] = '\0';
    result = EEPROMread((const uint8_t *)loopBuffer,
                        READ_THIS_MUCH_DATA,
                        EEPROM_ADDRESS,
                        false);

    if (result != EEPROM_noError) {
        USARTwriteText("In main(), EEPROMread() error: ");
        USARTwriteInt(result);
        USARTwriteText("\r\n");
    }

    // Strings must be terminated.
    loopBuffer[READ_THIS_MUCH_DATA] = '\0';
    USARTwriteTextln(loopBuffer);
    _delay_ms(1000);
}
}
```

The loop part of the main() function is as simple as the Arduino version. It begins by initializing the buffer, then reading some data from the EEPROM. Unlike the Arduino sketch, the AVR code *does* check for errors when reading the data; however, it still continues even if there was an error.

The data read from the EEPROM needs to be terminated prior to being displayed by the USART.

Unlike the Arduino, there's no handy Serial Monitor to be used by PlatformIO code. To see messages, there are a number of options:

- In *VSCode*, there's an icon on the PlatformIO status bar at the bottom. It looks like a US/European power plug. Click that and the USART's output will be displayed.

- Run the command `screen /dev/ttyUSB0 9600` in a terminal session. The USART output can be seen there too. Use CTRL+A followed by "k" to kill the session.
- Use `Putty` on the command line, `putty -serial /dev/ttyUSB0 -sercfg 9600`, and again the USART output will be displayed. Close the *putty* application when you get bored of it!
- Use `CoolTerm`. Use the Connection ▷ Options ▷ Serial Port, then set the port to `/dev/ttyUSB0` and the baud rate to 9600.

10.4   Initializing EEPROM Data at Compile Time

In theory, it is possible to define data to be written to the EEPROM at upload time, as this snippet of code shows:

```
uint8_t EEMEM Hello[] = "Hello EEPROM World!";
uint8_t HelloAgain[] EEMEM = "Hello again EEPROM World!";
```

Note
Yes, the EEMEM attribute can go either before or after the variable name.

When compiled, the EEMEM attribute causes the compiler to locate the data in a separate "eep" file, ready to upload to the device. Unfortunately, at least up until Arduino IDE version 1.8.13, and also version 2.0.2,[5] the "eep" file is *never uploaded*. If you turn on verbose uploading in the IDE, you will see that the only file uploaded is the "hex" file for the sketch; the "eep" file is created but never touched afterward.

In order to initialize the EEPROM data for a sketch, there are three main options:

- Initialize the EEPROM data using the "eep" file, and manually upload it with *avrdude*.
- Use PlatformIO, or similar, to initialize and upload the EEPROM data.
- Write a separate sketch to initialize the EEPROM data, then write and upload the sketch that uses the data. If you are using an ICSP, you must configure it to avoid wiping the entire chip when uploading a sketch's code.

The following sections demonstrate three different methods.

10.4.1 Initializing the EEPROM Using Avrdude

If you *really* want to mess with *avrdude*, this sequence of steps will work for the Arduino IDE, *sort of* :

- Write the sketch with the EEMEM attributes as previously described.
- Compile the sketch.
- Upload the sketch in verbose mode. This can be set in your IDE preferences.

---

[5]This is the current release candidate for the brand-new Arduino IDE version 2.

- Capture the lines in the output where the IDE calls *avrdude* to upload the "hex" file for the sketch. It will look similar to the following but all on one line:

```
/path/to/avrdude -C/path/to/avrdude.conf
-v -V -patmega328p -carduino
-Uflash:w:/tmp/../sketch.ino.hex:i
```

- Copy that whole line, and paste into a text editor.
- Edit the command and change the word -Uflash to -Ueeprom, then change .hex:i to .eep:i, as indicated in the highlighted parts of this command:

```
/path/to/avrdude -C/path/to/avrdude.conf
-v -V -patmega328p -carduino
-Ueeprom:w:/tmp/../sketch.ino.eep:i
  ^^^^^^                        ^^^
```

- Copy the edited command and paste it into a command-line session – Windows users, do not be afraid – when you press the RETURN key, the command will be executed and the "eep" file uploaded.

I said that the code "sort of" works, which is true, but the problem is that you have to mess about in the command line with *avrdude*. The Arduino IDE doesn't have an option to upload any EEPROM data directly, plus the command line you have to use will change if you change the board or switch to using an ICSP rather than the bootloader, and so on.

Listing 10-29 shows an example of how it *should* be possible to upload EEPROM data and use the data in the sketch directly, but, unfortunately, the Arduino IDE doesn't let you *easily* upload the EEPROM data. Now, beware as this is where things get a little strange.

Uploading a sketch's code using the Arduino bootloader will not affect the contents of the EEPROM, but you cannot upload any EEPROM data, in "eep" files, using the IDE.

You have to use another method to upload the EEPROM data. If you subsequently use *avrdude* to upload the EEPROM data using the Arduino bootloader, you will see messages on screen advising you that the the data have been uploaded and verified with no errors. *This is a lie!* The EEPROM has not been changed at all. The Arduino bootloader cannot, at present, upload EEPROM data, but what it does do is to tell *avrdude* that the requested operations worked fine!

If, on the other hand, you upload a sketch's code with an ICSP device, it will, by default, erase the whole chip including the EEPROM. This will reduce the EEPROM's life span and wipe any data that you have already uploaded to the EEPROM. However, this can be easily fixed. If you are using a USBtiny device, then you need to add the -D option to the command line to upload the "hex" file to avoid wiping out the EEPROM data (and reducing the life of the EEPROM itself). How exactly would we do this? For the Arduino IDE version 1.8.13:

- Open the Arduino IDE.
- Select File->Preferences.
- Select the Settings tab.
- Scroll down, if necessary, until you see the text "More preferences can be edited directly in the file."

- Beneath that line, you will see the location of the `preferences.txt` file. Mine is located in `/home/norman/.arduino15`; make a note of the location.
- Click the filename. It should open a file explorer at the desired location.
- Very importantly, close the Arduino IDE.
- In the file explorer session, navigate to the location of the `programmers.txt` file; in my case, this was to `packages/arduino/hardware/avr/n.n.n`. The "n.n.n" part of the name is a version number which changes from time to time; mine was 1.8.5.
- Find the `program.extra_params` entry for your ICSP device; because I use a USBtiny, I need the `usbtinyisp` specific line.
- Add the `-D` option to the end of the current line. (Mine was blank.)
- Save the file and reopen the IDE. Uploading with an ICSP should now leave the EEPROM untouched.

To my mind, this should be the IDE's default option – do not wipe the whole chip when uploading a sketch. Given the limited life span of the EEPROM, it seems pointless to erase it every time a sketch is uploaded as most sketches probably don't even use the EEPROM.

For the IDE version 2.0.2, this technique will not work. The way of working with settings and so on doesn't appear to have stabilized yet. A settings file, `settings.json`, does exist in `/home/norman/.arduinoIDE`, but it only handles settings that are configurable from within the IDE, and there are only a few that can be changed. There doesn't appear to be an equivalent for the `programmers.txt` file, yet.

10.4.1.1 Example Sketch
Listing 10-29 shows a quick sketch to demonstrate how easy it *should* be to initialize the EEPROM with data, without jumping through hoops.

Listing 10-29 EEPROM_Icsp_Init sketch

```
// EEPROM_icsp_Init.
//
// A sketch to create an eep file with a single byte, to be
// uploaded to the EEPROM on an Arduino Uno. The data byte will
// be used to update a pre-initialised variable with a new
// value.
//
// The code is suitable for an Arduino or PlatformIO sketch
// -- the latter with a suitable "platformio.ini" file.
//
// The before and after values will be displayed on the Serial
// Monitor.
//
// If the after value is 255, then it didn't work (and your
// EEPROM is blank!).
//
// Norman Dunbar
// 13 March 2020.

// PlatformIO needs this for the Arduino framework
```

```
// to be used.
#include "Arduino.h"

// Interesting. This gets optimised away if it isn't marked
// used volatile etc.
uint8_t eepromDataByte __attribute__ ((used)) EEMEM = 77;

uint8_t dataByte = 2;

void setup() {
    Serial.begin(9600);

    Serial.print("Before: ");
    Serial.println(dataByte);

    dataByte = eeprom_read_byte(&eepromDataByte);

    Serial.print("After: ");
    Serial.println(dataByte);
}

void loop() {
// Nothing to see here!
}
```

Everything happens in the setup() function. The loop() is empty.

The variable eepromDataByte is initialized to the value 77 and is declared with EEMEM to place it in the EEPROM data file and __attribute__ ((used)) to avoid the "eep" file being empty because the compiler optimized eepromDataByte away as "unused." I spent quite some time wondering why I always got 255 as the "after" value – it's the value in a "blank" EEPROM cell – before I dumped out the contents of the "eep" file, to find that it was empty. You can also declare the variable to be volatile, but that's not really the best option.

The variable dataByte is initialized with the value 2, and this variable will be amended by the call to eeprom_read_byte(). The new value will be that taken from the EEPROM at the address of the eepromDataByte variable, in the EEPROM. Because eepromDataByte is the first, and only, EEPROM data variable, the address will be EEPROM address 0. The call to eeprom_read_byte() takes the address of eepromDataByte in order to read the correct byte.

You should now follow the instructions given in Section 10.4.1, "Initializing the EEPROM Using Avrdude," to locate the "eep" file and upload it to the board. The board will reset and display the value of dataByte before and after it was updated from the EEPROM data. If you see that the "after" value is 255, then your EEPROM upload didn't work, and you should investigate the output for errors.

Well, *that* was simple eh?

So, with regard to the Arduino IDE, the following summary should help:

• The IDE has no option to allow you to upload the EEPROM data for a sketch, using either the bootloader or an ICSP device.

- The command line can be used with *avrdude* to upload the sketch's EEPROM data, but only with an ICSP device, not using the bootloader. The latter will appear to have worked, but it has done nothing.
- Uploading EEPROM data with *avrdude* and an ICSP device will wipe the whole chip, including your sketch, unless the appropriate *avrdude* options for the programmer are determined and added to the `programmers.txt` file.
- Likewise, uploading a sketch with *avrdude* and an ICSP device will wipe the whole chip, including the EEPROM, unless *avrdude* options, as already explained, prevent this.

10.4.2 Initializing the EEPROM Using PlatformIO

The sketch code in Listing 10-29 can also be used, completely unchanged, in PlatformIO using the settings from Listing 10-30 in the `platformio.ini` configuration file.

Listing 10-30 EEPROM_Icsp_Init application for PlatformIO

```
[env:uno]
platform = atmelavr
board = uno
framework = arduino

; Required to use USBtiny ICSP when uploading code or EEPROM
; data.
upload_protocol = usbtiny
```

To compile, upload, and monitor the sketch, use the commands in Listing 10-31. This is for the command line, obviously. In VSCode, there are clickable options to do the same.

Listing 10-31 Compiling EEPROM_Icsp_Init

```
# Compile
pio run

# Upload sketch with USBtiny
pio run -t upload

# Upload EEPROM with USBtiny
pio run -t uploadeep

# Remove USBtiny, plug USB cable
# into Arduino UNO

# Startup Serial Monitor
pio device monitor
```

The command to upload EEPROM data with PlatformIO is `pio run -t uploadeep`, and this command actually creates the "eep" file before attempting the upload. You do of course have to have compiled the code first, to be able to generate the EEPROM data file with this command. The whole process would normally be that shown in Listing 10-31.

If you run the command in verbose mode, `pio run -t uploadeep -v`, you will see the *avrdude* command line contains the -D option to prevent wiping the whole chip before uploading.

The sketch in Listing 10-29 can be found in the PlatformIO `EEPROMupload` directory in the code on disk for this chapter.

10.4.3 Initializing the EEPROM Using a Sketch

When your sketch contains the data you wish to write into the EEPROM, then after the data has been written, it's now in the EEPROM but also is still in your Flash RAM. This can be fine, if your sketch fits nicely into the available Flash RAM; however, if you are tight for program space, this is not ideal. There are some 3D printers, running Marlin,[6] where certain functions have to be disabled in order to have enough Flash RAM for some other, more desirable, functions – you, as the 3D printer owner, have to determine which functions you need and which you have to live without.

An ideal situation would be to write the data into the EEPROM and then get rid of it from Flash RAM. This isn't really possible – SPM Assembly Language instruction nonetheless – so what can be done is write one sketch to initialize the EEPROM with the required data, then a second sketch which doesn't have to worry about holding a copy in Flash RAM and simply uses the data from EEPROM.

Listing 10-32 is a small sketch which writes a message to the EEPROM using the AVR-lib EEPROM handling functions. As the code uses `eeprom_update_block()` instead of `eeprom_write_block()`, it only writes the data if it has changed. The `loop()` in the sketch is there to prove that the data were written correctly to the EEPROM.

Listing 10-32 EEPROMinit sketch

```
#include <avr/eeprom.h>

// Example data for the EEPROM.
uint8_t helloEEPROM[] = "Hello EEPROM World Again!";

// We need the zero terminator to be written too.
uint8_t dataSize = strlen(helloEEPROM) + 1;

void setup() {
    Serial.begin(9600);

    // Write the EEPROM data.
    Serial.println("Writing ...");
    eeprom_update_block(helloEEPROM, 0, dataSize);
    Serial.println("Done.\n");

    // Effectively deletes the data.
    helloEEPROM[0]='\0';
}
```

---

[6] https://marlinfw.org/

```
void loop() {
    // Read the data back.
    eeprom_read_block(helloEEPROM, 0, dataSize);
    Serial.print("Reading...: ");
    Serial.println((char *)helloEEPROM);
    delay(1000);
}
```

You will hopefully notice that I write one byte more than the length of the data string; this is to ensure that the (invisible) zero byte which terminates the string is also written. This means that when reading data back, it will be safely terminated without me having to remember to do so. Lazy? Me?

Once this sketch has been uploaded, it will write the required data to the EEPROM, and this can be very useful if you do not have an ICSP device to upload EEPROM data; the method explained here *can* use the Arduino bootloader.

After uploading the initialization sketch, you can write and upload the sketch that requires the EEPROM data without having to worry about using up valuable Flash RAM to hold a copy of the data. When you come to upload the latter sketch, the data already written to the EEPROM is safe and will not be overwritten if you are using the bootloader.

If you are using an ICSP device, then you must upload the sketch using the option to preserve the contents of the EEPROM from a full chip wipe; otherwise, the EEPROM data will be deleted.

10.5   Interrupt Flag

Unusually, the EEPROM Ready interrupt does not have a flag bit in any register to indicate that it has been triggered, whether or not an ISR exists for it.

10.6   Is It All Worth It?

So, that's EEPROM interrupts for you. Was it worthwhile? Some AVR Programming Notes, on the use of the EEPROM, do say that using the EEPROM interrupt is more efficient than using polling methods. I remain somewhat skeptical I have to say; however, with the code in this chapter, we now have interrupt controlled EEPROM access. If we want to use polling, we have the AVRlib functions or the EEPROM library built in to the Arduino IDE. I would even go so far as to state that the use of the EEMEM attribute is the ideal way to write data to the EEPROM, but due to the limitations of the Arduino IDE, it is not easily usable. Other IDEs, such as PlatformIO, do allow this facility to be used.

I have noticed, on the Arduino Forums, a number of postings where the EEPROM library is, apparently, not well received and not at all loved by everyone.

My own opinion is this: if possible, try to use the EEMEM attribute – at least for writing initial data to the EEPROM – which will save you having to remember where you stored the data in the EEPROM. Unfortunately, this method requires a separate upload if you are using the Arduino IDE as it cannot upload the EEPROM data.

Remember,[7] if you are using an ICSP to separately upload the EEPROM data and the sketch, your EEPROM will be wiped out on every upload – reducing its lifetime. You need to follow the

---

[7]And I might have mentioned this already!

instructions given earlier in this chapter to set up the programmer's extra command-line options to prevent a full erase of the device.

10.7 Register Summary

There are three registers used when accessing the EEPROM: the *EEPROM Address Register*, EEAR, which holds the next EEPROM address to be read from or written to; the *EEPROM Data Register*, EEDR, which holds the byte just read from the EEPROM or the byte that will be written to it; and the *EEPROM Control Register*, EECR. Only the latter is involved in the use of the *EEPROM Ready* interrupt, and only those relevant bits will be discussed here.

See the data sheet for details of the other registers and the relevant bits, if necessary.

7	6	5	4	3	2	1	0
N/A	N/A	N/A	N/A	EERIE	N/A	EEPE	N/A

EERIE   Setting this bit enables the *EEPROM Ready* interrupt. An interrupt will be triggered each time that the EEPE bit is cleared.

EEPE   This bit is cleared by the hardware whenever it is safe to carry out a new read or write access to the EEPROM.

10.8 Key Takeaways

In this chapter, we learned that

- Reading and writing data to and from the EEPROM is not difficult whether or not our code is using interrupts.
- The EEPROM access procedures should consider whether the Flash RAM is being written to at the same time and must not attempt to write the EEPROM and Flash RAM concurrently.
- There is a timed instruction sequence required to write to the EEPROM, but this is not required to read from it.
- After a write to the EEPROM has taken place, the main CPU is halted for two clock cycles before the next instruction can be executed.
- After a read from the EEPROM has taken place, the main CPU is halted for four clock cycles before the next instruction can be executed.
- We should bear in mind that the EEPROM has a limited life span as far as write operations are concerned. It is worth considering that our code should only write to the EEPROM if the data byte we wish to write is different from that currently stored in the EEPROM. This will extend the life of the device.
- The Arduino IDE cannot, currently, upload data to the EEPROM. The EEPROM data must be uploaded by a manual process.
- By default, the Arduino IDE will not erase the EEPROM when uploading a sketch using the bootloader. It *will* erase it if an ICSP is being used, unless the configuration has been changed to prevent this.

10.9   Coming Up

That's the EEPROM dealt with. The next chapter takes a close look at the ATmega328P's Analog Comparator – a device that compares voltages on two pins and triggers an interrupt when the voltages differ in some way.

Analog Comparator Interrupt

11

This chapter takes a look at the Analog Comparator's single interrupt. I think this is my favorite feature of the ATmega328P, and I will use it later on in this book when I give an example of a real-world application using interrupts. I have yet to see any articles or projects which make use of this interesting feature.

This chapter will explain how you can get to grips with this much underused hardware device and its interrupt of course.

11.1   Let's Compare Voltages

The Analog Comparator interrupt has the Vector 23 slot in the Interrupt Vector Table.

The ATmega328P has an internal component named the *Analog Comparator* (AC). When enabled, all it does is to compare the voltages on its positive and negative input pins, with respect to GND.

If the positive input voltage is higher than the negative input, then the ACO (that's a letter O, for Output, not a digit zero) bit in the *Analog Comparator Control and Status Register*, ACSR, will be set to 1.

If, on the other hand, the voltage on the positive input is equal or lower to that on the negative input, then the ACO bit will be cleared to 0.

The positive input pin is named AIN0 and is Arduino pin D6, and this can be configured to read a reference voltage from

- An internal 1.1 V bandgap reference voltage
- An external voltage on pin AIN0

The negative input is AIN1 which is Arduino pin D7; however, this can be configured to be one of the ATmega328P's Analog-to-Digital Converter (ADC) input pins PC0 through PC5 which correspond to the Arduino pins A0 through A5.[1]

---

[1]On the ATmega328P in its 28 pin dual in line package, it is pins A0 through A5. If your Arduino board has a surface mount ATmega328AU package, then you can also use Arduino pins A6 and A7 – if those are connected to a header somewhere on the board. Some Uno clones, mine included, have this feature.

© The Author(s), under exclusive license to APress Media, LLC, part of Springer Nature 2024
N. Dunbar, *Arduino Interrupts*, Maker Innovations Series,
https://doi.org/10.1007/978-1-4842-9714-8_11

As well as setting or clearing the ACO bit, an interrupt can be configured to trigger when

- ACO is rising from low to high.
- ACO is falling from high to low.
- ACO is toggling from low to high or from high to low.

Note
Your code should not attempt to write a value to the ACO bit as it is read-only, and the write will not have any effect.

The ACO bit can also be used to trigger Timer/counter 1's *Input Capture Unit* (ICU). The Input Capture Unit has been described previously, in Section 6.5, "Input Capture Event Interrupt," in Chapter 6, "Timer/Counter Interrupts." Later on in this chapter, we will see how to connect the Analog Comparator to the Input Capture Unit.

11.2   Analog Comparator Setup

The Analog Comparator is quite easily set up in code by following these steps:

- Disable all interrupts for the Analog Comparator.
- Enable the Analog Comparator by disabling its disable bit.[2]
- Disable digital I/O on the AIN0 and AIN1 pins, D6 and D7 on an Arduino.
- Configure the positive input voltage source for AIN0 to either the internal bandgap reference or an external voltage on pin AIN0 itself.
- Configure the negative input voltage source for AIN1 to either pin AIN1 itself or any of the six (or eight) ADC input pins.
- Configure when we want the Analog Comparator interrupt to trigger by configuring bits ACIS0 and ACIS1 in the ACSR register.
- Clear the Analog Comparator interrupt flag bit, ACI in the ACSR register.
- Enable the Analog Comparator interrupt.

The steps listed assume that global interrupts are, of course, enabled.

For the remainder of this chapter, I shall ignore the use of the ADC pins as negative inputs to the Analog Comparator and concentrate only on the AIN1 pin itself. If you wish to dig deeper into the Analog Comparator, then my book *Arduino Software Internals* covers the matter in some depth.

The setupComparator() function (see Listing 11-1) is a good starting point when configuring the Analog Comparator for use in either an AVR C++ application or an Arduino Sketch.

Listing 11-1   The setupComparator() function

```
//============================================================
// This function initialises the analog comparator with pin
// AIN0/D6 as the reference voltage and AIN1/D7 (-ve input)
// as the voltage to be compared with AIN0/D6 (+ve input).
```

---

[2]Yes, that's what we do; we have to disable the Analog Comparator's disable bit!

```
//
// When AIN0/D6 is higher than AIN1/D7 then the ACO bit
// will be set and this will trigger the interrupt.
//
// This function sets up the comparator to fire an interrupt
// each time the ACO bit toggles. It doesn't consider the
// use of the internal bandgap voltage, or any of the ADC
// input pins either.
//=============================================================

void setupComparator() {

    // Disable AC interrupts.
    ACSR &= ~(1 << ACIE);

    // Enable AC by disabling the AC Disable bit!
    ACSR &= ~(1 << ACD);

    // Disable digital I/O on D6 and D7.
    DIDR1 |= ((1 << AIN0D) | (1 << AIN1D));

    // D6 will be the reference voltage.
    ACSR &= ~(1 << ACBG);

    // D7 to compare with D6.
    ADCSRB &= ~(1 << ACME);

    // Fire AC interrupt on ACO toggle.
    ACSR &= ~((1 << ACIS1) | (1 << ACIS0));

    // Clear AC Interrupt flag.
    ACSR |= (1 << ACI);

    // Enable AC Interrupt.
    ACSR |= (1 << ACIE);
}
```

The function follows the steps outlined previously to configure the Analog Comparator to use the voltage on pin AIN0/D6 as the reference and to compare it with the voltage on pin AIN1/D7. The interrupt will trigger whenever the ACO bit toggles.

The setupComparator() function can be used in Arduino or AVR C++ code.

The two bits ACIS0 and ACIS1, in the ACSR register, control the Analog Comparator's interrupt trigger conditions. Table 11-1 shows the four different settings that are possible for these two bits.

Table 11-1 Analog Comparator interrupt trigger settings

ACIS1	ACIS0	Interrupt triggers
0	0	Whenever ACO toggles
0	1	Reserved – Do not use
1	0	Whenever ACO is falling
1	1	Whenever ACO is rising

11.3   Setting Up Arduino Interrupts

As with many interrupts, the Arduino Language does not facilitate the easy setup of this interrupt for use in your code. There are no functions, or indeed libraries, that I am aware of which allow the use of the Analog Comparator in an Arduino sketch. To this end, an Arduino sketch which requires to use the Analog Comparator and its interrupt will require the use of the setupComparator() in Listing 11-1 and also a suitable ISR to handle the interrupt.

The Arduino sketch, in Listings 11-2 through 11-4, sets up pin D6 with a reference voltage of 3.3 V from the Arduino board's own voltage regulator. Pin D7 is connected to the middle pin of a 10 KΩ potentiometer – but any reasonable value can be safely used – and the voltage on this pin will be compared with the voltage on pin D6. As long as D6 is at a higher voltage than D7, the LED will light; it will extinguish if the 3.3 V on pin D6 is lower, or equal, to the voltage from the potentiometer on pin D7.

Figure 11-1 shows the breadboard layout for the circuit which will be used for the Arduino sketch and also the AVR application in the next section.

The setupComparator() function, in Listing 11-1, is used unchanged and is not shown in the listings. However, it can be found between the ISR and the setup() function in the actual sketch on disk.

Listing 11-2 AnalogComparator sketch – ISR

```
// ==============================================================
// The ISR simply sets pin D8 HIGH or LOW according to the
// ACO bit in the ACSR register. The !! is sneaky as it will
// return 1 if the bit is 1 and 0 if the bit is 0. 1 and 0
// correspond to HIGH and LOW so the LED takes on the correct
// state.
//==============================================================
ISR(ANALOG_COMP_vect) {
    // Read the ACO bit and if on, light the LED on D8.
    // otherwise, extinguish it.
    digitalWrite(8, !!(ACSR & (1 << ACO)));
}
```

The ISR, in Listing 11-2, in keeping with best advice, keeps things short and simply extracts the eight-bit value from the ACSR register; this will be either 0 or 2^5 (32) depending on whether the ACO bit is set, then we "not not" the value to get a 0 or a 1. That final value is then used to set the LED's state.

As the D6 pin is tied to the Arduino's 3.3 V line, the LED will remain on for as long as the voltage output by the potentiometer is lower than 3.3 V – as soon as it rises to, or above, 3.3 V, the LED will extinguish.

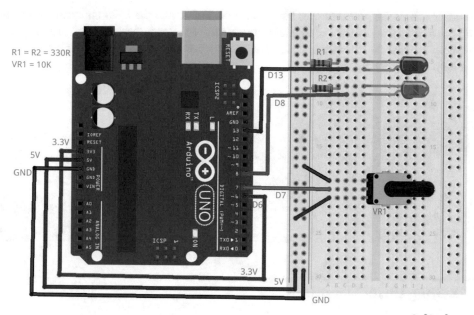

Figure 11-1 AnalogComparator breadboard layout

Listing 11-3 AnalogComparator sketch – setup() function

```
void setup() {
    setupComparator();
    pinMode(LED_BUILTIN, OUTPUT);
    pinMode(8, OUTPUT);
}
```

The setup() function sets the comparator up as previously described and makes sure that the built-in LED and pin D8 are defined as outputs. There's no need to define pins D6 and D7 as they are disconnected from digital I/O by the setupComparator() function.

Listing 11-4 AnalogComparator sketch – loop() function

```
void loop() {
    // Flash the built in LED every 5 seconds.
    digitalWrite(LED_BUILTIN, HIGH);
    delay(5000);
    digitalWrite(LED_BUILTIN, LOW);
    delay(5000);
}
```

And finally, the loop() function is doing the usual "work" of flashing the built-in LED every five seconds.

In operation, turn the potentiometer back and forth and watch the LED attached to pin D8 light and extinguish as appropriate and completely separate from the main flashing sequence of the built-in LED. You can see that the interrupt code is always executed immediately and doesn't have to wait for the main loop to stop calling delay().

> **Note**
>
> Interestingly enough, I noticed that you can set the potentiometer to a position where the LED on D8 will come on at exactly the same time as the built-in LED. I can't measure the voltages accurately or quickly enough, but I suspect that when the built-in LED is enabled, there's enough of a fluctuation of the voltage on pin D7 or pin D6, which is causing the ACO bit to be toggled, thus lighting or extinguishing the LED.
>
> Moving the potentiometer ever so slightly away from that particular setting stops this from happening.

11.4   Setting Up AVR Interrupts

Most of the work involved in setting up the Analog Comparator to fire interrupts is already done in the setupComparator() function shown in Listing 11-1 – if you need the interrupt to fire when the ACO bit toggles of course.

I leave it as an exercise for the reader[3] to amend the setupComparator() function so that it takes a couple of parameters to indicate whether the interrupt should be enabled and to indicate which stimulus will trigger the interrupt, even if not enabled.

Listings 11-5 and 11-6 are the AVR version of the Arduino sketch to show how the Analog Comparator is used. It will be using exactly the same breadboard layout as shown in Figure 11-1.

The setupComparator() function (see Listing 11-1) is used, unchanged, and as such is not shown in the listings; however, it can be found just after the ISR in the actual source file on disk.

Listing 11-5 AnalogComparator AVR application – ISR

```
#include "avr/io.h"
#include "avr/interrupt.h"
#include "util/delay.h"


// =============================================================
// The ISR simply sets pin D8 HIGH or LOW according to the
// ACO bit in the ACSR register.
//=============================================================
ISR(ANALOG_COMP_vect) {
    // Read the ACO bit and if on, light the LED on PB0
    // otherwise, extinguish it.
    if (ACSR & (1 << ACO)) {
        PORTB |= (1 << PORTB0);
    } else {
```

---

[3]This is something that authors normally say when something is either too difficult, too simple, or they just can't be bothered. None of this is the case here of course!

```
            PORTB &= ~(1 << PORTB0);
    }
}
```

Nothing much of interest here to be honest; the ACO bit is checked, and bit PORTB0 in the PORTB register is set or cleared accordingly to turn pin PB0 high or low. This corresponds to the Arduino pin D8.

As the AIN0 pin is tied to the Arduino board's 3.3 V line, the LED will remain on for as long as the voltage output by the potentiometer is lower than 3.3 V – as soon as it rises to, or above, 3.3 V, the LED will extinguish.

The setupComparator() function will be found after the code in Listing 11-5 – but is not shown here. Listing 11-6 is the main() function which encapsulates the setup and main loop of the code.

Listing 11-6 AnalogComparator AVR application – main() function

```
int main() {

    // Setup:
    setupComparator();
    sei();

    // PB5 = LED_BUILTIN, PB0 = D8.
    DDRB = ((1 << DDB5) | (1 << DDB0));

    // Loop:
    while (1) {
        // Flash the built in LED every 5 seconds.
        PINB |= (1 << PORTB5);
        _delay_ms(5000);
    }
}
```

The setup part of the main() function sets the comparator up as previously described and makes sure that the built-in LEDs on pin PB5 and pin PB0 are defined as outputs. There's no need to define pins AIN0 and AIN1 as they are disconnected from digital I/O by the setupComparator() function.

It is, however, very much necessary to enable global interrupts with the sei() function call. If you forget this simple matter, then you might spend some time wondering why the ISR is not executing and the LED is not lighting up. I always forget.

The loop part of the main() function just flashes the built-in LED on PB5 every five seconds as a pretense that the device is actually doing some work!

As with the Arduino sketch, turning the potentiometer back and forth will – at some point – cause the Analog Comparator to toggle its output, and the ISR will execute and turn the LED attached to pin PB0 on and off as appropriate.

11.5   The Analog Comparator Interrupt Flag

The Analog Comparator, like many other interrupts, has a flag to tell your code whether the interrupt was triggered or not. It is the `ACI` bit in the `ACSR` register. It will be set to a 1 any time that the interrupt is triggered and will remain set until cleared. The bit will be cleared by code writing a 1 to it – yes, I know – or by the ISR executing, when the hardware will clear the flag bit automatically.

The `ACI` bit must also be cleared when setting up the Analog Comparator – as has been done in the `setupComparator()` function shown in Listing 11-1. This will prevent the Analog Comparator's ISR from executing if the flag bit happens to be set when interrupts are enabled.

If you have interrupts disabled, the flag bit will still be set if the conditions are right for the interrupt to be triggered – had they been enabled. Given that most registers default to the value 0 when the device is started up, this would mean that even with the Analog Comparator not configured, the `ACSR` register would be all zero bits, which would configure the following:

- Bit 7, the `ACD` bit being clear would mean that the Analog Comparator is powered on.
- Bit 6, the `ACBG` bit being clear would select `AIN0/D6` as the positive input.
- Bit 5, the `ACO` bit being clear would show no output yet from the Analog Comparator.
- Bit 4, the `ACI` bit being clear would show that no interrupts have occurred yet.
- Bit 3, the `ACIE` bit being clear would show that the *Analog Comparator* interrupt is not enabled.
- Bit 2, the `ACIC` bit being clear would disable the connection between the Analog Comparator and Timer/counter 1's *Input Capture Unit*.
- Bits 1 and 0, the `ACIS1` and `ACIS0` bits, being clear would configure the interrupt to trigger when the `ACO` bit toggles.

In theory then, given the same circuit setup as in Figure 11-1, should we see that the `ACO` bit toggles even in a sketch with absolutely no setup of the Analog Comparator itself? Listing 11-7 is a sketch that shows whether we do or not.

Listing 11-7 ACResetState sketch

```
void setup() {
    Serial.begin(9600);
}

void loop() {
    Serial.print("ACO = ");
    Serial.println(!!(ACSR & (1 << ACO)));

    // Clear the interrupt flag.
    ACSR |= (1 << ACI);
}
```

Upload this to your Arduino and see what you get reported back in the Serial Monitor as you turn the potentiometer back and forth. It proves that the ATmega328P will record the appropriate stimulus even with no configuration. In addition, if the ATmega328P was put to sleep in idle sleep mode (see Appendix B, "Sleep Modes," for sleep mode details), then twiddling the potentiometer knob would wake the device from that particular sleep mode. It wouldn't have any effect on the other sleep modes however, plus, the Arduino software is configured to trigger an interrupt roughly every millisecond, which will wake the board from any sleep mode.

11.6 Arduino Analog Comparator and Input Capture Unit

I mentioned previously that the Analog Comparator could direct its ACO bit to the *Input Capture Unit* (ICU). To do this, we must configure the Analog Comparator with the ACIC bit in the ADSR register set to 1. This links the ACO bit directly to the Input Capture Unit's input circuitry and causes the Input Capture Unit to register an event when the ACO bit shows the required stimulus – a RISING or FALLING edge. The Analog Comparator itself can use its own interrupt for any other suitable purpose, even with ACO connected to the Input Capture Unit.

For the demonstration sketch, we will toggle an LED attached to pin D9 when the ACO bit toggles. When the ACO is set, the LED will be lit, and it will be extinguished when ACO is clear.

The ACO bit will also be connected to the Input Capture Unit, and we will configure that to toggle another LED on pin D8 when the Input Capture Unit sees a FALLING edge. This means that when ACO goes from 1 to 0, the second LED will toggle. In effect, we are turning two LEDs on and off by turning a potentiometer.

Figure 11-2 is the breadboard layout, and you can see that I've only added an additional LED and resistor to the circuit in Figure 11-1.

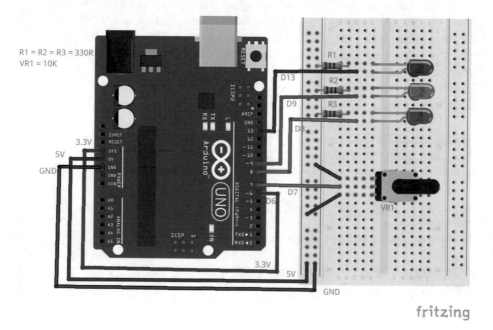

Figure 11-2 Timer1AnalogCompICU breadboard

When the potentiometer is turned and causes the Analog Comparator to toggle its ACO bit, the Analog Comparator interrupt will trigger, and the LED attached to pin D8 will follow the value in the ACO bit – it will be on when the bit is set and off when the bit is clear. The ACO bit is also connected to the Input Capture Unit input, which will cause the Input Capture Unit to register an event and the Input Capture Unit interrupt to trigger when the ACO bit changes from 1 to 0; this will cause the LED on pin D9 to toggle. The Analog Comparator is now controlling two separate LEDs.

In testing, I noticed that there is a bit of "bounce" from my potentiometer – it's well used! The ACO bit flickers occasionally between 1 and 0 a few times as the potentiometer "crackles."

I checked with the Serial Monitor and a couple of debugging Serial.println() lines in the sketch and found that ACO was indeed flickering between 1 and 0 at a certain setting of the potentiometer. The Input Capture Unit obviously noticed this flickering and toggled its LED accordingly. This is especially noticeable if I turn the potentiometer very slowly past the point where the voltage output from it is around the 3.3 V mark.

Listings 11-8 through 11-10 show the various functions in the Arduino sketch in which we connect the Analog Comparator to the Input Capture Unit and control two different LEDs with the Analog Comparator. Listing 11-8 shows all the setup that is required.

The function setupComparator() is mostly unchanged from Listing 11-1 and so is not shown in full; however, the one line that was changed is shown. The only change is to enable the link to the Input Capture Unit by setting bit ACIC in the ACSR register.

The function enableTimer1ICU() is completely unchanged from that in Listing 6-15 in Chapter 6, "Timer/Counter Interrupts," and so is not shown in the listings. When using the Analog Comparator as the Input Capture Unit's input, you only have to configure the Analog Comparator differently, not the Input Capture Unit.

Listing 11-8 Timer1AnalogCompICU sketch – setup() function

```
//===============================================================
// A sketch to use the Analog Comparator, connected to the
// Timer/counter1 Input Capture Unit, to light one LED on
// D8 when the ACO toggles, plus, gets the ICU Interrupt to
// turn on another LED on D9 when it sees a FALLING edge
// from the ACO bit.
// The main loop spends all its time flashing the built in
// LED on a 5 second delay.
//
// Norman Dunbar.
// 27th February 2020.
//===============================================================


void setupComparator() {
    // Mostly unchanged from original in text.
    ....
    // Enable the AC Interrupt and the ICU link.
    ACSR |= ((1 << ACIE) | (1 << ACIC));
}


void enableTimer1ICU() {
    // Unchanged from original described in text.
    ....
}

void setup() {
    pinMode(LED_BUILTIN, OUTPUT);
    pinMode(8, OUTPUT);
    pinMode(9, OUTPUT);
    setupComparator();
```

```
        enableTimer1ICU();
}
```

In this version of the `setup()` function, pins D8, D9, and D13 are all output pins – we are not using a switch to cause an Input Capture Unit event in this sketch, we are using the Analog Comparator. We also make a call from `setup()` to `setupComparator()` and `enableTimer1ICU()` to initialize the Analog Comparator and the Input Capture Unit as required.

Listing 11-9 shows the two ISRs we require for this sketch. The first is the Analog Comparator interrupt handler, which uses Arduino Language functions to toggle the LED on pin D8 every time that the `ACO` bit itself toggles.

The second ISR is for the Input Capture Unit interrupt, which will trigger each time that the Input Capture Unit registers a `FALLING` edge on its input. In this case, the input is the `ACO` bit. This ISR uses AVR code to toggle its LED on pin D9.

Listing 11-9 Timer1AnalogCompICU sketch – ISR

```
// ============================================================
// The ISR simply sets pin D8 HIGH or LOW according to the
// ACO bit in the ACSR register.
//=============================================================
ISR(ANALOG_COMP_vect) {
    // Read the ACO bit and if on, light the LED on D8.
    // otherwise, extinguish it.
    digitalWrite(8, !!(ACSR & (1 << ACO)));
}



//=============================================================
// Toggle D9 every time a FALLING ACO event is seen by the ICU.
//=============================================================
ISR(TIMER1_CAPT_vect) {
    // Toggle pin D9 (PB1) every interrupt.
    PINB |= (1 << PINB1);
}
```

You may once again recognize the code in Listing 11-10 as it's the same old `loop()` function which flashes the built-in LED every five seconds over and over again!

Listing 11-10 Timer1AnalogCompICU sketch – loop() function

```
void loop() {
    // Flash the built in LED every 5 seconds.
    digitalWrite(LED_BUILTIN, HIGH);
    delay(5000);
    digitalWrite(LED_BUILTIN, LOW);
    delay(5000);
}
```

When this sketch has been uploaded to your Arduino, it will allow you to turn the LEDs on and off with the potentiometer; all the while the built-in LED is taking up all of the main CPU's time, flashing and delaying.

11.7   AVR Analog Comparator and Input Capture Unit

Listings 11-11 to 11-14 are the AVR equivalent of the `Timer1AnalogCompICU.ino` sketch in the previous section. The application begins with Listing 11-11 detailing the three header files that are pretty much always required when programming for the AVR using interrupts.

Listing 11-11   Timer1AnalogCompICU – AVR application – included files

```
//==============================================================
// A sketch to use the Analog Comparator, connected to the
// Timer/counter1 Input Capture Unit, to light one LED on
// PB0 when the ACO toggles, plus, gets the ICU Interrupt to
// turn on another LED on PB1 when it sees a FALLING edge
// from the ACO bit.
// The main loop spends all its time flashing the built in
// LED on a 5 second delay.
//
// Norman Dunbar.
// 27th February 2020.
//==============================================================


#include "avr/io.h"
#include "avr/interrupt.h"
#include "util/delay.h"
```

Following on is Listing 11-12, showing the two ISRs. The first ISR is triggered when the `ACO` bit changes in any way. That change causes the LED attached to pin `PB0` to be set according to the setting of the `ACO` bit – the LED will be on when `ACO` is a 1 and off when it is a 0.

The second ISR is for the Input Capture Unit interrupt and is triggered only when the `ACO` bit is changing from a 1 to a 0, a `FALLING` edge in other words. This causes the LED on pin `PB1` to be toggled.

Listing 11-12   Timer1AnalogCompICU – AVR application – ISR

```
// ================================================================
// The ISR simply sets pin PB0 HIGH or LOW according to the
// ACO bit in the ACSR register.
//================================================================
ISR(ANALOG_COMP_vect) {
    // Read the ACO bit and if on, light the LED on PB0.
    // otherwise, extinguish it.
    if (ACSR & (1 << ACO)) {
        PORTB |= (1 << PORTB0);
```

```
        } else {
            PORTB &= ~(1 << PORTB0);
        }
}


//================================================================
// Toggle PB1 when a FALLING ACO event is seen by the ICU.
//================================================================
ISR(TIMER1_CAPT_vect) {
    // Toggle pin D9 (PB1) every interrupt.
    PINB |= (1 << PINB1);
}
```

The `setupComparator()` and `enableTimer1ICU()` functions in Listing 11-13 are *mostly* identical to those listed in the text elsewhere. The only change required is in the `setupComparator()` function, to write a 1 to the `ACIC` bit in the `ACSR` register to connect the `ACO` bit to the Input Capture Unit input. The `enableTimer1ICU()` function remains as per the text.

Listing 11-13 Timer1AnalogCompICU – AVR application – setup functions

```
//================================================================
// This function sets up the comparator to fire an interrupt
// each time the ACO bit toggles. It doesn't consider the
// use of the internal bandgap voltage, or any of the ADC
// input pins either.
//================================================================

void setupComparator() {
    // Mostly unchanged from the text.
    ...

    // Enable AC Interrupt and ICU input.
    ACSR |= ((1 << ACIE) | (1 << ACIC));
}


void enableTimer1ICU() {
    // Unchanged from the text.
    ....
}
```

Listing 11-14 is the `main()` function where we carry out all the required setup and then enter into the, by now, almost obligatory, loop to flash the built-in LED, PB5, every five seconds.

Listing 11-14   Timer1AnalogCompICU – AVR application – main() function

```
int main() {

    // Setup:
    setupComparator();
    enableTimer1ICU();
    sei();

    // PB5 = LED_BUILTIN, PB0 = D8, PB1 = D9.
    DDRB = ((1 << DDB5) | (1 << DDB0) | (1 << DDB1));

    // Loop:
    while (1) {
        // Flash the built in LED every 5 seconds.
        PINB |= (1 << PORTB5);
        _delay_ms(5000);
    }
}
```

In practice, this code suffers from the same flickering problem as the Arduino sketch does, which is understandable with such a noisy potentiometer. I know we can use code, an R/C filter, or a dedicated chip to debounce a *switch*, but how do you debounce a potentiometer I wonder!

11.8   Register Summary

The Analog Comparator has a single register for its control and status. This register contains six bits which are of interest when using interrupts. Those bits are described next; however, you should refer to the data sheet if you require to investigate the other bits and how they can be used.

The *Analog Comparator Control and Status Register,* ACSR, has the following bits relevant to interrupts:

7	6	5	4	3	2	1	0
N/A	N/A	ACO	ACI	ACIE	ACIC	ACIS1	ACIS0
9							

ACO   This bit toggles with the Analog Comparator output. When the voltage on the positive input is higher than the voltage on the negative input, the bit is 1; otherwise, it is a 0.

ACI   This is the Analog Comparator's interrupt flag bit. When the Analog Comparator's output matches the stimulus configured by bits ACIS1 and ACIS0, this bit will be set to 1. It is automatically cleared if an ISR is in use; otherwise, the application code must clear the bit.

ACIE   Setting this bit to a 1 will enable the *Analog Comparator* interrupt.

ACIC   Setting this bit to a 1 will enable Timer/counter 1's Input Capture Unit to be triggered by the Analog Comparator. Bit ACO is effectively connected to the Input Capture Unit.

ACIS1   This bit and ACIS0 define the triggering stimulus for the *Analog Comparator* interrupt. Table 11-1 has the full details of the configuration.

ACIS0   This bit and `ACIS1` define the triggering stimulus for the *Analog Comparator* interrupt. Table 11-1 has the full details of the configuration.

11.9   Key Takeaways

In this chapter, we learned about the Analog Comparator; specifically, we learned

- How to configure the Analog Comparator to use the interrupt to toggle an LED when the comparator output bit changed.
- How to attach the Analog Comparator's interrupt to the Input Capture Unit of Timer/counter 1.
- That there are three different stimuli which will trigger the *Analog Comparator* interrupt.
- How to access the features of the Analog Comparator from an Arduino sketch.

11.10   Coming Up

The next chapter covers the *Two-Wire Interface* interrupt. TWI is a name that Atmel gave the feature originally because the Philips company had exclusive rights to the I²C name. They are both the same thing though. It's another form of serial communications but designed originally to allow the chips in Philips TVs to communicate with each other.

The amount of work that the *Two-Wire Interface* interrupt will have to carry out on each interrupt does rather negate the rule to keep ISR code to a minimum. Read on for all the gory details!

TWI Interrupt

12

In this chapter, we will delve deep into the world of I^2C, also known as the Two-Wire Interface, TWI, in the Arduino world. This is quite a complicated system in which to use interrupts, but it can be done. This chapter starts easily with a discussion on device addresses – which occasionally can lead to confusion – followed by a simple polled example. This is then expanded to create a sketch using TWI to read and write from and to a temperature sensor before fully expanding our discussion to implement, with a little help from Chris Herring, a full TWI interrupt-driven library.

Normally, code in an interrupt handling routine should be kept as small as possible. TWI only has a single interrupt, so a fully implemented TWI library has a lot of code in the handler, as you will see.

12.1   TWI Also Known As I^2C

The TWI interrupt is located in Vector 24 in the Interrupt Vector Table.

The *Two-Wire Interface* or TWI feature of the ATmega328P is a hardware implementation of what was once trademarked by Philips, and is now owned by NXP Semiconductor, as the I^2C or Inter-Integrated Circuit serial bus. It is currently known by many names to avoid infringing the trademark. You may see I^2C, I2C, IIC, and, on the Arduino, Wire, after the library that is used to access the feature. I shall be referring to the feature as *TWI* for the rest of this chapter.

The Two-Wire Interface is a serial communications system which, according to the ATmega328P's data sheet, is ideally suited for typical microcontroller applications. The protocol allows *up to* 128 different devices to be connected together, each with a unique address, using only two bidirectional lines, one for the clock, SCL, and one for data, SDA. Additionally, it may be necessary to apply two pull-up resistors to these lines as they are designed to be high when idle.

> **Note**
> Some Arduino clones may have dedicated pin header locations for these two lines. This makes connecting devices a little easier as the headers are usually marked correctly. Those devices lacking the headers will use pins A4 for the SDA line and A5 for the SCL line.

© The Author(s), under exclusive license to APress Media, LLC, part of Springer Nature 2024
N. Dunbar, *Arduino Interrupts*, Maker Innovations Series,
https://doi.org/10.1007/978-1-4842-9714-8_12

> **Tip**
> The full I^2C specification and User Manual is available from NXP Semiconductor at www.nxp.com/docs/en/user-guide/UM10204.pdf.

12.2   Determining Device Addresses

In theory, TWI devices can have an address in the range between 0 and 127 which accounts for the 128 devices that can be connected to the bus, as previously mentioned. Unfortunately, this is not quite correct. The I^2C specification recently[1] reserved a total of 16 seven-bit addresses: 0x00 to 0x07 and 0x78 to 0x7F. These addresses are used for special purposes and should no longer be used for sensors or devices.

> **Note**
> Those reserved addresses look like eight-bit hexadecimal numbers. Beware, they are seven-bit addresses. The bit value in bit 7, zero here, is going to be obliterated when the seven-bit address is converted to eight bits as everything is shifted up one bit and the read or write bit merged into bit 0.

> **Note**
> If you see devices advertised with eight-bit addresses, they are really counting the read/write bit as part of the address.

The reservation of those 16 addresses reduces the legal range of the TWI device, seven-bit addresses, to between 8 and 119 inclusive and means a maximum of only 112 devices on the bus.

If your device or sensor has an address outside of this range, it might not work correctly.

> **Note**
> The ATmega328P's data sheet only mentions that address 0 is reserved and doesn't mention the other 15 reserved addresses.

Many sensors have configuration pads or links, so that they can be adjusted to give a different address to all the other TWI sensors on the bus. I have a pair of CJMCU-75 temperature sensors with an LM75A as the actual sensor. The LM75A is a surface mount component, so the CJMCU-75 is a breakout board to make it easier to use on breadboards and so on.

On the breakout board, I have three bits of the address that I can tie high or low by soldering those three address lines to VCC or to GND as required. The configuration changes the bit values in address bits 2, 1, and 0 of the seven-bit address. My two devices are configured as addresses 0x49 and 0x4F in hexadecimal. You cannot have more than one device with the same address on the bus.

---

[1] Well, back in, or around, the year 2000.

In use, when communicating with the sensor, the seven-bit address is shifted one bit position to the left – multiplied by two – and the now free lowest bit, bit 0, is used to indicate a read operation by setting it to 1 or a write by clearing it to 0. Using my CJMCU-75 with seven-bit address 0x49 as an example, Figure 12-1 shows the actual read address for this sensor. Figure 12-2 shows the same sensor's write address. We can now see why those sensors are advertised with *two eight-bit addresses*. My sensor will be addressed as 0x92 when writing to it and 0x93 when reading from it regardless of the fact that its seven-bit address is 0x49.

Tip
Read addresses are always *odd*, while *write* addresses are always *even*.

Bit Number	7	6	5	4	3	2	1	0
Usage	A6	A5	A4	A3	A2	A1	A0	R/W
7 bit address	1	0	0	1	0	0	1	x
Read address format	0x49							1
8 bit read address	0x93							

Figure 12-1 CJMCU-75 read address format

Bit Number	7	6	5	4	3	2	1	0
Usage	A6	A5	A4	A3	A2	A1	A0	R/W
7 bit address	1	0	0	1	0	0	1	x
Write address format	0x49							0
8 bit write address	0x92							

Figure 12-2 CJMCU-75 write address format

The read/write bit is there to inform the sensor that the controller will be reading from it or writing to it in the coming conversation.

There are many TWI scanners available on the Internet; however, if you have an Arduino, then there is one built in. In the IDE, File->Examples->Wire->i2c_scanner will load it for you. The sketch can be compiled and uploaded to a board, and if your sensors are all connected, the sketch will sit in a loop, displaying all the addresses it finds.

> **Note**
> The scanner sketch uses the Wire library, provided with the IDE, to carry out the communications. You should be aware that some older versions of this library are unable to work correctly with a number of sensors. This is because the library did not implement the sending of a "repeated start." (Repeated starts are discussed later in this chapter.)
>
> The Wire library included with the Arduino IDE version 1.0.1 onward is able to send a repeated start.

12.3   Chapter Terminology

In any TWI communication, only two devices are involved. One of these will be the *controller* and is responsible for initiating the conversation and controlling the clock line for the TWI bus. The other device is the *peripheral* and will respond to a request from the controller only if the controller has sent the peripheral's address at the beginning of the communication.

There is also a *transmitter* and a *receiver* involved, and either of the two devices can be one or the other of these, and this may change during the course of the communication. A summary of these devices is shown in Table 12-1.

Table 12-1 TWI device terminology

Term	Description
Controller	The device which initiated and controls the communication. This device controls the clock line for the bus
Sensor/peripheral	The device being addressed by the controller
Transmitter	The device which is currently transmitting data. This can obviously be the controller or the peripheral
Receiver	The device which is currently receiving data. This can obviously be the controller or the peripheral

12.4   TWI Communications Steps

As I previously mentioned, the SCL and SDA lines idle at a high state. Both lines should be pulled up by a resistor connected to VCC if the peripheral doesn't do this internally. The actual value of the pull-up resistors varies from device to device, so you should consult the data sheet for your particular device to determine the correct value. In the case of my CJMCU-75 temperature sensors, the data sheet advises a 10 KΩ resistor for each line.

The controller is in charge of communications. It is responsible for starting and stopping communications, telling the peripheral whether it wishes to read from it, write to it, and so on. The controller also generates the clock pulses on the SCL line to keep the peripheral in step. The clock is controlled by the hardware in the ATmega328P; there's no need for your own code to worry about it.

For those of us using Arduino boards where the TWI bus lines have not been broken out to separate, clearly labeled, header pins, the SCL line is on Arduino pin A5, AVR pin PC5, while the SDA line is on Arduino pin A4 which equates to the AVR pin PC4.

12.4.1 Transferring Data

The standard defines how data will be transferred over the TWI bus. Data are transmitted as eight-bit bytes with the most significant bit, bit 7, being sent first. There is no limit to the number of bytes that can be transferred. Each byte is transferred on the bus with nine clock cycles from the controller. The first eight clock cycles are for the eight bits of the data, while the ninth clock cycle allows the receiver to acknowledge the receipt of the data bits.

When transferring data, the state of the SDA line, high or low, must be stable when the clock line, SCL, is high. This is the signal for the receiver to read the state of the SDA line to determine if the current bit of the data is a 1 or a 0. There will be a clock pulse generated for each data bit transferred.

> **Note**
>
> The state of the SDA line can only be changed when the SCL line is low when sending data bits. Changing the state of the SDA line while the SCL line is high will indicate a start, repeated start, or stop condition with possible unintended results. Thankfully, the TWI hardware takes care of all this.

After every data byte (eight bits) has been transferred, with the exception of the final byte, the receiver should send an *acknowledgment* bit, ACK, to say "data byte received." The final byte of the data will have a *not-acknowledgment*, or NACK, which is the state of the line when SDA is allowed to float back up to high.

During a transfer of data, the sensor which is transmitting can pull the SCL line low and hold it there to get a bit more time, a process known as *clock stretching*. This prevents the controller from generating any more clock pulses. The data transfer will continue when the sensor releases the SCL line.

Currently, the most common devices communicate with an SCL clock speed of 100 KHz or 400 KHz, but much faster devices up to 5 MHz are becoming available. The data sheet for your device should document its maximum speed. Beware, however, some data sheets specify a maximum of 400 KHz, but speeds above 100 KHz don't appear to work. This *could* be caused by capacitance on the bus or by the pull-up resistors being the wrong value and slowing things down.

> **Note**
>
> Breadboards can have detrimental effects on high speed communications due to the stray capacitance between rows of connectors. You might find a sensor which claims to operate at 400 MHz, but on a breadboard you *may* have problems getting valid results above 100 KHz.

The value written to the *TWI Bit Rate Register*, TWBR, determines the SCL clock frequency, F_{SCL}, as per this equation:

$$F_{SCL} = \frac{F\_CPU}{(16 + (2 * TWBR) * PreScaler)}$$

The frequency is in Hertz (Hz).

The prescaler defaults to 1 and is almost invariably left at that setting as the data sheet advises. This simplifies the equation to

$$F_{SCL} = \frac{F\_CPU}{16 + (2 * TWBR)}$$

This is all very well, but given that we usually know the clock frequency and actually need the TWBR value, we have to reorganize things to get this equation instead:

$$TWBR = \frac{\left(\frac{F\_CPU}{F_{SCL}}\right) - 16}{2 * PreScaler}$$

Again, the frequency is in Hz, and as the prescaler is normally left at the default value, 1, this simplifies the equation to

$$TWBR = \frac{\left(\frac{F\_CPU}{F_{SCL}}\right) - 16}{2}$$

which can itself be simplified to a format useful for declaring a C++ macro:

$$TWBR = 0.5 * ((F\_CPU/F\_SCL) - 16)$$

If our sensor runs at 200 KHz and we are running an ATmega328P at 16 MHz with the default prescaler for the TWI clock, we get this formula:

$$TWBR = 0.5 * ((16,000,000/200,000) - 16)$$

Working all that out results in a value of 32 for the TWBR register. If we need to check our calculation result, we can feed 32 back into the formula for F_{SCL} and get this equation:

$$200,000 = \frac{16,000,000}{16 + (2 * 32)}$$

The result is indeed 200,000 Hz (or 200 KHz) and is exactly what we need.

Warning
The ATmega328P data sheet advises that the CPU frequency, F_CPU, must be *at least* 16 times higher than the freq of the TWI clock, F_{SCL}. In this example, we have F_{SCL} at 200 KHz and F_CPU at 16 MHz, which is 80 times higher. For an Arduino running at 16 MHz, the maximum TWI clock speed is limited to 1 MHz.

12.4.1.1 Starting Communications

All TWI communications begin with one device executing a start condition. In timing diagrams, this is usually denoted as a capital "S." If the device successfully transmits the start condition, then it becomes the controller for the duration of the conversation, and the bus is considered to be busy.

When the bus is busy, no other controllers should attempt to send a start condition. If one does, then bus arbitration will be initiated by the hardware.

A start condition is denoted by pulling the SDA line low, while the SCL line remains high.

When the peripherals on the bus see a start condition, they wait to see if the address that will be sent next is their own address.

A controller may need to send a repeated start if it needs to change from writing to reading, for example, and does not wish to relinquish control of the bus by sending a stop and another start. If it did this, another potential controller could grab control of the line between the stop and the start. A repeated start condition is simply another start condition, without a preceding stop, and keeps control of the bus.

12.4.1.2 Stopping Communications

All TWI communications end when the controller executes a stop condition. In timing diagrams, this is usually denoted as a capital "P." Once the device successfully transmits the stop condition, then the conversation is over and the bus will soon become free for other conversations to take place.

The bus does not immediately become free, there is a small delay, as the current controller may wish to start a new conversation; the delay allows for this to happen before any other potential controllers are able to send a start condition and take control of the bus.

A stop condition is denoted by allowing the pull-up resistors to raise the SDA line high, while the SCL line is currently pulled high.

It is an error to raise a stop condition immediately after raising a start or repeated start.

12.4.1.3 Communications Summary

- A *start* condition occurs when the SDA line is pulled low, while the SCL line remains high.
- A *stop* condition occurs when the pull-up resistors raise the SDA line high, while the SCL line is high.
- A *repeated start* condition is a new start condition being raised, by the current controller, without a preceding stop condition.
- A stop cannot immediately follow a start or repeated start.

12.4.2 Acknowledgments

When the transmitter has sent out all eight bits of a single data byte, the *receiver* is required to tell it whether or not the data byte was received correctly. It does this by sending a single 0 bit, an ACK. In order for the receiver to do this, the transmitter releases the SDA line, allowing it to float back to high while keeping the SCL line low. This allows the receiver to pull SDA low to acknowledge receipt. When the SCL line is next at a high state, the transmitter can read the state of the SDA line and determine if the byte was transferred successfully.

If the SDA line was read as high by the transmitter, that is deemed to be a not-acknowledge or NACK and indicates that the receiver didn't receive the data being transmitted. The transmitter should then decide on the correct course of action which is normally to send a stop condition or a repeated start and retry the transfer.

The I^2C User Manual states that there are five separate reasons why a NACK would be received during a conversation:

- There is no peripheral on the bus with the address sent by the transmitter immediately after raising the start condition.

- The receiver is unable to receive or transmit because it is performing some real-time function and is not ready to start communication with the controller.
- During the transfer, the receiver gets data or commands that it does not understand.
- During the transfer, the receiver cannot receive any more data bytes.
- A controller, which is receiving data, needs to signal the end of the transfer to the peripheral which is currently transmitting the data. In other words, the final byte of a data transfer is not acknowledged by the receiver.

The manual doesn't mention what application code should do in each of these circumstances; that's for the designer or developer to determine.

12.4.3 Reading Data

When the controller wishes only to read data from a device, a CJMCU-75 temperature monitor, for example, it will

- Raise a start condition to obtain control of the bus.
- Transmit the peripheral's eight-bit address with the lowest bit set to indicate a read request.
- Wait for the peripherals to acknowledge receipt of its address. If a NACK was received, the controller should send a stop condition to release the bus.
- Read all bytes of data, *except for the final byte*, from the peripheral and, for each byte received, send an ACK bit after each one received. This does imply that the controller knows how many bytes it will read. The peripheral's data sheet will have the details of how much data will be sent.
- Read the final byte of data from the peripheral but send a NACK after it. This signals the end of receipt of the data.
- Raise a stop condition on the bus.

When an LM75A temperature sensor is powered on, it initializes itself and sets the default register for read operations to be that of the temperature data register, or register zero. This makes the LM75A quite simple to use as a read-only TWI peripheral, as all the controller has to do is read the data – there's no writing to the LM75A or any other configuration required.

12.4.4 Writing Data

When the controller wishes only to write data to a device, an LCD, for example, it will

- Raise a start condition to obtain control of the bus.
- Transmit the peripheral's eight-bit address with the lowest bit clear, indicating a write operation.
- Wait for the peripheral to acknowledge receipt of its address. If a NACK was received, the controller should send a stop condition to release the bus.
- Write all but the final data byte to the peripheral and wait for it to raise an ACK on receipt of each byte.
- Write the final byte to the peripheral but will not expect, or wait for, an acknowledgement.
- Raise a stop condition on the bus which will release it.

12.4.5 Reading and Writing

Some devices, like the LM75A, power up in a default state which allows a controller to read data from it without having to configure it first. This is not the case with all peripherals.

When the controller has to write some data to the device or sensor, before it can safely read some data back from it, it will

- Raise a start condition to obtain control of the bus.
- Transmit the peripheral's eight-bit address with the lowest bit clear, indicating a write operation.
- Wait for the device or sensor to acknowledge receipt of its address. If a NACK was received, the controller should send a stop condition to release control of the bus.
- Write one or more bytes to the device or sensor, to set the required configuration of the peripheral, and wait for an ACK after each byte.
- Without sending a stop condition, raise a new start condition. This is a *repeated start*.
- Transmit the peripheral's eight-bit address with the lowest bit set to indicate a read operation.
- Wait for the peripheral to acknowledge receipt of its address. If a NACK was received, the controller should send a stop condition to release the bus.
- Read all bytes of data, *except for the final byte*, from the peripheral and, for each byte received, send an ACK after each one received.
- Read the final byte of data from the peripheral and send a NACK. This signals the end of receipt of the data.
- Raise a stop condition on the bus.

The LM75A mentioned previously has a few data registers that it can read and write. The default register is the temperature data register, which normally doesn't need configuring. If the controller wishes to read, or set, the maximum temperature before the sensor raised an alarm, for example, it would have to use these steps to configure the correct register.

Some LCD displays are similar in that they need to be configured before they can begin to be used to display any data.

12.4.6 Multicontrollers and Arbitration

I suspect that most of us are hobbyists and have a few Raspberry Pis[2] or Arduinos in use for various projects, but do we ever connect them together? It's all very well having up to eight separate LM75s in a circuit all taking temperature measurements, but what happens when you have a couple of Arduinos or Raspberry Pis in the system? Each of which is a *potential* controller of a TWI conversation.

A situation to avoid is where multiple potential controllers attempt to take control of the bus at the same time. The TWI system caters for this with a feature called *arbitration*. In arbitration, the hardware in all controllers attempting to control the bus will synchronize their clock pulses and then monitor the SDA line. The first controller to transmit a 1 bit on the bus loses the battle and must relinquish control. This will continue until only one controller remains in charge of the bus.

The winning controller, the one which did not send a 1 bit, will carry on as if nothing had happened and doesn't need to worry about its data transfer being corrupted by the other controllers attempting to take control of the bus.

---

[2]What exactly *is* the plural of Raspberry Pi?

The I^{2}C User Manual goes into more detail than I have, but this is a book about interrupts as opposed to the fiddly bits of the I^{2}C interface!

12.5   A Read-Only Polled Example

The simplest TWI usage is when a peripheral is being read with no configuration or writing required. The LM75A is an ideal subject for this. On power-on, it defaults to allowing read access to the temperature data register without any further configuration. Listings 12-1 through 12-4 show the code for a small Arduino sketch named `TWI_Read.ino`, which can be used to read an LM75A most likely mounted on a breakout board such as the CJMCU-75.

> **Note**
> The Arduino comes supplied with the Wire library to handle TWI communications. It uses interrupts under the hood. The code in this chapter should, hopefully, better explain how it all works, rather than us users just blindly making use of a supplied library.

To create the sketch, start a new Arduino project in the IDE and add the `twi_defines.h` header file on a new tab in the normal manner. Listing 12-1 is the header file mentioned. It contains a few definitions that will be used in the main sketch.

Listing 12-1   TWI_Read sketch – twi_defines.h header file

```
#ifndef TWI_DEFINES_H
#define TWI_DEFINES_H


//-----------------------------------------------------------
// DEFINES FOR CONTROLLER RECEIVER. (CRX) (No Interrupts)
//-----------------------------------------------------------

// TWCR settings ...

#define CRX_START            (1 << TWINT) | \
                             (1 << TWSTA) | \
                             (1 << TWEN)

#define CRX_REP_START        (CRX_START)

#define CRX_STOP             (1 << TWINT) | \
                             (1 << TWSTO) | \
                             (1 << TWEN)

#define CRX_READ_NACK        (1 << TWINT) | \
                             (1 << TWEN)


#define CRX_READ_ACK         (CRX_READ_NACK) | \
```

```
                          (1 << TWEA)

#define CRX_SEND_READ_ADDRESS (CRX_READ_NACK)

#define CRX_TRANSMIT          (CRX_READ_NACK)

// TWSR Status codes.

#define CRX_STATUS ((TWSR) & 0xF8)

#define CRX_INVALID_START_STOP 0x00

#define CRX_START_SENT        0x08
#define CRX_RESTART_SENT      0x10
#define CRX_ARBIT_LOST        0x38
#define CRX_SLAR_ACK_RCVD     0x40
#define CRX_SLAR_NACK_RCVD    0x48
#define CRX_DATA_ACK_SENT     0x50
#define CRX_DATA_NACK_SENT    0x58


# endif // TWI_DEFINES_H
```

The header file is effectively split into two parts; the first part defines all required TWI transmission bits for the *TWI Control Register*, TWCR, which is used to tell the TWI hardware what to do next. When writing to this register, the *TWI Interrupt Flag* bit, TWINT, must always be set to 1 as must the *TWI Enable* bit, TWEN; otherwise, nothing will work. The TWINT bit is set when the TWI hardware has finished performing an action. This pauses the interface until it is subsequently informed that it can continue, which is done by clearing the TWINT bit in the normal AVR manner of writing a 1 to it.

The second part of the header file defines all the expected status codes, returned in the *TWI Status Register*, TWSR, which tell the code how successful the previous TWI operation was. Bit 2 of this register always reads as a zero, and bits 1 and 0 of the register are not used in the status codes – they are the prescaler bits. For these reasons, those three bits are masked out in the define for CRX_STATUS. The ATmega328P data sheet gives details of which status codes are to be expected after each action.

Listing 12-2 is the setup() function for TWI_Read.ino. The code begins by including the header file from Listing 12-1, then defines the seven-bit address of my own LM75A sensor. You will need to change the code to suit the address of your sensor.

Listing 12-2 TWI_Read sketch – setup() function

```
#include "twi_defines.h"

#define LM75A_ADDRESS 0x4F

// Default prescaler = 1. Atmel says leave alone!
#define PSCALER 1

// Calculate TWBR from desired SCL frequency.
```

```
#define SCL_HZ_TO_TWBR(F)    (0.5 * PSCALER) * ((F_CPU/(F)) - 16)

void setup() {
    Serial.begin(9600);
    Serial.println("LM75A - Temperature Measurement\n");
    pinMode(LED_BUILTIN, OUTPUT);
    digitalWrite(LED_BUILTIN, LOW);

    // VERY VERY IMPORTANT!
    // Set  the SCL clock speed to 200 KHz.
    TWBR = SCL_HZ_TO_TWBR(200000);
}
```

After the sensor address, there is a macro to handle converting the SCL frequency to the required setting for the *TWI Bit Rate Register*, TWBR. This register is used to generate the appropriate SCL clock for the attached sensors.

The setup() function doesn't have much to do, only setting up the Serial Interface and writing a small heading to it and configuring the built-in LED as an output before setting it low. In the event of any TWI errors, the LED will be turned on to indicate a problem. However, the function does have one important function to perform; it must configure the SCL frequency for the TWI hardware to match that of the LM75A sensor attached. My sensor can operate at speeds up to 400 KHz, but as I'm using the sensor on a breadboard, I'm not going to push it too fast, it works fine at 200 KHz.

Listing 12-3 is the waitForStatus() function for TWI_Read.ino. The function's purpose is to wait for the TWI action just requested to complete and to obtain the status byte for that action.

The wait for completion is a busy loop waiting for the TWINT bit in the TWCR register to be set to 1. This bit is set by the hardware whenever a TWI action has completed or failed. The status of the now completed action is obtained using the CRX_STATUS macro, which simply reads the TWSR register and masks out the three unwanted bits.

Listing 12-3 TWI_Read sketch – waitForStatus() function

```
void waitForStatus(byte requiredStatus) {

    // Wait for the TWI to respond.
    while (!(TWCR & (1 << TWINT))) ;

    // Grab the status byte.
    byte crxStatus = CRX_STATUS;

    // Did we expect that status?
    if (crxStatus != requiredStatus) {
        Serial.print("Invalid status, expected 0x");
        Serial.print(requiredStatus, HEX);
        Serial.print(", received 0x");
        Serial.println(crxStatus, HEX);

        // Light the LED on errors.
        digitalWrite(LED_BUILTIN, HIGH);
```

```
        // Try to stop TWI communications.
        TWCR = CRX_STOP;

        // Loop the loop forever.
        while (1) ;
    }
}
```

If the status returned is the expected status, the function is finished and returns to the caller; otherwise, it fills the Serial Monitor with useful information, lights the built-in LED to indicate a problem, and enters an infinite loop to prevent any further actions taking place. It will attempt to send a stop condition to relinquish control of the bus, but that action might not always be possible.

Listing 12-4 is the `loop()` function for `TWI_Read.ino`.

Reading the temperature data from the LM75A is a simple matter of reading a pair of bytes. The first byte holds the sensor temperature, as a two's complement value, in degrees Centigrade.[3] The second byte has the top bit set if there is an additional 0.5 degrees to add; all other bits are unused. As we only require two bytes, a small array is set up to hold the result from the sensor.

The controller starts communicating with the TWI hardware by sending out a start condition, then waiting for the appropriate status to be returned.

Once the controller has the bus in its possession, it transmits the LM75A address as an eight-bit value. The seven-bit address is shifted one bit to the left and a 1 is added to indicate a read action from the sensor is being initiated. The address is transmitted by writing it to the *TWI Data Register*, TWDR, then we wait for the acknowledgment to be returned.

Listing 12-4 TWI_Read sketch – loop() function

```
void loop() {
    byte tempData[2];

    // Send start condition.
    TWCR = CRX_START;
    waitForStatus(CRX_START_SENT);

    // Send LM75A read address.
    TWDR = (((LM75A_ADDRESS) << 1) | 1);
    TWCR = CRX_SEND_READ_ADDRESS;
    waitForStatus(CRX_SLAR_ACK_RCVD);

    // Read two bytes, first with ack, second with nack.
    TWCR = CRX_READ_ACK;
    waitForStatus(CRX_DATA_ACK_SENT);
    tempData[0] = TWDR;

    TWCR = CRX_READ_NACK;
    waitForStatus(CRX_DATA_NACK_SENT);
```

---

[3] Sorry America!

```
    tempData[1] = TWDR;

    TWCR = CRX_STOP;


    // Did we get a temperature?
    Serial.print(" ");
    Serial.print(tempData[0]);
    Serial.println((tempData[1] & 0x80) ? ".5 C" : ".0 C");

    delay(5000);
}
```

The first of two data bytes must now be read from the sensor and acknowledged. Every byte read from the sensor must be acknowledged by the receiver, the controller in this case, except for the final byte. The lack of an acknowledgment informs the LM75A that the current communication is complete. Reading is facilitated by setting the TWCR register to read a byte and to acknowledge it, then waiting for the action to complete. Once complete, we can read the received data from the TWDR register.

The second data byte will not be acknowledged as it is the final one. The TWCR register is set with the bit pattern to read a byte with no acknowledgment which initiates the action; we then wait for completion in the normal manner before obtaining the data from the TWDR register.

At this point, communication is complete, so we close down the bus by sending a stop condition.

We now have our two bytes of temperature data and can display the current temperature on the Serial Monitor. The LM75A sends a 16 bit register value in two separate eight-bit bytes. The most significant byte is sent first which is the actual temperature, followed by the fractions of a degree in the topmost bit of the second data byte. All other bits are discarded; the sensor's register is 16 bits wide, but only 9 bits are used for the data.

In the code on disk for this sketch, there are a number of commented out lines which print various values and status codes to the Serial Monitor. If you are having problems, it might be helpful to uncomment these lines and upload the code again – it may give you a clue as to where the problem is. Those lines have not been shown in the listings.

Figure 12-3 shows the breadboard layout for this test sketch. Although the image of the Arduino Uno does show two extra pins on the top-right header, they are not labeled. Experimenting in Fritzing shows that these are the two TWI bus lines, SCL and SDA. As they are not labeled in Fritzing, I have taken the liberty of using the A4 and A5 pins in Figure 12-3 to avoid potential confusion.

Resistors R1 and R2 are the two pull-up resistors, and both are 10 KΩ. These may not be necessary on some breakout boards for the LM75A. My own CJMCU-75 boards do have their own 10 KΩ pull-up resistors installed, so additional ones are not necessary.[4]

Once the project has been set up and uploaded, you should be able to see the current temperature reported to the Serial Monitor every five seconds. We know that the sensor is working, we have the

---

[4]Having said that, I did use them on my test setup for a while before I discovered that the board has them built in, but everything still worked fine at 200 KHz clock frequency.

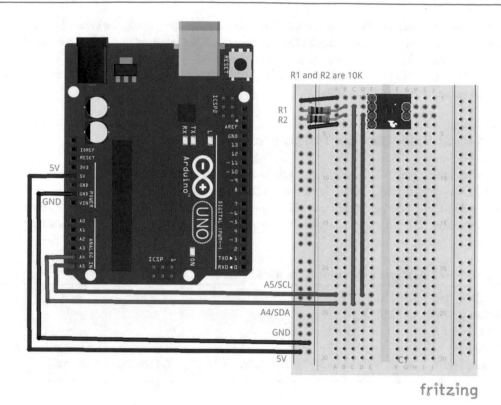

Figure 12-3 TWI_Read sketch – breadboard layout

correct address for it, and we have working code to read from a TWI sensor. Can we convert this to use interrupts?

12.6 Using the TWI Interrupt

There is only one interrupt allocated to the TWI hardware. It is triggered when global interrupts are enabled and the TWINT bit is set in the *TWI Control Register*, TWCR; the TWI hardware will set this bit each and every time that it has carried out an action, regardless of whether the action succeeded or not. The *TWI Status Register*, TWSR, will show any error codes.

To convert the sketch in Listings 12-1 through 12-4, to use interrupts, all we need to do is create an ISR and write some code to determine what just happened and to initiate the next action. We will, of course, require setting the TWIE bit in the TWCR register to ensure interrupts are on. How hard can all that be?

12.6.1 The Arduino Wire Library

The Arduino-supplied Wire library is used for the TWI communications, among other things, and is itself using the TWI interrupt. The code in the remainder of this chapter describes Arduino and PlatformIO sketches which do not use the Wire library.

If you decide to use the Wire library for TWI communications, please, feel free, but you cannot use the code here with the Wire library as there is only one TWI interrupt and either Wire or this code will grab the interrupt handler, and no end of "undocumented" problems will occur.

Even if you decide to continue using the Wire library, having a look over the code in this chapter may help you to understand how it works.

12.7   Read-Only Using the TWI Interrupt

We need to amend the `TWI_Read.ino` sketch to make sure that all the previously defined macros, with the exception of `CRX_STOP`, have the `TWIE` bit set. If this bit is not set, then interrupts will not be enabled, and nothing of interest will happen. Listing 12-5 shows the changes made to create the new version of the `twi_defines.h` header file. The interrupt-driven sketch will be named `TWI_Read_Interrupt.ino`.

Listing 12-5   TWI_Read_Interrupt sketch – twi_defines.h header file

```
#ifndef TWI_DEFINES_H
#define TWI_DEFINES_H

//------------------------------------------------------------
// DEFINES FOR CONTROLLER RECEIVER. (CRX) (Interrupts used)
//------------------------------------------------------------



// TWCR settings ...

#define CRX_START               (1 << TWINT) | \
                                (1 << TWSTA) | \
                                (1 << TWEN)  | \
                                (1 << TWIE)

#define CRX_REP_START           (CRX_START)

#define CRX_STOP                (1 << TWINT) | \
                                (1 << TWSTO) | \
                                (1 << TWEN)

#define CRX_READ_NACK           (1 << TWINT) | \
                                (1 << TWEN)  | \
                                (1 << TWIE)


#define CRX_READ_ACK            (CRX_READ_NACK) | \
                                (1 << TWEA)


#define CRX_SEND_READ_ADDRESS (CRX_READ_NACK)
```

```
#define CRX_TRANSMIT              (CRX_READ_NACK)


// TWSR Status codes.

...

# endif // TWI_DEFINES_H
```

Only the TWCR-related macros have been changed; there are no changes required to the TWSR status codes, so that part of the file has not been shown in Listing 12-5.

Listing 12-6 is the new setup() code. It begins, as before, by defining a couple of macros to enable the sensor's clock frequency to be set. There are four new volatile global variables defined in this new code. These are

- A small array, tempData, to store the two bytes of data received from the sensor
- A flag, tempAvailable, to show when both bytes have been received
- A flag, twiStatus, to show if there were errors in the ISR
- An optional counter, isrCount, just to show how many times we enter the ISR to obtain a reading from the sensor

Listing 12-6 TWI_Read_Interrupt sketch – setup() function

```
#include "twi_defines.h"

#define LM75A_ADDRESS 0x4F

// Default prescaler = 1. Atmel says leave alone!
#define PSCALER 1

// Calculate TWBR from desired SCL frequency.
#define SCL_HZ_TO_TWBR(F) (0.5 * PSCALER) * ((F_CPU/(F)) - 16)

// Storage for two data bytes from the sensor. The ISR will
// fill these in, so they are declared volatile. However we
// also need to be sure we have received both data bytes.
volatile byte tempData[2];
volatile byte tempAvailable;

// An error flag. If the ISR can't deal with a problem,
// this will tell us and the loop() will sort it out.
volatile byte twiStatus;

// Just how many times do we enter the ISR, out of curiosity?
volatile unsigned int isrCount;
```

```
void setup() {
    Serial.begin(9600);
    Serial.println("LM75A - Temperature Measurement\n");
    pinMode(LED_BUILTIN, OUTPUT);
    digitalWrite(LED_BUILTIN, LOW);

    // VERY VERY IMPORTANT!
    // Set  the SCL clock speed to 200 KHz.
    TWBR = SCL_HZ_TO_TWBR(200000);

    // No ISR entries yet.
    isrCount = 0;
}
```

The actual setup() function is the same as in the polled version of the code, other than it now initializes the isrCount counter variable to show that we have not yet executed the ISR.

You may remember Listing 12-3 where we saw the waitForStatus() function. If so, that is now totally removed as all of its work will be done in the ISR instead.

Much of the loop() function has also been removed as the ISR takes care of things there too. Listing 12-7 shows the new improved loop() function.

Listing 12-7 TWI_Read_Interrupt sketch – loop() function

```
void loop() {
    // Send start condition with interrupts enabled.
    TWCR = CRX_START;

    // Did we get a temperature?
    if (twiStatus != -1) {
        if (tempAvailable) {
            Serial.print(isrCount);
            Serial.print(": ");
            Serial.print(tempData[0]);
            Serial.println((tempData[1] & 0x80) ? ".5 C" :
                                                  ".0 C");
        }
    } else {
        // Oops! problems in the ISR.
        digitalWrite(LED_BUILTIN, HIGH);
        while (1) ;
    }

    delay(5000);
}
```

Each time that the `loop()` function executes, it sends a start condition to the bus to gain control. That's all! The ISR takes over and processes everything including shutting down communications when necessary.

> **Note**
>
> The `delay()` function call at the end of the loop ensures that more than enough time passes for the temperature sensor to respond and pass the data back to the Arduino and for the ISR to terminate the conversation. Obviously, a five-second delay is far more than is normally required.
>
> Sending a start condition each time through a speedy `loop()` might not leave enough time for the communications to complete. Normally, or hopefully, the processing done in the code after requesting data will take enough time to allow the interrupt handling code to obtain the data requested.
>
> In a proper sketch, the code would be off elsewhere doing something useful while the TWI interface obtains the requested data, and a `delay()` call, like the one here, would not be necessary.

The `loop()` function checks the ISR status for errors and, if there were none, checks if the temperature data is available yet. If the data is present, it is displayed on the Serial Monitor, as before, with the count of the number of times we had to enter the ISR as a prefix on each line. You will see from the output that it takes four executions of the ISR to obtain the two bytes of data.

If any errors were detected by the ISR, the `twiStatus` variable will be holding –1, and the Arduino will light the built-in LED to indicate a fault, before entering an endless loop to stop further processing.

Listing 12-8 is the new ISR function where the TWI communications are now handled. Whenever this function is executing, we can be sure that the TWI hardware has completed an action of some kind. The first task of the ISR is to ensure that the status code from the TWI hardware is saved away safely. The ISR error flag is then cleared, and, just for my own curiosity, the counter which tells me how many times we have executed the ISR is incremented.

The `loop()` function (see Listing 12-7) started communications when it sent a start condition to the TWI hardware. When that action completes, the interrupt will trigger and the ISR will be executed. However, all other TWI actions will also trigger the ISR, so we need to be aware of what status codes we have received.

Consulting the ATmega328P's data sheet shows that when in Controller Receiver mode, as we are now, the status codes in our amended `twi_defines.h` header file are the ones we want. We need to determine what action just took place and act accordingly. The `switch` statement takes care of those checks and actions for us.

It makes sense, to me anyway, to check the status code in the order we would expect to receive them. This may not be the most efficient order however, which we should bear in mind as we should be keeping ISR code paths as short as possible. However, when we get to a full-blown ISR to handle transmission and receipt of data, determining the order becomes more onerous, so don't lose any sleep over it!

The first check is to ensure that after the `loop()` function raised a start condition, it was actually raised. If so, we need to send the sensor address which we do by writing it into the `TWDR` register as before, and then we set the `TWCR` register to transmit the sensor address. After that, the ISR exits leaving the TWI hardware to get on with the task of sending out the sensor address.

Listing 12-8   TWI_Read_Interrupt sketch – ISR

```
ISR(TWI_vect) {
    // Get the status for the action which just completed.
    byte crxStatus = CRX_STATUS;

    twiStatus = 0;
    isrCount++;

    switch (crxStatus) {
        case CRX_START_SENT:
            // Start sent ok. Send the sensor read address,
            // flag up no data available yet.
            tempAvailable = 0;
            TWDR = (((LM75A_ADDRESS) << 1) | 1);
            TWCR = CRX_SEND_READ_ADDRESS;
            return;

        case CRX_SLAR_ACK_RCVD:
            // Sensor responded to its address. Request one
            // data byte and send an acknowledgement.
            TWCR = CRX_READ_ACK;
            return;

        case CRX_SLAR_NACK_RCVD:
            // Sensor not responding, sent a stop and
            // clear the TWIE bit to disable interrupts..
            TWCR = CRX_STOP;
            return;

        case CRX_DATA_ACK_SENT:
            // We have received a byte of data and sent an
            // acknowledgement. This is the first of two
            // bytes we need. Fetch the byte and request the
            // next one.
            tempData[0] = TWDR;
            TWCR = CRX_READ_NACK;
            return;

        case CRX_DATA_NACK_SENT:
            // We have received a byte of data and NOT sent
            // an acknowledgement. This is the last of two
            // bytes we need. Fetch the byte and stop the
            // TWI communications and the interrupt.
            tempData[1] = TWDR;
            TWCR = CRX_STOP;

            // We have all our data.
```

```
                    tempAvailable = 1;
                    return;

            default:
                    // Oops! Problem.
                    TWCR = CRX_STOP;
                    twiStatus = -1;
                    return;
        }
}
```

On the second entry to the ISR, we should be looking for the response from the sensor with an acknowledgment bit set – alternatively, without the acknowledgment. In the case of the former, we know that the sensor is present and responding, so we simply ask it to send over one byte of data and tell the TWI hardware to acknowledge that byte when it is received.

In the event that we didn't get an acknowledgment from the sensor, the ISR code simply stops the communications and drops control of the bus. It doesn't flag this as an error however, but we cannot really continue as the sensor is either physically not present or disconnected or is too busy doing something else to respond.

The third entry to the ISR should be after a data byte, the first one, has been received from the sensor. The controller will already have sent an acknowledgment to the sensor. The data byte received is the temperature in degrees Centigrade, and it is copied from the TWDR register into the first byte of our storage array. We request the TWI hardware to send a new request for a data byte, but this time, we tell it not to acknowledge receipt of the data – because this will be the final byte requested – and we then exit from the ISR.

The fourth and final entry to the ISR, this time around the loop() function, is when we should have received the second and final data byte from the sensor. The byte is copied into the second location in our storage array, and the TWI hardware is instructed to send a stop condition and relinquish control of the bus. As we have collected all the required data from the sensor, we indicate this to the loop() function by setting the tempAvailable variable.

In the unlikely event that we have a problem at any time in the TWI communications, the error flag twiStatus is set and communications terminated, if possible, and the bus released. The loop() function will detect the error flag and light up the built-in LED to show that a problem has occurred.

This sketch uses exactly the same breadboard layout as shown in Figure 12-3.

12.8 PlatformIO TWI Code

If you wish to take a look at the code for the PlatformIO infrastructure, then there are two corresponding sketches on the code repository for this chapter. The PlatformIO code has not been discussed here as there are very few differences, only in how information is written to the Serial Monitor; all the TWI-specific code is identical in both development environments.

12.9   Fully Extending the Interrupt Code

The interrupt handler in Listing 12-8 is quite useful, as long as you only need to read a pair of bytes. How could the code be modified to read, or write, any number of bytes of data? It's actually quite simple, and these are the steps to follow to amend the existing code to allow the changes to be made:

- Create a buffer to hold the data for transmission and also a buffer for received data.
- Create a small number of helper functions to transfer data to and from the buffers and to start and stop the TWI conversation, and interrupts, as and when required.
- Extend the interrupt handling code to cater for all the other status codes that can be received.

This is not hard to do really. Once you get your head around the data sheet that is, but one of the joys of open source is that someone out there has probably already had the same itch to scratch as you do and has written something helpful. In this case, it's a gentleman named Chris Herring who wrote TWILib,[5] back in 2014–2015, for use in plain C programs.

I have forked his code to my GitHub[6] and modified it to compile under C++, to allow the clock speed to be selected, and to work with the Arduino, PlatformIO, and other non-Arduino development systems. I also fixed a couple of bugs and discovered that Chris' tutorial, on his website, is out of date with even his version of the code. It seems he changed the return values from the transmit and receive functions but didn't update his error trapping to suit. It took me some time to figure that out!

The modified library code can only be used to communicate with sensors and other peripherals. It is not suitable, for example, to be used to communicate between two Arduino boards as only the controller code is implemented[7] – it's on my own to-do list to get the sensor handling code written at some point in the future. Having mentioned this apparent shortcoming, the library does allow data to be written to a sensor to configure it, for example, and data can be read back from the sensor for use by the application. This is all we need in this example and in other applications where real-time clocks, temperature sensors, Liquid Crystal Displays, and so on, are used.

The TWI_Read_Interrupt sketch in Listings 12-6 through 12-8 can be rewritten to use the AVRTWIlib library. In this version of the sketch, however, I shall demonstrate writing configuration data to the sensor prior to reading temperature data back from it – just to exercise the whole library. With the LM75A, this is not strictly necessary as the sensor defaults to using the temperature register on power-up.

The outline of the program code is as follows:

- Initialize the AVRTWIlib library and the Serial Monitor.
- Write configuration data to the temperature sensor to ask it to send us some, ahem, temperature data. This is actually how the sensor configures itself on power-up, but it can be done manually, as demonstrated here.
- In the loop() function, read two bytes of temperature data and display it on the Serial Monitor.

---

[5]https://github.com/c-herring/AVRTWIlib

[6]https://github.com/NormanDunbar/AVRTWIlib

[7]The library implements Master Transmitter and Master Receiver modes only. Slave Transmitter and Slave Receiver modes are "pending" and have been since 2015. The terminology used here is the old style, unfortunately.

Listing 12-9 is the start of the code for the sketch entitled TWI_Interrupt, which uses the AVRTWIlib by Chris Herring and myself, to read and write data to a sensor. The listing shows the global variables required by the sketch.

By defining NO_ERROR_DATA_REQUIRED, we are telling the compiler not to bother bringing in the entire list of potential TWI error messages. In the event of errors, only the status codes will be shown on the Serial Monitor. If you comment out the macro definition, you will get full error messages.

TWIlib.h is the header file that we need to include to be able to use the AVRTWIlib code.

TWI_READY_DELAY is the number of milliseconds we should wait for TWI to become available after initializing the AVRTWIlib library.

Listing 12-9 TWI_Interrupt sketch – globals

```
//-----------------------------------------------------------
// A sketch to use direct register access to read data from
// an LM75A temperature sensor.
//
// This version uses Norman Dunbar's slightly amended version
// of Chris Herring's TWIlib -- an interrupt driven TWI library
// for the ATmega328P et al microcontrollers.
//
// https://github.com/NormanDunbar/AVRTWIlib
//
//
// Norman Dunbar
// 17th April 2022
//-----------------------------------------------------------

// Save RAM by not using the error messages
#define NO_ERROR_DATA_REQUIRED

// Get the TWI library
#include "TWIlib.h"

// Delay, milliseconds to wait for the TWI to become ready
// or before attempting another try.
#define TWI_READY_DELAY 100


//-----------------------------------------------------------
// Global variables.
//-----------------------------------------------------------

// LM75A 7bit & 8bit write address
const byte LM75A_ADDRESS = 0x4F;
const byte LM75A_WR_ADDRESS = (LM75A_ADDRESS << 1) & 0xfe;

// LM75A register zero configuration data.
```

```
const byte LM75A_TEMP_REGISTER = 0x00;

// Configure the LM75A to use register zero.
byte configData[2] = {LM75A_WR_ADDRESS,
                      LM75A_TEMP_REGISTER};
```

LM75A_ADDRESS is the address of one of my LM75A breakout boards. This is its seven-bit address, and the code in Listing 12-9 uses this to configure LM75A_WR_ADDRESS, the address we use when initiating a write to the sensor.

The code continues and initializes LM75A_TEMP_REGISTER. This is the register we need to read temperature data from, so we will write some configuration data to the sensor to ensure that this register is selected for read operations. The configuration data is defined next in the array configData. The data consist solely of the write address for the sensor and the register we wish to read from. The data sheet for the sensor explains what configuration data is required when reading and writing to and from other registers.

The sketch's code continues in Listing 12-10 where the code to check the result of a TWI action is shown. As the comments explain, in normal circumstances, the TWI communication would be set up and initiated. The sketch would then go and do some useful work while the TWI hardware operates in the background. However, for the purposes of this demonstration, there's nothing important that needs to be done – unless we, perhaps, flash an LED – so this code is used to check each action for success or failure.

Listing 12-10 TWI_Interrupt sketch – checkTWIAction() function

```
//-------------------------------------------------------------
// Checks for success or failure of a TWI action.
//-------------------------------------------------------------
void checkTWIAction(const char *function) {
    // Normally, we would go off and do something and leave
    // the interrupts to get on with it. But here we will wait
    // for the transmit to complete. It's done when we get a
    // status code that isn't TWI_NO_RELEVANT_INFO.
    while (TWIInfo.errorCode == TWI_NO_RELEVANT_INFO)
        delay(1);

    // Grab the error code.
    byte errorCode = TWIInfo.errorCode;

    // Did it work?
    if (errorCode != TWI_SUCCESS) {
        Serial.println("");
        Serial.print(function);
        Serial.print(": Error: 0x");
        Serial.print(errorCode);
#ifndef NO_ERROR_DATA_REQUIRED
        Serial.print(' ');
        Serial.print(TWIGetLastError(errorCode));
#endif
```

```
        Serial.println();
    }
}
```

The code here considers whether or not the full error messages are to be displayed when errors are detected, by checking for NO_ERROR_DATA_REQUIRED at compile time and either including or excluding the code to display the errors.

Not including the various error messages has the advantage of reducing the amount of space required for your sketch and the disadvantage of not being able to see more than an error code when something bad happens.

Listing 12-11 TWI_Interrupt sketch – waitForTWI() function

```
//----------------------------------------------------------------
// Waits for TWI to complete the previous action. This is
// required as this example sketch is not doing any useful
// work between requesting data and reading it. If it was
// then this function would not normally be required.
//----------------------------------------------------------------
void waitForTWI() {
    while (!isTWIReady()) {
        delay(TWI_READY_DELAY);
    }
}
```

Listing 12-11 is a short function which waits for the AVRTWIlib library to become ready for the next action. This is required after initialization and between actions as the interrupt handler may still be running in the background to process a transmission or receipt. The TWI hardware can only be used to carry out one action at a time.

Listing 12-12 shows the code to send the configuration data to the sensor. It sets the error code in the TWIInfo structure to a meaningless value, which is impossible to receive back from the TWI hardware. It continues by attempting to initiate a transmission of the configuration data passed to sendConfig() as parameters and will try repeatedly until it manages to initiate successfully or receives an error. CheckTWIAction() from Listing 12-10 is then called to determine if the configuration data was successfully transmitted, in full, to the sensor.

Listing 12-12 TWI_Interrupt sketch – sendConfig() function

```
//----------------------------------------------------------------
// Send some configuration data and wait for it to be written.
// We will be reading next, so request a repeated start.
//----------------------------------------------------------------
void sendConfig(void *data, byte size) {

    // Wait for the transmit to successfully initiate.
    TWIInfo.errorCode = TWI_NO_RELEVANT_INFO;
    byte TXInitiated = TWI_TX_RX_NOT_READY;
```

```
    // This could hang if the TWI bus is up that famous creek!
    while (TXInitiated == TWI_TX_RX_NOT_READY)
        TXInitiated = TWITransmitData(data, size, true);

    // Did it work?
    checkTWIAction("sendConfig");
}
```

The code to read some data back from the sensor is next and is shown in Listing 12-13. In this function, we again set the error code to a meaningless value and attempt to initiate a data read from the sensor. This could fail if the TWI system is still busy from a previous action, so we loop until we get a response back that indicates success or a different error to the "not ready yet" one. CheckTWIAction() from Listing 12-10 is again called to determine if the data was successfully received, in full, from the sensor.

Listing 12-13 TWI_Interrupt sketch – readData() function

```
//-----------------------------------------------------------
// Read some data back from the TWI. We don't need a repeated
// start, so we don't request one. We only need 2 bytes here.
//-----------------------------------------------------------
void readData(byte TWIaddress, void *data, byte size) {
    // Try to get a successful read initiated. First, clear
    // any TWI Error codes.
    TWIInfo.errorCode = TWI_NO_RELEVANT_INFO;

    // Then initialise the read.
    byte TXInitiated = TWI_TX_RX_NOT_READY;

    // This could hang if the TWI bus is up that famous creek!
    while (TXInitiated == TWI_TX_RX_NOT_READY)
        TXInitiated = TWIReadData(TWIaddress, size, data, false);

    // Did it work?
    checkTWIAction("readData");
}
```

Listing 12-14 shows the code for the setup() function. Here, we initialize the AVRTWIlib library with the sensor running at 200 KHz. I'm choosing the speed even though the data sheet advises that the LM75A will operate at speeds up to 400 KHz. On a breadboard, you may not be able to communicate properly at full speed due to stray capacitance and other weird quantum effects.

The Serial Monitor is also initialized at 9600 baud here, my favorite speed for the Serial Monitor, and a sign-on message is displayed.

Listing 12-14 TWI_Interrupt sketch – setup() function

```
void setup() {
    // Initialise the TWIlib to 200 KHz
```

```
        TWIInit(200);

        Serial.begin(9600);

        // Sign on message;
        Serial.println("\nLM75A Interrupt Driven Example\n");



        // Make sure that TWI is initialised before we send
        // the configuration data.
        waitForTWI();
        sendConfig((void *)configData, 2);
}
```

After displaying the sign-on message, we wait for the TWI library to become ready for use, and when it does so, we initialize the LM75A sensor by writing the two bytes of configuration data which will configure it to process read operations from its register zero.

Within the `loop()` function, which can be seen in Listing 12-15, we create an array of two bytes into which the temperature data will be written and then attempt to read two bytes from the sensor. On receipt of both data bytes, the current temperature is displayed on the Serial Monitor in the usual manner.

The `delay()` call at the end of `loop()`, in this case, is no longer to allow the TWI hardware to complete its communications, but so that the temperature data isn't being displayed on the Serial Monitor constantly.

Listing 12-15 TWI_Interrupt sketch – loop() function

```
void loop() {
    byte temperature[2];

    // Make sure that TWI is ready for use again before we
    // read the temperature data. ReadData handles converting
    // the 7 bit address to the SLA+R address in 8 bits.
    waitForTWI();
    readData(LM75A_ADDRESS, (void *)temperature, 2);

    Serial.print("Current temperature: ");
    Serial.print(temperature[0]);
    Serial.println(temperature[1] & 0x80 ? ".5" : ".0");

    // Delay for a bit.
    delay(5000);
}
```

Once again, the code for this chapter includes a similar sketch for PlatformIO which is almost identical to the `TWI_Interrupt.ino` code that it needs no explanation here.

The AVRTWIlib library can be used to talk to sensors, LCD displays, and other TWI devices using code similar to these examples. This is especially useful if you are not using the Arduino IDE, which, as mentioned previously, has similar functionality in its Wire library. If you are not using the Arduino Language, then Wire is not available to you; this version of Chris Herring's AVRTWIlib is a suitable replacement.

A full description of the AVRTWIlib can be found in Appendix D, "AVRTWIlib."

12.10 Register Summary

The registers used for the TWI interrupt are described, in summary only, in this section. Only the bits relevant to the TWI interrupt are considered. While other bits may be used elsewhere, they are marked here as not applicable. Consult the data sheet for full details of the registers involved.

12.10.1 TWI Bit Rate Register

The *TWI Bit Rate Register*, TWBR, is used to determine the frequency of the communication between the controller and the sensor. All eight bits are used. This register should be set to match the data sheet requirements for the sensor in question.

7	6	5	4	3	2	1	0
TWBR7	TWBR6	TWBR5	TWBR4	TWBR3	TWBR2	TWBR1	TWBR0

12.10.2 TWI Status Register

The *TWI Status Register*, TWSR, should be examined after every TWI operation which takes place. It holds the response code for any errors that may have been detected by the TWI hardware built in to the ATmega328P. The lower two bits are used to define the prescaler for the frequency calculations carried out using the TWBR register.

7	6	5	4	3	2	1	0
TWS7	TWS6	TWS5	TWS4	TWS3	-	TWPS1	TWPS0

Bit 2 is not used and always reads as zero.

TWPS1 and **TWPS0** set the prescaler value for the TWBR register's frequency calculation. The data sheet advises that this should always be configured so as to give the prescaler the value 1 which requires both bits to be zero, which happens to be the power on default.

TWS7 through **TWS3** are the five bits making up the status code from the TWI operation which just took place. These bits are read-only. The status code read is an eight-bit value, but the code should always mask out the lower three bits giving a result of the form 0bxxxxx000, and this is the format used in the data sheet to describe the numerous status codes.

12.10.3 TWI Control Register

The *TWI Control Register*, TWCR, as its name implies, controls the TWI hardware.

7	6	5	4	3	2	1	0
TWINT	**TWEA**	**TWSTA**	**TWSTO**	**TWWC**	**TWEN**	-	**TWIE**

Bit 1 is not used for any purpose and always reads as zero.

TWINT is set by the TWI hardware when the TWI has finished its current operation and signals that the application code should respond accordingly. If global interrupts are enabled and TWIE is set, the TWI interrupt handler will be executed. This bit must be cleared by software by writing a 1 to it. The flag will be automatically cleared if the TWI interrupt handler is executed; otherwise, the code must clear the flag.

While the TWINT flag remains set, the SCL low period is stretched, and the TWI hardware will not progress with the next operation.

Clearing this flag, automatically or manually in code, continues the operation of the TWI hardware, so the code must ensure that all required access to any of the other TWI registers has completed *before* clearing this flag.

TWEA controls generation of the ACK pulse. If this bit is set to 1, the ACK pulse will be generated by the TWI hardware as necessary.

If the application code clears this bit to zero, the sensor can be virtually disconnected from the two-wire serial bus temporarily. Address recognition can then be resumed by writing the bit to one again.

TWSTA will be written to 1 whenever the controlling device wishes to take control of the bus. The TWI hardware checks if the bus is available and generates a start condition on the bus if it is free. If the bus is not free, the TWI hardware will wait until it sees a stop condition on the bus and will try again to assert a start condition to claim the bus. Once the application code receives a notification that the start condition has been asserted, it must clear this bit.

TWSTO will be written to 1 when the controlling device wishes to relinquish control of the bus and generate a stop condition. Once the stop condition is asserted on the bus, this bit is cleared automatically. If a TWI device is not the controller, then it can set this bit to recover from an error condition. This will not generate an actual stop condition, but the TWI hardware in the sensor will return to an unaddressed mode and will release the SCL and SDA lines to a high impedance state. The controlling device is expected to restart (or abort) the communication.

TWWC will be set by the hardware if an attempt is made by the application code to write to the *TWI Data Register* while the TWINT flag is low. The flag will be cleared when the application code next writes to TWDR when TWINT is high.

TWEN activates the TWI hardware and enables the next TWI operation. If the bit is set to 1, the TWI hardware takes control of the I/O pins connected to the SCL and SDA pins. If this bit is cleared to zero at any time, the TWI hardware is immediately disabled off, and all current TWI communications are terminated.

TWIE enables the TWI interrupt if written to 1. Global interrupts must also be enabled for the TWI interrupt handler to execute. In this case, the interrupt handler will be activated each time TWINT is set by the hardware.

12.10.4 TWI Data Register

The *TWI Data Register*, TWDR, is used to hold the next byte to be transmitted or to hold the byte just received. The register remains valid for as long as the TWINT flag remains set.

7	6	5	4	3	2	1	0
TWD7	TWD6	TWD5	TWD4	TWD3	TWD2	TWD1	TWD0

All eight data bits are used and can be read and written. Writing is only permitted when there are no TWI communications currently ongoing – that is, when TWINT in TWSR is high.

12.10.5 TWI Address Register

The *TWI Address Register*, TWAR, holds a seven-bit address which the device will respond to when not configured as a controlling device. The seven-bit address is shifted left into the top seven bits of the register.

The address in this register is not used when this device is acting as a controller, only when configured as a sensor.

7	6	5	4	3	2	1	0
TWA6	TWA5	TWA4	TWA3	TWA2	TWA1	TWA0	TWGCE

TWA6 through **TWA0** hold the seven bits of the address.

TWGGE, if set, enables the recognition of a "general call" given over the TWI bus. The data sheet has full details.

12.10.6 TWI Address Mask Register

The *TWI Address Mask Register*, TWAMR, holds a value which acts as a mask to be applied to any sensor address placed on the bus. Any bit which is a 1 causes the corresponding bit in TWAR to be ignored when comparing the requested address on the bus and the device's own address in TWAR. This allows the device to respond to numerous address requests on the bus, if required.

This register is not used when this device is a controlling one.

7	6	5	4	3	2	1	0
TWAM6	TWAM5	TWAM4	TWAM3	TWAM2	TWAM1	TWAM0	-

Bit 0 is not used and is read-only, always returning a zero.

TWAM6 through **TWAM0** comprise the mask value. Any of these being set to a 1 indicates a "don't care" when comparing the address value on the bus and in the TWAR register.

12.11 Key Takeaways

In this chapter, we learned about the Two-Wire Interface and its single interrupt, in particular:

- The steps involved in reading, writing, and configuring a sensor device so that it responds to the controlling device.
- How to set the TWI frequency to ensure that communications can actually be understood.
- We wrote an interrupt handler to allow us to read temperature data from a TWI temperature sensor.
- We then, using a suitable library, generalized the code to enable any TWI communications to take place.

12.12 Coming Up

This chapter concludes the description of the numerous interrupts available on the ATmega328P. The astute reader will have noticed that the SPM interrupt has not been covered. This is simply because it is exceedingly difficult to find any documentation which covers this interrupt in any detail at all. I'd love to explain it to you and show examples of how to use it, but as yet, this is pretty much impossible. Sorry. I think it would be quite a challenge to create an interrupt-driven bootloader for the Arduino using the SPM interrupt, but, sadly, information is sparse on the matter.

Coming up in the next chapter, I will discuss a real-world example of using interrupts for something useful. The project is a small night light device, based initially on the Arduino Uno using the Arduino Language, but then progresses to using AVR C++ to reduce code size. This reduced version is further converted by using an ATtiny85 microcontroller as the brains. The Uno is too big and expensive to use in an actual working device; the ATtiny series is perfect when only a limited number of pins are required.

A Real-World Example

13

After reading this far, you should be aware of the available interrupts on your ATmega328P and how to start using them. Maybe it would be nice to have a real-world example project to practice with?

A project that I have in the prototype stage right now is an Arduino-powered night light, which illuminates an LED when the light level in a room falls below a preset level. This uses the Analog Comparator's interrupt to compare the current light level with a preset setting, and if they differ, an LED is lit or extinguished depending on the state of the ACO bit in the ACSR register. I'm currently using the prototype on a breadboard to enable me to find my office light switch in the dark. My office is currently[1] underground and so is in darkness almost all the time, and the light switch is on the wrong end of the room!

The project uses a light-dependent resistor to determine the current light level. The required darkness setting is facilitated using a $10\,K\Omega$ trimpot. In the final project, I will be using an ATtiny85 rather than an ATmega328P, but the code is the same.

13.1   The LDR

The light-dependent resistor, or LDR, is a small two-legged component which is usually made of selenium. This has a resistance which varies depending on the amount of light that falls upon the top surface. These are used in those small, cheap, LED lights that people have in their gardens. If you examine one carefully, there's usually a solar panel, and close by, on the top surface, there's a small round dimple where the LDR is hiding.

Unfortunately, the Arduino cannot directly measure resistance, so we have to convert the resistance to a voltage and use the Analog Comparator to compare the detected voltage representing the light level with the desired light level setting. How do we do this? Simple, we use the LDR as one half of a voltage divider.

When the LDR is in darkness, it has a high resistance which can be a few mega ohms in value. As the light levels increase, the resistance drops and in full light can be as low as a few ohms.

---

[1] By *currently*, I mean that I'm in the process of moving house, and not in the process of raising my office to ground level.

© The Author(s), under exclusive license to APress Media, LLC, part of Springer Nature 2024
N. Dunbar, *Arduino Interrupts*, Maker Innovations Series,
https://doi.org/10.1007/978-1-4842-9714-8_13

13.1.1 Voltage Dividers

Figure 13-1 shows a schematic diagram of a voltage divider.

Figure 13-1 Voltage
divider

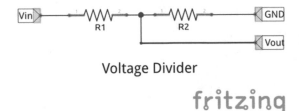

Voltage Divider

fritzing

We can see from Figure 13-1 that we have a simple circuit consisting of two resistors in series, with an input voltage, V_{in}, connected at one end and ground at the other. The output voltage, V_{out}, is obtained from the center point between the two resistors.

https://en.wikipedia.org/wiki/Voltage_divider has more details on voltage dividers and how they work, if you are interested.

If one of the Arduino's analog input pins is connected to the join between the two resistors, V_{out}, then a voltage will be detected on that pin which is dependent on the value of the input voltage and the ratio between the two resistors given by the equation:

$$V_{out} = V_{in} * \frac{R2}{R1 + R2}$$

If R1 and R2 have the same value, then the output voltage is half of the input voltage; otherwise, we have to do the calculations ourselves.

If we replace one of the resistors with an LDR, then the output voltage will vary as the light levels themselves vary. This allows the Arduino to determine the light levels based on the output voltage. Normally, a 10 KΩ fixed resistor is used as R1 in series with the LDR which acts as R2; however, some diagrams out on the Internet have the components reversed. It may be worth experimenting to determine which variant is best!

13.2   The Arduino Sketch

Figure 13-2 shows the breadboard layout for the sketch. The Arduino supplies the voltage divider with 5V and ground and reads the output voltage on its `AIN1/D7` pin. The trimpot's[2] output is read by the Arduino's `AIN0/D6` pin which is the Analog Comparator's reference voltage pin.

The LED is a white one even though it is shown as yellow in the image. This is because a white LED in Fritzing doesn't show up in the exported images!

The sketch is incredibly simple. Listings 13-1 through 13-4 show the entire sketch, for the Arduino Uno, with most of the comments removed for brevity.

---

[2]A potentiometer is another form of voltage divider.

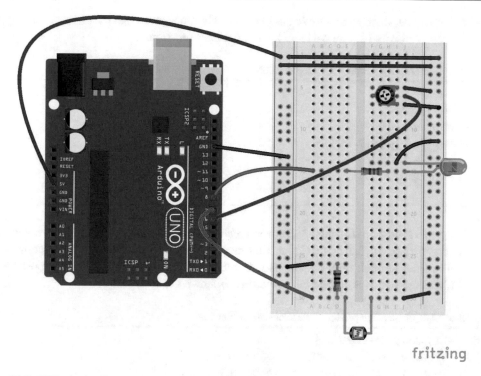

Figure 13-2 LDR_AnalogComparator breadboard layout

Listing 13-1 LDR_AnalogComparator – setup function

```
// We need to sleep.
#include "avr/sleep.h"

// LED pin.
const uint8_t LED = 8;

void setup() {
    // Disable Timer0. Millis() delay() won't work.
    // Timer0 overflow wakes from idle sleep.
    TCCR0B &= ~(1 << CS02 | 1 << CS01 | 1 << CS00);
    pinMode(LED, OUTPUT);
    set_sleep_mode(SLEEP_MODE_IDLE);
    setupComparator();
}
```

Listing 13-1 is the `setup()` function, and this sets the LED pin, pin D8, to be an output pin; sets the sleep mode to the lightest sleep possible, idle mode, as this is the only sleep mode which the Analog Comparator can wake up the ATmega328P; and calls the `setupComparator()` function, in Listing 13-3, to enable the comparator.

As we are using the Arduino Language, we need to be aware that Timer/counter 0 is set up to cause an overflow interrupt every 1024 microseconds. This is used to increment the `millis()` counter used by `delay()` and other built-in Arduino functions. Because an interrupt will wake the ATmega328P from idle sleep mode, we need to disable this interrupt. This does mean that `millis()`, `micros()`, `delayMicroseconds()`, and `delay()` will no longer function.

Listing 13-2 LDR_AnalogComparator – loop function

```
void loop() {
    noInterrupts();
    sleep_enable();
    sleep_bod_disable();
    interrupts();
    sleep_cpu();
}
```

The `loop()` function, in Listing 13-2, doesn't really have much to do. All the hard work is carried out by the comparator, so the `loop()` function merely puts the board back to sleep until the next wake-up call comes through from the comparator. Sleep has to be disabled as soon as possible after the board wakes up, so this is carried out in the ISR as shown in Listing 13-4.

Listing 13-3 LDR_AnalogComparator – setupComparator function

```
void setupComparator() {
    // Initialise the ACSR register to:
    // Disable AC interrupt (ACIE=0).
    // Enable the AC. (ACD = 0).
    // D6/PD6/AIN0 is reference voltage. (ACBG = 0).
    // D7/PD7/AIN1 is compare voltage. (ACME = 0).
    // Trigger AC interrupt on AC0 toggle. (ACIS0 = ACIS1 = 0).
    ACSR = 0;

    // Disable digital I/O on D6 and D7.
    DIDR1 |= ((1 << AIN0D) | (1 << AIN1D));

    // Clear pending interrupts.
    ACSR |= (1 << ACI);

    // Enable AC Interrupt.
    ACSR |= (1 << ACIE);
}
```

Listing 13-3 is where the Analog Comparator is initialized. Setting the `ADSR` register to zero has the effect of

- Disabling the AC interrupt as bit `ACIE` is cleared.
- Powering on and enabling the comparator as the AC Disable bit, `ACD`, is cleared.
- Enabling `D6/AIN0` as the reference voltage pin. `ACBG` is clear.
- Enabling `D7/AIN1` as the compare voltage pin. `ACME` is clear.
- Configuring the currently disabled AC Interrupt to trigger when the `ACO` bit toggles. `ACIS0` and `ACIS1` are both clear.

Normal GPIO operations on pins D6 and D7 are then disabled to ensure that the comparator can use these two pins for its comparisons. This configuration is facilitated by setting bits AIN0D and AIN1D in the DIDR1 register.

As we are using interrupts, any that may be pending should be cleared before enabling interrupts. This happens when we set the ACI bit. Finally, the AC Interrupt is enabled by setting the ACIE bit in ACSR.

Listing 13-4 LDR_AnalogComparator – analog comparator ISR

```
ISR(ANALOG_COMP_vect) {
    // Disable sleep mode, we are awake.
    sleep_disable();

    // Read the ACO bit and if on, light the LED on PB0/D8.'
    // otherwise, extinguish it.
    if (ACSR & (1 << ACO)) {
        digitalWrite(LED, HIGH);
    } else {
        digitalWrite(LED, LOW);
    }
}
```

The Analog Comparator interrupt's ISR is shown in Listing 13-4. The first task it carries out is to disable sleep mode. The data sheet advises that whenever the microcontroller wakes up from a sleep, it should have sleep disabled until it is necessary to enable it again.

After disabling sleep mode, the state of the ACO bit in the ACSR register is checked, and if set, the LED will be turned on; otherwise, it will be turned off.

After the ISR finishes its work, control will return to the loop() function, where sleep mode will be re-enabled and the board put back to sleep until the next time that the ACO bit toggles.

13.3 AVR C++ Conversion

The LDR_AnalogComparator.ino sketch just discussed is only 870 bytes in size plus 9 bytes of Static RAM. It's not large, especially when there is 32 KB of Flash RAM available on the ATmega328P. However, we can convert it to AVR C++ quite simply and save a few more bytes. I shall leave this as an exercise for the reader, but my version is now only 230 bytes of Flash RAM and no bytes at all of Static RAM.

If you decide to accept this challenge, then you will need to make code changes to

- Combine setup() and loop() into a single main() function.
- Use direct DDRx manipulation to configure the output pin for the LED.
- Use direct PORTx accesses to enable and disable the LED in the ISR.
- The sleep functions will remain the same.
- You will no longer need to disable Timer/counter 0. It is not enabled in AVR C++ unless you specifically enable it.

If you decide against accepting this challenge, then have a look in the code for this chapter on disk; there's a sketch named `LDR_AnalogComparator_AVR_C.ino` with all the changes already made for you.

Obviously, it's not necessary to save bytes in this manner for this project; there's more than enough Flash RAM, even on an ATtiny25, to hold the compiled code. However, some projects might benefit from a conversion to AVR C++, or even Assembly Language, rather than using the Arduino Language, which can get a little large at times.

13.4   ATtiny85 Conversion

While the Arduino Uno is a handy board for prototyping projects, there comes a time when a production-ready setup needs to be created. Unos are quite expensive, even the cheap clones that are available, and bulky. They are not really suited to production quality project.

A breadboard version of the Uno is possible, but requires a number of additional components, such as capacitors, pull-up resistors, reset switches, and so on, to create a minimal Uno clone for a project – all of which results in some bulk and a bit more battery power consumption. The Uno runs at 16 MHz and, as such, requires 5 V power. The ATtiny85 also runs at 16 MHz but can be configured to operate at a measly 1 MHz, which reduces the power requirements, and can be operated quite happily from 3 V batteries.

As this project only needs three pins plus power, the ATtiny25 would be suitable here. I only have the ATtiny85 variant, so I'm using one of those.

Figure 13-3 shows the amended breadboard layout. Battery power is supplied using the GND and VCC connections at the top left. I run mine with a 3 V Lithium battery.

In Figure 13-3, GND connections are shown with black wires; red wires indicate VCC connections. Signal wires are yellow and orange.

Listings 13-5 through 13-7 show the conversion from the AVR C++ version of the Uno sketch to a suitable sketch for an ATtiny85 microcontroller.

Figure 13-3
LDR_AC_ATtiny85
breadboard layout

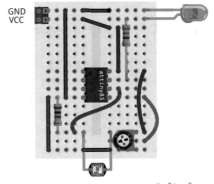

Listing 13-5 LDR_AnalogComparator_ATtiny85 – analog comparator ISR

```
// We need to sleep.
#include <avr/sleep.h>


ISR(ANA_COMP_vect) {
    // Make sure we disable sleep mode.
    sleep_disable();

    // Read the ACO bit and if on, light the LED on PB2.
    // otherwise, extinguish it.
    if (ACSR & (1 << ACO)) {
        PORTB |= (1 << PORTB2);
    } else {
        PORTB &= ~(1 << PORTB2);
    }
}
```

Listing 13-5 reads the header file required to use the various sleep functions, then defines the ISR to handle the Analog Comparator interrupt. The only difference between the ATtiny85 and Uno code is the pin name for the LED.

Listing 13-6 LDR_AnalogComparator_ATtiny85 – setupComparator

```
void setupComparator() {
    ACSR = 0;

    // Disable digital I/O on PB0 and PB1.
    DIDR0 |= ((1 << AIN0D) | (1 << AIN1D));

    // PB1/AIN1 to compare with PB0/AIN0.
    ADCSRB &= ~(1 << ACME);

    // Clear pending AC Interrupts.
    ACSR |= (1 << ACI);

    // Enable AC Interrupt. ACIE = 1.
    ACSR |= (1 << ACIE);
}
```

Setting up the comparator for the ATtiny85 is slightly different from the Uno. Listing 13-6 shows the code. ACSR is cleared, as before, to initialize and enable the comparator; however, we are using different pins for the reference and comparison voltages. On the ATtiny85, we have an additional register, ACSRB, which we use to ensure that we are comparing the reference voltage on PB0/AIN0 with the voltage on PB1/AIN1.

Pending interrupts are again cleared before enabling the interrupt.

```
int main() {
    // PB2 is the "night-light" LED.
    PORTB = 0;
    DDRB = (1 << DDB2);

    setupComparator();

    // Set idle sleep mode.
    set_sleep_mode(SLEEP_MODE_IDLE);

    // Don't forget!!
    sei();

    while (1) {
        // The main loop, simply puts the board back to sleep.
        cli();
        sleep_enable();
        sleep_bod_disable();
        sei();
        sleep_cpu();
    }
}
```

Listing 13-7 is our `setup()` and `loop()` functions combined – in AVR C++, there are no separate functions. The Arduino Language hides this detail from you and silently creates a hidden `main()` function which calls your sketch's `setup()` and `loop()`. In AVR C++, we have to do this ourselves.

The setup part of main() sets the PB2 pin as an output after making sure that all pins on PORTB are set low. This avoids the LED lighting spuriously. Next, the comparator is configured and enabled as discussed previously.

The final part of our setup enables interrupts. This is quite important when writing code that doesn't use the Arduino Language and is another feature that the Arduino Language does in the background. If you have read ahead in the code, you may be wondering why I enable interrupts when the main loop also enables them. From the point interrupts are enabled, the Analog Comparator is working to determine light levels. If the current light level is too low, the LED would light at this point, even before the main loop is entered.

Obviously, the time gap between enabling the interrupts here and later on in the loop is tiny in this example; it may be important in other projects.

The main loop of our sketch happens in the `while` loop in Listing 13-7. As with the Uno sketch, the loop simply puts the board back to sleep any time it has been woken up by the Analog Comparator.

13.5   Coming Up

That's it, I'm afraid; only the appendixes are to follow and the index of course. The appendixes cover the internals and operation of circular buffers; the ATmega328P's sleep modes, explaining which are usable and which are best avoided; how to use software and/or hardware to debounce push-button switches to prevent all sorts of weird goings on when you use them in a project; and finally, an explanation of the AVRTWIlib library, discussed in brief in the previous chapter.

Circular Buffers

A

I glossed over circular buffers in Chapter 8, "USART Interrupts", so it may be best to try and explain how they work so that you have a better understanding of the code for that chapter. The examples given in this chapter are suitable for use on your desktop PC or laptop, as opposed to on your Arduino board. This makes it easier for you to see the output from the code as it runs.

The code used in the USART examples from Chapter 8 are only slightly different in operation, but the concepts explained here will be sufficient for you to understand those examples as well.

A.1   How Circular Buffers Operate

A circular buffer is nothing more than a contiguous number of bytes of memory, set aside to store and retrieve data in a "First In First Out" manner, a FIFO as this sort of thing is usually known, or even simpler, a queue.

The code to implement circular buffers is a little more efficient if the buffer size is a power of two as this makes the arithmetic modulus operator easier to implement. If the buffer is 2^4 bytes long, then the modulus operator is simply a bitwise AND operation with the value $2^4 - 1$; otherwise, a divide, subtract, and multiply are required, and multiplication and division are quite intensive operations in an embedded device's CPU.

There are a number of implementations of circular buffers around. The simplest, and those used in Chapter 8, use a pair of indexes normally named "head" and "tail" to record where the most recent byte was written (at the head) or read (at the tail). The code in that chapter is slightly different from the code presented here. This appendix contains a generalized set of functions which can be used in numerous applications rather than being specific to the USART operations described in Chapter 8.

There are a few things to remember when dealing with circular buffers as implemented in this appendix's code files:

- The *head* index is where the most recent data was written and will be incremented before the next request to write more data.
- The *tail* index is where the most recent data was read from and will be incremented before the next read request.
- The maximum number of bytes that the buffer can accommodate is always less than the buffer size.
- When $head = tail$, the buffer is empty.
- When $(head + 1) \, MOD \, buffer\_size = tail$, the buffer is full up.
- $(Current\_value + 1) \, MOD \, buffer\_size$ is how to increment the head or tail indices.
- $(Current\_value + buffer\_size - 1) \, MOD \, buffer\_size$ decrements the head or tail indices.

- $(Buffer\_size + head - tail)\ MOD\ buffer\_size$ results in the amount of data in the buffer which has yet to be read by the sketch code.
- $(Buffer\_size - 1) - space\_used$ will inform you as to how much free space remains in the buffer.

In the code folder for this appendix, you will find an example of a circular buffer implementation. There are three files:

- `main.cpp` which is the main application code. This creates a buffer and uses it, reporting on its state as it uses the buffer to store and retrieve bytes of data.
- `cBuffer.h` is the required header file to allow the use of the circular buffer code.
- `cBuffer.cpp` contains the code to implement the circular buffer.

To use it, you simply need to include the header file `cBuffer.h` and compile your code along with the file `cBuffer.cpp`. No special command-line parameters are required. The compilation command is a simple one-liner:

```
gcc -o cBuffer main.cpp cBuffer.cpp
```

The example used a 32-byte buffer which is easily changed in `cBuffer.h` by changing the definition for `BUFFER_SIZE`.

> **Note**
> If you need to change the size, make sure you use a power of two – this allows for a much more efficient modulus operation when incrementing, decrementing, or wrapping around in the buffer.
> If you go above 255, then you will need to change the `uint8_t` pointers to `uint16_t` in the header as well as changing the various functions to suit.

A.1.1   The Library Code

This section describes the two files used to build the circular buffer handling library.[1]

> **Note**
> The code for this appendix is general purpose. It is not specific to any microcontroller and as such can be used in other projects not necessarily for embedded devices.
> The code in disk for the USART, for example, which also uses circular buffers, *is* specific to the ATmega328P microcontroller and the Arduino environment. It is, therefore, slightly different to the code in this appendix.

---

[1]It's not a real library, it's simply compiled alongside your code as an additional source and header file. There's no static or dynamic library linking going on here.

A.1.1.1 The cBuffer Header File

Listing A-1 shows *most* of the header file, cBuffer.h. The missing parts are only some of the comments.

The file starts and ends with the usual markers to prevent the file being included more than once and the inclusion of the stdint.h header file which allows the use of uint8_t and similar data types. These define exactly how many bits are to be found in the variables as opposed to relying on int or short and so on, which may not be as you might expect on another CPU or microcontroller.

Listing A-1 Circular buffers – cBuffer.h

```
#ifndef CBUFFER_H
#define CBUFFER_H

#include <stdint.h>

//=================================================================
// The HEAD index is where the most recent byte was added to
// the buffer.
//
// The TAIL index is where the most recent byte removed from
// the buffer was located.
//
// For best results, the buffer should be a power of two in
// size. It will hold one less byte than the size of the
// buffer.
//
// The buffer is EMPTY when HEAD == TAIL.
//
// The buffer is FULL when HEAD + 1 = TAIL.
//
// The next index is (index + 1 ) MOD buffer_size.
//
// The previous index is (index - buffer_size - 1) MOD
//                        buffer_size.
//
// Bytes used so far is (buffer_size + head - tail) MOD
//                      buffer_size.
//
// Bytes free is buffer_Size - 1 - bytes used so far.
//=================================================================


#define BUFFER_SIZE 32


typedef struct circularBuffer {
    uint8_t headIndex;
    uint8_t tailIndex;
```

```
    uint8_t cBuffer[BUFFER_SIZE];
} circularBuffer;

// Initialise a new buffer.
void cBufferInit(circularBuffer *buf);

// Anything in a buffer to read? Unsigned return, buffers are
// always a positive length!
uint8_t cBufferBytesUsed(circularBuffer *buf);

// Any space in buffer to add to? Unsigned return, buffers are
// always a positive length!
uint8_t cBufferBytesFree(circularBuffer *buf);

// Add a byte to a buffer.
bool cBufferAdd(circularBuffer *buf, uint8_t aByte);

// Get a byte from a buffer.
bool cBufferGet(circularBuffer *buf, uint8_t *aByte);

// Is the buffer empty?
bool cBufferEmpty(circularBuffer *buf);

// Is the buffer full?
bool cBufferFull(circularBuffer *buf);

#endif // CBUFFER_H
```

The BUFFER_SIZE macro is the first to be defined and determines the size of all circular buffers in the application. This is easily changed but should be a value which is a power of two and, as we are using eight-bit indices, must be less than 256.

Following the buffer size, we see the definition of a circular buffer itself. In this example code, a circular buffer is a self-contained structure. This means that it contains the buffer and the two indices to be used for inserting and retrieving data. This avoids the need for numerous global variables when more than one buffer is used in an application. The remainder of the header file defines the function prototypes for the buffer handling code we will see in cBuffer.cpp.

Tip
You can easily change the buffer size to be 256 or bigger. If you do, however, you will need to change the indices to uint16_t. This will not be a problem when used in non-AVR code.

In AVR code however, this can be a source of intermittent errors. The AVR doesn't have a 16-bit register load instruction, so 16-bit values are loaded into two 8-bit registers in two separate instructions. If an interrupt occurs between loading the two 8-bit values, then the ISR may execute instructions with the affected variables having incomplete values.

To avoid this problem with interrupts, you *must* write the code in a manner where interrupts are disabled when updating any of the affected 16-bit variables.

A.1.1.2 The cBuffer Code File

In the matching C++ file, `cBuffer.cpp`, we see a number of functions to manipulate circular buffers. These are shown in Listings A-2 to A-6. We begin with the function `cBufferInit()`, shown in Listing A-2, which will initialize a new buffer.

Listing A-2 Circular buffers – cBufferInit() function

```cpp
//-------------------------------------------------------------
// Initialise the circular buffer. Sets the two pointers to
// the start of the buffer and as they are equal, this means
// empty.
//-------------------------------------------------------------
void cBufferInit(circularBuffer *buf) {
    // Make sure buffer is empty.
    buf->headIndex = buf->tailIndex = 0;
}
```

As you can see, all that needs to be done is to initialize the head and tail indices to zero. This indicates that the buffer is currently empty as both head and tail are the same value. The value given to the two indices is simply the offset into the buffer and in the example is zero, but *any* value within the buffer dimensions can be used provided both indices get the same value.

A circular buffer has no start and no end, metaphorically speaking, just like a circle. Provided that the buffer initialization gives the head and tail indices the same value, the buffer is empty. In use, regardless of the starting index, adding data to the buffer in sufficient quantities will wrap around and start using the "missed" indices. Try it for yourself – change the zero initial index value to something else; the numbers will be different, but the action and results will be the same.

Listing A-3 shows the `cBufferBytesUsed()` function which we can use to determine if there is anything in the buffer to be retrieved.

Listing A-3 Circular buffers – cBufferBytesUsed() function

```cpp
//-------------------------------------------------------------
// Any data in buffer to get? Unsigned return, buffers are
// always a positive length!
//-------------------------------------------------------------
uint8_t cBufferBytesUsed(circularBuffer *buf) {
    // Return number of bytes written to buffer so far.
    return ((BUFFER_SIZE + buf->headIndex - buf->tailIndex) %
            BUFFER_SIZE);
}
```

The calculation looks a bit on the wild side, but work through an example with me, and all will be clear. If we assume that the buffer is 64 bytes in size and that the head pointer is at index 60 with the tail at 50, then we obviously have a 10-byte difference between the two indices. This is "obvious" as it is a simple subtraction; what if the head pointer has wrapped around to index 12, while the tail has moved up to index 62? Follow the maths!

$$64 + (12 - 62) \ MOD \ 64$$

$$64 + (-50) \ MOD \ 64$$

$$14 \ MOD \ 64$$

The result is 14 available bytes. There are two bytes from the tail at index 62 to the end of the buffer at index 63, plus 13 bytes from index 0 up to the head at index 12 minus 1 byte because the tail's data item has *already* been retrieved, giving 14. Remember, the tail is where the most recent data item was retrieved from, so doesn't count in the calculation. The head is where the most recent data byte was added, so has yet to be retrieved and is still available. A picture might help visualize things.

0	1	2	3	4	5	6	7	8	9	10	11	12	...	62	63
												H		T	

Moving quickly away from the maths, Listing A-4 shows the cBufferBytesFree() function which returns the amount of space left in the buffer which can be written to before the buffer becomes full.

Listing A-4 Circular buffers – cBufferBytesFree() function

```
//-----------------------------------------------------------------
// Any space in buffer to add to? Unsigned return, buffers are
// always a positive length!
//-----------------------------------------------------------------
uint8_t cBufferBytesFree(circularBuffer *buf) {
    // Return BUFFER_SIZE minus space used minus 1.
    return (BUFFER_SIZE - 1 -
            cBufferBytesUsed(buf));
}
```

This is a simple function which returns the buffer size minus the bytes already written but not yet read, minus one. That final 1 being subtracted is required because a buffer of 64 characters can only hold 63 bytes of data, as has been explained.

Listing A-5 is the code to add a new byte of data to a buffer.

Listing A-5 Circular buffers – cBufferAdd() function

```
//-----------------------------------------------------------------
// Add a byte to a buffer.
//-----------------------------------------------------------------
bool cBufferAdd(circularBuffer *buf, uint8_t aByte) {
    // Any free space? Add the byte.
    if (!cBufferFull(buf)) {
        uint8_t nextPut = (buf->headIndex + 1) % BUFFER_SIZE;
```

```
        buf->cBuffer[nextPut] = aByte;
        buf->headIndex = nextPut;
        return true;
    }


    // Buffer full.
    return false;
}
```

The cBufferAdd() function will return false if the buffer is already full. Otherwise, it calculates the index where the next data byte added will be stored and stores the new data byte at that location. After adding the new byte, the current head index is updated to the position where the byte was just stored, and the code returns a value of true for success. The calculation for the next head index takes care of wrapping around based on the size of the buffer.

The calculation for the next available position in the buffer, in Listing A-5, is responsible for the loss of one byte of storage from the buffer's capacity. Imagine that your buffer is only two bytes in size and is currently empty with the head and tail indices both at 0.

The first byte to be added will cause the head index to be incremented to 1, and the byte will be stored there, leaving index 0 unused as yet.

Attempting to add a second byte will cause the head index to wrap around from 1 to 0; however, the tail index is still at 0, so the code will return a buffer full error even though only a single byte has been stored. Simple? A buffer is full when $(head + 1) = tail$.

Listing A-6 is how a byte is extracted from a circular buffer.

Listing A-6 Circular buffers – cBufferGet() function

```
//---------------------------------------------------------------
// Get a byte from a buffer.
//---------------------------------------------------------------
bool cBufferGet(circularBuffer *buf, uint8_t *aByte) {

    // Test if buffer is empty? If not, fetch a byte.
    if (!cBufferEmpty(buf)) {
        uint8_t nextGet = (buf->tailIndex + 1) % BUFFER_SIZE;
        *aByte = buf->cBuffer[nextGet];
        buf->tailIndex = nextGet;
        return true;
    }

    // Buffer is empty..
    return false;
}
```

The `cBufferGet()` function first checks to see if the buffer is empty. If it is not, the index of the next data byte to be retrieved is calculated and may equal the current head index. The calculation for the next tail index takes care of wrapping around whenever the new value for the tail index would exceed the size of the buffer. If the byte is successfully removed from the buffer, the tail index is updated and the code returns `true`.

If the buffer was found to be empty, `false` is returned so that the calling code can take appropriate action.

Listing A-7 is the code which will test a buffer to determine if it is empty.

Listing A-7 Circular buffers – cBufferEmpty() function

```
//------------------------------------------------------------
// Is this buffer empty? Head == Tail
//------------------------------------------------------------
bool cBufferEmpty(circularBuffer *buf) {
    return buf->headIndex == buf->tailIndex;
}
```

A circular buffer is empty if the head index is the same as the tail index.

Listing A-8 is the code to test if a buffer is currently full up.

Listing A-8 Circular buffers – cBufferFull() function

```
//------------------------------------------------------------
// Is this buffer full? If ((head + 1) MOD BUFFER_SIZE) == Tail
//------------------------------------------------------------
bool cBufferFull(circularBuffer *buf) {
    return (buf->headIndex + 1) % BUFFER_SIZE ==
                    buf->tailIndex;
}
```

A circular buffer is full up if the *head index* + 1, wrapped around if necessary, is the same as the tail index.

A.1.2   The Test Harness

Now that the "library" code has been covered, we are ready to look at the actual demonstration code. Listings A-9 and A-10 show the code, in the file `main.cpp`, which uses and abuses a circular buffer.

We begin with Listing A-9 which is the `displayBufferSpace()` function and displays the current state of a circular buffer. This function is called a number of times during the demonstration to show what is happening in the buffer.

Listing A-9   Circular buffers – displayBufferSpace() function

```c
#include <stdio.h>
#include "cBuffer.h"


void displayBufferSpace(circularBuffer *buf) {

    uint8_t freeSpace = cBufferBytesFree(buf);
    uint8_t usedSpace = cBufferBytesUsed(buf);

    printf("\n---------------------------------------------"
           "-------------\n");

    // Check the available space (for writing).
    printf("The buffer has %d free bytes for writing to.\n",
            freeSpace);

    // Check the available space (for reading).
    printf("The buffer has %d bytes to be read from.\n",
            usedSpace);

    // Print the buffer indices.
    printf("Buffer headIndex = %d, tailIndex = %d.\n",
            buf->headIndex, buf->tailIndex);

    // Full? Empty?
    if (cBufferEmpty(buf))
        printf("Buffer is EMPTY.\n");

    if (cBufferFull(buf))
        printf("Buffer is FULL.\n");

    printf("---------------------------------------------"
           "-------------\n");
}
```

This code should be easy to understand. It begins, after the required include statements, by grabbing the buffer's free and used space and displaying the two values. The two buffer indices are then displayed, and if the buffer is currently full or empty, a suitable message is displayed.

Listing A-10 is where it all takes place. This code begins by creating a new circular buffer and a pointer to it. The pointer is used in the various function calls to identify the buffer that we are operating on; there could be more than one. The buffer is initialized with a call to cBufferInit(), and the buffer details are dumped out on screen to show the state of an empty buffer.

The code continues by checking how many bytes it can write into the buffer before proceeding to fill the buffer to its maximum capacity. In the demonstration, the buffer is 32 bytes in size, allowing for 31 bytes of usable storage space. Each byte written has its details displayed on screen. Once the buffer is full, the current state is dumped out again.

Listing A-10 Circular buffers – main() function

```
int main() {
    // Define a new circular buffer.
    circularBuffer demoBuffer;

    // Create a pointer to the buffer.
    circularBuffer *buf = &demoBuffer;

    // Initialise the buffer.
    cBufferInit(buf);
    printf("\n1. The buffer has been initialised.\n");

    // Check the available space.
    displayBufferSpace(buf);


    // We have (BUFFER_SIZE - 1) bytes of space available.
    uint8_t freeSpace = cBufferBytesFree(buf);

    printf("\n2. Filling buffer with %d bytes.\n\n", freeSpace);

    for (uint8_t x = 0; x < freeSpace;  x++) {
        if (cBufferAdd(buf, (x + '0'))) {
            printf("cBufferAdd(): Byte %2d = '%c'\n",
                    x + 1, x + '0');
        } else {
            printf("cBufferAdd() failed with x = %d\n", x);
        }
    }

    // Check the available space.
    displayBufferSpace(buf);


    // Try adding one more byte, should fail.
    printf("\n3. Adding one more byte - this will fail!\n\n");
    if (cBufferAdd(buf, '!')) {
        printf("cBufferAdd() OK! Something wrong here!\n");
    } else {
        printf("cBufferAdd() failed, as expected.\n");
    }


    // Remove 10 bytes.
    printf("\n4. Removing 10 bytes.....\n\n");
    for (uint8_t x = 0; x < 10; x++) {
        uint8_t ch;
```

```
        if (!cBufferGet(buf, &ch)) {
            printf("cBufferGet() failed with x = %d\n", x);
            break;
        }

        printf("cBufferGet(): Byte %2d = '%c'\n", x + 1, ch);
    }

    // Check the available space.
    displayBufferSpace(buf);

}
```

After filling the buffer, the code attempts to write one more byte and expects this to fail. It does indeed fail and advises the user of the failure.

Finally, the demonstration code removes ten bytes of data from the buffer. This should free up ten bytes for further inserts. The first ten bytes which were added and are now being removed are displayed on the screen. These bytes will match up exactly with the first ten bytes that were displayed earlier when the buffer was filled up.

The buffer state is again dumped to the screen and will display that ten bytes are now free.

The test harness can be compiled with this command:

```
gcc -o cBuffer main.cpp cBuffer.cpp
```

If there are no errors, an executable named *cBuffer* will be created.

Listing A-11 shows the output from a demonstration run on Linux.

Listing A-11   Circular buffers – example output

```
1. The buffer has been initialised.

------------------------------------------------------------
The buffer has 31 free bytes for writing to.
The buffer has 0 bytes to be read from.
Buffer headIndex = 0, tailIndex = 0.
Buffer is EMPTY.
------------------------------------------------------------

2. Filling buffer with 31 bytes.

cBufferAdd(): Byte  1 = '0'
cBufferAdd(): Byte  2 = '1'
cBufferAdd(): Byte  3 = '2'
cBufferAdd(): Byte  4 = '3'
cBufferAdd(): Byte  5 = '4'
cBufferAdd(): Byte  6 = '5'
cBufferAdd(): Byte  7 = '6'
```

```
cBufferAdd():  Byte   8 = '7'
cBufferAdd():  Byte   9 = '8'
cBufferAdd():  Byte  10 = '9'
cBufferAdd():  Byte  11 = ':'
cBufferAdd():  Byte  12 = ';'
cBufferAdd():  Byte  13 = '<'
cBufferAdd():  Byte  14 = '='
cBufferAdd():  Byte  15 = '>'
cBufferAdd():  Byte  16 = '?'
cBufferAdd():  Byte  17 = '@'
cBufferAdd():  Byte  18 = 'A'
cBufferAdd():  Byte  19 = 'B'
cBufferAdd():  Byte  20 = 'C'
cBufferAdd():  Byte  21 = 'D'
cBufferAdd():  Byte  22 = 'E'
cBufferAdd():  Byte  23 = 'F'
cBufferAdd():  Byte  24 = 'G'
cBufferAdd():  Byte  25 = 'H'
cBufferAdd():  Byte  26 = 'I'
cBufferAdd():  Byte  27 = 'J'
cBufferAdd():  Byte  28 = 'K'
cBufferAdd():  Byte  29 = 'L'
cBufferAdd():  Byte  30 = 'M'
cBufferAdd():  Byte  31 = 'N'


--------------------------------------------------------------
The buffer has 0 free bytes for writing to.
The buffer has 31 bytes to be read from.
Buffer headIndex = 31, tailIndex = 0.
Buffer is FULL.
--------------------------------------------------------------


3. Adding one more byte - this will fail!

cBufferAdd() failed, as expected.

4. Removing 10 bytes.....

cBufferGet():  Byte   1 = '0'
cBufferGet():  Byte   2 = '1'
cBufferGet():  Byte   3 = '2'
cBufferGet():  Byte   4 = '3'
cBufferGet():  Byte   5 = '4'
cBufferGet():  Byte   6 = '5'
cBufferGet():  Byte   7 = '6'
cBufferGet():  Byte   8 = '7'
cBufferGet():  Byte   9 = '8'
```

```
cBufferGet(): Byte 10 = '9'

------------------------------------------------------------------
The buffer has 10 free bytes for writing to.
The buffer has 21 bytes to be read from.
Buffer headIndex = 31, tailIndex = 10.
------------------------------------------------------------------
```

A.2   Key Takeaways

In summary, the code in this example of a circular buffer implementation is *related* to the code in Chapter 8, "USART Interrupts", but is not exactly the same. ISRs run at unexpected times and cannot easily pass an error code back easily, for each and every character processed.

> **Tip**
> It *is* possible to have the ISR return an error code for every byte. I have seen it done in interrupt-driven USART communications. While the sending of data to the USART for transmission is byte oriented, the receipt of data is 16-bit word oriented. The higher eight bits contain the error code, if any, and the lower eight bits contain the actual data byte received.

Other implementations of circular buffers have the ability to use all the bytes in the buffer; however, in order to do so, they require a few more variables to indicate full or empty buffers and so on – it's a trade-off as to which version you use. My preference, and that of the Arduino developers, is to use a pair of indices and "take the hit" on losing one byte.

Hopefully, this appendix has made circular buffers a bit more clear.

"What do sleep modes have to do with interrupts?" I hear you think. Well, sleep modes are useful as they can be used to shut down various parts of the ATmega328P to save power, and interrupts will wake the device up to do some work, before going back to sleep again. There are six different sleep modes available on an ATmega328P; however, two of them are not usable on an Arduino, and another is *almost* useless on an Arduino, as will become clear.

The data sheet covers a lot of details on the various sleep modes and points of note when using them; I will note the salient points in the discussions to follow.

B.1   Sleeping

In order to send the board to sleep, there are a number of steps that must be applied. Some of the steps are time limited – if you don't make the changes fast enough, nothing will happen. The steps required to put a device to sleep are

- Set an appropriate sleep mode by setting bits SM2:SM0 (three bits) in the *Sleep Mode Control Register*, SMCR. This can be done in the setup code for the application as it will not change during or after a sleep.
- Set the Sleep Enable bit, SE, in SMCR.
- Execute the sleep instruction. This is an Assembly Language instruction, but C/C++ programmers have the sleep_cpu() function which does exactly the same thing.

Life is not always so simple. The data sheet warns that

When entering a sleep mode, all port pins should be configured to use minimum power. The most important is then to ensure that no pins drive resistive loads.

In sleep modes where both the I/O clock (clkI/O) and the ADC clock (clkADC) are stopped, the input buffers of the device will be disabled. This ensures that no power is consumed by the input logic when not needed. In some cases, the input logic is needed for detecting wake-up conditions, and it will then be enabled.

If the input buffer is enabled and the input signal is left floating or has an analog signal level close to VCC/2, the input buffer will use excessive power. For analog input pins, the digital input buffer should be disabled at all times. Digital input buffers can be disabled by writing to the *Digital Input Disable Registers*, DIDR1 and DIDR0.

An analog signal level close to VCC/2 on an input pin can cause significant current even in active mode.

This means a bit of work before going into sleep and then, when waking up, reconfiguring the device to get ready to continue.

© The Author(s), under exclusive license to APress Media, LLC, part of Springer Nature 2024   273
N. Dunbar, *Arduino Interrupts*, Maker Innovations Series,
https://doi.org/10.1007/978-1-4842-9714-8

> **Tip**
>
> I have read somewhere, but of course I can no longer find it when I need it, that pins should be put into "High-Z" prior to sleeping. This means make them inputs. On waking, they must be reconfigured as outputs again.

Looking at the data sheet for the various sleep modes, there are two main modes that are particularly usable for makers and developers, *Power Down Mode* and *ADC Noise Reduction Mode*. It may also be possible to use *Idle Mode* on Arduino boards, if Timer/counter 0's overflow interrupt can be disabled and no other timer/counters are configured to interrupt.

The remainder of this section briefly discusses all of the ATmega328P's sleep modes; for each mode, an example of enabling this mode is given and assumes that the `avr/sleep.h` header file has been included in the sketch.

B.1.1   Idle Mode

This mode is configured by

- Setting bits `SM2:SM0` to 000 in the *Sleep Mode Control Register*, `SMCR`

or

- By calling `set_sleep_mode(SLEEP_MODE_IDLE)`

This mode is *almost* useless on an Arduino. It is not possible to disable the BOD in this mode.

It *can* be used, but only if you disable Timer/counter 0 beforehand. Timer/counter 0 has its overflow interrupt in use to accumulate the `millis()` counter. With a 16 MHz system clock running, the timer/counter overflows every 256 timer clock cycles, which only takes 1024 microseconds before the interrupt will wake the board.

In this mode, only the CPU and Flash RAM clocks are stopped, so the input buffers are still active, as are the timer/counters, ADC, Analog Comparator, and so on. It is not possible to disable the BOD in this mode. Attempting to do so will appear to work, but the BOD will remain enabled.

This is a very light sleep mode, and most peripherals are still running. The device will be woken up by

- An external reset
- An INT0 interrupt – both level and edge interrupts
- An INT1 interrupt – both level and edge interrupts
- Any Pin Change interrupt – level or edge
- A TWI Address Match interrupt
- Any Timer/counter interrupt
- An SPM/EEPROM Ready interrupt
- The ADC Conversion Complete interrupt
- The Watchdog Timer interrupt
- Any "Other I/O" interrupt (as the data sheet mentions, but does not explain!)

- The Analog Comparator interrupt
- A BOD-initiated reset

The data sheet advises that the Analog Comparator should be powered off if not required to wake the device by writing a 1 to the ACD bit in the ACSR register.

B.1.2   ADC Noise Reduction Mode

This mode is configured by

- Setting bits SM2:SM0 to 001 in the *Sleep Mode Control Register*, SMCR

or

- By calling set_sleep_mode(SLEEP_MODE_ADC)

This mode is usable on an Arduino. It is not possible to disable the BOD in this mode.

The main purpose of this mode is to disable any peripherals that might cause excessive noise while the ADC is taking a reading. Because the BOD cannot be disabled in this mode, attempting to do so will appear to work, but the BOD will remain enabled.

In this mode, the CPU, I/O, and Flash RAM clocks are stopped while the remaining clocks continue to run. This means that while the AVR microcontroller is unable to access the Flash memory, use the I/O pins (except for the analog pins obviously), or actually run any instructions, peripherals, such as the ADC, USART, SPI, ADC, TWI, Analog Comparator, the three Timer/counters, and the Watchdog Timer, will continue to run and all can be used to wake the device.

As the ADC is most likely to be configured and enabled when this sleep mode is used, executing the sleep instruction will cause the ADC to initiate a new conversion. When the conversion completes, and assuming no other interrupts have occurred in the meantime, the device will wake up.

This mode is quite a light sleeper and will be woken by

- An external reset
- An INT0 low level interrupt
- An INT1 low level interrupt
- Any Pin Change interrupt – level or edge
- A TWI Address Match interrupt
- A Timer/counter 2 asynchronous interrupt (not usable on an Arduino)
- An SPM/EEPROM Ready interrupt
- The ADC Conversion Complete interrupt
- The Watchdog Timer interrupt
- A BOD-initiated reset.

B.1.3   Power Down Mode

This mode is configured by

- Setting bits SM2:SM0 to 010 in the *Sleep Mode Control Register*, SMCR or

- By calling `set_sleep_mode(SLEEP_MODE_PWR_DOWN)`

This mode is usable on an Arduino. It is also possible to disable the BOD in this mode.

This is a deep sleep and saves the most power. Consequently, it has fewer wake-up stimuli. In power down mode, *all* clocks are stopped. This means that the AVR microcontroller is effectively powered off; however, the Watchdog Timer can continue to run, and a level INT0 or INT1 interrupt or any Pin Change interrupts will also wake the device as will a TWI Address Match interrupt.

This is the most useful mode for saving power but, unfortunately, has the fewest wake-up stimuli. I have used this mode on a plant watering device which looks after my citrus tree (lime) when I'm away from home. It uses the Watchdog Timer on an ATtiny85 to wake every eight seconds, and after "enough" of those wake-up calls have occurred, it checks if the tree needs water before watering as necessary and going back to sleep.

This mode is a heavy sleeper, but can be woken by

- An external reset
- An INT0 low level interrupt
- An INT1 low level interrupt
- Any Pin Change interrupt – level or edge
- A TWI Address Match interrupt
- The Watchdog Timer interrupt
- A BOD-initiated reset, provided BOD has not been disabled

B.1.4   Power Save Mode

This mode is configured by

- Setting bits `SM2:SM0` to 011 in the *Sleep Mode Control Register*, SMCR

or

- By calling `set_sleep_mode(SLEEP_MODE_PWR_SAVE)`

This mode is not advisable on an Arduino. It is also possible to disable the BOD in this mode.

This is another deep sleep mode; however, it is slightly less a deep sleep than the Power Down Mode. This sleep mode is not advised on an Arduino as the asynchronous mode for Timer/counter 2 is not enabled.

In this mode, all clocks are stopped except Timer/counter 2's asynchronous clock. The data sheet advises that Power Down Mode should be used, instead of this sleep mode, if Timer/counter 2 is not running in asynchronous mode.

The microcontroller is pretty much powered off in this mode although the Watchdog Timer can continue to run. If this is not an Arduino board, and Timer/counter 2 is configured in asynchronous mode, then Timer/counter 2 can wake the device from this sleep mode with either an overflow or a compare match interrupt. This isn't possible on an Arduino though as the pins required for the external crystal for that particular timer mode are used for the main oscillator and have a 16 MHz crystal attached.

In summary, if you have an Arduino, use Power Down Mode. Otherwise, use this mode only if Timer/counter 2 is running asynchronously.

This mode can be woken by

- An external reset
- An INT0 low level interrupt
- An INT1 low level interrupt
- Any Pin Change interrupt – level or edge
- A TWI Address Match interrupt
- A Timer/counter 2 asynchronous interrupt (not usable on an Arduino)
- The Watchdog Timer interrupt
- A BOD-initiated reset, provided BOD has not been disabled

B.1.5   Standby Mode

This mode is configured by

- Setting bits SM2:SM0 to 110 in the *Sleep Mode Control Register*, SMCR

or

- By calling set_sleep_mode(SLEEP_MODE_STANDBY)

This mode is usable on an Arduino. It is also possible to disable the BOD in this mode.

The data sheet advises not to use this sleep mode unless there is an external crystal running the main clock. This is appropriate for Arduino boards as they have a 16 MHz crystal connected to run the main system oscillator. This mode is almost identical to the Power Down Mode described previously.

When sleeping, *all* clocks are again stopped. This means that the AVR microcontroller is effectively powered off; however, the Watchdog Timer can be configured to run and can be used to wake the device.

This mode can be woken by

- An external reset
- An INT0 low level interrupt
- An INT1 low level interrupt
- Any Pin Change interrupt – level or edge
- A TWI Address Match interrupt
- The Watchdog Timer interrupt
- A BOD-initiated reset, provided BOD has not been disabled

B.1.6   Extended Standby Mode

This mode is configured by

- Setting bits SM2:SM0 to 111 in the *Sleep Mode Control Register*, SMCR or

- By calling `set_sleep_mode(SLEEP_MODE_EXT_STANDBY)`

This mode is not usable on an Arduino. It is possible to disable the BOD in this mode.

The data sheet advises not to use this sleep mode unless there is an external crystal running the main clock and Timer/counter 2 is running asynchronously. All clocks are stopped, and once more, the AVR microcontroller is powered off to all intents and purposes. The Watchdog Timer does continue to run if configured to do so.

This mode can be woken by

- An external reset
- An INT0 low level interrupt
- An INT1 low level interrupt
- Any Pin Change interrupt – level or edge
- A TWI Address Match interrupt
- A Timer/counter 2 asynchronous interrupt (not usable on an Arduino)
- The Watchdog Timer interrupt
- A BOD-initiated reset, provided BOD has not been disabled

B.2   Power Reduction

Before going into a sleep mode, a number of the ATmega328P's internal peripherals can be powered off if not required. The *Power Reduction Register*, PRR, has eight bits to control eight peripherals, but only seven are used. The bits used in the PRR are

7	6	5	4	3	2	1	0
PRTWI	PRTIM2	PRTIM0	N/A	PRTIM1	PRSPI	PRUSART0	PRADC

If your code is not using a specific peripheral, you can use this register to shut off power to that particular part of the ATmega328P and save a few microamps of power. This can help prolong battery life if your device is battery powered. You can also power down these peripherals prior to entering a sleep and restore power on waking up afterward.

- **PRTWI**, bit 7, controls the Two-Wire Interface, also known as I^2C. To turn off power to the TWI circuitry, write a 1 to this bit position. If TWI is powered off before sleeping, it must be reconfigured on waking up. It will not be able to continue from where it was when it went to sleep.
- **PRTIM2**, bit 6, controls Timer/counter 2. To turn off power to Timer/counter 2, write a 1 to this bit position. On waking up again, the timer/counter will continue from where it went to sleep without needing any reconfiguration.
- **PRTIM0**, bit 5, controls Timer/counter 0. To turn off power to Timer/counter 0, write a 1 to this bit position. On waking up again, the timer/counter will continue from where it went to sleep without needing any reconfiguration.
- Bit 4 is not used. It is defined as read-only in the data sheet.

- **PRTIM1**, bit 3, controls Timer/counter 1. To turn off power to Timer/counter 1, write a 1 to this bit position. On waking up again, the timer/counter will continue from where it went to sleep without needing any reconfiguration.
- **PRSPI**, bit 2, controls the Serial Peripheral Interface, also known as SPI. To turn off power to the SPI circuitry, write a 1 to this bit position. If SPI is powered off before sleeping, it must be reconfigured on waking up. It will not be able to continue from where it was when it went to sleep.
- **PRUSART0**, bit 1, controls the USART interface. To turn off power to the USART, write a 1 to this bit position. If the USART is powered off before sleeping, it must be reconfigured on waking up. It will not be able to continue from where it was when it went to sleep.
- **PRADC**, bit 0, controls the Analog-to-Digital Converter, also known as ADC. To turn off power to the ADC, write a 1 to this bit position.

Other features of the ATmega328P can also be disabled to save a little power. The Analog Comparator can be disabled by writing a 1 to the ACD bit in the *Analog Comparator Status Register*, or ACSR. I wonder why Atmel didn't just use bit 4 of the PRR?

The Watchdog Timer can be disabled also. This feature doesn't have a disable bit as such; it will be disabled by calling the wdt_disable() function.

The ATmega328P has a peripheral known as the Brown Out Detector or BOD, which watches over the power supply to make sure it doesn't fall below a certain level for too long. If power does drop, the BOD holds the RESET pin at GND potential causing the device to stop, pending a reset. If power comes back up, the BOD releases RESET and the board resets. If power remains low, the BOD holds the device in a *nonrunning and ready to reset* state, until power goes off completely and everything shuts down.

The BOD can be disabled during sleep on some AVR microcontrollers, including the ATmega328P. Disabling the BOD requires a timed instruction sequence and must be done within the three clock cycles prior to sleep instruction executing; otherwise, the BOD stays enabled.

B.3   Waking Up

When the ATmega328P wakes up from a sleep, and the wake-up call originated from an interrupt, then

- The system will delay while the CPU wakes up and will then halt for four clock cycles.
- The interrupt which woke the microcontroller will then be handled by the appropriate ISR.
- Program control then returns to the instruction after the sleep instruction which initiated the sleep mode from which the device has been wakened.
- The BOD, if it was disabled during the sleep, will be enabled automatically.

Once awake, the data sheet advises that sleeping should be disabled until ready to resume sleeping. This is done by clearing the SE bit in SMCR, which requires a zero to be written to it.[1] Then, all the considerations carried out prior to sleeping must be undone in order to resume. This may require the TWI, SPI, and/or USART to be reconfigured, but the three timer/counters, the ADC, and Analog Comparator are all ready to continue from where they left off when the device was put to sleep.

---

[1]Unusually for an AVR device, clearing a bit by actually clearing it!

B.4   A Sleep Template

This section describes a template for putting your ATmega328P to sleep. This applies regardless of whether you are using the Arduino IDE or otherwise. If you follow the steps outlined, you should have no problems using the sleep facilities.

B.4.1   In the Code Setup

In the setup code for the application or sketch

- Set the sleep mode that you wish to use. For most of us, this will be either ADC Noise Reduction Mode or Power Down Mode. The best way to set sleep modes is to `#include "avr/sleep.h"` and then call `set_sleep_mode()` passing the appropriate sleep mode.

The sleep mode can be set in the setup code as it never changes during or after a sleep.

B.4.2   In the Code Loop

In the loop for the application, prepare to sleep:

- Permit the microcontroller to be able to sleep using the `sleep_enable()` function.
- Prior to sleeping, make sure to follow the data sheet advice on disabling pins, turning off digital I/O, and so on, as necessary.
- Prior to sleeping, the internal peripherals may be powered down to save a little more power. The easiest method of setting the sleep mode is to `#include "avr/power.h"` and then call the various `power_xxx_disable()` functions, using the required "xxx" as necessary.
- *Immediately* prior to sleeping, disable the BOD, if required. There is a strict time limit between disabling the BOD, using `sleep_bod_disable()`, and going to sleep. You only have three clock cycles to execute the `sleep_cpu()` command after disabling the BOD.

```
#include "avr/sleep.h"
#include "avr/interrupt.h"
...
cli()
sleep_enable();
sleep_bod_disable();
sei();
sleep_cpu();
...
```

You should note that `sleep_bod_disable()` and `sleep_cpu()` are not *proper* functions; otherwise, the three clock cycle timeouts would always expire. They are defined as inline assembly which has no function call overheads to disrupt the timings.

The `sleep_cpu()` function will put the ATmega328P to sleep. You will note that interrupts must be re-enabled before going to sleep, or, depending on the sleep mode, nothing will be able to wake the board!

After the device wakes from sleep, the code should

- Disable sleeping until ready to sleep again by calling the `sleep_disable()` function
- Power on any peripherals which were powered off during the sleep
- Reconfigure TWI, if necessary
- Reconfigure SPI, if necessary
- Reconfigure the USART, if necessary
- Return pins to their desired modes and re-enable the digital I/O if necessary

The device is now ready to continue from where it left off.

Debouncing Switches

C

Many of the sketches in this book have made use of push-button switches. These little components are very handy for lots of things, but they have a few drawbacks. The biggest of these is the fact that they are imperfect; they *bounce*. Bouncing switches are a problem in electronic circuits as microcontrollers, even a relatively slow one like the ATmega328P, are able to test the state of a switch numerous times before it stops bouncing. In addition, when interrupts are involved, the bouncing registers as a new, *single* interrupt which will trigger the handler almost immediately after it has completed processing the first interrupt, leading to LEDs that don't light when they should and so forth.

This appendix will explain what we can do to allow the microcontroller the ability to read a steady, nonbouncing state from our switches. We will examine a simple hardware solution as well as a couple of software variants.

C.1   Why Do Switches Bounce?

When you press the button, the internals of the switch slam together quite violently and, on making contact, bounce back apart again before making and breaking a few more times before they settle into the required state.

If you have the switch connected to an interrupt handler via a pin, then when the contacts make contact for long enough to be registered, the ISR will start executing. This execution will clear the interrupt flag and disable further interrupts. Unfortunately, the bouncing contacts will cause another interrupt to be noted, and this will set the interrupt flag again to show a pending interrupt is waiting to be processed.

Once the ISR finishes executing, and your LED is shining brightly, the ISR will execute again, after four clock cycles, and most likely turn the LED off again. This is particularly noticeable in ISRs that toggle something in response to an interrupt – you press the button and nothing appears to happen, so you try again and again and, eventually, it happens. This is caused by the switch bouncing.

In my circuits, for example, Figure 3-1 in Chapter 3, "External Interrupts INT0/INT1", you can see that I'm using an MC14490P hex debounce chip to stop spurious effects when I use switches. This IC allows up to six different switches to be debounced quite easily. However, other forms of debouncing can be used, and a couple of the most common are described in the following sections.

© The Author(s), under exclusive license to APress Media, LLC, part of Springer Nature 2024
N. Dunbar, *Arduino Interrupts*, Maker Innovations Series,
https://doi.org/10.1007/978-1-4842-9714-8

C.2   Resistor-Capacitor Debouncing

The resistor-capacitor debouncing circuit is pretty much what the MC14490P is using internally. If you only have a couple of switches to debounce, and you have room on the breadboard, then this is a good way to debounce a switch. The additional components you will require are a couple of 10 KΩ resistors and a 100 nanofarad capacitor (0.1 microfarad).

The circuit diagram can be seen in Figure C-1 and represents the switch connected to Arduino pin D2 in Figure 3-1 in Chapter 3, "External Interrupts INT0/INT1".

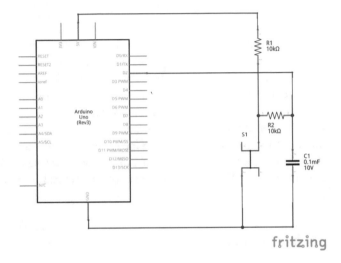

Figure C-1 RC debouncing – schematic

When the switch is open, capacitor C1 charges from the Arduino's 5 V pin through R1 and, as the switch is open, through R2. When the button is pressed, C1 discharges through resistor R2 and, obviously, the switch to ground. Charging and discharging a capacitor through a resistor take a certain amount of time, and with the values used in the circuit shown, even the worst switches will have finished bouncing well before the voltage on the capacitor rises or falls below the value required for the Arduino pin to see a high or low value. What exactly are those voltage values?

- An ATmega328P running on a VCC of 5 V, on an Arduino board, for example, will see a high when the voltage on the pin is 3 V or higher and a low if the voltage is 1.5 V or lower. Voltages between 1.5 and 3 V will be deemed floating and are to be avoided.
- An ATmega328P running on a VCC of 3.3 V will see a high when the voltage on the pin is 2 V or higher and a low if the voltage is 1 V or lower. Voltages between 1 and 2 V will be deemed floating and are to be avoided.

There is a slight drawback though; reading the switch will return a value as if the switch has been configured with pull-up resistors enabled – INPUT_PULLUP in Arduino speak. A closed (pressed) switch will cause a low value on the Arduino pin, while an open (unpressed) switch will show a high value. Why?

- While the switch remains unpressed, the capacitor is charged to *almost* VCC, and the Arduino pin is connected to the positive side of the capacitor, so reads a voltage level very close to VCC. This is therefore a high.
- When the switch is pressed, the capacitor will begin to discharge, and the pin will follow the charge state of the capacitor as it discharges.

Figure C-2 shows the corresponding breadboard layout that I used for this experiment.

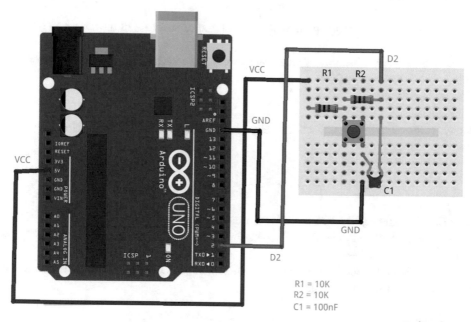

Figure C-2   RC debouncing – breadboard layout

I find the circuit layout in Figure C-1 to be perfectly adequate to debounce switches when I'm not able, or willing, to use an MC14490P.

If we are lacking in the components required to use hardware debouncing, we can still use software. However, before we delve into the software manner of debouncing a switch, we can take a look at the theory behind the time it takes to change and discharge a capacitor in an RC circuit. What's that? You don't care? Skip to Section C.3, "Software Delay Debouncing", in that case!

If you want the full details about capacitor charging and discharging, then *Electronics Tutorials* has all you should need at www.electronics-tutorials.ws/rc/rc_1.html. Why might you need this information? If your circuit is such that even with the values given, the switch *still* bounces, you need to know how to adjust the resistor or capacitor values to increase the delay time to get the voltage across the capacitor to be at the correct logic level for the pin to be accurately read.

C.2.1   RC Charging

Charging a capacitor through a resistor takes a certain time. As charging begins the current is highest, then as the capacitor charges, the current reduces and the voltage across the capacitor increases. The time it takes is dependent on the value of the resistance in ohms and the value of the capacitor in farads. If we multiply those two figures together, we get the value T or the *Time Constant* for the RC circuit.

Given that in our RC debouncing circuit, the charging resistance is $R1 + R2$; we have $20\,K\Omega$, which is $20{,}000\,\Omega$, and 100 nanofarads, which is 100^{-9} farads. Our value for T is therefore $(20{,}000) *$ (100^{-9}) or $(20{,}000) * (0.0000001)$, which equals 0.002 seconds.

However, T is the time taken for the voltage across the capacitor, V_c, to rise to 63% of the source voltage, V_s. This means that

- After one period T, the voltage on the fully discharged capacitor will have risen to 63% of 5 V or 3.15 V.
- After another T period has passed, the voltage will have risen to 63% of the *remaining* voltage (that between 3.15 V and VCC).
- And so on in 63% steps.

The voltage across a charging capacitor at any given time, t, after charging starts, is given by the equation:

$$V_c = V_s * \left(1 - e^{-t/RC}\right)$$

where e is Euler's number,[1] 2.7182, and t is the time period of interest.

A capacitor is considered to be fully charged after $5 * T$ and has reached 98% of VCC. This time is known as the *Transient Period*.

Can we prove that after one T, the capacitor voltage will be 3.15? Yes, we can; substitute our values into the equations and see what comes out:

$$V_c = 5 * \left(1 - 2.7182^{-0.002/0.002}\right)$$

$$V_c = 5 * \left(1 - 2.7182^{-1}\right)$$

$$V_c = 5 * (1 - 0.3686)$$

$$V_c = 5 * 0.6314$$

$$V_c = 3.157$$

Note
I have rounded the figures to four decimal places in the calculations. You can use a decent calculator (or spreadsheet) and get a more accurate set of figures if you wish.

This is a high enough voltage to see a high on the pin, so unless the code reads the switch state within 0.002 seconds of power-on, the switch will still be debounced and will show a high when not pressed.

---

[1] See www.mathsisfun.com/numbers/e-eulers-number.html for much more detail.

C.2.2 RC Discharging

When the switch is pressed, the capacitor starts to discharge; however, it discharges through R2 only. The Time Constant, T, is now calculated as $(10{,}000) * (100^{-9})$ or $(10{,}000) * (0.0000001)$ which equals 0.001 seconds. After $1 * T$ period of time, 63% of the capacitor's charge will have gone. After a second T period, 63% of the remaining charge will have leaked away and so on in 63% steps. After $5 * T$, the capacitor is deemed to be fully discharged.

The voltage across a discharging capacitor at any given time, t, after discharging starts, is given by the equation:

$$V_c = V_s * e^{-t/RC}$$

where, as before, e is Euler's number, 2.7182, and t is the time of interest.

Taking our RC circuit under discussion, what will the voltage across the capacitor be after T seconds? Well, we know that T is 0.001 seconds, so

$$V_c = 5 * 2.7182^{-0.001/0.001}$$

$$V_c = 5 * 2.7182^{-1}$$

$$V_c = 5 * 0.3679$$

$$V_c = 1.8395$$

This value is 36.79% of VCC, which, given I've rounded the figures to four decimal places, is showing that 63.21% of the charge has leaked away. However, this is still showing a high as the voltage is more than 1.5 V. We need to keep going!

The voltage after $2 * T$ seconds is

$$V_c = 5 * 2.7182^{-0.002/0.001}$$

$$V_c = 5 * 2.7182^{-2}$$

$$V_c = 5 * 0.1353$$

$$V_c = 1.6765$$

And this is a low enough voltage to be read as a low when the switch state is checked. This means that unless the code checks the switch state somewhere between 0.001 and 0.002 seconds after the switch was pressed, it will still read a high value and see the switch as *not pressed*. Is this a problem? It's unlikely; not many people can hold a switch down for such a short period of time, so the code will most likely be checking more than once while the switch is down, and as such, it will see the pressed state.

C.3 Software Delay Debouncing

How do we use software to debounce a switch? Well, there are numerous different methods, but the simplest is to note when the switch changes state and start a delay running. After the delay is complete, and assuming it is not too long or too short, the switch should settle down and a valid reading can be obtained.

www.arduino.cc/en/Tutorial/BuiltInExamples/Debounce, on the Arduino website, has an excellent example of using software to debounce a switch. The example sketch there is based on a sketch written by Limor Fried of Adafruit, but modified slightly so that the switch reads high when closed and low when open. This is completely the opposite to the RC debouncing circuit previously discussed and is entirely due to the switch being configured with a pull-down resistor, R1, which you can see in the schematic in Figure C-3.

You will most likely notice that this is the normal manner in which a switch is configured with a pull-down resistor; there's nothing special here.

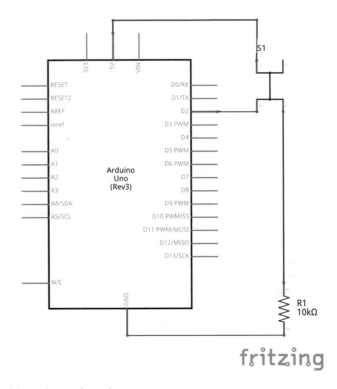

Figure C-3 Software debouncing – schematic

There's a problem though; when using interrupts, the `millis()` function doesn't get updated while the ISR is executing because interrupts have been disabled and it's interrupts which update the `millis()` and `micros()` return values. However, this method of debouncing a switch is useful when polling, so I've included it here for reference.

Figure C-4 is the breadboard layout for this experiment.

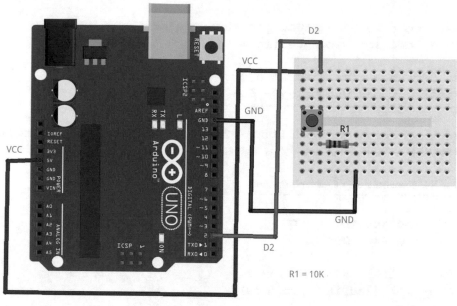

Figure C-4 Software debouncing – breadboard layout

As shown in Figure C-4, the switch is attached to Arduino pin D2, and the built-in LED is, as ever, attached to pin D13.

Listings C-1 through C-3 show the code for the sketch, which is in the public domain.

We begin with a number of constants and variables in Listing C-1. Other than the switch and LED pins, we need to keep hold of the current state of the LED, and ledState is used for this purpose. ButtonState will be used on each pass through the loop() function to read the current state of the switch *after* it has been debounced. This will be compared with lastButtonState to see if the switch has changed state; if it has, then we need to start running the delay. Finally, debounceDelay is used to determine how long to delay before presuming that the switch has stopped bouncing.

Listing C-1 SW debouncing sketch – variables

```
// The number of the pushbutton pin
const int buttonPin = 2;

// The number of the LED pin
const int ledPin = 13;

// The current state of the output pin
int ledState = HIGH;

// The current reading from the input pin
int buttonState;

// The previous reading from the input pin
int lastButtonState = LOW;
```

```
// The last time the output pin was toggled
unsigned long lastDebounceTime = 0;

// The debounce time; increase if the output flickers
unsigned long debounceDelay = 50;
```

The setup() function is shown in Listing C-2 and simply configures the switch and LED pins and sets the LED to the initial state which is high and therefore illuminates the LED.

Listing C-2 SW debouncing sketch – setup() function

```
void setup() {
  pinMode(buttonPin, INPUT);
  pinMode(ledPin, OUTPUT);

  // Set initial LED state
  digitalWrite(ledPin, ledState);
}
```

Listing C-3 is where the action takes place. The loop() function reads the current state of the switch into reading, a temporary variable defined within the loop() function itself. The value in reading is potentially invalid if the switch is still bouncing; however, it is compared to the state the button was in on the previous pass through the loop() function – lastButtonState.

If this is different from the current state, then either a bounce occurred or the button was pressed; in either case, the millis() value is saved in lastDebounceTime. This value is not updated if the two button state readings are the same – either because the switch has not been pressed or it has finally stopped bouncing.

Listing C-3 SW debouncing sketch – loop() function

```
void loop() {
  // Read the state of the switch into a local variable:
  int reading = digitalRead(buttonPin);

  // Check to see if you just pressed the button
  // (i.e. the input went from LOW to HIGH), and you've waited
     long enough
  // since the last press to ignore any noise:

  // If the switch changed, due to noise or pressing:
  if (reading != lastButtonState) {
    // Reset the debouncing timer
    lastDebounceTime = millis();
  }

  if ((millis() - lastDebounceTime) > debounceDelay) {
    // Whatever the reading is at, it's been there for
```

```
    // longer than the debouncedelay, so take it as
    // the actual current state.

    // If the button state has changed:
    if (reading != buttonState) {
      buttonState = reading;

      // Only toggle the LED if the new button state is HIGH
      if (buttonState == HIGH) {
        ledState = !ledState;
      }
    }
  }

  // Set the LED:
  digitalWrite(ledPin, ledState);

  // Save the reading. Next time through the loop, it'll be the
     lastButtonState:
  lastButtonState = reading;
}
```

If `millis()` is now higher than the `lastDebounceTime` by at least `debounceDelay` milliseconds, then we can be sure that the button was pressed and has stopped bouncing. The value in `reading` can be considered to be the actual state of the debounced button.

If this is different from the last state of the button, stored in `buttonState`, then we need to store the new state and then check if the LED needs to be toggled. If you recall, the switch pin will be high when pressed, so if `buttonState` is high, we need to toggle the LED. We do this by toggling `ledState`, and the new value will shortly be applied to the LED.

The LED is then toggled, if necessary, and the new, debounced state of the switch is stored in `lastButtonState` ready for the next pass through the loop.

It takes a few reads to get your head around the code, but it works!

C.4   Switch History Debouncing

My own preferred method for software debouncing is to read the switch a number of times and keep a history of the last 32 readings. When all 32 are the same, we should have a settled switch. The `debounce()` function in Listing C-4 carries out the reading of the switch and storing the history. It only returns a value when the switch has settled.

The function will return the value `true` of a switch being pressed and `false` if it is released. This is always the same regardless of whether the switch pin has a resistor pulling it down to ground, is configured as `INPUT_PULLUP`, or has a resistor pulling it up to VCC.

Listing C-4 SW debouncing with history – debounce() function

```
// Masks for the pressed/released bit patterns
#define ALL_ONES 0xFFFFFFFF
#define ALL_ZEROS 0x00000000

bool debounce(uint8_t pinNumber, bool pullUpEnabled) {
    uint8_t switchState = 0;      // Current state
    uint32_t stateHistory = 0;    // 32 State history

    // Loop around until we read the same value from
    // the switch, 32 times in succession.
    while (1) {
        // Get 0 or 1 from the switch.
        switchState = !!(digitalRead(pinNumber));

        // Add it to the stateHistory.
        stateHistory = (stateHistory << 1) | switchState;

        // If we have read 32 consecutive high or low
        // values from the pin, we are done.
        if (stateHistory == ALL_ONES || stateHistory == ALL_ZEROS)
            // Return true if switch is pressed, false if released

            return ((stateHistory == ALL_ONES) != pullUpEnabled);
    }
}
```

The code is quite simple and, to my mind, less messy than Listing C-3; however, your mileage may differ, so I present you with a choice.

The variable switchState holds the current state of the switch, which could still be bouncing, and stateHistory holds a record of up to 32 previous states for the switch.

The main part of the code is the while loop which loops around constantly until such time as the stateHistory holds either all 1 bits or all 0 bits. Each bit in the history is read from the switch by calling digitalRead() and using the C++ "!!" operator to convert to a 1 or a 0 "bit" for the switch state. If the switch is being pulled up, then

- A pressed switch will register a 0.
- A released switch will register a 1.

If, on the other hand, the switch is being pulled down by a resistor, then

- A pressed switch will register a 1.
- A released switch will register a 0.

The bit recorded is added to the stateHistory after each read of the switch.

After each read of the switch, the history is checked to see if it contains 32 identical bits. If this is not the case, the loop continues executing; however, once the history is found to contain 32 identical bits, we exit from the code returning a value of `true` if the switch was pressed or `false` if it was released.

The result is obtained by comparing the `stateHistory` with `ALL_ONES` and then making sure that differs from the passed in parameter for the pin's pull-up state.

Listing C-5 shows an example sketch utilizing this function to debounce a switch attached to pin D2 and using the result to toggle the built-in LED. This sketch used the same breadboard layout as already seen in Figure C-4.

The `setup()` function simply sets the switch pin to be an input pin, then the built-in LED is set as an output and turned off. The Serial Monitor is then set to 9600 baud and a prompt displayed to get the user interested!

Listing C-5 SW debouncing with history – example sketch

```
#define SWITCH_PIN 2

void setup() {
    pinMode(SWITCH_PIN, INPUT);
    pinMode(LED_BUILTIN, OUTPUT);
    digitalWrite(LED_BUILTIN, LOW);

    Serial.begin(9600);
    Serial.println("Press the switch ...");
}

void loop() {
    // The previous state of the switch when last read.
    static bool switchPreviousState = false;

    // Current state of the LED, true = on.
    static bool ledState = false;

    bool switchState = debounce(SWITCH_PIN, false);

    if (switchState != switchPreviousState) {
        switchPreviousState = switchState;

        if (switchState) {
            ledState = !ledState;
            digitalWrite(LED_BUILTIN, ledState);
        }
    }
}
```

The `loop()` function uses a `static` variable, `switchPreviousState`, to record the previous state of the switch and another, `ledState`, to record whether the built-in LED is on or off. The LED is initially off. Static variables are initialized only on the first execution of the function. On the second and subsequent executions of `loop()`, they will hold on to their most recently assigned value.

Tip
You can use static variables in place of global variables, much loved in Arduino sketches.

The current `switchState` is read by calling the `debounce()` function from Listing C-4. If the switch has changed state since the last execution of the `loop()` function, then the new state is recorded. If the new switch state is pressed, the LED's state is toggled and used to toggle the LED.

AVRTWIlib

D

In Chapter 12, "TWI Interrupt", I mentioned that I had made some modifications to Chris Herring's AVRTWIlib for AVR microcontrollers. This appendix describes the operation of my new version of Chris' code.

D.1   The AVRTWIlib Library

The library consists of the following three files:

- `TWIlib.h` is the main header file. This file should be included in any sketch or application which requires the library.
- `twiErrors.h` should be included if you wish to use the `TWIGetLastError()` function. If you do not wish to use the verbose error messages, then define the macro `NO_ERROR_DATA_REQUIRED` and only include the file if this macro has not been defined.
- `TWIlib.cpp` is the implementation file for the library. This has been slightly bug-fixed and updated since Chris originally wrote it. This file needs to be added to any application or sketch that uses the library.

D.2   Structures and Enums

The library provides a global structure named `TWIInfo` which is defined as follows:

```
// In TWIlib.h
typedef struct TWIInfoStruct{
    TWIMode mode;
    uint8_t errorCode;
    uint8_t repStart;
} TWIInfoStruct;

extern TWIInfoStruct TWIInfo;

// In TWIlib.cpp
TWIInfoStruct TWIInfo;
```

© The Author(s), under exclusive license to APress Media, LLC, part of Springer Nature 2024
N. Dunbar, *Arduino Interrupts*, Maker Innovations Series,
https://doi.org/10.1007/978-1-4842-9714-8

The three fields indicate the mode of operation, any error codes detected, and whether a repeated start has been requested. The interrupt handler returns error codes through this global structure.

The mode field is an enumeration and may take any of the following values:

```
// In TWIlib.h
typedef enum {
    Ready,
    Initializing,
    RepeatedStartSent,
    MasterTransmitter,
    MasterReceiver,
    SlaveTransmitter,
    SlaveReciever,
    SlaveReceiver = SlaveReciever,      // Spelling mistake fix!
    Initialising = Initializing
} TWIMode;
```

D.3   Macros Provided

The following macros are defined in TWIlib.h:

- TWI_TX_RX_SUCCESS which has the value 0
- TWI_TX_RX_NOT_READY which has the value 1

Those are potential returns from TWITransmitData() and TWIReadData() to indicate if the TWI system is ready and able to initiate a transmission or receipt of data.

- TWI_SUCCESS which has the value 0xFF

This is the return value from TWIInit() returned via the TWIInfo structure.

- TWI_BUSY which has the value 0
- TWI_READY which has the value 1

Those are potential returns from isTWIReady() to indicate if the AVRTWIlib library is ready to be used, or otherwise.

- TWI_STATUS

This macro is used whenever the ISR is executing. It extracts the actual status code for the operation which has just completed and masks out the unwanted bits (bits 0–2) which are not part of the status code.

- TWISendStart()

This macro is called in `TWITransmitData()` to initiate a TWI communication. It will also be used in the ISR when handling repeated starts after a number of different status codes have been received. It has been defined to resemble a function call.

- `TWISendStop()`

This macro is called in the ISR whenever an error is detected or when a conversation is completed. The macro causes the TWI system to be disconnected and the bus made available for other uses. It has been defined to resemble a function call.

- `TWISendTransmit()`

This macro is called from the ISR to make sure that all requested bytes are sent. It is also used in the `TWITransmitData()` function to continue a transmission after a repeated start has been sent. It has been defined to resemble a function call.

- `TWISendACK()`

This macro is called in the ISR whenever a data byte or a device read address is to be received. When receiving data, this macro will be called to request each byte and, apart from the final one, will return an ACK to the device transmitting the data. It has been defined to resemble a function call.

- `TWISendNACK()`

This macro is called whenever the last byte is to be requested from a device. On successful receipt of this final byte, the TWI system will return a NACK to the sender, indicating the end of the transmission. It has been defined to resemble a function call.

The following macros are from Chris' original library and are defined to match the various status codes that TWI_STATUS can extract from the `TWSR` register after each and every TWI operation. These are for use in the ISR which is described in Section D.9.3, "The Interrupt Handler".

- `TWI_START_SENT` which has the value 0x08
- `TWI_REP_START_SENT` which has the value 0x10
- `TWI_MT_SLAW_ACK` which has the value 0x18
- `TWI_MT_SLAW_NACK` which has the value 0x20
- `TWI_MT_DATA_ACK` which has the value 0x28
- `TWI_MR_SLAR_ACK` which has the value 0x40
- `TWI_MR_SLAR_NACK` which has the value 0x48
- `TWI_MR_DATA_ACK` which has the value 0x50
- `TWI_MR_DATA_NACK` which has the value 0x58
- `TWI_LOST_ARBIT` which has the value 0x38
- `TWI_NO_RELEVANT_INFO` which has the value 0xF8
- `TWI_ILLEGAL_START_STOP` which has the value 0x00

D.4   Functions Provided

The library provides all Chris Herring's original functions, some slightly amended, and a couple of new additions.

D.4.1   TWIInit

```
void TWIInit(uint32_t freqSCLKHz = 100);
```

This function initializes the library and sets the clock frequency to 100 KHz, unless otherwise defined. Any required clock frequency can be supplied, but so far, only speeds up to 400 KHz have been tested. This is only because I have no devices that operate above this speed.

The required speed is passed, in KHz, in the freqSCLKHz parameter.

This function returns values via the TWIInfo structure:

- TWIInfo.mode = Ready
- TWIInfo.errorCode = TWI_SUCCESS

D.4.2   isTWIReady

```
uint8_t isTWIReady();
```

This function should be called before attempting to initiate a transmission or reception of data. It returns one of two results:

- TWI_READY if the AVRTWIlib library system has been successfully initialized
- TWI_BUSY if the library is currently in use, facilitating a transmission or reception of data

D.4.3   SCLfreq

```
uint32_t SCLfreq();
```

This function calculates the current clock frequency for the TWI hardware. It should match up with that passed to TWIInit().

D.4.4   TWITransmitData

```
uint8_t TWITransmitData(void *const TXdata,
                        uint8_t dataLen,
                        uint8_t repStart);
```

This function initiates a transmission of data. Data are transmitted from a buffer, TXdata, which is user defined and must remain in scope until after the transmission has completed. The first byte of the first transmission must be the eight-bit write address for the device to be communicated with. If there are more data to be sent, the second and subsequent transmissions need not send the device address again. The size of the data to be sent is passed in dataLen.

A repeated start should be requested, via repStart, if, for example, the data being sent configures a sensor and will be followed by a read operation to retrieve data from the newly configured device. If no repeated start is requested, then the TWI bus will be released after the current transmission completes or errors out.

D.4.5 TWIReadData

```
uint8_t TWIReadData(uint8_t TWIaddr,
                    uint8_t bytesToRead,
                    void *RXBuffer,
                    uint8_t repStart);
```

This function initiates data reception. Received data are written into a buffer, RXBuffer, which is user defined and must remain in scope until after the reception has completed. The buffer must be big enough to hold all the received data. Only bytesToRead bytes will be returned.

The device address passed in TWIaddr is the seven-bit address – the code internally handles converting this into an eight-bit address with the lowest bit set.

A repeated start should be requested, via repStart, if, for example, the data being read is to be followed by a subsequent write operation to the same device. If no repeated start is requested, then the TWI bus will be released after the current transmission completes or errors out.

D.4.6 TWIGetLastError

```
const char *TWIGetLastError(uint8_t errorCode);
```

This function is only available if twiErrors.h has been included, and the macro NO_ERROR_DATA_REQUIRED has *not* been defined. It will, for any passed status code, return a meaningful error message (in English) for use in reporting problems to the user.

D.5   Library Initialization

To use the library, the code should initialize the library and determine if verbose error messages are to be used.

- Optionally define NO_ERROR_DATA_REQUIRED to show that verbose errors are not required. Verbose errors will be used if this macro is *not* defined.
- Include the TWIlib.h header file *after* defining the NO_ERROR_DATA_REQUIRED macro, if you do not wish to see the expanded error messages.

- Optionally, based on NO_ERROR_DATA_REQUIRED, include the twiErrors.h header. This file should be included if NO_ERROR_DATA_REQUIRED is not defined.
- Enable global interrupts.
- Initialize the AVRTWIlib library and set the speed of the TWI clock by calling TWIInit() passing the required clock speed in KHz.

An example of the library initialization would therefore resemble Listing D-1.

Listing D-1 AVRTWIlib initialization

```
// Comment out the next line to get verbose errors.
#define NO_ERROR_DATA_REQUIRED

// We need the AVRTWIlib header
#include "TWIlib.h"

// Optional verbose errors.
#ifndef NO_ERROR_DATA_REQUIRED
    #include "twiErrors.h"
#endif

// Initialise the library to 200 KHz.
void initTWI() {
    sei();
    TWIInit(200);
}
```

D.6   Data Transmission

To transmit data, the code should

- Create a buffer holding the data to be transmitted, and ensure that the first character in the buffer is the write address of the device. The write address is the seven-bit device address shifted left one bit and ANDed with 0xFE to clear bit zero. This buffer should remain in scope until after the transmission has completed.
- Call isTWIReady() in a loop, perhaps with a delay, until the result returned is equal to TWI_READY; alternatively, just loop until a nonzero value is returned. This indicates that the library has been initialized and is ready for use.
- Initialize TWIInfo.errorCode with TWI_NO_RELEVANT_INFO. This value is not able to be returned from the TWI hardware, so cannot ever be a valid error status.
- Initialize a transmission by calling TWITransmitData(), passing the buffer address, the size of the data to transmit, and whether or not a repeated start is required after the transmission completes. When initiating a new transmission, the first byte in the data buffer must be the eight-bit write address of the device you wish to communicate with.

To initialize a data transmission, the code may resemble Listing D-2.

Listing D-2   AVRTWIlib data transmission

```
// Initialise the sensor with config data and
// request a repeated start as we need to read
// data back afterwards.

// Sensor 7 bit address.
const uint8_t LM75A_ADDRESS = 0x4F;

// Sensor temperature register number.
const uint8_t LM75A_TEMP_REGISTER = 0x00;

// Data to configure reads from temperature register.
uint8_t configData[2] = {
    (LM75A_ADDRESS << 1) & 0xFE,
    LM75A_TEMP_REGISTER
};

// Wait for TWI. TWI_BUSY has the value zero.
while(!isTWIReady()) {
    _delay_ms(50);
}

// Initiate the transmission of data.
TWIInfo.errorCode = TWI_NO_RELEVANT_INFO;
uint8_t TXInitiated = TWI_TX_RX_NOT_READY;
while (TXInitiated == TWI_TX_RX_NOT_READY) {
    TXInitiated = TWITransmitData(configData,
                                  2,
                                  true);
}
```

D.7   Data Reception

To receive data, the code should

- Create a buffer big enough to hold the desired data from the TWI device you wish to read from. This buffer must remain in scope until after the data reception has completed.
- Call isTWIReady() in a loop, perhaps with a delay, until the result returned is equal to TWI_READY; alternatively, just loop until a nonzero value is returned. This indicates that the library is ready for use.
- Initialize TWIInfo.errorCode with TWI_NO_RELEVANT_INFO. This value is not able to be returned from the TWI hardware, so cannot ever be a valid error status.

- Initialize a data receipt by calling TWIReadData(), passing the seven-bit device address,[1] the buffer address, the size of the data to receive, and whether or not a repeated start is required after the transmission completes.

To initialize data receipt, the code may resemble Listing D-3.

Listing D-3 AVRTWIlib data reception

```
// Read data back from a sensor. The address and configuration
// data has been previously written and a repeated start has held
// the TWI bus for this read to take place.

// Sensor data buffer.
uint8_t temperature[2];

// Wait for TWI. TWI_BUSY has the value zero.
while(!isTWIReady()) {
    _delay_ms(50);
}

// Initiate the reception of data. A repeated start is not
// required as the reading of the data will indicate the end
// of this transmission. The bus will be freed.
TWIInfo.errorCode = TWI_NO_RELEVANT_INFO;
uint8_t RXInitiated = TWI_TX_RX_NOT_READY;
while (RXInitiated == TWI_TX_RX_NOT_READY) {
    RXInitiated = TWIReadData(LM75A_ADDRESS,
                             2,
                             temperature,
                             false);
}
```

D.8   Checking Success or Failure

After every attempt to transmit or receive data, the status of the operation should be checked.

Now, in a polling application, the code would initiate the action and then sit in a loop waiting for it to complete. With interrupts, it happens in the background, and the main code can get on with some useful work, and only a periodic check to determine the action has completed will be required.

There's nothing to stop you writing code to immediately check for completion as soon as the request has been initiated of course, but surely it's more useful to flash an LED[2] instead of just waiting for the TWI action to finish!

To check for success or failure, the code should

---

[1]Note, this is different from TWITransmitData() which requires an 8-bit address.

[2]It is a fact that the only useful work that any microcontroller carries out is flashing LEDs!

- Loop until `TWIInfo.errorCode` is not equal to `TWI_NO_RELEVANT_INFO`. This is the impossible[3] value that you set before initiating the data transmission or receipt.
- Extract the error code from `TWIInfo.errorCode`.
- Test for errors and handle them appropriately[4] by indicating an error condition, displaying a message or similar. `TWI_SUCCESS` indicates that all went well and that the action completed successfully.
- If the macro `NO_ERROR_DATA_REQUIRED` has not been defined, then the code may use the function `TWIGetLastError()` to retrieve meaningful error messages as opposed to just the status codes.

Code to check for success or failure may resemble the `checkTWIAction()` in Listing D-4.

Listing D-4 AVRTWIlib checkTWIAction() function

```
// Checks for success or failure of a TWI action.
void checkTWIAction(const char *functionName) {
    // Wait for completion. It's done when we get a
    // status differs from TWI_NO_RELEVANT_INFO.
    while (TWIInfo.errorCode == TWI_NO_RELEVANT_INFO)
        _delay_ms(1);

    // Grab the error code.
    uint8_t errorCode = TWIInfo.errorCode;

    // Did it work?
    if (errorCode != TWI_SUCCESS) {
        printf("TWI/I2C Error: 0x%x in %s.\n", errorCode,
            functionName);

#ifndef NO_ERROR_DATA_REQUIRED
        printf(" %s\n", TWIGetLastError(errorCode));
#endif
    }
}
```

The error handling code could also light up an LED to show a fault or some other manner of giving the user some feedback.

D.9   How It Works

In this section, I will discuss the salient points of how the library works. Most of what follows is detailed in the ATmega328P data sheet, but it's not in a great format for easy understanding there I'm afraid. Some of the status codes in the data sheet have more than one option that can be taken when the status code is detected. Where there are multiple options available for a status code, Chris' code takes the best one.

---

[3]Impossible because no TWI action returns that specific status value.

[4]Well now! There's a cop-out if ever I heard one.

D.9.1   Data Transmission

```
uint8_t TWITransmitData(void *const TXdata,
                        uint8_t dataLen,
                        uint8_t repStart);
```

When you pass a buffer, with the first character set to the device's *eight*-bit write address, or SLAW, the code in the TWITransmitData() function initiates the transmission and then, almost immediately, returns control to your code. Everything related to the transmission happens in the background under control of the hardware and the interrupt handler. Listing D-5 shows the code for this function.

The code begins by making sure that the TWI system is ready for use. If not yet ready, TWI_TX_RX_NOT_READY will be returned to the caller. On receipt of this status, the calling code should attempt another transmission with the same parameters – perhaps after a small delay.

Assuming that the system is not busy, the TWIInfo.repstart field is updated to hold the repeated start request. This will be used in the interrupt handler to send a repeated start if one is required. The passed buffer address is copied over to an internal variable for use by the interrupt handler as is the data size. The current buffer pointer is initialized to point at the start of the buffer.

Listing D-5   AVRTWIlib TWITransmitData() function

```
uint8_t TWITransmitData(void *const TXdata,
                        uint8_t dataLen,
                        uint8_t repStart)
{
    if (!isTWIReady()) {
        return TWI_TX_RX_NOT_READY;
    }

    //-----------------------------------------------------------
    // Set repeated start mode.
    //-----------------------------------------------------------
    TWIInfo.repStart = repStart;

    //-----------------------------------------------------------
    // Copy data  buffer address into the transmit buffer
    // pointer.
    //-----------------------------------------------------------
    TWITransmitBuffer = (uint8_t *)TXdata;

    //-----------------------------------------------------------
    // Copy transmit info to global variables.
    //-----------------------------------------------------------
    TXBuffLen = dataLen;
    TXBuffIndex = 0;

    //-----------------------------------------------------------
```

```
    // If a repeated start has been sent, then devices are
    // already listening for an address and another start
    // does not need to be sent.
    //-------------------------------------------------------
    if (TWIInfo.mode == RepeatedStartSent) {
        TWIInfo.mode = Initializing;

        //---------------------------------------------------
        // Load data to transmit buffer.
        //---------------------------------------------------
        TWDR = TWITransmitBuffer[TXBuffIndex++];

        //---------------------------------------------------
        // Send the data
        //---------------------------------------------------
        TWISendTransmit();
    } else {
        //---------------------------------------------------
        // Otherwise, just send the normal start signal
        // to begin transmission.
        //---------------------------------------------------
        TWIInfo.mode = Initializing;
        TWISendStart();
    }

    //-------------------------------------------------------
    // All's well.
    //-------------------------------------------------------
    return TWI_TX_RX_SUCCESS;
}
```

The code next checks to see if a repeated start was recently sent. If so, then some device out there is waiting for the data, and the code loads up the TWDR register with the next byte from the buffer, before setting the TWSR register's bits to initiate the transmission by calling the macro TWISendTransmit().

If no repeated start was sent, we are beginning a new transmission and just call the macro TWISendStart().

The current mode of operation is set to Initializing (or Initialising if you wish to use English rather than American spelling) after sending a start or repeated start, and the code exits, returning a value of TWI_TX_RX_SUCCESS. The interrupt handler handles all further transmission of the data from the buffer. The user code is free to continue doing other useful work in the meantime; however, the buffer passed into this function must remain in scope until the transmission has ended.

D.9.2   Data Receipt

```
uint8_t TWIReadData(uint8_t TWIaddr,
                    uint8_t bytesToRead,
                    void *RXBuffer,
                    uint8_t repStart);
```

Data reception requires that you pass the *seven*-bit address of the device you wish to receive data from. The TWIReadData() function will correctly convert this address into an eight-bit read address, SLAR, and call TWITransmitData() to send the start condition and the SLAR address. Once these two bytes have been sent, the ISR will take over the rest of the communication and copy each received byte into the supplied buffer.

Listing D-6 is the code for TWIReadData().

Listing D-6 AVRTWIlib TWIReadData() function

```
uint8_t TWIReadData(uint8_t TWIaddr,
                    uint8_t bytesToRead,
                    void *RXBuffer,
                    uint8_t repStart) {

    //------------------------------------------------------------
    // Reset buffer index and set RXBuffLen to the number
    // of bytes to read. Any read operation will start from
    // the beginning of the Receive buffer.
    //------------------------------------------------------------
    RXBuffIndex = 0;
    RXBuffLen = bytesToRead;
    TWIReceiveBuffer = (uint8_t *)RXBuffer;

    //------------------------------------------------------------
    // Create the one value array for the address to be
    // transmitted.
    //------------------------------------------------------------
    uint8_t TXdata[1];

    //------------------------------------------------------------
    // Shift the address left and AND a 1 into the
    // read or write bit (set to write mode).
    //------------------------------------------------------------
    TXdata[0] = (TWIaddr << 1) | 0x01;

    //------------------------------------------------------------
    // Use the TWITransmitData function to initialize the
    // transfer and address the slave.
    //------------------------------------------------------------
    uint8_t txStat = TWITransmitData(TXdata, 1, repStart);
```

```
    if (txStat == TWI_TX_RX_NOT_READY) {
        return TWI_TX_RX_NOT_READY;
    }


    //------------------------------------------------------------
    // All's well.
    //------------------------------------------------------------
    return TWI_TX_RX_SUCCESS;
}
```

D.9.3   The Interrupt Handler

After `TWITransmitData()` and/or `TWIReadData()` have initiated a conversation, the vast majority of the hard work is carried out by the TWI hardware and the interrupt handler.

Listings D-7 through D-10 show the different tasks that the ISR has to carry out depending on the action which has just completed. The hardware signals that the ISR should be executed by setting the interrupt flag bit, `TWINT`, in register `TWCR`. This causes the handler to interrupt whatever code was being executed and begin executing its own code.

Listing D-7 shows the code in the ISR to handle most of the work when the TWI system is running in Master Transmitter (MT) mode. The ISR always begins by extracting the current status code from the `TWSR` register using the `TWI_STATUS` macro. Once the status byte has been extracted, the correct modes and actions can then be initiated.

On receipt of the `TWI_MT_SLAW_ACK`, `TWI_START_SENT`, or `TWI_MT_DATA_ACK` status, the next action is always to send a byte to the bus. The byte is written to the `TWDR` register and transmitted by setting the `TWCR` register accordingly. The byte to be sent obviously depends upon the status code received:

- Receipt of the `TWI_START_SENT` status requires that the device address byte be sent. In MT mode, this is assumed to be the SLAW or device write address; this is stored in the first byte of the transmission buffer, so the code handling `TWI_MT_DATA_ACK` will fetch the address and move it into the `TWDR` register ready for transmission.
- Receipt of the `TWI_MT_SLAW_ACK` status indicates that the SLAW address has been successfully acknowledged by the device with that address, and the first data byte can be sent next. Again, the code handling `TWI_MT_DATA_ACK` will pick up the correct byte from the transmission buffer and move it into the `TWDR` register ready for transmission.
- On receipt of the `TWI_MT_DATA_ACK` status, or on a "drop down" from the other two status bytes mentioned, a test is carried out to check whether we have transmitted the final byte from the buffer. Assuming this is not the case, the next available data byte is copied from the transmission buffer to the `TWDR` register, and `TWCR` is configured, using the `TWISendTransmit()` macro, to initiate a transmission with a request for an ACK on receipt by the device.

If the data byte was indeed last to be transmitted, we either send a repeated start, if we need one to keep control of the bus, or terminate the communications by sending a stop condition.

Listing D-7 AVRTWIlib Master Transmitter

```
ISR (TWI_vect)
{
    switch (TWI_STATUS) {

    //===========================================================
    //                      MASTER TRANSMITTER
    //===========================================================

    //-----------------------------------------------------------
    // SLA+W transmitted. ACK received from the addressed
    // sensor.
    //-----------------------------------------------------------
    case TWI_MT_SLAW_ACK:
        // Set mode to Master Transmitter.
        // Drops in below.
        TWIInfo.mode = MasterTransmitter;

    //-----------------------------------------------------------
    // Start condition has been transmitted. The next data
    // byte sent will be the SLA+W or SLA+R address byte.
    //-----------------------------------------------------------
    case TWI_START_SENT:
        // Drops in below.

    //-----------------------------------------------------------
    // A data byte has been transmitted, ACK has been
    // received from the sensor. The code in this library
    // sends ALL bytes from the MT to the sensor and asks
    // for an ACK for all of them. TWI_MT_DATA_NACK is not
    // really possible as a status, unless some error
    // occurrred in the hardware or or the bus.
    //-----------------------------------------------------------
    case TWI_MT_DATA_ACK:
        if (TXBuffIndex < TXBuffLen) {
        // There is more data to be sent, so, load the
        // next data byte to transmit register.
        TWDR = TWITransmitBuffer[TXBuffIndex++];
        TWIInfo.errorCode = TWI_NO_RELEVANT_INFO;
        TWISendTransmit(); // Send the data
        } else
            if (TWIInfo.repStart) {
                // This transmission is complete however
                // do not release bus yet.
                TWIInfo.errorCode = TWI_SUCCESS;
                TWISendStart();
            } else {
```

```
                       // All transmissions are complete, exit.
                       TWIInfo.mode = Ready;
                       TWIInfo.errorCode = TWI_SUCCESS;
                       TWISendStop();
                   }
            break;
```

In Master Receiver mode, the code for which is shown in Listing D-8, the ISR handles receipt of data from a device or sensor. There are three possible status codes in this mode:

- On receipt of the `TWI_MR_SLAR_ACK` status, the mode is recorded as Master Receiver as the SLAR address, the eight-bit read address for the device, has been received and acknowledged by the sensor. If we are expecting more than a single byte, we request the first one and signal the hardware to send an ACK when the byte is received. If there is only one byte left to receive, the code requests it from the hardware and signals that a NACK will be sent on successful receipt of the final byte.
- When the hardware indicates that the `TWI_MR_DATA_ACK` status is current, we know that one byte has been received and an ACK has been returned to the sensor or device. The data byte is copied from the `TWDR` register into the next available slot in the receive buffer. If there is more than one byte remaining to be received, it is requested, and the hardware is signaled to send an ACK on receipt; otherwise, the final byte is requested, and the hardware will send a NACK on receipt.
- The `TWI_MR_DATA_NACK` status indicates that the final byte we expected to read from the sensor or device has been received, and a NACK has been sent back. This indicates the end of the communications, unless a repeated start is required to keep control of the bus. If so, one is sent; otherwise, the STOP condition is sent to terminate the communications and release the bus.

Listing D-8 AVRTWIlib Master Receiver

```
//==============================================================
//                      MASTER RECEIVER
//==============================================================

//--------------------------------------------------------------
// SLA+R has been transmitted, ACK has been received
// from the adresses sensor. Request some data.
//--------------------------------------------------------------
case TWI_MR_SLAR_ACK:
    // Switch to Master Receiver mode
    TWIInfo.mode = MasterReceiver;

    // If there is more than one byte to be read,
    // request the next data byte and send an ACK
    // when it is received.
    if (RXBuffIndex < RXBuffLen-1) {
        TWIInfo.errorCode = TWI_NO_RELEVANT_INFO;
        TWISendACK();
    } else {
```

```
            // Otherwise request the final data byte and
            // send a NACK when it is received.
            TWIInfo.errorCode = TWI_NO_RELEVANT_INFO;
            TWISendNACK();
        }
    break;

//----------------------------------------------------------
// Data has been received from sensor, ACK has been
// transmitted back to say we got it. Request more data
// if any outstanding.
//----------------------------------------------------------
case TWI_MR_DATA_ACK:

    // Copy data byte to receive buffer.
    TWIReceiveBuffer[RXBuffIndex++] = TWDR;

    // If there is more than one byte still to be read,
    // request another data byte and return an ACK.
    if (RXBuffIndex < RXBuffLen-1) {
        TWIInfo.errorCode = TWI_NO_RELEVANT_INFO;
        TWISendACK();
    } else {
        // Otherwise request the final data byte and
        // when it is received, return NACK.
        TWIInfo.errorCode = TWI_NO_RELEVANT_INFO;
        TWISendNACK();
    }
  break;

//----------------------------------------------------------
// Data byte has been received from sensor, NACK has
// been transmitted. End of conversation.
//----------------------------------------------------------
case TWI_MR_DATA_NACK:

    // Copy data byte to receive buffer.
    TWIReceiveBuffer[RXBuffIndex++] = TWDR;

    // This transmission is complete however do not
    // release bus yet if a repeated start was
    // requested.
    if (TWIInfo.repStart) {
        TWIInfo.errorCode = TWI_SUCCESS;
        TWISendStart();
    } else {
        // All transmissions are complete, exit.
```

```
            TWIInfo.mode = Ready;
            TWIInfo.errorCode = TWI_SUCCESS;
            TWISendStop();
        }
    break;
```

Listing D-9 shows code which is common to both Master Transmitter and Master Receiver modes. There are four status codes in common, and all are handled in the same manner by the TWI_LOST_ARBIT handling code. This code simply checks if a repeated start is required and, if so, sends one; otherwise, the bus is freed by sending a STOP condition.

TWI_MR_SLAR_NACK and TWI_MR_SLAW_NACK indicate that no response was received when the SLAR or SLAW address was transmitted. This means that the sensor is either not online or is too busy doing other work to respond.

If the status was TWI_MT_DATA_NACK, then the sensor or device has received a data byte from the Master Transmitter, but didn't ACK it, so the MT has decided to close down communications and release the bus as it was expecting an ACK.

Listing D-9 AVRTWIlib common code

```
//================================================================
//                  COMMON CODE - MT and MR
//================================================================


//-----------------------------------------------------------------
// SLA+R transmitted, NACK received. We are done here.
//-----------------------------------------------------------------
case TWI_MR_SLAR_NACK:
    // Drops in below.


//-----------------------------------------------------------------
// SLA+W transmitted, NACK received. We are done here.
//-----------------------------------------------------------------
case TWI_MT_SLAW_NACK:
    // Drops in below.


//-----------------------------------------------------------------
// Data byte has been transmitted, NACK has been
// received. We are done here.
//-----------------------------------------------------------------
case TWI_MT_DATA_NACK:
    // Drops in below.


//-----------------------------------------------------------------
// Arbitration has been lost. Return error and send
// stop and set mode to ready. If a repeated start was
// previously requested, send a start - this will
// succeed when the bus becomes free.
//-----------------------------------------------------------------
```

```
    case TWI_LOST_ARBIT:
        if (TWIInfo.repStart) {
            // Repeated start wanted. Try to get one when
            // the bus is next free.
            TWIInfo.errorCode = TWI_STATUS;
            TWISendStart();
        } else {
            // All transmissions are complete, exit.
            TWIInfo.mode = Ready;
            TWIInfo.errorCode = TWI_STATUS;
            TWISendStop();
        }
      break;

    //-----------------------------------------------------------
    // Repeated start has been transmitted. Set the mode
    // but DO NOT clear TWINT as the next data is not yet
    // ready.
    //-----------------------------------------------------------
    case TWI_REP_START_SENT:
        TWIInfo.mode = RepeatedStartSent;
        break;
```

Listing D-10 completes the ISR code and shows the handling of the miscellaneous status codes which don't belong in any of the previously discussed categories.

TWI_NO_RELEVANT_INFO is a status that cannot legally be received from the TWI hardware; if it is somehow received, it is ignored. The final status byte that does need handling is TWI_ILLEGAL_START_STOP which is returned if a STOP condition is sent immediately following a START, repeated or otherwise. This is forbidden by the rules of TWI, and if detected the library code simply closes down communications and resets the status of the library to ready, so that further communications can be initiated.

Listing D-10   AVRTWIlib ISR miscellaneous states

```
    //===========================================================
    //                 MISCELLANEOUS STATES
    //===========================================================


    //-----------------------------------------------------------
    // It is not really possible to get into this ISR on
    // this condition Rather, it is there to be manually
    // set between operations
    //-----------------------------------------------------------
    case TWI_NO_RELEVANT_INFO:
        break;


    //-----------------------------------------------------------
    // Illegal Start+Stop transmitted. Abort and return an
```

```
    // error code.
    //-------------------------------------------------------------
    case TWI_ILLEGAL_START_STOP:
        TWIInfo.errorCode = TWI_ILLEGAL_START_STOP;
        TWIInfo.mode = Ready;
        TWISendStop();
        break;
    } // end switch.
} // end ISR
```

Note

The AVRTWIlib library does not implement Slave Transmitter or Slave Receiver modes.

Index

Adafruit, 288
Analog Comparator interrupt, 201–215
 triggers, 204
Analog-to-Digital Converter interrupt, 159–166
Arduino IDE, compiling AVR code, 31
Arduino interrupts, 1
Arduino Software Internals, 6, 72, 79, 164, 202
ATmega328P pinout, 38
attachInterrupt, 136
AVRTWIlib, 238–244, 295–313

BOOTRST fuse bit, 8

Capacitor time constant; T, 286, 287
Circular buffers, 133, 136, 259–271

Debouncing
 resistor-capacitor, 284
 software delays, 285, 287
 switch history, 291
Debouncing Switches, 283–294
Doorbell interrupts, xxv

EEPROM Ready interrupt, 169–199
EspoTek Labrador oscilloscope, 77
Euler's number; e, 286, 287
External interrupts INT0/INT1, 21–35

Fried, L., 288
Fritzing, xxvi

Herring, C., 217, 295
Hood, N., 39

Interrupt
 ADC, 159, 160, 164
 ANALOG COMP, 201, 202, 204, 206, 209, 211, 212, 275

EE READY, 169, 176, 177, 180, 185, 198, 274, 275
INT0, 2, 21, 22, 28, 29, 32, 34, 38, 39, 274–278
INT1, 2, 21, 22, 28–30, 32, 34, 38, 39, 274–278
PCINT0, 37, 52, 53
PCINT1, 37, 52, 53
PCINT2, 37, 42, 45–49, 52, 53
RESET, 1, 2, 8, 11
SPI STC, 95, 104–106, 110, 115
SPM READY, 274, 275
TIMER1 CAPT, 69, 86, 211, 212, 274
TIMERn COMPA, 69, 79, 83, 84, 274
TIMERn COMPB, 69, 79, 83, 84, 274
TIMERn OVF, 69–71, 73, 74, 76, 77, 83
TIMETn OVF, 274
TWI, 217, 231, 232, 235, 237, 274–278, 307
USART RX, 3, 125, 127, 132, 156
USART TX, 125, 127, 132, 156, 157
USART UDRE, 3, 125, 127, 132, 156, 157
WDT, 55, 56, 59–62, 274–278
Interrupt flags, 4–6, 32, 51, 70, 73, 208
Interrupt flags, Clearing, 5, 9, 32, 51, 61, 70, 73, 126, 132, 155, 166, 208, 227, 245
Interrupt priority, 2
Interrupt processing, 3
Interrupts, edge triggered, 3
Interrupts, level triggered, 3, 5, 23, 32, 33
Interrupt vector, 1, 3, 8, 9, 11, 37, 69

LyX, v

Nested interrupts, 3
Normduino, 99, 162

Pin Change interrupt, 37–53, 274–278
PlatformIO, 31, 48
printf() function, 133–134

Real world example, 249–257
Reset interrupt, 11, 18
Resistor-capacitor charging, 285
Resistor-capacitor discharging, 287

Printed in the United States
by Baker & Taylor Publisher Services